On the History of the Id~~ ~f T

On the History of the Idea of Law is the first book ever to trace the development of the philosophical theory of law from its first appearance in Plato's writings to today. Shirley Robin Letwin finds important and positive insights and tensions in the theories of Plato, Aristotle, Augustine, and Hobbes. She finds confusions and serious errors introduced by Cicero, Aquinas, Bentham, and Marx. She harnesses the insights of H. L. A. Hart and especially Michael Oakeshott to mount a devastating attack on the late twentieth-century theories of Ronald Dworkin, the Critical Legal Studies movement, and feminist jurisprudence. In all of this, Dr. Letwin finds the rule of law to be the key to modern liberty and the standard of justice.

This is the final work of the distinguished historian and theorist SHIRLEY ROBIN LETWIN: a major figure in the revival of conservative thought and doctrine from 1960 onwards, Dr. Letwin died in 1993. Her principal academic publications include *The Pursuit of Certainty: David Hume, Jeremy Bentham, John Stuart Mill, Beatrice Webb* (Cambridge University Press, 1965), and *The Gentleman in Trollope: Individuality and Moral Conduct* (Harvard University Press, 1982). This manuscript has been prepared for publication by Noel B. Reynolds.

On the History of the Idea of Law

Shirley Robin Letwin

Edited By

Noel B. Reynolds

CAMBRIDGE
UNIVERSITY PRESS

CAMBRIDGE UNIVERSITY PRESS
Cambridge, New York, Melbourne, Madrid, Cape Town, Singapore, São Paulo, Delhi

Cambridge University Press
The Edinburgh Building, Cambridge CB2 8RU, UK

Published in the United States of America by Cambridge University Press, New York

www.cambridge.org
Information on this title: www.cambridge.org/9780521854238

First published 2005
Reprinted 2007
This digitally printed version 2008

A catalogue record for this publication is available from the British Library

ISBN 978-0-521-85423-8 hardback
ISBN 978-0-521-09090-2 paperback

Contents

Editor's preface

Almost six months before she died, Shirley Robin Letwin mentioned in a letter to her friend, Milton Friedman, that she had "not been well," but that she seemed "to be mending" and was finally "able to finish the long overdue 'law book'."[1] This book, which she intended to be her career contribution to the academic debates about theories of law – her central intellectual passion – had been her principal project for at least a decade, but was repeatedly delayed as she took on other more urgent projects, such as her book on Margaret Thatcher (*The Anatomy of Thatcherism*, New Brunswick, NJ: Transaction, 1993).

For many years, her husband William Letwin, and her son Oliver Letwin, nurtured the hope of being able to complete the manuscript. Shirley had secured a tentative offer of publication from an American university press, but it would require some important revisions. Bill's declining health, and Oliver's ascending political career conspired to stall their project. Finally, in 2001, I took advantage of a casual encounter with Kenneth Minogue, a close Letwin family friend and London School of Economics colleague to inquire about the status of the manuscript. We shared the view that this would be an important contribution to legal philosophy, and that outside help would probably be needed to bring it to publication. By this time Oliver was completely consumed by his political career as Shadow Home Secretary, and was also managing most of his father's affairs. He welcomed Minogue's suggestion that I be asked to pick up the project, and within weeks I had received the manuscript in my office at Brigham Young University.

The importance of this manuscript was immediately obvious. In what was clearly her *magnum opus*, Shirley Letwin chose not to engage the hundreds of lesser issues that occupy the pages of the legal philosophy

---

[1] Letwin died June 19, 1993. Friedman quoted her January letter in the obituary he wrote for her and published in *National Review*, vol. 45, issue 14, July 19, 1993, 20. She told very few of her friends about the illness. When I arrived in Dover and called her home to set up a time that my daughter and I could stop by for a visit on our way home from a sabbatical year in Jerusalem, her husband Bill informed me that she had died just that morning.

journals where all the twists and turns of contemporary theories are examined and criticized in discussions that soon lose their currency, but rarely address the most general questions that have motivated philosophers in every age. Rather, she addressed the same fundamental questions to every philosopher from Plato to the present who has made a substantial contribution to our understanding of the nature of law. What is law? What is the rule of law? While the book explains and criticizes the legal theories of the most important philosophers from Plato to the present, it has as its primary target those theories of the twentieth century which in one way or another reject the classical understanding of law as illusory, and treat the idea of rule of law as a conservative mantra or a misnomer for rights.

From Letwin's perspective, these recent movements have misunderstood the important issues. Since the legal realists launched their attack on the objectivity of judicial decision-making early in the twentieth century, the underlying assumption of successive movements in legal philosophy has been that unless judicial reasoning could be shown to be objective, the rule of law must be an illusion. But as Letwin clearly shows, the classical defenders of the rule of law understood the limitations of judicial decision-making, and they still championed the rule of law as the best possible regime for human beings who wished to establish and preserve the individual freedom necessary for human virtue to flourish. The waves of criticism of rule of law, based on the insight that judicial decisions are never fully predictable by objective criteria, all share the same mistake. They have focused their attack on an assumption that was never an essential plank of the case for the rule of law. The right question would be this: under what conditions would a wise and informed people choose to be governed by law, fully recognizing the limitations of judicial reasoning and other persistent sources of potential error in legal administration?

However critical Letwin might be of these twentieth-century apostasies, she is not a pessimist. For this same time period saw the rise of other theorists who did grasp and revere the achievements of the rule of law in the classic sense. While it may well have been her early exposure to F. A. Hayek at the University of Chicago that focused her attention on this question, she went on to find the most comprehensive development in understanding the rule of law ever – in the writings of the English philosopher, Michael Oakeshott, the subject of her final chapter.

Letwin's critiques of legal realism, Ronald Dworkin, Critical Legal Studies, and feminist jurisprudence were written in the mid-1980s when these writers were seen as revolutionary and controversial. Two decades later, our perspective on their positions has matured considerably, and the list of important representatives of these views, has evolved as well. As the 1992 peer reviewers of the manuscript had already seen, some rewriting of these chapters was required to allow readers to see Letwin's critique firmly engaged with the most significant and mature positions that had emerged out of these movements. Letwin's original manuscript will be available at the Brigham Young University Library for anyone who would like to read her 1980s treatment of these topics.

The most time-consuming part of editing Letwin's manuscript, however, has been the footnotes. It was not the author's custom to include full citations in the draft versions of her manuscript. At this point no one knows whether she had recorded full citations in a separate file, now unavailable, or whether she planned to complete them during the editing process. Of the approximately 800 citations, only a small number were complete. I mention this primarily to give credit to a series of research assistants who spent hundreds of hours searching for translations and sources that would match the text. After we had exhausted the resources of the normally very adequate Brigham Young University Library, we turned to Inter-Library Loan. But still a hundred citations remained mysterious. Finally, on an extended trip to London, with the help of my wife Sydney, who proved better than I at finding these, we combed through Letwin's personal library and the stacks of the London Library, where Letwin did much of her work. In a few cases, where we could not verify a reference, we were forced to adjust the text or use alternative translations. A very few nonessential references were simply deleted, and a couple of important ones have been left in the text with imperfect citations that we have not been able to confirm. In my judgment, this imperfection is of less consequence than the potential damage to her argument that would occur from omitting them. Certainly, our eventual success in finding 99.8 percent of her citations justifies the presumption that she did have access to the sources she cites for the handful that we could not verify. Hopefully, readers of this volume will recognize these missing sources and report them to me.

This project has benefited from the labors of numerous other individuals, including research assistants, secretaries, editors, and my wife. I wish to thank Sydney S. Reynolds, Joan L. Naumann, Ryan A. Davis, Clark D. Asay, Joseph Reed Callister, John Andrew West, Jason S. Schofield, Ari Bruning, John J. Nielsen, Alison Coutts, Adam W. Bentley, and Margene H. Jolley for their invaluable assistance. The editorial staff of Cambridge University Press has been most helpful, and, in particular, I want to thank Richard Fisher, who as group director seemed as pleased as I was to see Letwin's last book, like her first, published by Cambridge University Press. I have also benefited from the generous support of

Brigham Young University and the Earhart Foundation in bringing this project to conclusion, and wish to state my deep appreciation for both institutions.

In conclusion, I wish to thank Oliver and William Letwin, as Shirley's literary executors, for their enthusiastic encouragement and for the free reign that they offered from the beginning of the project. While I would have been quite happy to accommodate special directions or restrictions from them, they imposed none. I am sure the author would be as pleased as I to see this volume dedicated to them.

NOEL B. REYNOLDS
OREM, UTAH

Introduction: The idea of law

The idea of law has been at the heart of Western civilization since its beginnings in ancient Greece. All that we consider distinctive about our civilization, above all its genius for maintaining a peaceful communal life that leaves room for a remarkable variety in thought and action, is bound up with the idea of law.

Yet why that is so, or even whether it is so, despite a long and rich history of reflection on the meaning, merits, and intricacies of the idea of law, has remained obscure. Indeed, so marked has been the indifference to examining our understanding of the idea of law (as opposed to studying the operation of legal systems) that attempts to repudiate the idea of law have gone unnoticed. As a result, we stand in danger of losing our greatest blessing without having learned to understand or appreciate it.

But if the nature of the idea of law, and the pattern of its development, has remained elusive, the starting point for such an inquiry is easily discerned in ancient Greece. In the fifth century B.C., where the story begins, the word used to denote law was *nomos*, and the historical phenomenon to which the discussion of *nomos* referred is readily identified. The *nomoi* of Athens were the rules collected by a group of *anagrapheis* or "inscribers" who had been empowered to engrave them on stone. These rules were thought of, probably not altogether accurately, as having been derived from Draco's Code of 621–620 B.C. and its revisions in the next century by Solon (who had used the word *thesmoi* to describe his rules). As Aristotle tells us in the *Athenian Constitution*, Solon's laws were written up on "the Boards" (three four-sided structures of wood or perhaps stone revolving on pivots), which were set up in the Royal Colonnade. And Solon prescribed that the laws should remain unaltered for a hundred years.[1]

---

[1] Aristotle, *Athenian Constitution* 7.1, in *Athenian Constitution; The Eudemian Ethics; On Virtues and Vices*, trans. H. Rackham (London: Heinemann, 1935).

In 403–402 B.C., there was a general review of these laws, and the additions and changes prepared by the *nomothetai* or "lawmakers" were recorded on the stone wall along with the already existing laws. It was declared that no law passed before 403–402 B.C. was valid unless it was included in the new inscriptions made between 410 and 403 B.C.; no charge for offenses committed before that year could be brought, and no new regulations could override the law thus established. A central record office was set up to keep public records on rolls of papyrus that could be brought into court and read out. And the records of laws passed after the fifth century B.C. include the date, the procedure, and the official bodies by which the law was passed, along with the name of the proposer. There was also a regular procedure for inspecting the laws in order to weed out inconsistencies and redundancies. Judgments given in court were recorded and regarded as precedents. That anyone who proposed a measure that contravened established law was subject to severe punishment was only one of the precautions against reckless or inconsistent innovations. To ensure that magistrates observed the law, every citizen had a right to charge a magistrate with illegal conduct. And the *graphe paranomon*, or indictment for illegality, was regularly used.

The pride of the ancient Greeks in the fact that Athens was, as Theseus says in *Oedipus at Colonus*, "A state that rules by law, and by law only," is evident throughout their literature.[2] Although the law came under attack almost as soon as it was established, and various aspects of the law became subjects of dispute, it was agreed that the rule of law is the mark of a high civilization and that its opposite, lawless tyranny, reduces its subjects to slaves and is characteristic of barbarism. Expressions of this veneration for law appear regularly throughout the fifth and fourth centuries B.C. in the tragedies, the histories, and the arguments of the orators.

When the wife of Darius, in Aeschylus' *Persians*, asks who is the master of the army, she is told that the Greeks are neither the slaves nor the subjects of any man, just as in Herodotus, Darius is assured that the Greeks are both free and able to act together as an army because they fear the law as much as Darius' subjects fear him. In *Prometheus Bound*, Zeus is described as a "tyrant" because he exercises power capriciously according to no fixed known law: "I know that he is savage," says

---

[2] Sophocles, *Oedipus at Colonus* 1040–44, in *The Complete Greek Tragedies*, vol. II, *Sophocles*, ed. David Grene and Richmond Lattimore (Chicago: University of Chicago Press, 1959).

Prometheus, "and his justice a thing he keeps by his own standard."[3] Euripides' Jason tells Medea that in following him she received more than she gave because "instead of living among barbarians," she had inhabited a Greek land and learned "how to live by law instead of the sweet will of force."[4] In *The Suppliant Woman*, Theseus reproves the herald from Thebes for "seeking a master here" because "this city is free, and ruled by no one man." He explains that "nothing is worse for a city than an absolute ruler," for whereas without law, "one man has power and makes the law his own," once there is written law, both rich and poor "have recourse to justice." And "if the little man is right, he wins against the great."[5]

Theseus' words were echoed by the orator, Isocrates, who said that the mark of Athens' greatness is that "finding the Hellenes living without laws and in scattered abodes, some oppressed by tyrannies, others perishing through anarchy, she delivered them from these evils by taking some under her protection and by setting to others her own example; for she was the first to lay down laws and establish a polity. This is apparent from the fact that those who in the beginning brought charges of homicide, and desired to settle their mutual differences by reason and not by violence, tried their cases under our laws."[6] Later, in the fourth century B.C., in the debates about the proper response to Macedonian power, Aeschines distinguished monarchy and oligarchy which "are governed by the will of the rulers" from democratic regimes which are governed by "established laws," and "it is the laws that guarantee the security of citizens in a democratic city." And Aeschines' opponent, Demosthenes, made the same point: "The laws, Athenians, you have sworn to obey; through the laws you enjoy your equal rights; to the laws you owe every blessing that is yours. . . ."[7]

Law, its admirers believed, was opposed to both decrees (*psephesmata*) and to custom. It was opposed to decrees, by which they meant particular, occasional decisions applying to one individual, because they identified

---

[3] Aeschylus, *Prometheus Bound* 184–85, in *The Complete Greek Tragedies*, vol. I, *Aeschylus*, ed. David Grene and Richmond Lattimore (Chicago: University of Chicago Press, 1959).
[4] Euripides, *The Medea* 532–36, in *The Complete Greek Tragedies*, vol. III, *Euripides*, ed. David Grene and Richmond Lattimore (Chicago: University of Chicago Press, 1959).
[5] Euripides, *The Suppliant Women* 400–60, in *The Complete Greek Tragedies*, vol. IV, *Euripides*, ed. David Grene and Richmond Lattimore (Chicago: University of Chicago Press, 1959).
[6] Isocrates, *Panegyricus* 39–40, in *Isocrates*, vol. I, trans. George Norlin (Cambridge, MA: Harvard University Press, 1928).
[7] Demosthenes, *Against Meidias* 188, in *Demosthenes*, vol. III, trans. J. H. Vince (Cambridge, MA: Harvard University Press, 1935).

law with permanent rules which define wrongdoing and its corresponding punishment equally for all Athenians. Demosthenes thus warns Athenians that if particular legislative acts are allowed to prevail over rules, then "our laws are no better than so many decrees." And he points out as well, what is implicit in this view of law, that law has nothing to do with bargaining or arbitration between parties of opposed interests. That is why, Demosthenes argues, his opponent was obliged "to prove that he has not done what I have charged him with. . . . He may argue as if the question at issue were whether he is to be delivered unto Demosthenes' hands," but "the truth is quite otherwise," because "you never 'deliver' a malefactor to his accuser; for when someone has been wronged, you do not exact the penalty in such a form as the injured party urges upon you in each case." Demosthenes goes on to state what appears as a leading theme in the philosophical discussions, that "laws were laid down by you before the particular offences were committed, when the future wrongdoer and his victim were equally unknown. What is the effect of these laws? They ensure for every citizen the opportunity of obtaining redress if he is wronged. Therefore, when you punish a man who breaks the laws, you are not delivering him over to his accusers; you are strengthening the arm of the law."[8]

Law was contrasted to custom because it was held that the rules of law had to be recorded. The history of the word *nomos* suggests, however, that this was not definitely established before the fifth century. Herodotus used *nomos* in the sense of both written and unwritten law; he speaks of Solon's *nomoi*, which are clearly statutes, but he also uses *nomos* when he says that the Corinthians' "law did not allow the ships to be given for nothing," which was not likely to have been written. In Thucydides as well, when Pericles speaks of the *nomos* of delivering funeral orations or of the Corcyrean *nomos* about the cutting of vine poles or about the rules of succession to the priesthood of Hera of Argos, it is not clear whether he is referring to statutes. But generally, from the fifth century onwards it is taken for granted that law must be written. For otherwise, it was argued, law cannot acquire that formal character and permanent definiteness that ensures the kind of security for which the law is valued.

Reliance on "unwritten law" was accordingly denounced as a rejection of law and a resort to tyranny. When Andocides reproved magistrates for undermining the law, he equated arbitrary decisions with "unwritten law." Allowing magistrates to appeal to "unwritten law," he says firmly,

---

[8] Ibid., 28–30.

introduces arbitrariness because it enables the magistrate to ignore the established law and make whatever law he pleases. Since "unwritten law," or custom, consists of the conflicting materials out of which the formal rules of law have been fashioned, giving custom precedence over law is tantamount to letting the magistrate make his own selection. The same point is made in Euripides' *Orestes*. When Menelaus is charged with having acquired barbarian ways because he remains friendly to Orestes after he had murdered his mother, Menelaus' excuse that, "It is a Greek custom, I think, to honor your kin," is scornfully dismissed: "But not to put yourself above the laws."[9]

In short, it was agreed in the popular discourse of ancient Greece that law consists of rules made without reference to any particular outcome as opposed to commands, designed to produce substantive consequences here and now; that they were easy to identify as such because they had been formally defined and authentically recorded; and that observing such rules consists in conforming to impersonal conditions.

The agreement on the opposition of law both to the commands of tyrants and to custom served to identify the law. But once attention was turned to scrutinizing systematically the character of the law itself, there was no such unanimity even among the ancient Greeks. And from the fifth century B.C. to the present, there has been a continuous conversation about the character and significance of the idea of law. That conversation is the subject of this book. It is, in other words, an account of what has been thought about a certain sort of social arrangement, which consists of a set of recorded rules, recognized to have been made by human beings and subject to being changed by them, for regulating an association whose members subscribe to these rules. My object is to relate not what the law has been at any time or place, but how it has been understood and how that understanding has changed. Only systematic discussions of the law are considered, and then only such discussions as have introduced important departures from what has been said before. Reflections on "law" in any other sense, such as the commands of a divinity or of a tribal chieftain, the regularities of nature, or usages and regulations that have not been articulated as changeable rules, except insofar as any of these is taken to have some connection with law in the sense used here, are excluded.

This book is not designed to provide anything like a complete history of reflection about the nature of law. Rather, what the reader can find here is

---

[9] Euripides, *Orestes* 480–90, in *The Complete Greek Tragedies*, vol. IV.

an exposition and analysis of the main questions that have, since ancient times, been asked about the idea of law and the pattern of the answers that they have received. The omission of many important and distinguished discussions, both of the past and present, has been imposed partly by the constraints of time and space, but also by the leading concern of this book. That concern is to disengage from a vast literature what has been deemed essential to the idea of law, and to show how, in the course of being explored and refined, the idea of law has become confused and exposed to attack, and how that attack has been, and can be, resisted by those who wish to preserve that peculiar achievement of Western civilization, the marriage of order with diversity.

Part I

Law anchored to a cosmic order

1   Plato

No philosopher is more emphatic about the opposition between law and tyranny than Plato. He defines a tyrant as a ruler who is at liberty to do what he pleases, to kill, to exile, to follow his own pleasure in every act, and he condemns tyranny in a number of different contexts. In the *Seventh Letter*, he urges that Sicily should not be subject to the despot, but to law. In the *Eighth Letter*, he says that "either servitude or freedom, when it goes to extremes, is an utter bane. . . . The due measure of servitude is to serve God. The extreme of servitude is to serve man. The god of sober men is law." To substitute the rule of law for tyranny ought to be the aim of every ruler, for only in that way could a city prosper. Indeed, so obvious is this truth, Plato concludes, that anyone disposed to establish a tyranny should "turn back and to flee for their lives. . . . Let them endeavor to put on the form of a king and to be subject to kingly laws, enjoying the highest honors by the consent of willing subjects and of the laws."[1] In the *Statesman*, Plato describes as the best of all constitutions "The rule of one man, if it has been kept within the traces, so to speak, by the written rules we call laws," and he warns that when the rule of one man is "lawless it is hard, and the most grievous to have to endure."[2] In the *Laws*, the Athenian Stranger says that rulers should be called "ministers of the law" because "the preservation or ruin of a society depends on this more than on anything else. Where the law is overruled or obsolete, I see destruction hanging over the community; where it is sovereign over the authorities and they its humble servants, I discern the presence of salvation and every blessing Heaven sends on a society."[3]

[1] Plato, *Eighth Letter* 354e–356e, in *Thirteen Epistles of Plato*, trans. L. A. Post (Oxford: Clarendon, 1925).
[2] Plato, *Plato's Statesman* 302e–303a, ed., trans. J. B. Skemp (New Haven, CT: Yale University Press, 1952).
[3] Plato, *The Laws of Plato* IV, 715d–e, trans. A. E. Taylor (London: Dent, 1934).

The Stranger emphasizes, moreover, that it is because the law consists of rules that are framed when the wrongdoer and his victim are equally unknown that the law secures the stability of the city. For otherwise, whoever achieves power could not be restrained from governing in his own interest, which would provoke others to try to replace him, thus producing endless turmoil. And it is essential to the character of law that it be written because "legal enactments, once put into writing, remain always on record, as though to challenge the question of all time to come . . . since even the dull student may recur to them for reiterated scrutiny."[4]

Law must also be sharply distinguished from custom. This distinction appears in Plato's reference in the *Laws* to an age when men did not "so much as possess an alphabet, but regulate[d] their lives by custom and what is called *traditionary* law." Then men lived not in cities, but separately in families as did the Cyclopes who, according to Homer, had not even "gatherings for councils nor oracles of law, but . . . each one utters the law to his children and his wives, and they reck not one of another." But when many different families came together into a larger settlement, the Stranger explains, as each family brought its own "habits of conduct" and "preferences," they could live together only by agreeing to accept common rules. And these had to be framed by a legislator who adopted what he deemed to be best among the variety of customs brought into the larger community by the smaller groups of which it is composed. The laws may be such local customs "as have our approval" or they may be drawn "from other quarters." Where the laws come from is of no consequence.[5] What matters is a clear determination of what customs constitute law. In other words, law replaces custom; law makes a definitive selection out of a variety of conflicting customs.

Plato is equally uncompromising about the obligation to obey the law. The history of systematic reflection on the idea of law may be said to open with the argument between Socrates and his friends in the *Crito*. There Socrates addresses himself to explaining why he is obliged to obey the law, and in doing so, he answers the more general question: Does the idea of law include an unqualified obligation to observe it? Although Socrates knows himself to be innocent of the crime for which he had been sentenced to die, when Crito urges him to attempt to escape, Socrates replies that though his sentence was unjust, refusing to submit to it would constitute an even graver injustice. And he establishes his obligation by arguing that though he might at any time have left Athens, he had chosen not to do so. He had in all ways enjoyed the benefits of the kind of life

[4] *Laws* X, 890e–891a.   [5] *Laws* III, 680e–681a; III, 702.

that the laws of Athens secured for him and had even brought children into the world in Athens. In all these ways, he had tacitly accepted membership in the community and had thereby undertaken an obligation to obey its laws. Therefore, if he now attempted to escape from what the law had imposed on him, the laws might justly rebuke him by saying: "Although we have brought you into the world and reared you and educated you, and given you and all your fellow-citizens a share in all the good things at our disposal, nevertheless by the very fact of granting our permission we openly proclaim this principle: that any Athenian, on attaining to manhood and seeing for himself the political organization of the state and us its laws, is permitted, if he is not satisfied with us, to take his property and go away wherever he likes . . . not one of our Laws hinders or prevents him from going away wherever he likes, without any loss of property. On the other hand, if any one of you stands his ground when he can see how we administer justice and the rest of our public organization, we hold that by so doing he has in fact undertaken to do anything that we tell him . . . you are behaving like the lowest type of menial, trying to run away in spite of the contracts and undertakings by which you agreed to live as a member of our State . . . you are breaking covenants and undertakings made with us, although you made them under no compulsion or misunderstanding, and were not compelled to decide in a limited time."[6]

What is important here is not merely the argument that the citizens are obliged to obey the law even when it conflicts with their interests, but also the *reason* why Socrates considers this obligation intrinsic to law. Socrates' argument clearly attaches law to an association made by subscription to rules governing it. And he emphasizes that this kind of association, the *polis* or city-state, is not imposed by nature but made by men. This implies, on the one hand, that men may renounce their membership in a *polis* by leaving it, as they cannot do by leaving their families or tribes. But on the other hand, it implies that a *polis* exists only insofar as its members observe its laws. Once its members cease to subscribe to the law, the *polis* ceases to exist. And that is why Socrates says that if he disobeyed the law, he would be unable to refute the charge that he would thereby be destroying Athens. For the laws would say to him: "Can you deny that by this act which you are contemplating you intend, so far as you have the power, to destroy us, the Laws, and the whole State as well? Do you imagine that a city can continue to exist and

---

[6] Plato, *Crito* 51c–52a, in *The Last Days of Socrates*, trans. Hugh Tredennick (London: Penguin, 1954).

not be turned upside down, if the legal judgements which are pronounced in it have no force but are nullified and destroyed by private persons? . . . Shall we say 'Yes, I do intend to destroy the laws, because the State wronged me by passing a faulty judgement at my trial?'" If he left, he would become a "destroyer of law," whom every city would shun because members of "the higher forms of human society" must regard such a man as an enemy of civilization.[7]

The *Crito* postulates three points about the law. First, the law shapes an association (the *polis*), which is a formal association, that is to say, an association constituted not by agreement to achieve any particular substantive purpose, but by subscription to a common set of rules. The rules of law are designed to secure the order and peace on which the life of the city depends, instead of being designed to pursue any particular substantive projects. In other words, rules of law that constitute the *polis* are by definition noninstrumental.

The second point – related to the noninstrumental character of law – is the connection of law with an association of people of different families and tribes, whose only necessary connection is their subscription to the same rules. Law is equated with an association that contains a variety of households and tribes. Thus the idea of a law, according to Socrates in the *Crito*, postulates a sharp distinction between a *polis* and a family or tribe, and it follows that tribal law is a self-contradictory idea.

The third point is that the idea of law is inseparable from an unqualified obligation to observe it, regardless of whether one likes the consequences. Although the *polis* is an association that its members may choose to leave, if they remain within the *polis* they must have no choice but to obey the laws that secure the life of the *polis* that they are enjoying.

These conclusions are supported also in Xenophon's account of Socrates, where he tells the Sophist, Hippias, that the laws are written rules that the citizens of the city have agreed to observe. And when Hippias asks how one can be obliged to respect laws that are changed by the very people who made them, Socrates replies that such changes no more detract from the validity of the law than the fact that men who have fought in wars, but who settle down to peaceful occupations afterwards, detracts from their valor as soldiers. Cities where the laws are respected are happiest in peace as well as in war, Socrates explains, because the agreement on which the life of the city depends is not that the citizens all "like the same things, but that they may obey the laws."[8] Obedience to the

---

[7] *Crito* 50a–c; 53–4; cf. Plato, *Statesman* 300a–e.
[8] Xenophon, *Memorabilia* IV, iv.16, in *Memorabilia and Oeconomicus*, trans. E. C. Marchant (London: Heinemann, 1923).

laws is what the gods ordain, and by obeying the laws of their city, whatever they are, men honor the gods.

In the *Crito*, Socrates is at one with the Sophists, who also argued that the mere existence of a legal order imposed an unqualified obligation to observe the law. It is the same argument that Cleon makes in the debate about Mytilene: "The most alarming feature in the case is the constant change of measures with which we appear to be threatened, and our seeming ignorance of the fact that bad laws which are never changed are better for a city than good ones that have no authority. . ."[9]

Saying that the laws need to be obeyed is not, however, by any means the same as saying that they are perfect. On the contrary, Plato recognized that the very fixity of law, which is required if it is to prevent disorder, is far from an unmitigated blessing. In a number of different contexts, Plato draws attention to the disparity between the stability and generality of rules of law and the changing variety of the human world. In the *Statesman*, for example, he compares the law to a "self-willed, ignorant man who lets no one do anything but what he has ordered and forbids all subsequent questioning of his orders even if the situation has shown some marked improvement on the one for which he originally legislated." And the reason for this accusation is that the differences in human personality and the variety of men's activities, i.e., the fact that nothing in the human world is permanent, make it impossible for invariable rules to dictate what is appropriate at any given time. The law is necessarily defective because it is impossible "for something invariable and unqualified to deal satisfactorily with what is never uniform and constant."[10]

In this context, Plato describes rules of law as a kind of "generalization," that is to say, a proposition about what is true in a majority of cases. The legislator makes the law "for the generality of his subjects under average circumstances," which Plato describes as the "bulk method" and the opposite of individual treatment. Such "bulk" prescription Plato considers inescapable under the rule of law.[11] And this defect in the law is only a particular instance of the gap between the universal and the particular, between the written word and life with which Plato was concerned throughout his philosophy. Written discourse cannot adapt itself to diverse individual cases or choose the most apt argument, he says in the *Phaedrus*, and because the written word, given its stiffness, is always imperfect, teaching by dialogue is the only mode of initiation. In the same

---

[9] Thucydides, *The History of the Peloponnesian War* III.37, trans. R. W. Livingstone (London: Oxford University Press, 1943).
[10] Plato, *Statesman* 294c.   [11] Ibid., 294d–295a.

way, law is both static and general and consequently at odds with the changing particularities of the concrete world. That is why law is necessarily a second best alternative to the ideal, which is a ruler of perfect wisdom who can make the right decision for every particular question. If such a ruler were available, it would be as ridiculous to hamper him by legal codes as for a patient to prefer the instructions left by the doctor when he travels abroad to the doctor's personal prescription on the spot. As such an all-wise ruler is not available in the real world, law is the best substitute for him. But its capacity for remedying disorder necessarily entails a degree of inappropriateness in its prescriptions because law is inseparable from rigidity. Any attempt to mitigate that rigidity, Plato insisted, must destroy the law.

It is not the function of judges to rid law of its rigidity. Judges are there to decide what is just or unjust according to the standards "embodied in the legal rules." And a judgment "shows its peculiar virtue by coming to an impartial decision on the conflicting claims it examines, by refusing to pervert the lawgiver's ordinance through yielding to bribery or threats or sentimental appeals, and by rising above all considerations of personal friendship or enmity."[12] To adjust the law to take account of unusual circumstances is a corruption of law: "Equity and indulgence, you know, are always infractions of the strict rule of absolute and perfect justice."[13] Here Plato is making the same point that Isocrates made in *Areopagitica*, where he condemns the corruption of Athens and urges a return to the regime of Solon: "For they saw that in cases of contract the judges were not in the habit of indulging their sense of *equity* but were strictly faithful to the laws; and that they did not in trying others seek to make it safe for themselves to disobey the law."[14] But whereas Isocrates suggests, as do others, that qualifying the law by equity might sometimes be beneficial even though it is too dangerous to allow, Plato holds that equity is not in any way compatible with law. Rather, it is the opposite of law, for it is the nature of law to be rigid and unresponsive to the intricate, changeable contours of the human world. Law is thus an alternative to both the perfect concrete decisions of the wise ruler and the capricious decrees of the despot. The former, though more desirable, is unattainable, while the latter is the greatest of all evils. The only protection against this evil is the inflexible law.

Even the suggestion that a law should be amended or replaced, whenever it is found wanting, was firmly and repeatedly rejected by Plato. In

---

[12] Ibid., 305b–c.   [13] *Laws* IV, 757e.
[14] Isocrates, *Areopagiticus* 33–34, in *Isocrates*, vol. II, trans. George Norlin (Cambridge, MA: Harvard University Press, 1929).

Book I of the *Laws*, he praises the rules in Sparta and Crete that required all criticism of laws to be made in secrecy. Although Plato admitted that changes might sometimes be inescapable, he proposed that the two functions of "preserving" and "rectifying" the laws be united in the guardians of the laws, to be chosen with great care among people over fifty years of age. And he hedged the provisions for change with impediments to rashness. No change should be made for ten years during which the laws were to be observed for imperfections, and once that period elapsed, the law could be altered only by the agreement of all the magistrates, the people, and the oracles.

In what he says about the dangers of changing the law as about the obligation to obey the law, Plato clearly takes the essence of law to be that it is a human arrangement for securing order in the contingent human world. When, however, he turned to considering the kind of skill required of the legislator, he endowed law with a different character. This view of law appears in answer to the argument that law is an instrument of power, put forward by Callicles in the *Gorgias* and by Thrasymachus in the *Republic*. Callicles argues that the law is a contrivance for enabling the weak to triumph over the strong and is therefore opposed to nature, where the strong rule over the weak. Whether Callicles echoes the argument of the Sophist, Antiphon, or whether he is an invention of Plato's with no historical foundation, his conception of law as an instrument for protecting the weak is one that reappears not only in Thucydides and Demosthenes, but also throughout the history of jurisprudence. Although Thrasymachus, who represents the common man's view of law, argues for a different conclusion, that the law is made by the most powerful to serve their interests, he, too, sees the law as a means for satisfying certain interests. And he accordingly concludes that there is no obligation to obey the law when it conflicts with the satisfaction of one's interests. To refute the view, represented by Callicles and Thrasymachus, that the obligation to obey the law rests on its ability to satisfy the interests of those subject to it, Plato radically revises the view of law that appears in the *Crito* and introduces a non-human element into the idea of law.

Socrates defeats both Callicles in the *Gorgias* and Thrasymachus in the *Republic* by arguing that they misunderstand the satisfaction that they seek. What they really want is the kind of order that only the rule of reason can produce. Here Socrates describes law as the rational element in the life of the *polis*, with law performing the same function in the community as does reason in the soul. The wants of the individual members of the *polis* are the analogues of the passions in the soul, and law reduces the unruly and changing variety of individual wants to order by directing them in conformity with the rational principle that governs the universe and transforms it into an ordered cosmos. Thus Plato suggests that *nomos* is derived from *nous* (understanding)[15] and says that while pain and pleasure act as "the cords, or strings, by which we are worked; they . . . pull us with opposite tensions in the direction of opposite actions . . . a man must always yield to one of these tensions without resistance, but pull against all other strings – must yield, that is, to that golden and hallowed drawing of judgment which goes by the name of the public law of the city."[16]

This argument implies that the legislator must have a special sort of knowledge that transcends the human world. It is knowledge of something eternal, of the eternal form of justice, which he must endeavor to copy in framing the laws. Only a state ruled by lawmakers who possess such knowledge may be said to possess "a real constitution."[17] Here the question about the obligation to observe the law is turned by Plato into a question about how to ensure the "justice" of law. Against the Sophists, who denied that there is a fixed, non-human standard for law, Plato argued that rules can qualify as law only if they are "written copies of scientific truth in the various departments of life they cover, copies based as far as possible on the instructions received from those who really possess the scientific truth on these matters."[18] Law-making then becomes an activity of discovery rather than creation. And we are told that the law must be obeyed not because, as in the *Crito*, it cannot be infringed without destroying the city, but because "there can be no claim to possess wisdom greater than the wisdom of the laws."[19] It follows that the obligation to obey the law depends on its justice, and there can be no obligation to obey a rule that is "unjust."

That this conclusion in the *Statesman* contradicts Socrates' position in the *Crito* is not its only oddity. In both the *Republic* and the *Statesman*, Plato makes clear that if true wisdom were available to the ruler, he could use this knowledge to do what is correct in all the contingencies of the human world, which ideal would be far superior to the rigidity of law. But this means that to see law as a copy of an eternal reality necessarily leads to self-contradiction because the knowledge needed to make law renders the making of law superfluous, indeed harmful. For if human legislators could know the correct answer for all contingencies, they could decide each question as it arose. There would thus be no need for rigid rules of law that, by virtue of being rules, are necessarily defective.

---

[15] Plato, *Laws* IV, 714a.
[16] Ibid., I, 644e–645a.
[17] *Statesman* 293d–294a.
[18] Ibid., 300c. [19] Ibid., 299c–d.

This difficulty is acknowledged indirectly in what Plato says about the impossibility of finding in the human world a true statesman. The philosopher king of the *Republic* is an ideal ruler, not a real one. In the *Statesman*, Plato lowers the requirement so as to suggest that the superiority wanted in legislators is of the sort that can be found only in the few rather than in the many: "in no community whatsoever could it happen that a large number of people received this gift of political wisdom and the power to govern by pure intelligence which would accompany it. Only in the hands of the select few or of the enlightened individual can we look for that right exercise of political power which is itself the one true constitution." Nevertheless, the Stranger and the young Socrates conclude that such "right exercise of political power" is not to be expected, and they agree in the end with the Sophists, who argued that no standards for law could be shown to be universally, eternally, and indisputably correct, and that without such standards, there is no rational ground on which men might refuse to obey the laws of their city. This conclusion is accepted by the Stranger when he says that the survival of law depends on "strict adherence to a rule which we admit to be desirable though it falls short of the ideal," the rule that "none of the citizens may venture to do any act contrary to the laws, and that if any of them ventures to do such act, the penalty is to be death or the utmost rigor of punishment. This is the justest and most desirable course as a second-best when the ideal we have just described has been set aside."[20]

In short, Plato presents us with two distinct views of law. One, contained in the *Crito* (and some parts of the *Statesman*), suggests that the law is a set of noninstrumental, general, highly determinate and necessarily somewhat defective written rules, created by an association (a *polis*), purely for the sake of maintaining the association, and which (despite their defects) are to be obeyed by the members for the sake of peaceful coexistence. The second view, which appears most sharply in the *Republic*, the *Gorgias*, and parts of the *Statesman*, suggests on the contrary that the laws are to be obeyed only because (and hence presumably only to the extent that) they are the products of and embody a human wisdom that is the nearest thing in the changing world to the unchanging verities of Reason.

The difficulty of reconciling Plato's two different conceptions of law appears also in the aims that he attributed to legislators in the *Statesman* and the *Republic*. In the *Statesman*, Plato says that the rulers "may purge

---

[20] Ibid., 297b–e.

the city for its better health by putting some of the citizens to death or banishing others. They may lessen the citizen body by sending off colonies like bees swarming off from a hive, or they may bring people in from other cities and naturalize them so as to increase the number of citizens."[21] In the *Republic*, the legislator is likened to a shepherd, a goatherd, a horsebreeder, and also to a weaver, because his job is to separate out the different components of the community, to dispose of the useless or detrimental ones, and then to arrange them into a harmonious whole. The ideal described in the *Laws* is the same: "The first-best society, then, that with the best constitution and code of law, is one where. . . all means have been taken to eliminate everything we mean by the word 'ownership' from life; if all possible means have been taken to make even what nature has made our own in some sense common property, I mean, if our eyes, ears, and hands seem to see, hear, act, in the common service; if, moreover, we all approve and condemn in perfect unison and derive pleasure and pain from the same sources – in a word, when the institutions of a society make it most utterly one, that is a criterion of their excellence than which no truer or better will ever be found. . . ."[22] Although this picture is described as an ideal, which suggests that it can never be realized in practice, it is the only account that Plato gives of the legislator's task. He is obliged to ask himself, Plato insists: "What is my intent?" "Do I hit the mark in this, or do I miss it?"[23]

But if the object of law is to create a community in which everyone is like one another, the city ruled by law acquires a character very different from that which Socrates describes in the *Crito*. It is not an association whose members are independent individuals bound together only by their observation of the same laws, but an association with a particular substantive object: the creation of a certain sort of person. In other words, the *polis* acquires the character of an educational enterprise designed to produce and impose an all-embracing discipline. The object of the laws is to teach virtue to the individuals who constitute the city. Rules of law are instrumental imperatives, a set of directions for how to behave. They direct behavior and distribute censure and praise in such a way as to ensure that all the members of the community will pursue the right satisfactions in the right order. Thus, the law directs individuals to marry between thirty and thirty-three years of age, to take meals in common, to have a certain amount of physical exercise; the laws even decide in what manner the funeral rites of each class of citizen should be celebrated, and what marks of respect should be assigned to them. In short, the law

[21] Ibid., 293d–e.   [22] *Laws* V, 739b–d.   [23] Ibid., V, 744a.

becomes a detailed pattern for how to live. It directs individuals to perform certain functions in the city. It is an instrument for creating an organic unity. And so it is said in the *Laws* that the intelligence of the lawmaker will "knit the whole into one, and keep it in subjection to sobriety and justice, not to wealth or self-seeking."[24]

What distinguishes the law of the *polis* from the commands of the tribe is not – in this version of Plato's account – its formal but its substantive character due to its being made by men who possess the knowledge needed to direct the rest towards fashioning a virtuous unity. As the formality that distinguishes it from custom is no longer of its essence, the relation of law to custom changes. Custom is no longer the antithesis of law, but rather a supplement, a mortar that fills the gaps.[25] There is also a change in the relation of law to theory and practice. Whereas in the *Statesman* the law is described as a prescription "in bulk" as if it were a practical generalization, in answering the arguments of Protagoras and Hippias in the *Protagoras*, Plato gives law the character of a theoretical idea of justice. He gives this character to law also in the *Laws* when he requires that every law has a preamble that justifies the prescription and is designed to persuade those subject to the law of the desirability of observing it. The presence of such preambles in all laws, we are told, distinguishes them from a "dictatorial prescription"[26] and makes the law an instrument of instruction rather than coercion.

The underlying thought common to both of Plato's views is that the idea of law is an answer to the fundamental difficulty of the human condition: how to bring some fixity into a world from which change and multiplicity cannot be eradicated. But in attempting to resolve the conflict between the mutable reality of the human world and the need for fixity and reason, Plato endows the idea of law with a highly ambiguous character. It is not clear whether the rational character of law is due to its being a set of fixed rules or to its conformity to a given, non-human, standard. And this ambiguity about the rationality of law is connected with an ambiguity in Plato's conception of reason. For reason is seen, on the one hand, as the governing principle of the universe and, on the other hand, as an attribute of human beings. That the law is a product of reason may therefore mean for Plato that it is a human artifact whose purpose is to maintain an association that permits variety without conflict (by providing fixed rules); or it may mean that law is a reflection of a non-human reality whose purpose is to reduce this variety and multiplicity to

[24] Ibid., IV, 721a–e; I, 631a–632c.   [25] Ibid., VII, 793b–794d.
[26] Ibid., IV, 722c–723d.

unity by imposing a substantive pattern that conforms to a given non-human model of justice. Put another way, Plato wavers between two meanings of justice – one that takes justice to be the opposite of arbitrariness and equates it with consistent, regular, dependable rules governing the relations between rulers, subjects, and among subjects, which rules are to be obeyed because they bring peace; the other identifies justice with the "right" rules in the sense of a particular substantive pattern for living, which are rules to be obeyed because they are "right." In his attempt to accept both of these conflicting meanings of justice, Plato introduced a conflict between a formal and a substantive idea of law that all his successors have struggled to resolve.

2   Aristotle

Aristotle, like Plato, understood the character of law by analogy with a conception of the universe as a cosmos in which the elements of disorder are reduced to unity by reason. Just as reason governs the soul of a human being, so law is the source of order in communal life: "He who commands that law should rule may thus be regarded as commanding that God and reason alone should rule; he who commands that a man should rule adds the character of the beast. Appetite has that character; and high spirit, too, perverts the holders of office, even when they are the best of men. Law [as the pure voice of God and reason] may thus be defined as 'Reason free from all passion.'"[1] Moreover, Aristotle made the distinction between arbitrary government and the rule of law the foundation of his analysis of the varieties of political life. The manner of selecting the ruler or of apportioning offices was for him secondary to the question: Are all public decisions subject to rules of law? Monarchy, aristocracy, and *politeia* are all legitimate forms of government, Aristotle says, because they are all ruled by law, but a democracy, where the majority decide as they please from one moment to the next, is just as tyrannical as rule by one man without law because in both there is the same subjection to arbitrary will.

But Aristotle addressed himself, as Plato had not, to considering the precise character of the order created by law. He self-consciously wrestled with the difficulty, which appears only as a tension in the thought of Plato, of how to answer the question: What kind of unity does law give to a community? Plato's view that "the greatest possible unity of the whole polis is the supreme good" was sharply criticized by Aristotle. If a *polis* "goes on and on, and becomes more of a unit," he argued, it "will eventually cease to be a polis at all." It will become first "a household instead of a polis and then an individual instead of a household. . . It

---

[1] Aristotle, *The Politics of Aristotle* III, 1287a, trans. Ernest Barker (Oxford: Clarendon, 1946).

follows that, even if we could, we ought not to achieve this object: it would be the destruction of the polis."[2] Although a *polis* "belongs to the order of 'compounds', in the same way as all other things which form a single 'whole'," Aristotle explains, it is a peculiar kind of whole. While it is composed of a number of different parts, these parts are not strictly speaking parts, but are wholes in themselves, because they are citizens capable of ruling as well as being ruled. What welds these independent individuals into a whole is the constitution to which they subscribe. Therefore, if the constitution changes, the *polis* changes even though the people remain the same. But the constitution does not create a unity in which the parts lose their distinctiveness because the parts are not reduced to mere organs or functions in the whole, nor are they unified by coming to resemble one another. On the contrary, a *polis* is "composed of unlike elements," that is to say, of individuals who have many different relations to one another – as man and wife, parent and child, soldier and civilian, ruler and ruled – and who engage in many different occupations, "which enables them to serve as complements to one another, and to attain a higher and better life by the mutual exchange of their different services."[3] There cannot then "be a single excellence common to all the citizens, any more than there can be a single excellence common to the leader of a dramatic chorus and his assistants." That is why advancing a *polis* to the kind of unity that Plato advocated would destroy the essence of the *polis*: "It is as if you were to turn harmony into mere unison, or to reduce a theme to a single beat."[4]

When Aristotle says that the members of the *polis* are made a unity by the constitution, which "is a scheme established [in order to regulate the distribution of political power] among the inhabitants of a polis,"[5] he implies that the law is the unifying element of a *polis* and that between persons connected by law, there is a special relationship – "justice" – which is distinct from the kind of relationship that exists between members of a household or tribe.[6] Much that Aristotle says elsewhere re-enforces this view of law. He speaks of law as concerned with distributing the offices required in a *polis*, and says that these offices are connected with regulating the "market-place, the city-centre, the harbours, and the country-side"; with administering "the law-courts, the registration of contracts, the enforcement of penalties, the custody of prisoners, and the reviewing, scrutiny, and audit of the accounts of

[2] Ibid., II, 1261a.   [3] Ibid., III, 1274b32, 1277a, 1261a.
[4] Ibid., III, 1276b31, 1263a–b.   [5] Ibid., III, 1274b–1275a.
[6] Aristotle, *Nicomachean Ethics* VI, 1134b1–15, in *The Complete Works of Aristotle*, ed. Jonathan Barnes, vol. II (Princeton, NJ: Princeton University Press, 1984).

magistrates"; and finally with "the functions connected with deliberation on public affairs."[7] In serving these functions, the purpose of the law is to make possible a peaceful communal life. The association created by law is "political" because its members are peers who have no necessary connections with each other and need the law only to regulate certain very complicated relations with one another that they have willingly entered into.

When, however, Aristotle turns to considering just how the law works to unify the *polis*, he endows it with a different character. This contradiction emerges from two difficulties. One is the difficulty of explaining how the unity of a *polis* could be less than that of a household or tribe and yet more than that of a military alliance, which is a mere aggregate united only for the sake of mutual help against a common enemy. Aristotle had to explain how law could create an all-embracing unity that would not destroy the independence and diversity of its members. The other difficulty arises from Aristotle's insistence that the law is impersonal. Law is preferred, he says, because it provides an impersonal answer to questions where personal interests are involved. Since those who are in office may try to do favors to themselves or to their friends, their subjects may prefer to be governed by rules, just as patients who "suspected physicians of conspiring with their enemies to destroy them for their own profit" might be "inclined to seek for treatment by the rules of a text-book." And for the same reason, when physicians themselves fall ill they turn to someone else, because they fear that their own judgment might be distorted by "the influence of their own feelings."[8] There is, besides, a quite different way in which law replaces personal judgments: The existence of stable rules is a substitute for decisions made by the members of the community on how to conduct themselves and leaves them free to devote themselves to other activities. Thus, in a moderate oligarchy, where the members do not have "so much property that they are able to enjoy a leisure free from all business cares," they prefer "that the law should rule for them."[9] But the fact that the law is impersonal and not a means to satisfying anyone's interests raises the question: How can law have a substantive content or purpose if it serves neither the ruler nor the ruled?

Aristotle's answer to both the questions – about how law gives unity to the *polis* and what gives law a substantive content – is shaped by a postulate about the nature of order, which he shares with Plato, that the cosmos, which is directed by a single rational principle to a single end, is the model of order. This implies that if the laws are not to be merely "a

---

[7] *Politics* VI, 1322–23.   [8] Ibid., III, 1287a–b.   [9] Ibid., IV, 1293a.

promiscuous heap of legislation," they must be directed "to a single object."[10] It follows that for a *polis* to be orderly, all the activities of its members have to be directed to serve a common purpose, as opposed to an alliance where a common objective exists alongside many diverse, unrelated ends. The end that shapes political order must be one to which everything that goes on in the *polis* is related as a means. Aristotle finds this end in "the good life," by which he means the realization of the higher potentialities of human "nature," as distinct from mere physical survival, which human beings share with animals. And he concludes that what distinguishes the *polis* from other associations like a household or alliance is its concern with achieving this all-embracing and therefore highest end for all of its members: "any polis which is truly so called, and is not merely one in name, must devote itself to the end of encouraging goodness. . . The end and purpose of a polis is the good life, and the institutions of social life are means to that end."[11]

Because the "good life" is an end that men may not renounce without renouncing their humanity, it is a universal and eternal end and distinct from the objectives of an alliance. But as the "good life" is an abstract end that can accommodate a variety of concrete activities, it does not impose a single objective on the members of a *polis* as does maintaining the economy of a household. Whereas in the latter, the members are all engaged in a single enterprise, the "good life" can comprehend a variety of enterprises.

Recognizing the "good life" as the end of a *polis* explains not only the unity of a *polis*, but also what determines the substance of law. For the law is then supposed to teach the members of the *polis* a particular way of living, and does so by imposing a "system of order" on the activities of all citizens. The object of law is education in its broadest sense, and this gives the unity of a *polis* its distinctive character: "Otherwise, a political association sinks into a mere alliance" and "law becomes a mere covenant – or (in the phrase of the Sophist Lycophron) 'a guarantor of men's rights against one another' – instead of being, as it should be, a rule of life such as will make the members of a polis good and just."[12] Because law gives a collection of men a common quality, Aristotle says that the law instructs, and that the art of the legislator molds the citizens. Legislators make men good by "forming habits in them," and those who fail to do so "miss their mark."[13] What distinguishes the "instruction" provided by the law from that of the family is the coercion attached to law. This is the only context in which Aristotle notices coercion as an attribute of law.[14]

[10] Ibid., VII, 1324b.   [11] Ibid., III, 1280a–b.   [12] Ibid., III, 1280b.
[13] *Nicomachean Ethics* II, 1103b1–5.   [14] Ibid., X, 1178b1–1180b13.

The fact that law is the public expression of the rational element that all human beings have in common gives it impersonality and makes its governance acceptable; although people "hate *men* who oppose their impulses," even when their opposition is right, "the law in its ordaining of what is good is not burdensome."[15] In short, in specifying its substantive content, Aristotle identifies the law with the rules of an educational enterprise.

Although Aristotle occasionally speaks of law as if it were the instrument of an economic enterprise, as when he criticizes the Spartan property laws for having led to a decline in her wealth and power, such remarks do not indicate more than a carelessness about distinguishing incidental from essential attributes of law. But a serious inconsistency does appear in another way, for Aristotle also regularly describes law as rules for distributing the offices required to regulate the public life of an association of equals. In this context, he implies that law sets conditions rather than aiming at bringing about certain substantive consequences and that the people it governs are capable of running their own lives and should be left free to do so. This is the view of law postulated when he speaks of the different sorts of constitutions that a *polis* may have. He includes among the varieties of the *polis* both "democracy," in which the citizens are concerned above all with doing as each likes, and "oligarchy," where wealth is honored above all other goods, thereby suggesting that the idea of law does not require any particular substantive content.[16]

By his more thorough exploration of the idea of law, Aristotle clearly exposed the conflict between the conception of law as a set of *noninstrumental* rules setting conditions that make possible a peaceful communal life, and the conception of law as a set of *instrumental* rules for shaping a particular kind of life and bringing about certain substantive consequences. In doing so, he raised a question that has continued to haunt the idea of law: Is the law a moral institution, or does its noninstrumental character mean that it is morally neutral? In other words, is the law an institution that imposes a unifying moral pattern on the life of all its subjects, or does the law enable its subjects to adopt a variety of moral patterns without coming into conflict? Throughout his discussion of law, Aristotle associates it with a judgment of what constitutes a good way to live. But he also says that law belongs to an association of equals who should not and do not want to be treated as children being educated. Acknowledging that law is associated with a certain idea of moral education seems to deny its connection with an association of equals. And this

---

[15] Ibid., X, 1180a14–24.   [16] *Politics* IV, 1289a–b.

acknowledgment obliges Aristotle to explain how an association governed by law can be distinguished from an alliance to defend certain interests without converting that association into a school for adults.

Aristotle has no answer to this question. He suggests that law is to be understood as the instrumental rules of an educational enterprise, but he also clearly distinguishes the subjects of law from children being led by the legislator's guiding strings, and he nowhere addresses himself to showing how the two views can be reconciled. He falls into this difficulty because he defines the purpose of law as promoting "the common good," and identifies the "common good" with a pattern for a "good life." He therefore cannot assign any purpose to law without making it the instrument of an educational enterprise and denying its noninstrumental character. Moreover, taking law to be an instrument for achieving the "good life" implies that law cannot have a moral content without being a set of directives for living. Whether this instrumentality of law is compatible with the diversity essential to the *polis* and the conception of a *polis* as an association of equals is not a question that Aristotle considers.

The question about how law acquires its moral quality is connected with what at first appears to be a separate question about whether law is made or discovered. Plato's emphasis falls on the "discovery" of law, that is to say, it is "found" by those who possess the quality requisite for a legislator: the wisdom to see the eternal Idea of Justice. The scheme presented in the *Laws* is the one good system of law, and every other scheme is deficient in the character of law. The Aristotelian picture is much more complicated because Aristotle makes distinctions of which there are, at most, only intimations in Plato.

Aristotle's conception of the relation between knowledge and law resembles Plato's insofar as he judges the desirability of law by its conformity to an eternal, universal standard. But this standard has a different character because it is a principle, not a Form. In Aristotle's picture, legislators are not obliged to copy an ideal, but rather to articulate in more particular and concrete terms what they have grasped as an abstract requirement. And Aristotle accordingly distinguishes between theoretical and practical reason. This distinction introduces an important element into the understanding of law that is wholly absent from Plato's discussion. It enables Aristotle to articulate different aspects of the idea of law far more completely and subtly. And whether his successors distinguish between theoretical and practical reasoning plays a crucial role in determining their view of the nature of law, a role that has become increasingly important in recent times.

Aristotle describes the operations of theoretical reason as "discovery" because they consist in "intuiting" first principles. These first principles give the legislator knowledge of the true purpose of legislation and of the nature of the good life in the abstract sense. Thus the legislator "discovers" for himself, or perhaps learns from a philosopher who has discovered it, that the human soul is composed of reason and passion; that the well-ordered soul is one in which reason governs; that the "good life" consists in fulfilling all the capacities of man in the right order, that is to say, in accordance with the cosmic hierarchy of being that ascends from matter to spirit; and that law plays the same role in the community as reason in the soul. But the actual business of making laws has a very different character. It is a practical activity, and the legislator has to attend to the contingent human world, where everything can be other than it is and nothing stands still. The activity of legislating is not concerned with disclosing the unchanging truth, but rather with interpreting it for particular circumstances.

Aristotle does not attempt to explain just how the legislator moves from knowledge of first principles to conclusions about what they require here and now (although his account of practical reasoning might serve as such an explanation). But he does make it clear that what is wanted in a legislator is not only "wisdom," or knowledge of eternal first principles, but also "prudence" – the ability to decide what the first principles require in the particular community where he works. In legislating, he is "making" rules in accordance with "discovered" knowledge of eternal truths. The substance of law is therefore always made. And by the same token, it is also "conventional," that is to say, not fixed by "nature," but changes from one place and time to another. Because the circumstances of different communities, or even of the same community at different times, are bound to vary, there can be no single perfect set of laws. As the work of legislating is a practical activity concerned with the contingent world, the rules it makes are bound to change with the circumstances for which they are intended.

The twofold character of law is described by Aristotle as if there were two sorts of law, which he calls "particular" and "universal." Particular law "is that which each community lays down and applies to its own members"; universal law "is the law of nature." Because "everyone to some extent divines" this "law of nature," we can know that it "really is," Aristotle says. And because of this divine element in human nature, there is a "natural justice and injustice that is common to all, even to those who have no association or covenant with each other." This is the law to which Antigone refers, Aristotle reminds us, when she refuses to obey the ruler of her city. In this passage in the *Rhetoric*, Aristotle states the heart of what has become known as "natural law theory." What is distinctive and crucial in this statement is Aristotle's articulation of the postulate on which the idea of "natural law" rests – that "there really is . . . a natural justice and injustice that is common to all" that "everyone to some extent divines."[17]

That everyone can "divine" the natural law follows from the definition of man, common to Plato and Aristotle, as a compound of reason and passion or of spirit and matter, or as a rational animal. This understanding of human nature implies that the rational or spiritual element in man is a participation in the ruling principle of the universe, and that the universe is a cosmos ordered by a rational and divine principle of which man's reason is a fragment. Aristotle makes it clear that men can claim to have knowledge of an unchanging "natural law" because they share in the divine reason that rules the universe, and this belief postulates a universe that incorporates within itself its divine ruling principle. In short, the idea of natural law rests on assuming that God is neither beyond and outside his creations nor incomprehensible, but is rather immanent in human reason.

Because Aristotle understands human life to have two aspects, one of which is "natural" and unchanging and the other "contingent" and "conventional," he distinguishes two varieties of justice. One is "natural," which "everywhere has the same force" and "does not exist by people's thinking this or that." The other is "legal" and is originally "indifferent," but "when it has been laid down is not indifferent."[18] In making this distinction, Aristotle was arguing against two sorts of opponent – those who insisted that justice is immutable and therefore "has everywhere the same force," and those who said that justice is whatever the laws ordain and therefore denied that the moral quality of law could be judged by a universal standard. Aristotle maintained that "legal justice" must be distinguished from "natural justice" and that this distinction must be made in all aspects of human life because life is governed by both "nature" and "convention": "And in all other things the same distinction will apply; by nature the right hand is stronger, yet it is possible that all men should come to be ambidextrous. The things which are just by virtue of convention and expediency are like measures; for wine and corn measures are not everywhere equal, but larger in wholesale and smaller in retail markets."[19]

But Aristotle's distinction between "natural" and "conventional" justice is confusing because he uses "conventional" in two different senses and relates law to the "immutable principles of justice" in two different ways. In

---

[17] Aristotle, *Rhetoric* I, 1373b, in *The Complete Works of Aristotle*, ed. Jonathan Barnes, vol. II (Princeton, NJ: Princeton University Press, 1984).
[18] *Nicomachean Ethics* V, 1134b18–20.   [19] Ibid., V, 1134b33–1135a3.

one sense, "conventional" means "indifferent by nature." When the law determines weights and measures, no one system can be said to conform to "immutable justice" more than another because these matters are "naturally indifferent." They enter the realm of "justice" only when they are made the subject of law. Other matters, however, are not "indifferent" by nature. Therefore, what the law determines may be said to accord more or less well with the immutable principles of justice. And about such matters, two different questions may be asked: What is "legally just?" and How well does "legal justice" conform to "natural justice?" Here, what is "legally just" is "conventional" in the sense that it may differ from one community to another, but all such legal systems are nevertheless subject to being judged by an unchanging standard.

Aristotle's failure to distinguish clearly between these two senses of conventional justice prevented him from giving a clear answer about the obligation to observe the law. Where the subject of "legal justice" is "naturally indifferent," the obligation would seem to be absolute, for there is no standard other than the law to which one could appeal. But in matters where "legal justice" can be required to conform to "natural justice," the "divine" element in men that gives each person natural knowledge of this higher justice would seem to give every person the right to refuse, as did Antigone, to observe an "unjust" law.

Although Aristotle appears to approve of Antigone's stand, he denied that citizens had a "natural right" to ignore whatever law they found to be "naturally unjust." Nor could he consistently have allowed such a right without denying the "practical" and "contingent" character of the law. For if law cannot be deduced from first principles, but involves knowledge of things that may be other than they are, there can be no indisputable knowledge of what constitutes "just law." And if there is no such indisputable knowledge, allowing citizens to defy whatever they might find undesirable in the law would be tantamount to destroying the force of the law altogether, as Socrates had argued.

This difficulty is ignored by Aristotle. Those passages that bear on it are uncharacteristically ambiguous:

Now some think that all justice is of this sort [legal], because that which is by nature is unchangeable and has everywhere the same force . . . while they see change in the things recognized as just. This, however, is not true in this unqualified way, but is true in a sense . . . with us there is something that is just even by nature, yet all of it is changeable; but still some is by nature, some not by nature [if we are asked to say which is which]. It is evident which sort of thing, among things capable of being otherwise, is by nature, and which is not but is legal and conventional, assuming that both are equally changeable . . . thus things which are just not by nature but by human enactment are not everywhere the same, since constitutions [on which law depends] also are not the same, though there is but one which is everywhere by nature the best.[20]

The same ambiguity appears in another passage, in the *Politics*: "We have to distinguish two senses of the rule of law – one which means obedience to such laws as have been enacted, and another which means that the laws obeyed have also been well enacted. (Obedience can also be paid to laws which have been enacted badly.)"[21] Nor does Aristotle give a more clear-cut answer when he says in the *Nicomachean Ethics*: "for the acts laid down by the legislative act are lawful, and each of these, we say, is just . . . the law . . . commanding some acts and forbidding others; and the rightly framed law does this rightly, and the hastily conceived one less well."[22] Aristotle's distinction between "natural" and "legal" justice is clear enough. But what follows from recognizing this distinction for the obligation to observe the law remains obscure. Aristotle did not find a satisfactory answer to the question that he had addressed: How can we acknowledge the subjection of law to "natural" standards without denying an obligation to observe the law?

Within the law itself, however, Aristotle distinguishes quite clearly between two different aspects – the general and the particular. He adds to the Platonic account a picture of law as descending from principles of nature, through constitutions and particular laws to judicial decisions. This picture endows the law with an important new attribute – that its rules may be more and less abstract, and that the relationship between these more and less abstract rules has a systematic character.

The most general aspect of law is what Aristotle calls "the constitution" and defines as the "organization of offices in a state, by which the method of their distribution is fixed, the sovereign authority is determined, and the nature of the end to be pursued by the association and all its members is prescribed."[23] The question about the "natural justice" of a community's laws applies to its constitution because the "constitution is the way of life of a citizen-body."[24] This view of the constitution is what makes the ambiguity in Aristotle's view of natural and legal justice so important. For if it is the constitution that is to be judged in accordance with an eternal ideal, it would follow that in none but a perfect community would there be any obligation to obey the law. Although Plato does not say this, he does describe constitutions other than the ideal as "mere imitations" of it: "Some are more perfect copies of it; others are grosser and less

---

[20] Ibid., V, 1134b24–1135a6.
[22] *Nicomachean Ethics* 1129b13–26.
[24] Ibid., IV, 1295a–b.

[21] *Politics* IV, 1294a.
[23] *Politics* IV, 1289a.

adequate imitations."[25] But this is not what Aristotle says. Although he discusses different sorts of constitutions and concludes that some are "wrong" or "perverted" and others "just," he also emphasizes that "in regard to constitutions generally, we have to inquire which constitution is desirable for which sort of civic body," and he goes on to say that "It is possible, for instance, that democracy rather than oligarchy may be necessary for one sort of civic body, and oligarchy rather than democracy for another." He points out that there are many varieties of each constitution – "there is not a single form of democracy, or a single form of oligarchy, but a number of varieties of either" – from which it follows that "the same laws cannot possibly be equally beneficial to *all* oligarchies or to *all* democracies." That there are many different varieties of constitutions must be borne in mind, Aristotle says, "in order to be able to enact the laws appropriate to each."[26]

All of this suggests that Aristotle would consider it wrong, that is to say, "unjust," to try to impose an ideal constitution on every community. Justice in Aristotle's view is never a matter only of discovering the pattern of perfection. It requires that the conditions of this world be considered and that the impossible not be attempted. The legislator must consider two different questions: Which is the best constitution? and What sort of constitution suits what sort of civic body? Both questions must be taken into account because a constitution is just only insofar as it conforms to an ideal, but the ideal constitution may be impossible to realize in real cities, because what is practicable will differ from one city to another. The good lawgiver and the true statesman must therefore have their eyes open not only to what is absolutely best, but also to what is best in relation to actual conditions. And an essential attribute of the "best possible" rules is that they are acceptable to those subject to them because the rule of law does not consist in the mere existence of a set of rules, or even of good rules; the rules must be obeyed.

In making particular laws, as distinguished from a constitution, the legislator must consider another kind of question about the relation of particular laws to the constitution: "whether any provision runs contrary to the principles and character of their constitutions *as actually established*."[27] The conformity of laws to the constitution is part of "legal justice," and no one may claim a right to violate the constitution because he finds it undesirable. Aristotle did not describe a constitution as a charter of basic "rights" as we are inclined to do today. Nor did he

[25] Plato, *Plato's Statesman* 297c, ed., trans. J. B. Skemp (New Haven, CT: Yale University Press, 1952).
[26] Aristotle, *Politics* IV, 1289a–b.   [27] Ibid., II, 1269a–b.

indicate any procedures for correcting "unconstitutional acts." Nevertheless, he clearly distinguished between a constitution and particular enactments and required that the latter conform to the former. The true statesman may try to move his community to a better condition by reforming the existing constitution, but he is obliged to observe the constitution as it stands.[28]

The law is not then just a collection of rules, but a systematic structure, consisting of more and less abstract aspects, which are to be shaped and judged by different criteria, and which are of varying degrees of steadiness and carry different degrees of obligation. Although Aristotle says little about the possible conflicts that may arise among these different aspects of law, or about the different qualities required to deal with them, he unequivocally denies both that legislating is merely a matter of enacting a pattern discovered in the sky and that every man has a right to disobey a law when he finds that it conflicts with "natural law."

The importance of distinguishing between the general and the particular in law is emphasized by Aristotle also in relation to the difference between rules of law and decisions in disputes about the meaning of these rules in particular cases. Aristotle makes it clear that law consists of general rules that do not indicate what should be done here and now by opposing laws to "decrees" which, he says, are related to laws as "particulars to their universal" and are "a thing to be carried out in the form of an individual act."[29] That is why, Aristotle explains, "the exponents of this act are alone said to take part in politics." Two other aspects of the difference between laws and decrees are indicated in the *Rhetoric*. For one thing, "laws are made after long consideration, whereas decisions in the courts are given at short notice, which makes it hard for those who try the case to satisfy the claims of justice and expediency." But more important and indeed crucial is the fact that "the decision of the lawgiver is not particular but prospective and general," whereas decrees decide "on definite cases." Furthermore, such judgments are likely to be obscured by personal interests and prejudices.[30]

Aristotle accordingly contrasts the judgment of the legislator to the decrees made by the public assembly on "definite cases." As the consequences of such decrees are immediately evident, the members find it

---

[28] The importance of constitutional law for Aristotle is generally denied. The common view is that of McIlwain: "Whatever the phrase 'an unconstitutional law' might have meant for Plato or for Aristotle, if he had ever used it, it would never have meant a law void on account of unconstitutionality; and, while a 'constitutional law' might conceivably have meant one concerned with the frame-work of the state, it could never have been a 'fundamental' law in our sense of that phrase." (C. H. McIlwain, *Constitutionalism Ancient and Modern* [Ithaca, NY: Cornell University Press, 1940], 38.)

[29] *Nicomachean Ethics*, VI, 1141b23–28.   [30] *Rhetoric* I, 1354b6–8.

difficult to be disinterested: "They will often have allowed themselves to be so much influenced by feelings of friendship or hatred or self-interest that they lose any clear vision of the truth and have their judgment obscured by considerations of personal pleasure and pain!"[31] The opposition between laws and decrees is also at the heart of Aristotle's distinction between the two different forms of democracy, though in both, the majority decides. A *politeia* is ruled by law and is therefore a just form of government. But in democracies where demagogic leaders refer "all issues to the decision of the people," decrees are substituted for laws and there "is no constitution." For "Decrees can never be general rules [and any real constitution must be based on general rules]. . ." Where "popular decrees are sovereign instead of the law," the people act as "a single composite autocrat made up of many members, with the many playing the sovereign, not as individuals, but collectively." Where law is sovereign, "the magistrates and the citizen body should only decide about details."[32] In other words, law consists of general rules, and a public decision that does not take the form of a general rule, however many may have participated in making it, is not a law.

Although he addresses himself more precisely than Plato did to considering the nature of the law's generality, Aristotle does not find it easy to explain just how "decisions about details" are related to the general rules that are laws. He speaks sometimes as if the law were a set of instructions telling magistrates how to think about the questions that come before them.[33] At other times, Aristotle suggests that the judge's decision is different in kind from the legislator's, as when he says that a judge should decide only about whether "the alleged fact is so or is not so, that it has or has not happened," because such questions cannot be foreseen by the legislator. A judge must therefore "decide for himself all such points."[34] But Aristotle also describes laws as if they were generalizations about what it is proper to do in most cases, which suggests that the judge usually has only to "apply the law" in a mechanical fashion, though occasionally he has to supply what the law has omitted to say.

Throughout his discussion of the law's generality, Aristotle takes it for granted that the law is at odds with the real world because "the matter of practical affairs is of this kind from the start." Because "In those cases . . . in which it is necessary to speak universally, but not possible to do so correctly, the law takes the usual case," the legislator necessarily

---

[31] Ibid., I, 1354b10–11.   [32] *Politics* IV, 1289a.
[33] Ibid., III, 1287a–b.   [34] *Rhetoric* I, 1354a29–31.

over-simplifies. But even though there is always a possibility of error because of an exceptional case, "it [the law] is none the less correct." Aristotle was constrained to recognize the possibility of "error" because he likened the law's generality to an "averaging" of cases. Whatever deviates from the "average case" therefore must produce an error. But he displayed discomfort with this formulation in his insistence on the "correctness" of the law. The error that is possible is not in the law, nor again in the legislator, but in the nature of the act to be dealt with. It is the stuff of action itself that has from the start this variable quality. Correcting the "errors" of law consists in adding to the law what the legislator had left out of it. Whether this is always necessary, Aristotle does not say, but at least in some cases the "gap" would seem to be unavoidable because of the nature of practical reason and the contingency of human affairs: "When the law speaks universally, then, and a case arises on it which is not covered by the universal statement, then it is right, when the legislator fails us and has erred by over-simplicity, to correct the omission – to say what the legislator himself would have said had he been present, and would have put into his law if he had known."[35]

Though he does not clearly specify the nature of "gaps" in legislation, Aristotle explicitly recognizes yet another way in which the law may fall into error. Circumstances may have changed since the enactment of a rule so as to produce results quite different than the legislator had intended. If the conditions that led to the enactment of the law have become "obsolete," the law must be amended by judicial discretion.[36] All such "gaps" in the law are the province of "equity" (*epieikeia*), which is "but a correction of legal justice." Providing for such correction is intrinsic to Aristotle's idea of law because he takes the generality of rules to mean that they are correct for the "average case": "The reason [for the existence of such a corrective] is that all law is universal but about some things it is not possible to make a universal statement which will be correct. . . . And this is the nature of the equitable, a correction of law where it is defective owing to its universality." Indeed, Aristotle goes even further to say that "this possible defect of law" will also explain why not all questions can be settled by law: "about some things it is impossible to lay down a law, so that a decree is needed. For when the thing is indefinite the rule is also indefinite. . . ."[37]

Whereas Plato saw only two possibilities, that the judge either applies the law strictly or departs from it, Aristotle introduced a third kind of decision in which the judge complements the work of the legislator. Plato

[35] *Nicomachean Ethics* 1137b20–24.   [36] *Rhetoric* I, 1375a22–b35.
[37] *Nicomachean Ethics* I, 1137b12–30.

described equity as a dispensation from the law, a kind of leniency that is a corruption of the justice embodied in law. To modify the law by *epieikeia* is therefore necessarily an abrogation of the law. But in Aristotle's usage, *epieikeia* takes on the connotation of a correction of the letter of the law. It is law adapted to particular circumstances, and this is the province of the judge. His duty is to act in place of the legislator, as if he were the legislator on the spot, so as to arrive at the decision that the legislator would have chosen if he had been confronted with the particular case. The law enables the judge to do this because it tells him how to think as did the legislator. By describing the judge's use of *epieikeia* as a bridging of the gap between the law and the concrete world, Aristotle made the judicial decision part of the shaping of the law and not just an enforcement of the legislator's will.

The gaps in the law that call for decisions according to "equity" also explain how advocates may defend cases that appear to run against the written law. If he wishes to win, Aristotle advises, the pleader

must appeal to the universal law and to equity as being more just. We must argue that the juror's oath "I will give my verdict according to my honest opinion" means that one will not simply follow the letter of the written law. We must urge that the principles of equity are permanent and changeless, and that the universal law does not change either, for it is the law of nature, whereas written laws often do change. . . . We shall argue that justice indeed is true and profitable, but that sham justice is not, and that consequently the written law is not, because it does not fulfill the function of the law. Or that justice is like silver, and must be assayed by the judges, if the genuine is to be distinguished from the counterfeit. Or that the better man will follow and abide by the unwritten law in preference to the written.[38]

In other passages, Aristotle suggests that the "gaps" in the law may also be filled by appeal to "unwritten law" in the sense of "what is customary." And at times, Aristotle speaks as if what is "equitable" may be identical with what is customary, as well as with "natural law."

Although all these arguments imply that law is necessarily defective, Aristotle does not conclude that the law should thus be disregarded whenever it seems to be undesirable. His emphasis falls rather on the need to supplement the law. But that his suggestions for correcting the law could destroy it, because the materials used to fill "the gap" are so various and undefined, is overlooked by Aristotle. Nowhere does he consider how an appeal to "equity" or "custom" may be distinguished from an attempt to promote selfish interests. Nor does he recognize that his account of adjudicating contradicts much else that he says. For it implies that a

---

[38] *Rhetoric* I, 1375a27–b8.

judicial decision is concerned with achieving certain consequences, and that the proper question for a judge to ask himself is: "What would be the right outcome here?" And this removes the distinction between the judge and the arbitrator on which Aristotle otherwise insists – "An arbitrator goes by the equity of a case, a judge by the law,"[39] which means that the judge should be concerned with maintaining what has already been established by the legislator, rather than with producing any particular results. Aristotle makes the same point in his distinction between laws and decrees, where he argues that rule by law is preferable because it means that decisions are not determined by the passions of the moment, but by the judgment of the legislator, which "is not particular, but prospective and general."[40] Aristotle thereby implies that decisions according to law should not be concerned with producing any particular substantive consequences here and now. In short, Aristotle was troubled in the same way as Plato by the difficulty of reconciling the impersonality and generality of law, which enables it to secure men against arbitrary, self-interested rulers, with the recognition that these qualities put law at odds with the mutable and various reality of the world on which it tries to impose order.

Aristotle recognized that the shortcomings of law considered in his discussion of equity gave support to the opponents of the rule of law. In answer to them, he suggests that the rules of law should not be regarded as blueprints or designs to be copied, but rather as signposts, directions, or instructions for how to proceed in thinking about the correct answer. Law "[does the best it can: it] trains the holders of office expressly in its own spirit, and then sets them to decide and settle those residuary issues which it cannot regulate 'as justly as in them lies'." On the whole, "*All* persons in office who have been trained by the law will have a good judgment," and if there are a number of cases that law seems unable to determine, it is also true that a personal ruler would be no better able to find satisfactory answers for such cases.[41] Above all, Aristotle emphasizes the identity of law with reason by pointing out that a just ruler also necessarily decides in terms of general rules because he is governed by reason, and reason always looks to the universal: "Those who hold that kingship is expedient argue that law can only lay down general rules; it cannot issue commands to deal with various different conjunctures; and the rule of the letter of law is therefore a folly in any and every art. . . But we have to remember that general principles must also be present in the ruler's mind." Unlike Plato, Aristotle points out that even if we could find the "one best man to rule," he, too, would rule by law because that is the

---

[39] Ibid., I, 1374b21.   [40] Ibid., I, 1354b6–8.   [41] *Politics* III, 1287a–b.

only way in which he could make certain that his decisions were not tainted by passion: "That from which the element of passion is wholly absent is better than that to which such an element clings. Law contains no element of passion; but such an element must always be present in the human mind. . . . These considerations lead us to conclude that the one best man must be a law-giver, and there must be a body of laws (even in a state which is governed by such a man), but these laws must not be sovereign where they fail to hit the mark – though they must be so in all other cases."[42] The advantage of rule by the best man, according to Aristotle, is not that he would dispense with law, but that he would make better laws and fill their gaps more perfectly.

But this argument in defense of law only serves to underscore Aristotle's struggle with the difficulty of choosing between two views of the generality of law that have continued to trouble all his successors: The blueprint view of rules (to which Plato adhered completely) success-fully expresses their impersonality and stability, but excludes any possi-bility of adjusting law to circumstance. The signpost view of rules (which Aristotle developed) allows for flexibility, but at the cost of destroying the impersonality and stability of law. Much of Aristotle's discussion of the relation between general rules and particular decisions oscillates be-tween these alternatives, sometimes attempting to combine them, but never succeeding.

In addition, however, Aristotle suggested a third way of understanding the relation between rules and decisions. He speaks of the law as applying to "classes" of individuals and acts and describes the judge's decisions as "a perception akin to that by which we perceive that the particular figure before us is a triangle."[43] The logic by which a judge moves from a legal rule to a decision, which has been called "reasoning by example," is analyzed in the *Prior Analytics* as follows:

We have an "example" when the major term is proved to belong to the middle by means of a term which resembles the third. It ought to be known both that the middle belongs to the third term, and that the first belongs to that which resembles the third. For example let A be evil, B making war against neighbours, C Athenians against Thebans, D Thebans against Phocians. If then we wish to prove that to fight with the Thebans is an evil, we must assume that to fight against neighbours is an evil. Evidence of this is obtained from similar cases, e.g. that the war against the Phocians was an evil to the Thebans. Since then to fight against neighbours is an evil, and to fight against the Thebans is to fight against neighbours, it is clear that to fight against the Thebans is an evil. Now it is clear that B belongs to C and to D (for both are cases of making war upon one's

---

[42] Ibid., III, 1286a–b.   [43] *Nicomachean Ethics* VI, 1142a28–30.

neighbours) and that A belongs to D (for the war against the Phocians did not turn out well for the Thebans): but that A belongs to B will be proved through D. Similarly if the belief in the relation of the middle term to the extreme should be produced by several similar cases. Clearly then to argue by example is neither like reasoning from part to whole, nor like reasoning from whole to part, but rather reasoning from part to part, when both particulars are subordinate to the same term, and one of them is known. It differs from induction, because induction starting from all the particular cases proves (as we saw) that the major term belongs to the middle, and does not apply the syllogistic conclusion to the minor term, whereas argument by example does make this application and does not draw its proof from all the particular cases.[44]

This kind of reasoning is discussed also in the *Rhetoric*, where Aristotle describes it as the logic appropriate to deliberation that deals with things that are "probable," that is to say, that happen generally but not necessarily and "may be other than they are." In other words, Aristotle distinguishes a kind of reasoning suitable to practical affairs, which reasoning cannot issue in indisputable truth because it deals with contingent things and does not start from indisputable propositions, but which nevertheless has a distinct and orderly character.

Aristotle's "reasoning by example" has in recent years been rediscovered as a description of legal reasoning[45] which can explain how legal rules can be stable while decisions are adjusted to particular circumstances. But Aristotle himself did not make that connection. He bequeathed a clear idea that the law contains a movement from the general to the particular and suggested different ways of understanding this movement, but he did not devote himself to explaining it because the question about the logic of law was not at the center of his idea of law.

Aristotle emphasized not only that contingency is inseparable from the nature of law, but also that the contingency operates in two ways. It affects, on the one hand, the relation of law to the universal principles that are the standard for all law because these principles are not a pattern that human laws imitate, but rather highly abstract requirements that can be translated into concrete rules in many different ways, about which there may be reasonable, irresolvable disagreement. Therefore, even though it is certain that human laws can be judged by eternal universal principles to which human reason has access, whether the judgment made is correct cannot be known with certainty. On the other hand, there is contingency in the relation of law to particular cases due to the generality of rules of

---

[44] Aristotle, *Prior Analytics* 68b–69a, in *The Works of Aristotle*, trans. W. D. Ross, vol. I (Oxford: Clarendon, 1928).
[45] Cf. Chapter 11.

law. There are consequently "gaps" in the law, and these are the proper subject for "equity," which adapts law to changing circumstances but cannot give indisputable decisions.

Both theoretical and practical reason enter into the law in another way that makes it impossible to purify the law of contingency. Theoretical reason enables men to know the abstract principles by which to judge their constitutions, but it cannot tell them how to construct a constitution for any particular historical community. Recognizing a constitution limits the area of disagreement about what rules to make here and now about particular matters, and the rules made by the legislator further limit the area of disagreement about how to resolve particular disputes. But in the end the judge must decide, and there can be no certainty about the correctness of his decision. The law accordingly has the character of an inverted pyramid in which reason operates at increasingly concrete levels to restrict disagreement about conclusions that are irremediably contingent, but without ever removing altogether the possibility of disagreement.

The effect of Aristotle's treatment of law is to emphasize its uncertainty and fragility. Although this suggests that making changes in the law is a perilous operation, he considers why allowing the law to be changed may nevertheless be desirable. In arts, such as medicine and physical training, he points out, there have been great improvements, and as politics is also an art or form of skill, "it can be argued logically that the same must also be true of politics." The ancient usages were simple and uncivilized, and the relics that still remain "are utterly absurd." Since men "as a rule, seek to follow, not the line of tradition, but some idea of the good," it would seem ridiculous to remain constant to what is established. Such considerations are even more pertinent to written laws than to "unwritten custom" because the first form of a law is bound to be "inexact" and "need[s] to be changed in the light of further experience of men's actions in detail." Nevertheless, Aristotle concludes by emphasizing the reasons for refraining from making changes in the law: "When we reflect that the improvement likely to be effected may be small, and that it is a bad thing to accustom men to abrogate laws light-heartedly, it becomes clear that there are some defects, both in legislation and in government, which had better be left untouched." The benefit of the change will be less than the loss that will likely result "if men fall into the habit of disobeying the government." Indeed the analogy from the arts is false. Changing the practice of an art does not have the same effect as changing the law because "It is from habit, and only from habit, that law derives the validity which secures obedience. But habit can be created only by the passage of time; and a readiness to change from existing to new and different laws will accordingly tend to weaken the general power of law."[46]

In this discussion, Aristotle enlarges the idea of law to include "a habit of obedience." He thereby adds a different kind of consideration to discussions about the desirability of altering the law. Not only must the direct consequences of a change in law be considered, but also its indirect effects on the attitude towards law. This is, of course, entirely consistent with Aristotle's emphasis on the need to consider the effectiveness of law and the importance of learning in all aspects of human life. And he concludes, much as Cleon argues in Thucydides, that it is better to have imperfect but stable laws rather than good laws that do not command obedience because the benefit of change is likely to be less than the damage resulting from weakening the habit of obedience.

Along with Plato and others in ancient Greece, Aristotle took the essence of law to be that it provides men with something fixed which protects them against the disorder to which their mortal condition exposes them. Just as Plato says in the *Laws* that if men lived without laws, they would be no different from the most savage beasts, so Aristotle says in the *Politics*, "Man, when perfected, is the best of animals: but if he be isolated from law and justice he is the worst of all."[47] His picture of law as a hierarchy of regulations of increasing degrees of fixity and generality is rich enough to accommodate apparently incompatible qualities and can explain how the law imposes order and unity at an abstract level while allowing change and heterogeneity to reign at more concrete levels. It can explain how, even though the law cannot wholly eliminate injustice and uncertainty, it can impose a moral order and ensure stable expectations. It can also explain how the justice and stability of a legal order can allow a constantly changing diversity to flourish.

Aristotle's explanation of how the law can provide a fixed barrier against the fluidity of the human world and at the same time accommodate it is made possible by his distinction between theoretical and practical reasoning. That distinction rests on his assumption that human beings can achieve indisputable knowledge of a cosmic order and reason from that knowledge to conclusions about the contingent human world. When that assumption was rejected by Aristotle's modern successors, the distinction between theoretical and practical reasoning was lost. And until its restoration on a new basis well into the twentieth century, it became impossible to reconcile the fixity of law with its contingency.

Aristotle did not succeed, however, in resolving another problem raised by Plato. By describing law both as a pattern for "the good life" and as

[46] *Politics* II, 1268b–1269a.   [47] Ibid., I, 1253a.

the bond of a *polis*, characterized by the diversity and independence of its members, he produced a sharper version of the tension between Plato's two senses of justice. In Aristotle's account, this tension takes the more definite shape of what in modern times would be described as a conflict between justice and liberty. In other words, we have inherited from the ancient Greeks two ideas of law, one as a means to preserving peace among heterogeneous associates and the other as a means to achieving perfection. In addition, Aristotle opened but did not answer the question: How can we acknowledge standards other than legal without denying an obligation to observe the law? It was left to his medieval successor, Aquinas, to struggle with that question and to his modern successors to dismiss it.

3   Cicero

The discussion of law takes a radically different turn with Cicero. He departs not only from Plato, whom he regarded as his master, but also from the entire Greek tradition by taking little interest in what the Greeks emphasized: that law consists of rules that are clear and fixed and publicly known to be so. One reason for this may be that Cicero was reflecting on the very different experience of the Roman Republic where there was little law in the form familiar to Plato and Aristotle, that is to say, explicitly formulated rules authoritatively declared to the public. The Twelve Tables, which were supposedly based on Greek models and enacted in the middle of the fifth century, were not a set of rules, but decisions on certain matters that were commonly disputed. Their provisions varied in form as well as substance and, taken as a whole, the Twelve Tables hardly constituted a comprehensive system of law. Nor is it clear how they were related to the many different sources of *lex* or rules for both private and public actions.

Although in the early Republic *lex* was generally spoken of as a declaration of the unchanging law, it was by no means obvious whether such rules were enactments of new law or merely declarations of existing law. And what constituted existing "law" was far from clear. Not only the edicts of a great variety of magistrates, but also informal arguments were used to settle disputes. There was besides "jurist-law," developed by people who dedicated themselves to knowing and making what were regarded as authoritative decisions, but who had no official position either as legislators or judges. These "jurists" were the only people who were acquainted with the whole field of private law. They provided what were described as *"regulae"* which were "standards" or "criteria" for deciding disputes but were not, strictly speaking, rules of law.

Little or nothing was done officially to publish legal rulings. Magistrates had a remarkable degree of discretion. The Greek practice of allowing individuals to charge a magistrate with failing to provide due legal protection was unknown among the Romans. Though the magistrate could be called to account when his term of office expired, he was later made immune to legal prosecution. If in practice there was little interference by officials in the private sphere of the individual, there was no formally established limit to the officials' powers. It was rather assumed that magistrates had unlimited discretion to grant or withhold rights. The rule, "no crime without law, and no punishment without law," was unknown. Legislation and adjudication were regularly confounded by being lodged in the same hands and by indifference to keeping the distinction clear. And juristic discussions were concerned not with whether a rule was clearly established, but with whether the effects of a particular decision were desirable. The Roman Republic's way of dealing with law has been commended for its love of flexibility and as the source of later Roman legal inventiveness, but it also suggests that the Republic was not much concerned with securing the rule of law in the sense that concerned Aristotle.

Certainly Cicero shows no great concern with the fixity of law. The most obvious sign of this indifference is his use of the terms *ius* and *lex*. In the traditional usage of his time, *lex* referred to a declaration of an authoritative decision, and *ius* referred to the ground of this declaration. *Ius* sometimes denoted custom or unwritten law as opposed to the written law or *lex* expressed in the Twelve Tables. It has also been suggested that *ius* referred to the king's law or to patrician law, as opposed to the law of the Republic or plebeian law. But it is generally agreed that *ius* referred to the broader body of prescriptions or ideas about right and wrong of which *lex* was a particular determination. Cicero reversed the traditional usage. He either used *lex* to denote the broader sense of *ius* or treated the two terms as synonymous.

He similarly transformed the meaning of *ius gentium*. In its earliest meaning, *ius gentium* meant "the law common to nations," that is to say, a convention that was an appendage to the *ius civile* and was intended to facilitate dealings with foreigners. Later *ius gentium* denoted common usages observed in commerce and general intercourse. By the second century B.C., it had become a quasi-technical term that distinguished universal and informal usage from the *ius civile*. But, writing in the first century B.C., Cicero, in *De Officiis*, speaks of *ius gentium* as "universal law" that derives its sanction from nature and belongs with the idea of the common brotherhood of man that transcends national differences. It becomes, in other words, a synonym for natural law and, as such, a standard for civil codes that requires them to respect man's essential nature. Cicero accordingly insisted that "Law is not a product of human thought" nor any enactment of peoples, but "something eternal which rules the whole universe by its wisdom." Its commands and prohibitions are one with "the primal and ultimate mind of God, whose reason directs all things either by compulsion or restraint." Thus Cicero implies that law and reason came into being together – "reason did not first become Law when it was written down, but when it first came into existence; and it came into existence simultaneously with the divine mind." And there- fore, "just as that divine mind is the supreme Law, so, when [reason] is perfected in man, that also is Law. . . ."[1] For when reason is "firmly fixed and fully developed in the human mind," it is law.[2] And as "that Law which the gods have given to the human race" is the "reason and mind of a wise lawgiver applied to command and prohibition,"[3] everything done in the human world is done by the gods who are "the lords and rulers of all things."[4] In short, Cicero identified "law" with "reason," and by reason he meant the directing principle of the universe.

The conception of the cosmos as a rational order and of human reason as a participation in that order, on which this description of law rests, was not of course peculiar to Cicero. But the difference between Cicero's picture and that of Plato or Aristotle is due to a gross simplification of how cosmic reason is related to its operation in the human world. The symptom of this simplification is Cicero's use of the word *lex* to describe what Plato called the Forms or Ideas and Aristotle called "first principles." By describing the cosmic order as *lex*, and by refusing to recognize any distinction or gap between the human faculty of rationality and the cosmic principle of reason, Cicero evaded the difficulty that plagued his Greek predecessors, i.e., that of explaining how a purely spiritual ordering gets translated into human arrangements. Instead, he bluntly described reason as "the first common possession of man and God," and took this to be a necessary implication of recognizing that man "has been given a certain distinguished status by the supreme God who created him." He went on to say with utter confidence that "those who have reason in common must also have right reason in common. And since right reason is Law, we must believe that men have Law also in common with the gods. Further, those who share Law must also share Justice; and those who share these are to be regarded as members of the same commonwealth," a claim his Greek predecessors would certainly have considered disputable. And so Cicero concluded that "we must now conceive of this whole universe as one commonwealth of which both gods and men are members . . . men are grouped with Gods on the basis of blood relationship and descent."[5] The ground for this blood relationship,

---

[1] Marcus Tullius Cicero, *De Legibus* II. IV. 8; II. IV. 10–11, in *Cicero: De Republica, De Legibus*, ed. T. E. Page, trans. Clinton Walker Keyes (Cambridge, MA: Harvard University Press, 1928).
[2] Ibid., I. v. 19.   [3] Ibid., I. VI. 19 318.
[4] Ibid., II. VII. 16.   [5] Ibid., I. VII. 23–24 321–23.

Cicero explains, is that "while the other elements of which man consists were derived from what is mortal, and are therefore fragile and perishable, the soul was generated in us by God. Hence we are justified in saying that there is a blood relationship between ourselves and the celestial beings; or we may call it a common ancestry."[6]

Cicero was not just arguing, as had Plato and Aristotle, against the belief, taught by Epicurus, that God does not trouble himself about mortals. He wholly ignored the mortal element in man. His view of human reason as identical with the mind of God enabled Cicero to describe law as an innate idea present in all human beings and identical with the divine element in human nature. If only men were willing to consult it, the divinity within them would tell them what to do with complete certainty. Law need not, indeed could not, therefore be derived from edicts or from the Twelve Tables, but only from "the deepest philosophy."

It follows, Cicero concluded, that there is "only one principle by which men may live with one another, and that this is the same for all, and possessed equally by all."[7] This principle explains why love of truth and independence and propriety are natural and cruelty is contrary to nature,[8] and why virtue and vice are "judged by themselves and not by anything else" in just the same way as truth and falsehood. What confuses us into supposing otherwise is the variety in men's beliefs about moral questions. Because we do not find the same variation in the conclusions drawn from the senses, we conclude that Nature has made the senses accurate and that what they tell us is real, whereas those matters about which men disagree must be unreal. But the explanation for this discrepancy is simply that "our senses are not perverted by parent, nurse, teacher, poet, or the stage, nor led astray by popular feeling; but against our minds all sorts of plots are constantly being laid." Men's moral judgments are corrupted not only by such outside influences but also by "that enemy which lurks deep within us, entwined in our every sense." That enemy is "pleasure," that "counterfeit of good" and "the mother of all evils." Men fail "to discern clearly what things are by Nature good, because the same seductiveness and itching does not attend them" as the objects of pleasure.[9]

Because nature is governed by the "might, . . . reason, power, mind, will" of the gods,[10] human virtue consists in living according to human nature, which is identical with living in accordance with universal reason,

---

[6] Ibid., I. viii. 24 323.   [7] Ibid., I. xiii. 35.

[8] Marcus Tullius Cicero De Officiis I, 14. Cicero: De Officiis, ed. G. P. Goold, trans. Walter Miller, vol. XXI (Cambridge, MA: Harvard University Press, 1913).

[9] De Legibus I. xvii. 45–47.   [10] Ibid., I. vii. 21.

that is to say, with the directing reason of the universe. And this reason should be called *lex* because it is the only law by which men are obliged to be governed. Cicero accordingly derived *lex* from *legere*, to choose, because "Law is the distinction between things just and unjust, made in agreement with that primal and most ancient of all things, nature; and in conformity to nature's standard are framed those human laws which inflict punishment upon the wicked but defend and protect the good."[11] And he concludes that what men ordinarily call laws, that is to say, "those rules which, in varying forms and for the need of the moment, have been formulated for the guidance of nations," are not really *lex*. They bear that title "rather by favor than because they are really such"; they are what the populace thinks of as law, because the crowds "give the name of law to that which in written form decrees whatever it wishes, either by command or prohibition." But law properly understood is identical with justice: "every law which really deserves that name is truly praiseworthy," for "in the very definition of the term 'law' there inheres the idea and principle of choosing what is just and true."[12]

That the laws of the different nations are not all the same indicates only that they are lacking in justice. Cicero claimed that the failure to identify law with justice also explains why men wrongly suppose that it is fear of punishment, rather than an innate sense of justice, that makes men obey the law. But once we recognize that "true law is right reason in agreement with nature," then it necessarily follows that true law is "of universal application, unchanging, and everlasting," which "summons to duty by its commands, and averts from wrongdoing by its prohibitions." To alter this law, or to attempt to repeal any part of it, is a sin. In any case, it is impossible to abolish it, or to free ourselves from its obligations by the actions of magistrates, senates, or people. And once we recognize this true law, we see that "there will not be different laws at Rome and at Athens, . . . now and in the future, but one eternal and unchangeable law will be valid for all nations and all times" who will thus be subject to the one true master and ruler, God, who "is the author of this law, its promulgator, and its enforcing judge." Human beings need no one to expound or interpret this law; they need only look within themselves to discover it. And anyone who refuses to do so is "fleeing from himself and denying his human nature."[13]

At no point does Cicero stop to consider the question that both Aristotle and Plato addressed with such careful attention – how in a mortal world, where both human beings and things are constantly

---

[11] Ibid., II. v. 13.   [12] Ibid., I. vi. 19; II. iv. 11–12.
[13] *De Republica* III. xxii. 33.

altering, could unchanging law be equally suitable for all times and places. He says nothing about distinctions between more and less abstract principles, nor could he have done so without qualifying his simple conclusion that what is true law is absolutely certain and divinely ordained. For if in law there is a movement from more to less abstract principles, and if that is not a purely logical or automatic movement but a genuine attempt to take account of contingent circumstances, then there can be no such certainty. Nor does Cicero consider the implications of saying that we need not look outside ourselves for an expounder or interpreter of law.[14] For if, as he says, the true law is imprinted on all men, how can there be false interpretations? In short, Cicero's identification of law with justice and nature, and his insistence that the one true law is known intuitively by all men, takes no account of the mortal character of the human world.

Nor does Cicero attempt to explain why, if true law is imprinted on the souls of men, there is any need for law in the sense of human regulations among men who are as good as he exhorts them to be. Although he suggests that an innate disposition to seek pleasure is what distracts men into bad ways, he makes no attempt to consider the relation between this bad disposition and reason, nor to explain why there should be anything such as senates and magistrates deliberating about legislation and making judicial decisions, or why there should not be merely a policing body to administer punishment for violations of what all men naturally know to be law.

Only in one respect did Cicero pursue the implications of his view of law. He explicitly recognized that the postulate of believing that true law is known innately by men is that all men are alike, and that their individuality is merely a perversion of true human nature. The fact "that right is based, not upon men's opinions, but upon Nature," he says, "will immediately be plain if you once get a clear conception of man's fellowship and union with his fellow-men. For no single thing is so like another, so exactly its counterpart, as all of us are to one another. Nay, if bad habits and false beliefs did not twist the weaker minds and turn them into whatever direction they are inclined, no one would be so like his own self as all men would be like all others." Here the similarity among human beings described by Aristotle as the possession of the same set of faculties and the same place on the scale of being has been translated by Cicero into the conclusion that the same ideas are "imprinted on our minds, are imprinted on all minds alike."[15] In making this simplistic translation, Cicero was offering the view of human beings consistent with his view

---

[14] Ibid.   [15] *De Legibus* I. x. 30.

of law as one with nature and justice. Although Plato and Aristotle also regarded human individuality and mortality as a defect, they nevertheless recognized that the differences among human beings are an intrinsic quality of their humanity which made it unavoidable that even good men might disagree about what is right here and now. Both were seriously concerned with explaining how the variety in the laws suitable for the human world is related to the eternal, natural principles inherent in the cosmic order. No such concern appears in Cicero's discussion, which only reiterates, in different words, that law commands and prohibits what all men know innately to be right.

None of this is put in question by what is commonly described as Cicero's "skepticism." He denied the Stoic view that the relation between man and God, as he described it, could be demonstrated to be necessarily true by a formal argument. Theology is not a substitute for natural science, he said, and to base one's belief in God on dialectic could only weaken the case; the belief in God is too precious a possession to be imperilled by founding it on false dialectic. But though Cicero was in this sense a "skeptic," he nevertheless believed the truths that the Stoics tried to demonstrate, and he believed that those truths were manifest. He did not in the least doubt that the human soul is of divine essence, and that human reason is one with the divine reason that ruled the universe. In short, Cicero was not at all a skeptic in the sense of denying that human beings had access to indubitable truths. On the contrary, he was a much more thoroughgoing pantheist than his Greek predecessors, because he recognized none of the difficulties with which Plato and Aristotle struggled in their efforts to reconcile pantheism with the concrete contingent reality of the human world.

The simplistic pantheism of Cicero accounts for his reputation as the father of natural law. But it is a false reputation, because the foundation for natural law theory is as much present in Plato and Aristotle as in Cicero, and the doctrine was elaborated only much later, above all by Aquinas. It is true, however, that Cicero is the founder of what in the twentieth century is commonly taken to be the doctrine of natural law. For it is in Cicero that we find a totally unqualified identification of law with justice, reason, and nature, and a complete disregard for human individuality and the contingency of human existence, which characterizes the currently popular versions of natural law.

The simplistic character of Cicero's identification between law and justice is displayed, above all, in his complete indifference to the distinction that plays so important a part in Aristotle's view of law, the distinction between practical and theoretical reasoning. Cicero identified practical reasoning with fixed precepts of conduct for ordinary men telling them what to do in order to be good. His skepticism about theoretical proofs for God's existence and His dominion over the universe did not prevent Cicero from being completely dogmatic in the practical sphere. If he denied the possibility of producing logical proofs of ethical truths or of achieving certainty through dialectical reasoning, he did not deny the possibility, nor even the necessity, of maintaining certainty about what it is good to do. There is nothing in Cicero about the limitations on practical reasoning imposed by the contingency of the human world that Aristotle stressed. Nor is there any attempt to relate practical precepts to more abstract principles. Although Cicero links his study of duty in *De Officiis* with his study of *telos* and the *summum bonum* in *De Finibus*, he offers no understanding of how that link operates in practical reasoning. For Cicero's picture of knowledge contains no modulations, only a collection of manifest and certain truths, both about how things are and about what men ought to do.

What makes Cicero's neglect of practical reasoning especially striking is that his reflections on law are shaped by practical concerns much more exclusively than were the reflections of his Greek predecessors. Their view of law was an intrinsic part of a coherent philosophical theory and remained so even when their discussion of law included a response to the political events of their day. But Cicero, like many of those now concerned with reviving natural law, was interested only in persuading his contemporaries to adopt certain policies. He phrases the issue as a question about whether utility is the only criterion for law, or whether law need also be "just." And he connects "utility" with "self-interest," from which it follows that the only question to ask about law is whether it serves "self-interest" or "justice." But Cicero does not explore the character of self-interest nor indicate how the relation between law and various sorts of interests should be properly understood.

Instead, he concentrates on denying that the principles of justice are founded on the decrees of peoples, the edicts of magistrates, or the decisions of judges. If this were so, he argues, then "Justice would sanction robbery and adultery and forgery of wills, in case these acts were approved by the votes or decrees of the populace. But if so great a power belongs to the decisions and decrees of fools that the laws of Nature can be changed by their votes, then why do they not ordain that what is bad and baneful shall be considered good and salutary?"[16] This concern of Cicero's echoes one that appears also in both Plato and Aristotle, the concern to combat an infatuation with democracy that leads men to

[16] Ibid., I. xvi. 43–44.

conclude that the only standard for law is whatever the majority finds desirable. But the elaborate arguments and distinctions considered relevant to this question that appear in Plato and Aristotle are not to be found in Cicero. He simply insists that the only escape from the whims of the mob is to recognize a natural, universal, eternal standard of justice.

In saying so, Cicero jettisons the rule of law in the sense valued by the Greeks. Although he recognizes that law is commonly identified with written rules, he refers to that identification only in the most condescending and disapproving manner: "But since our whole discussion has to do with the reasoning of the populace, it will sometimes be necessary to speak in the popular manner, and give the name of law to that which in written form decrees whatever it wishes, either by command or prohibition. For such is the crowd's definition of law."[17] Given this view, it is not surprising that the opposition between law and custom, which is so essential for the Greeks, is denied by Cicero. Instead he identifies custom with natural law. At the source of law, he says, is what our ancestors considered good; the custom of our ancestors is one with law and virtue.

Whereas the Greek emphasis fell on the contrast between government by steady, effective rules and arbitrary government, Cicero emphasized rather the contrast between human judgments and nonhuman standards in order to establish that unless men rely on nonhuman standards, there can be no order. His fundamental distinction is not therefore between rule under law and rule without law, but between "just" and "unjust" governments. By "unjust" government, or when he speaks of tyranny and despotism, Cicero means nothing more than governments that do the wrong things. When he denies the "title of commonwealth" to a government in which "everything is subject to the power of the multitude," and likens it to the tyrannies at Syracuse, Agrigentum, and Athens, he does not dwell on the arbitrariness of mob rule and its similarity to the arbitrariness of tyrants, as did Aristotle, but emphasizes rather the desire of the multitude to do what is unjust and, in particular, to confiscate property: "For in the first place a people exists only when the individuals who form it are held together by a partnership in justice. . . Nor indeed is it right . . . that an insane multitude should be left in uncontrolled possession of the 'property of the people'."[18] When he argues that it is unimportant whether one, few, or the many rule, he does not say, as did Aristotle, that what really matters is whether whoever rules is subject to law, but rather "if wisdom rules the State, what difference does it make whether that wisdom is the possession of one person or of several?"[19]

[17] Ibid., I. vi. 19.   [18] *De Republica* III. xxxiii. 45.
[19] Ibid., III. xxxv. 47.

Nowhere does Cicero recognize that a degree of rigidity is inseparable from law and that this accounts for both the benefits and the drawbacks of law. Whereas Plato emphasized that rule by the philosopher king is preferable because such a ruler can make decisions perfectly suited to the changing circumstances of human life as rules of law cannot do, and Aristotle argues that even the wisest of rulers – being human rather than philosopher kings – would do well to rely on law, Cicero never raises this question about law. He praises rule by the wise man and identifies law with the rule of wisdom and justice, but never stops to consider the relation between law and steady, general rules, nor the injustice that is inseparable from submitting the changing multiplicity of the human world to fixed rules. Nor does he consider the problem of interpreting natural standards of justice for human conditions here and now. When arguing in favor of "natural law," he speaks as if what constitutes "true law" and the best possible regulation for every community at any time is obvious. And he identifies the view that laws are bound to differ in accordance with the different conditions of particular communities with an attempt to destroy the objectivity of law, to use it as an instrument to promote self-interest, and to deny the obligatory quality of law. Thus he argues that if justice consists in nothing but conformity to written laws and national customs, and if everything is to be tested by the standard of utility, then anyone who thinks it will be profitable to him will, if he is able, disregard and violate the laws.

Cicero is also uninterested in the tension between the need to obey positive law because it is a law and the ability to question the validity of a law or a legal judgment in the light of more general and abstract principles. He merely takes the simplistic view that there can be neither objectivity in the law nor any obligation to obey it if law is not perfectly just. In other words, Cicero denies not only what Socrates argues in the *Crito*, but what Plato and Aristotle took for granted throughout – that the obligation to obey a given law rests at least in part on its being recognized as law, that is, as the foundation of communal life rather than on its substantive desirability. He argues, just as did Callicles, whom Plato represents as the most radical challenger to the rule of law, that if men are not by nature inclined to love their fellows and to be virtuous, then there can be no distinction between right and wrong, just and unjust. Whereas Plato tells us that even among robbers there is law, Cicero says that "the many pestilential statutes which nations put in force . . . no more deserve to be called laws than the rules a band of robbers might pass in their assembly." Plato's analogy between the legislator and the doctor, on the grounds that theoretical knowledge does not suffice for prescribing what is wanted here and now, is put to a very different use by Cicero – "For if ignorant and unskillful men have prescribed deadly poisons instead of healing drugs, these cannot possibly be called physicians' prescriptions; neither in a nation can a statute of any sort be called a law, even though the nation, in spite of its being a ruinous regulation, has accepted it."[20] Thus Cicero declares that the Titian or Apuleian or Livian Laws were not "really laws at all," that true law "can neither be repealed nor abrogated,"[21] and claims to have proved that a government "cannot be carried on without the strictest justice."[22]

In Cicero's conception of "natural law" there is no ambiguity whatsoever about the relation between law and justice because he makes no distinction between them. And for the same reason, he makes no distinction between different kinds of order, but insists that there can be no communal order unless it is a perfectly just order.

Cicero's view of law as identical with justice necessarily implies that law is an instrument of education. For if law and justice are one, whatever in human life escapes from the rule of law must be unjust, and the aim of law must be to bring the whole of human life under its aegis and to shape it in accordance with the pattern of a good life. Thus the laws that Cicero suggests for an ideal republic include even detailed prescriptions for the rites of burial, the making of the grave, the monument, and the tomb. But whereas the educational purpose that Plato and Aristotle also attributed to law produced a serious tension in their general view of it, no such tension exists for Cicero because he took so much simpler a view of the relation between reason, law, and the contingent human world.

This simplicity does not, however, prevent Cicero from falling into a massive self-contradiction; indeed, it leads him to it. When required by the context, he abandons the view of law as a nonhuman pattern given to men and makes assertions that completely undermine his view of law. When he adopts this standpoint, Cicero argues in the manner of Callicles, but to a different conclusion, that nature always gives dominion to the better for the greater profit of the weak. Nature has provided, he says, "not only that those men who are superior in virtue and in spirit should rule the weaker, but also that the weaker should be willing to obey the stronger."[23] But he goes on to say that the proper analogy for the rule of kings, emperors, magistrates, fathers, and victorious nations is only partly the rule of the mind over the body. It is also partly like the rule of the mind over the body's lusts, or the master over his slaves, because it is coupled with coercion and repression. And this view of the role of the ruler is

---

[20] *De Legibus* II. v. 13.   [21] Ibid., II. v. 13–14.
[22] *De Republica* II. xliv. 70.   [23] Ibid., I. xxxiv. 51.

connected by Cicero with a sharp division of human nature between evil desires and divine reason. Our desires, he says, are masters over our thoughts, and, as they are forever active and can never be fully satisfied, they urge those inflamed by desire to every sort of crime. Therefore the ruler who uses the authority of magistrates and the penalties imposed by law to subdue men's desires is superior to the philosopher who enunciates the principles of ruling but rarely persuades even the few to heed his admonitions. In this connection, Cicero suggests – what is wholly absent from his discussion of the identity between law and justice – that coercion to enforce legal provisions is intrinsic to the idea of law.

Cicero moves even further away from the view of law as a nonhuman pattern given to man when he describes the goal of the leaders in a commonwealth as a "leisured dignity," which is what all good and prosperous men desire. This goal requires the maintenance of public worship, the powers of the magistrates and the authority of the Senate, along with the body of the law, ancestral custom, the courts, and the action of judges. The director of the commonwealth should aim to secure for his fellow citizens happiness fortified by such earthly goods as wealth, material resources, glory and honor. In *De Officiis*, where he is arguing against the confiscation or redistribution of wealth, Cicero declares that security of property is "the chief purpose in the establishment of constitutional state and municipal governments," and that "although it was by nature's guidance that men were drawn together into communities, it was in the hope of safeguarding their possessions that they sought the protection of cities."[24] Here he says, too, echoing Solon, that statesmen truly concerned to preserve the commonwealth will "above all . . . use their best endeavors that everyone shall be protected in the possession of his own property by the fair administration of the law and the courts, that the poorer classes shall not be oppressed because of their helplessness, and that envy shall not stand in the way of the rich, to prevent them from keeping or recovering possession of what justly belongs to them."[25]

Cicero thus dissociated law into two disparate ideas. One identifies law with a nonhuman pattern that he described indifferently as reason, nature, or justice, and which he took to exclude all contingency and uncertainty. The other idea of law identifies it with a fallible human contrivance for maintaining order, subject to all the defects of mortal arrangements. Cicero neither attempted to reconcile these two conceptions of law nor felt any need to do so because he avoided noticing any conflict between them by treating law as a synonym for justice. He moved from one conception of law to the other without recognizing that he was

[24] *De Officiis* II, 73.   [25] Ibid., II, 85.

identifying law both with indisputable eternal verities manifest to all human beings and with a changeable, disputable, and fallible mortal arrangement. The delicate balance maintained in the Greek discussion between two conflicting elements in the idea of law was broken by Cicero.

* * *

The ancient discussion makes it clear that the idea of law comprehends two conflicting ideas, of change and fixity, because the idea of law is an answer to the fundamental difficulty of the human condition: how to bring some fixity into a world from which change and multiplicity cannot be eradicated. Plato and Aristotle are notable for their self-conscious recognition that there is an unavoidable conflict between the mutable reality of the human world and the fixity imposed by law. They attempt to explain how the law could comprehend both a changing and an unchanging element. But they never confound the unchanging element, which they identified with the eternal pattern given by nature, with the whole of law. Instead, they distinguish two different aspects of law: what it actually commands or prohibits, and how far it satisfies the requirements of justice. In other words, they distinguish between the justice and the substance of law. Indeed, they go so far as to maintain that a degree of injustice is inseparable from subjection to law that, they nevertheless insist, is the essence of a civilized life. Even though this distinction gave rise to a serious ambiguity in their view of law, they never wholly lost sight of it.

Thanks to the two meanings that they attributed to justice, they did, however, bequeath to their successors an ambiguous idea of law. In one sense of justice, law has the following features: First, law constitutes the unity of a particular kind of association, which is distinguished from a tribe or family by the fact that its members can choose to join or leave it and are not necessarily associated by anything other than their subscription to common rules. Second, rules of law are noninstrumental, that is to say, they are not designed to promote any particular enterprise, neither the satisfaction of any interests nor the securing of any particular substantive results. This means that the purpose of law is to maintain conditions that enable people who do and believe different things to live and work together in peace. Third, the moral quality of justice is intrinsic to law because the rule of law is the condition for a civilized life in which the rational nature of human beings receives the respect and support due to it. Fourth, the obligation to obey the law is independent of its substantive content or outcome because it rests on an agreement to subscribe to the law. This agreement is implicitly made by anyone who continues to enjoy the life within an association made possible by the rule of law. Fifth, the justice of the substantive content of law is necessarily uncertain because the making and interpretation of law is an exercise of practical rather than theoretical reason. Human beings have access to indisputable knowledge only of eternal truths; and there is no indisputable way of moving from those truths to practical decisions about what it is right to do at a particular time and place because such decisions concern things that can be other than they are and are therefore necessarily disputable.

But a quite different meaning of justice, indeed what is usually taken to be the ancient idea of justice, appears in those contexts where Plato, Aristotle, and Cicero describe the law as a set of rules designed to produce and maintain the kind of discipline needed to fashion virtuous citizens. Here justice consists in the maintenance of a particular pattern of life. And the law is seen as an instrument for achieving the aims of an educational enterprise. In Aristotle's discussion the tension between the two different ideas of law associated with the two meanings of justice is mitigated by the importance that he attaches to the distinction between theoretical and practical knowledge. For the legislator's obligation to adapt the law to particular contingent circumstances may blur the conflicts between framing noninstrumental rules of law and using the law as an instrument for inculcating virtue. Nevertheless, Aristotle shared with Plato and Cicero the conception of justice as a pattern for virtue because he shared with them the same understanding of the relation between the human world and the universe.

They all understood the universe as a cosmos, that is to say, as a unity governed by a single pattern or principle. When they spoke of "nature," they meant an all-embracing cosmic order, from which it followed that the human social order is as much subject to nature as are all the other aspects of the universe. Although they recognized that the relationship of the human world to nature has a different character from that of the physical or biological world and disagreed on how that difference is to be understood, they agreed that nature provided the pattern for human life and that human activity ought to be directed to conform with this pattern. It follows that the products of man's art might conflict with nature, but only if art is improperly exercised. Art is rightly exercised necessarily in accordance with nature because art is the product of reason, and reason is the governing principle of nature. If law shapes the life of the city, then law is bound to shape it so as to conform with nature. And as nature is not merely orderly, but characterized by a particular kind of order, law ought to impose a substantive pattern of life. This view of nature, and hence of law, was put in question by Christianity.

Part II

The Christian revision

4　St. Augustine

Whereas in the ancient Greek tradition, there is a tension between law as a means of securing a peaceful communal life among individuals pursuing diverse purposes and law as a pattern for a good life, Augustine unequivocally denied that law is a pattern for goodness or an instrument of education. The question about whether peace or perfection is the proper purpose of law, which had before been merely an implicit issue in discussions of law, was made central by Augustine. It has since become, in somewhat different forms, peculiarly important in the modern discussion, and those who today deny that law is a moral pattern still give reasons which are in fact derived from Augustine, though seldom recognized as having this origin.

The tension between the two views of law (as an instrument of peace and an instrument of moral education) appears even within Augustine's own early writings because he initially accepted many of the classical ideas that he had discovered in Stoic thought and especially in Cicero. In these early writings, Augustine tended to speak of law, much as Cicero did, as one with a cosmic ordering principle manifest to men through their reason. He maintained that the *lex temporalis* is valid only if it is derived from or correctly embodies the eternal law,[1] and that any legislation lacking this quality could not be just and therefore did not deserve the name of law. Like his pagan predecessors, Augustine at this stage regarded law as a means to man's perfection, which he described as an ascent to God for "Order is that which will lead us to God, if we hold to it during life."[2] But it was not long before this Ciceronian identification of law with justice was qualified by Augustine. In *De Vera Religione* he did not say that legislation which failed to accord with eternal law was invalid, but rather that the temporal legislator, if he is a good and wise

---

[1] Augustine, *On Free Choice of the Will*, trans. Anna S. Benjamin and L. H. Hackstaff (Indianapolis, IN: Bobbs-Merrill, 1964), 13–15.
[2] Augustine, *Divine Providence and the Problem of Evil (De Ordine)*, in *Writings of Saint Augustine*, vol. I, ed. Ludwig Schopp (New York: CIMA, 1948), 264.

man, will bear the eternal law in mind so that he may lay down for his own time what is to be enforced and what is to be prohibited according to its unchanging rules.

This change in Augustine's view was due to a transformed understanding of man's earthly existence, and in particular, of the consequences of man's Fall. Instead of seeing mortal life as a stage in the perfection of man and regarding civil institutions as rungs on the ladder of ascent, he came to describe man on earth as a *peregrinus*, a foreigner, whose real home lies elsewhere, to which he is linked only by hope. And it followed that no human institution could be an agency of perfection.

Once Augustine repudiated the classical view of nature as a cosmos that includes the human world, he argued that the creation of man introduced a radical division in the universe. To understand Augustine's view of law, it is essential to see what this radical division in the universe implies about the human world. It means that the human world, which consists of the acts of human will and the resulting events, is distinct both from nature and from God. Human reason cannot then be continuous with the Divine Reason that orders the universe, and there can be no way of knowing that God approves of what men have willed. On the contrary, there is bound to be a discrepancy. What men call crimes need not be sins in the eyes of God. But, on the other hand, Augustine warns, deeds that go unpunished on earth might constitute sins because God's concern is with the inner state of the human soul, and He can know what is necessarily hidden from men: "Many a deed, then, which in the sight of men is disapproved, is approved by Thy testimony; and many a one who is praised by men is, Thou being witness, condemned; because frequently the view of the deed, and the mind of the doer, and the hidden exigency of the period severally vary."[3] Men cannot control their own destiny or work their own salvation as the pagan philosophers believed because perfection cannot be achieved on earth. The only society in which perfection can be found is the society of angels and saints in heaven. But as men nevertheless persist in trying to achieve perfection by their own efforts, the human condition is a tragedy. In the scriptural sentence quoted at the opening of the *City of God* – "God resisteth the proud, but giveth grace unto the humble" – Augustine expressed his condemnation of the pagan blindness to the tragic character of human existence.[4]

---

[3] Augustine, *Confessions* Book I, 17, in *A Select Library of the Nicene and Post-Nicene Fathers of the Christian Church*, vol. I, *The Confessions and Letters of St. Augustin*, ed. Philip Schaff (Grand Rapids, MI: Eerdmans, 1988).
[4] Augustine, *City of God* Book I, Preface, in *A Select Library of the Nicene and Post-Nicene Fathers of the Christian Church*, vol. II, *St. Augustin's City of God and Christian Doctrine*, ed. Philip Schaff (Grand Rapids, MI: Eerdmans, 1978).

The Christian recognizes that there is no way to bridge the chasm between his yearning for perfection and what he can do to achieve it. And Augustine described this chasm as a dichotomy between two cities, the earthly and heavenly. They are built by two different loves: "the earthly by the love of self, even to the contempt of God; the heavenly by the love of God, even to the contempt of self."[5] It is impossible to discern membership in the heavenly city by observing how a person behaves. Nor are any particular performances required, for membership in the heavenly city is determined by how a man understands what he does. Whether men are members of the heavenly city depends on what they love. But civil arrangements can affect only outward actions.

Law cannot therefore shape a heavenly city. While it can distribute and protect property, law cannot decide the spirit in which property is used. Law can punish the wrong done to others, but it cannot punish wrongful loving.[6] That is why no city on earth, even if it is a Christian theocracy, can ensure membership in the heavenly city. No civil or religious community can be identified with the heavenly city; that city finds its members in every nation and every state and among people of the most diverse habits and customs. Augustine accordingly rejects both the apocalyptic view, hostile to the civil order of Rome, and the Eusebian view, identifying Christianity with the Roman Empire. He emphasizes that we can expect to find citizens of both cities living a common life with others who are not like them, and it is impossible to identify the city to which anyone belongs.

Augustine denies the classical view that the need for civil association is intrinsic to man's rational nature. Instead, he attributes the divorce of the earthly from the heavenly city to man's Fall. Because men have fallen, they make things other than God the object of their love and accordingly pursue divergent purposes. And this diversity brings them into conflict with one another. There is besides another reason for conflict: men seek to impose their will on others, for they are driven by a passion to dominate. As a result, human beings are always threatened by violence from those among whom they live, as nothing is so social by nature and so antisocial by corruption as the human race. And that is why, in order to live with any security from violence, men need a civil order. In short, instead of being a means to perfection, civil order is a remedy for sinfulness. It is, moreover, a highly precarious remedy because, being a purely human arrangement for keeping chaos at bay, the civil community is always in danger of disintegrating.

---

[5] *City of God* Book XIV, 28.   [6] *On Free Choice* Book I, 15, 32.

This understanding of the civil order made it impossible for Augustine to accept the classical view of law. Whereas that rests (at least at one pole of the tension) on an identification of the civil order with the moral life, for Augustine, the moral life is wholly personal and independent of the civil order. What gives the Christian his sense of identity is not membership in a particular community but his faith that the world will be transformed in the future when Christ will defeat sin and death. This transformation depends wholly on God's will, and anyone who supposes that earthly projects can bring about such a transformation displays sinful pride: "Who can deny that future life is most blessed, or that, in comparison with it this life which now we live is most wretched, be it filled with all blessings of body and soul and external things? And yet, if any man uses this life with a reference to that other which he ardently loves and confidently hopes for, he may well be called even now blessed, though not in reality so much as in hope. But the actual possession of the happiness of this life, without the hope of what is beyond, is but a false happiness and profound misery. For the true blessings of the soul are not now enjoyed. . . ."[7]

Because the Christian considers every earthly project irrelevant to his ultimate allegiance, he is necessarily an alien in whatever community he finds himself. His proper concern is not with molding that community to a particular pattern, but with safeguarding an area within which he is left free to conduct himself as he believes he should.

The tension in the classical picture between the *polis* seen as an educational enterprise and the *polis* seen as an association distinguished by diversity thus disappears in Augustine's picture of the civil order. That he is wholly committed to the latter and does not regard the civil order as a natural organic unity is indicated by his use of the word *societas*.[8] This denotes an association produced by an agreement among individuals, each of whom is pursuing his own interests, as opposed to a *universitas*, which denotes an aggregate that has the unity of a natural person and pursues a single end. This distinction, and Augustine's insistence that a civil order has the character of a *societas*, gives law a new importance. For the only way that a *societas* can become orderly is by an agreement to observe the law. Without that, there would be merely a collection of individuals: "a civic community . . . is nothing else than a multitude of men bound together by some associating tie."[9]

[7] *City of God* Book XIX, 20.   [8] Ibid., Book XII, 1; Book XVI, 16.
[9] Ibid., Book XV, 8.

Augustine's repudiation of the classical view of man's relation to the cosmos thus led to a new conception of order, which laid the foundation for a wholly secular and apparently amoral conception of law. Order ceased to be identified, as in the classical view, with direction to a common end and the pursuit of a good life. Instead, order became a synonym for peace, in the most modest sense of an absence of violent conflict. Peace in this sense is, for Augustine, the closest that men can come in mortal life to the eternal peace which is their ultimate desire: "there is no word we hear with such pleasure, nothing we desire with such zest, or find to be more thoroughly gratifying."[10] And he maintains that wicked men love peace as much as do good men: "For even they who intentionally interrupt the peace in which they are living have no hatred of peace, but only wish it changed into a peace that suits them better. They do not, therefore, wish to have no peace, but only one more to their mind." Even those who wish to overthrow the established order must establish peace among themselves: "And in the case of sedition, when men have separated themselves from the community, they yet do not effect what they wish, unless they maintain some kind of peace with their fellow-conspirators." Likewise, criminals who live by disobedience nevertheless enforce obedience within their own ranks: "And therefore even robbers take care to maintain peace with their comrades. . . ." Indeed, the rebel who operates alone is constrained to adopt some associates: "And if an individual happens to be of such unrivalled strength, and to be so jealous of partnership, that he trusts himself with no comrades . . . yet he maintains some shadow of peace with such persons as he is unable to kill, and from whom he wishes to conceal his deeds. . . ."[11]

But if men must try to preserve peace, they cannot discover how to do so from an eternal pattern because there is no link between the human world and nature, or between human and divine reason. Ultimate truth is hidden from man, who inhabits a world that is full of violence and has no visible anchor to a cosmic order. In this perilous condition, man's chief resource against violence is the law, which is thus part of God's dispensation for punishing man's transgression and for dealing with the consequences of that transgression. The role of law in the human world is not then analogous to the governance of reason in nature as in the classical picture. In no sense can those who make and enforce the law draw on some higher, infallible reason. Law is not so much a protection against the dominion of tyrants as the only alternative to the violence of anarchy.

---

[10] Ibid., Book XIX, 11.   [11] Ibid., Book XIX, 12.

This does not, of course, endow law with an exalted character. On the contrary, Augustine's emphasis on the misery of a mortal condition is nowhere more evident than in his insistence on the inescapable defectiveness of earthly law. Although he continued to write about the "eternal law" as divine reason or the "will of God," in his later writings he speaks of human law not as a direct derivative from eternal law but rather as standing apart from the order of nature, which remains as an ultimate, but inaccessible and mysterious source and sanction.[12] Whereas his predecessors had exhorted men to remember that their reason gave them access to eternal truths, Augustine keeps reminding them that they are blind beings from whom the truth is hidden. The laws that they make are neither embodiments nor reflections of the "eternal law," but rather human artifacts subject to all the uncertainty inherent in human life.

To dream of establishing a perfect set of laws, suitable for all times and places and impervious to change, thus becomes a sin rather than a noble aspiration. Augustine never ceases to believe that the "most perfect law of God Almighty" is "the same always and everywhere," and that "Moses, and David, and all those commended by the mouth of God were righteous" and that those who judged them to be otherwise were "foolish men, judging out of man's judgment, and gauging by the petty standard of their own manners the manners of the whole human race." But that did not prevent him from insisting, and with a peculiar fervor, that the same laws cannot be suitable for all times and places: "Like as if in an armoury, one knowing not what were adapted to the several members should put greaves on his head, or boot himself with a helmet, and then complain because they would not fit. . . Such are they who cannot endure to hear something to have been lawful for righteous men in former times which is not so now; or that God, for certain temporal reasons, commanded them one thing, and these another, but both obeying the same righteousness; though they see, in one man, one day, and one house, different things to be fit for different members, and a thing which was formerly lawful after a time unlawful – that permitted in one corner, which done in another is justly prohibited and punished."[13]

But it does not follow, as fools might conclude, Augustine argues, that therefore justice is various and changeable. Wise men know that justice is unchanging, but that "the times over which she presides are not all alike, because they are times." Because men live for such a brief spell on earth

---

[12] Augustine, *A Select Library of the Nicene and Post-Nicene Fathers of the Christian Church*, vol. IV, *St. Augustin: The Writings against the Manichaeans and against the Donatists*, ed. Philip Schaff (Grand Rapids, MI: Eerdmans, 1988), 283–84, 288, 295–96.
[13] Augustine, *Confessions* Book III, 13.

and have such a constricted experience, they cannot connect what happened in other ages with that of which they have direct experience. Yet they need only remember that in their daily lives there is constant variation in what is suitable for any one body, day, season, person, or family. In the same way, the laws that are suitable for one age become unrighteous in another. For only by "diversities in the manners, laws, and institutions . . . earthly peace is secured and maintained."[14] But even though what is right at one time may be wrong at another just because "they are times," human arrangements "all tend to one and the same end of earthly peace." Because members of the heavenly city are so clearly aware of the distinction between mortal life and eternal bliss and know that contingency is inescapable on earth, they, least of all men, wish to abolish diversity. They strive rather to preserve and encourage it.[15] In his *Confessions*, Augustine accordingly blamed himself for not seeing "how that righteousness . . . in varying times . . . did not prescribe all things at once, but distributed and enjoined what was proper for each."[16]

Because the truth is hidden, just what the laws should be, and how they should be enforced, can be determined only by agreement on what constitutes the public concern (*res publica*). Far from embracing the whole life of the citizens, the public concern is that area in which divergent interests and loyalties of individuals coincide. The subject of these concerns is itself intrinsically changeable because it is what Aristotle described as "those goods that men fight about." As there is no eternal pattern for the law, and as it deals with mortal questions to which the answers are always provisional and partial, the law not only differs from one place and time to another but is necessarily subject to constant revision and renewal at any given place and time. Whereas in the classical picture change in the law is regularly decried, Augustine considers change in the law essential to keeping it just. His awareness of a long Roman history of law may have led him to take its existence more for granted and to feel confident that there can be changes in a system of law without endangering its existence. In any case, he was more impressed than his pagan predecessors with the need for constant revision of the law and was less fearful of the effects of change than the Greeks had been.

Augustine put a new stress not only on the variety and changeability of law, but also on the arbitrariness of its enforcement. He went much further than Plato or Aristotle in insisting that a painful degree of injustice is inseparable from law, that the tragic character of human existence is

---

[14] Ibid., 64; cf. *City of God* Book XIX, 17.   [15] *City of God* Book XIX, 17.
[16] *Confessions* Book III, 14.

nowhere more obvious than in the operation of law. Since there, as elsewhere, the truth is hidden, not only is every legal judgment bound to be in some degree defective, but men must also endure practices which they find repellent. Because a mortal judge, unlike God, "cannot discern the consciences of those at their bar," he must resort to torture to discover whether a man is innocent. Consequently, the innocent man, even if he is in the end released, may suffer torture undeservedly. Or he may die in the course of torture without confessing. If he chooses not to be tortured and to confess, he wrongly lets himself be taken for guilty. Or he may be put to death because he confesses under torture, even though he is innocent. Accusers may suffer in the same way. Though prompted only by a pure "desire to benefit society by bringing criminals to justice," they may be unable to prove their charges, or they may be traduced by witnesses who lie, or they may be tortured to produce evidence about crimes of which they are themselves not even accused:

Thus the ignorance of the judge frequently involves an innocent person in suffering. And what is still more unendurable – a thing, indeed, to be bewailed, and, if that were possible, watered with fountains of tears – is this, that when the judge puts the accused to the question, that he may not unwittingly put an innocent man to death, the result of this lamentable ignorance is that this very person, whom he tortured that he might not condemn him if innocent, is condemned to death both tortured and innocent. . . And, when he has been condemned and put to death, the judge is still in ignorance whether he has put to death an innocent or a guilty person, though he put the accused to the torture for the very purpose of saving himself from condemning the innocent; and consequently he has both tortured an innocent man to discover his innocence, and has put him to death without discovering it.[17]

Given such appalling possibilities, no man can take on the duties of a judge without exposing himself to suffering. Why, then, should any man consent to act as a judge: "If such darkness shrouds social life, will a wise judge take his seat on the bench or no?" Augustine answers: "Beyond question he will. For human society, which he thinks it a wickedness to abandon, constrains him and compels him to this duty." There is no end to the ways in which justice may be perverted by the operation of the law, and yet the wise judge does not consider "these numerous and important evils" to be sins. He recognizes that what matters before God is that he does not intend to do harm and that he is compelled to accept what harm he causes by his inescapable ignorance and by his duty as a judge. He cannot be a happy man, even though he is guiltless. He is bound to recognize "the misery of these necessities" and to shrink from his own

[17] *City of God* Book XIX, 6.

implication in that misery. He may cry to God, "From my necessities deliver Thou me," but, like the accused and the accusers, the judge must bear his undeserved suffering because that is the condition of fallen man. Anyone who tries to evade such sufferings brings upon himself the most serious kind of guilt, that of trying to escape from his sinful nature. The Christian can only "condemn human life as miserable."[18]

Given his conviction that whatever men do, they cannot avoid injustice, it is hardly surprising that Augustine firmly rejected Cicero's view that a "republic cannot be administered without justice." For Augustine that is tantamount to denying the existence of any earthly city. Against Cicero, he argued that "the Roman people is a people, and its weal is without doubt a commonwealth or republic."[19] The injustice in one city might be greater than in another, but the presence of some injustice in every city is as inescapable as the Fall of man.

For the same reason, coercion is, in Augustine's view, intrinsic and central to the law. The association of punishment with law had been taken for granted by Augustine's predecessors, but was regarded as merely an accidental attribute. This was because in the classical picture, the legislator has the character of an interpreter of cosmic reason for the education of the *polis*. He is, at least in one of the classical views, a teacher, not a master, and his use of force is only a means of making his teaching more effective. But since Augustine repudiated the conception of a ruler or legislator as an intermediary between the terrestrial community and the heavenly kingdom, and instead regarded the object of the legislator as being to remedy the disorder of "this hell upon earth,"[20] it is not surprising that he believes the legislator can achieve his ends only by repression, by dispensing punishment. Thus law ceases to be identified with reason as in the classical picture, and its association with force and punishment is of its essence.

The obligation to observe the law also acquires a different character. Although Augustine sometimes recommends that magistrates should perform their duties in the spirit of a kind father, he does not see the role of the civil ruler or legislator as analogous to that of the *paterfamilias*. Nor does he, in this connection, invoke the picture of a cosmic order where superior levels rule over inferior ones, although he continued to think in terms of such an order in other contexts. When speaking of law, he emphasizes that the order of the human world has no connection with a natural order, and that the ground for subordination in civil society is derived from the peculiar character of the human world, which imposes

---

[18] Ibid.   [19] Ibid., Book XIX, 21–24.   [20] Ibid., Book XXII, 22.

on fallen man an obligation to obey the powers that be. This duty of submission has nothing whatever to do with the Greek conception of law as an alternative to servitude, adopted by men because they are rational beings. It is, on the contrary, more nearly a form of servitude, an obligation to submit to superior power as the only means of preserving peace. Its moral quality is derived merely from its being a recognition of man's fallen nature, and an acceptance of the consequences of that Fall. Indeed, Augustine's view of the obligation to observe the law is strictly analogous to his view of illness; they are both unpleasant phenomena intrinsic to the human condition and beyond man's control. The Christian obeys the law because he is the sort of man who would not set himself up against the hidden ways of God.

In principle, then, Augustine offers at least as simple a view of law as Cicero does, but a view from the opposite pole of the Greek tension between law as a foundation of association and law as a moral education derived from eternal verities. Whereas Cicero had escaped that tension by arguing that the law has no justification other than its being in conformity with or a reflection of eternal reason, Augustine escapes the tension by arguing that the law has no justification other than its contribution to the peacefulness of a human association. But just as Cicero left his readers wondering how man can know with such certainty the content of eternal truth in its application to the contingent world, Augustine left subsequent generations with unresolved issues. In particular, he did not tell his successors how to determine the limits of obedience to a law that has no links to eternal verities, or to what extent they should regard eternal or natural law as at least a negative criterion which justifies disobedience to a human law that flies in the face of what the human subject conceives as divine law. These issues were directly addressed by Aquinas.

5   St. Thomas Aquinas

A much more complicated idea of law emerged from the project of St. Thomas Aquinas to reconcile the revealed Christian truth with the pagan philosophy of Aristotle. This project required Aquinas to restore the link between law and a cosmic order while at the same time acknowledging, as Christian doctrine required, that men cannot read the mind of God.

Aquinas' solution rests on accepting, in a modified form, the Aristotelian view of nature that Augustine had rejected. In the Thomistic picture, the model for order in human society is the cosmic hierarchy, in which the higher moves the lower by means of superior natural powers divinely assigned to the higher. The universe is a hierarchy of "movers," in which power descends from the first mover to subordinates in their due order, just as the plan of a work of art descends from the chief craftsman to the craftsmen who work under him. Just as in nature, where higher things move the lower because of the preeminent natural powers conferred upon them by God, so also in human affairs superiors impose their will upon inferiors because of the authority established by God. The submission not only of children to the father, but also of families to the political ruler is as natural as the rule of the soul over the body and of God over the world. As subjection to a ruler belongs to the chain of agencies provided by God for the perfection of each kind of being, it is ordained by God that the plan, or *ratio*, of what is to be done in the political community flows from the king's command to his chain of inferior administrators.

The political order is not then, as in the Augustinian picture, the result of man's Fall, but belongs to the natural order of things. Men need to be ruled because otherwise they would be a "plurality of individuals" without any unity and would be no more able to achieve their natural end than would the crew of a ship without a captain. To be orderly, every multiplicity has to be reduced to unity, and this can only be done by subjecting the many to the rule of one – "in nature, government is always by one. Among members of the body there is one which moves all the rest, namely, the heart: in the soul there is one faculty which is pre-eminent, namely, reason. . .

for all plurality derives from unity."[1] In the same way, rulers impose unity upon their subjects by directing them to a unitary end – the good. Whereas Aristotle's conclusion that the political community must pursue a unitary end is required by his conception of rational activity as activity directed to an object, for Aquinas the reduction of multiplicity to unity is part of God's dispensation for the governance of the universe.

Assuming that the most effective agent of unity is something which is itself a natural unity, just as the universe is governed by one ruler, so the best form of government is a monarchy because it is less given to dissension and tyranny than rule by the many. But on the other hand, Aquinas insists that the evil to be feared above all is the rule of a tyrant. He is as concerned as the pagan philosophers were with the distinction between rule by arbitrary will and rule by law, which he considers synonymous with the distinction between the rule of irrational passion and the rule of reason. Aquinas accordingly defines law as "nothing else than an ordinance of reason for the common good, made by him who has care of the community, and promulgated."[2] This "ordinance of reason" provides a "directive principle" for human actions because, by being promulgated, law "imprints" on those subject to it a rule that provides for them a "principle of action."[3] Law thus satisfies the natural need of rational mortals for direction by a rational principle.

That the rule of law belongs to the natural order does not, however, exclude its also being required by man's Fall. When "man turned his back on God, he fell under the influence of his sensual impulses: in fact this happens to each one individually, the more he deviates from the path of reason, so that, after a fashion, he is likened to the beasts that are led by the impulse of sensuality."[4] The rule of law is a means for restoring the rule of reason, which their sinfulness leads men to reject. And this relation between law and original sin leads Aquinas to conclude that the power to coerce those subject to it is one of law's distinctive qualities. What distinguishes the law from the commands of a father is not then, as Aristotle holds, that law rules a *polis* rather than a household, but that the law has "coercive power" and can inflict penalties. Aquinas, like Augustine, thus considers punishment intrinsic to the idea of law. The purpose of the punishments inflicted by the law is not to punish for punishment's sake, for "God does not delight in punishments for their own sake," and punishment of this kind belongs to the time of the last

[1] St. Thomas Aquinas, *De Regimine Principum*, in *Aquinas: Selected Political Writings*, ed. A. P. d'Entrèves, trans. J. G. Dawson (Oxford: Blackwell, 1948), 11, 13.
[2] St. Thomas Aquinas, *The "Summa Theologiae" of St. Thomas Aquinas*, I–II, 90, 4.
[3] Ibid., I–II, 93, 5.   [4] Ibid., I–II, 91, 6.

judgment. On earth, the purpose of punishment is rather "medicinal," to promote public peace, by curing the criminal of evil propensities and deterring others through the fear of punishment.[5]

Thus, the law has two different purposes because it is imposed on two different kinds of men. For those who have a good disposition, whether by nature or the gift of God, paternal training and custom, which proceed by admonition, are sufficient. The law serves such men more as a plan for unity than as a restraint on passion. They observe the law according to their "own free-will and not of constraint." But those who are depraved, prone to vice and not easily amenable to words, who have to be restrained from evil by force and fear, are tamed by law.[6] For them, the law is a deterrent and an educational device.

But a different purpose for the punishment associated with law, a retributive purpose, is suggested in Aquinas' distinction between "the guilty act" and "the consequent stain." In this context, he says that even when the act has ceased, the guilt remains because in injuring his fellow men, the criminal has transgressed "the order of Divine justice," and he can restore this order only by paying some sort of "penal compensation." This debt of punishment lasts as long as the stain in his soul remains. Therefore, the duration of punishment should be proportionate not merely to the act, but to the duration of the fault, that is to say, the punishment must be sufficient to heal the powers of the soul that had been "disordered by the sin committed." In addition, punishment serves "to remove the scandal given to others, so that those who were scandalized at the sin may be edified by the punishment." In all these ways, punishment helps to maintain the order of God's justice.[7]

But even though law is intrinsically associated with coercion, it is not, as for Augustine, essentially an instrument of repression. Instead, the law is identified by Aquinas with *ratio*, with a plan, a measure, or principle of order that provides rational direction for human activity. The difference between Augustine's view of law as an instrument of repression and Aquinas' emphasis on the rational quality of law arises from the difference in their understanding of the relation between God and the human world. Whereas in the Augustinian picture, the emphasis falls on the mystery of God's will, the Thomistic picture emphasizes rather God's having willed to rule by a rational plan that is imprinted on His creatures. In this way, Aquinas tries to preserve the Aristotelian view of the human world as part of nature without suggesting that the human intellect is one with the Divine Intellect.

---

[5] Ibid., I–II, 87, 3.   [6] Ibid., I–II, 96, 5.   [7] Ibid., I–II, 87, 6.

But in addition, Aquinas gives practical reasons for preferring government by steady, written rules to government by personal judgments or
decrees. And these reasons echo Aristotle's arguments: To find a few wise
men competent to frame just laws is easier than finding the many who are
capable of judging rightly in each single case. Those who make laws
consider long beforehand what laws to make, but judgment for each
single case has to be pronounced as soon as it arises, and to see what is
right by taking many instances into consideration, as the legislator can, is
easier than by considering only one solitary fact. Moreover, lawgivers in
principle judge universally and of future events, whereas those who judge
particular cases are more likely to be affected by personal interests and
feelings that pervert their judgment. For this reason, Aquinas adopts the
basic Greek conception of law as written rules, deriving *lex* from *legere*, to
read. Law, in his view, must be written so that it can be promulgated. As
little as possible should be left to judges to decide since "animated justice"
is not to be found in every man and is in any case easily distorted.[8]

To the objection that inflexible rules cannot take into account the
variations in particular cases, Aquinas answers that the law is like any
other measure. If there were as many measures as there are things to be
measured, the measure would be useless. So a law must be applied to
many different people and acts in order to provide the kind of direction
that human beings need in order to be unified into a community. No
legislator can take account of "every single case" in the words of a law;
but even if he could do so, he ought not to mention all cases because that
would only produce confusion. Instead, the aim should be to keep the
law simple. It should therefore be framed according to that which is "of
most common occurrence."[9]

Law plays the same role in the human world as God's plan in the
universe by articulating the pattern for the common good that is in the
mind of the good lawmaker. But the pattern for the common good is
not, as for Aristotle, identical with a pattern for the good life. In this
respect, Aquinas remains closer to Augustine than to pagan philosophy.
Although he speaks of the "good life," he says that "the aim of a good
life on this earth is blessedness in heaven." And therefore the ruler's
purpose is not to lead his subjects to perfection on earth, but rather "to
promote the welfare of the community in such a way that it leads
fittingly to the happiness of heaven." But Aquinas goes on to say that
the ruler "must insist upon the performance of all that leads thereto,"
and forbid, as far as is possible, whatever is inconsistent with this end.[10]

---

[8] Ibid., I–II, 95, 1.   [9] Ibid., I–II, 96, 6.   [10] *De Regimine* 79.

On the other hand, Aquinas emphasizes a distinction between public and private discipline that is foreign to Aristotle and which echoes Augustine's Christian doctrine that the earthly city must not be confused with the heavenly one. It is not the business of the law to command every act of virtue, but only those that are necessary for the sake of the public good. Human law must even tolerate many deeds that are against virtue, not because they are approved, but because it is preferable that they not be punished. Some undesirable actions must go unpunished by law because the imperfection of man's condition brings it about that human beings "would be deprived of many advantages, if all sins were strictly forbidden and punishments appointed for them." Thus, usury should be permitted by law, not because it is held to be just, but to avoid interfering with the useful activities of many persons. To the question "whether it is lawful to borrow money under a condition of usury" Aquinas answers, "it is lawful to make use of another's sin for a good end." For example, "a man who has fallen among thieves is allowed to point out his property to them (which they sin in taking) in order to save his life."[11]

Another reason for limiting the aegis of law is that it must be "imposed on men" of different aptitudes for virtue. There are many vices by which the virtuous are not tempted but which the mass of men find it impossible to resist. The law should forbid only those more grievous vices that are damaging to others and threaten social stability, and which can be avoided by the majority of men.[12] A third reason for distinguishing the "common good" from the "good life" is the one emphasized by Augustine, that virtue is a matter of "interior movements, that are hidden" and that men can judge only exterior acts. Whereas God who is able to judge "the inward movement of wills" and may punish "the man who wishes to slay, but slays not," men can see only "those things that appear."[13] Therefore, only insofar as virtue is exhibited in outward acts, which can be observed by men and which affect the common good, is virtue an object of law.

The most distinctive aspect of Aquinas' idea of law appears in his discussion of how the laws made by men are related to "natural law." There is a similarity to Cicero's "natural law" insofar as, unlike Aristotle's "first principles" and Plato's "Ideas" or "Forms," which are perceived only by philosophers, Aquinas' natural law is "imprinted" in human reason and is therefore evident to all human beings: "The natural law is promulgated by the very fact that God instilled it into man's mind so as to

---

[11] *Summa Theologiae*, I–II, 78, 1; 78, 4.   [12] Ibid., I–II, 96, 2.
[13] Ibid., I–II, 91, 4; 100, 9.

be known by him naturally."[14] It is not, then, something that has to be "discovered" by men; it is not a kind of knowledge that may or may not be acquired: "the natural law, in the abstract, can nowise be blotted out from men's hearts."[15] But what is "imprinted" is nothing like the specific rules that Cicero identified with natural law.

What Aquinas has to say about the natural law can be properly understood only by remembering its metaphysical context – the postulate that the universe is a cosmos ordered by a hierarchy of principles. Eternal Reason rules this hierarchy, and all things participate in Eternal Reason. But each does so in its own way. Because man is a rational creature, he "partakes thereof [Eternal Reason] in an intellectual and rational manner." And the participation of man in the Eternal Reason "is properly called a law, since a law is something pertaining to reason."[16] Not all that is in the Divine Mind is made known to man in this way. Some things are made known by direct revelation, and this is the Divine Law. And much, of course, can never be known by man. But as human beings possess rational understanding, they are capable of being aware of the cosmic hierarchy, their place in it, and of the "end" to which they ought to direct their activities: "the rational creature is subject to Divine providence in the most excellent way, in so far as it partakes of a share of providence, by being provident both for itself and for others. Wherefore it has a share of the Eternal Reason, whereby it has a natural inclination to its proper act and end: and this participation of the eternal law in the rational creature is called the natural law."[17]

In other words, the natural law is the cosmic link between the positive laws made by men that rule earthly cities and the Divine Law. This link or role does not make the natural law either a standard to which enactments have to conform in order to qualify as law, or a definition of the particular purposes that positive laws should pursue. Nothing in the way of "natural rights" is implied by Aquinas' doctrine of natural law. It establishes only that there is an eternal cosmic foundation for the laws made by human beings and that laws are consequently not just human acts of will: "Every act of reason and will in us is based on that which is according to nature. . . for every act of reasoning is based on principles that are known naturally, and every act of appetite in respect of the means is derived from the natural appetite in respect of the last end. Accordingly the first direction of our acts to their end must needs be in virtue of the natural law."[18] To recognize natural law means recognizing that human laws, for all their variety, changeability, and uncertainty, are part of

---

[14] Ibid., I–II, 90, 4; 91, 2.   [15] Ibid., I–II, 94, 6.
[16] Ibid., I–II, 91, 2.   [17] Ibid., I–II, 91, 2.   [18] Ibid., I–II, 91, 2.

God's dispensation and have a fixed place in the natural order. That is why all laws include natural law, just as all buildings include their foundation stones. When Aquinas says that "every human law has just so much of the nature of law, as is derived from the law a nature,"[19] he is defining law by its relation to the cosmic order and to the different operations of human reason. His statement is entirely analogous to saying that a structure has the character of a house insofar as it provides shelter, or that something is a part insofar as it is derived from a whole. And just as the definition of a house does not indicate whether a Georgian country house is superior to a high-rise block of flats, so the relation of positive law to natural law does not provide any ground for distinguishing better from worse laws. But natural law does enable men to distinguish the rules of a civil association from the rules of other kinds of association, because it enables them to recognize what is the proper object of law and its place in shaping the human world as part of the natural order.

The importance of natural law in the Thomistic picture rests on the sharp distinction that Aquinas makes between theoretical and practical reason and between higher and lower principles of practical reason. The natural law is superior to the laws made by men to order the human world because it contains the first principles of practical reason. When Aquinas says that every law is derived from the natural law, he is saying that legislation is an activity of practical reason, which means that lawmaking is directed to action in this world and is a self-conscious rational choice as opposed to the instinctive behavior of animals. Because man alone among living beings can understand his end and the relation between his actions and that end, the power of comprehension implanted in him by nature is, Aquinas says, properly described as the *lex naturalis*, whereas in other animals we speak instead of a natural "instinct."

Although Aquinas stressed the uncertainty and variability of human law, by anchoring it through natural law to the eternal order of the universe, he reconciled the rational character given to law by the pagan philosophy of Aristotle with the Christian doctrine that the universe is ruled by a Creator whose will cannot be known by his creatures. Like Augustine, he insists that what pertains to the earthly city has to be distinguished sharply from what pertains to the heavenly city. But Aquinas does not conclude, as Augustine had, that power rather than reason is the essence of law.

The first precept of the natural law is that *"good is to be done and ensued, and evil is to be avoided."* Or, in other words, whatever the practical reason naturally understands to be good is to be pursued. What

---

[19] Ibid., I–II, 95, 2.

is good for man is that for which he has a natural inclination. And this precept is not a mere tautology because the "natural desires" of man are given not by his will or instincts, but by his place in the cosmic hierarchy of being. With all other substances, he has in common an inclination to seek the preservation of his nature, and therefore, "whatever is a means of preserving human life, and of warding off its obstacles, belongs to the natural law." Next, man shares with other animals an inclination to reproduce and bring up offspring. Therefore, whatever is a means to perpetuating the human species belongs to the natural law. On the other hand, man has an inclination that distinguishes human rational beings, that is, to perfect his rational powers, which means that he wants to know the truth about God and to live in society. All virtuous acts belong to the natural law because "whatever pertains to this inclination belongs to the natural law."[20] In short, the natural law denotes the natural needs of man that can be perceived by human reason.

But no particular practical conclusions necessarily follow. Aquinas explains and repeatedly emphasizes that although we possess by nature "knowledge of certain general principles," we do not thereby know "each single truth" contained within these principles. What is specifically required by the principles of natural law, that is to say, all questions about particular positive laws, remains to be answered by practical reason, which cannot arrive at indisputable answers. The natural law requires that all laws should be designed to achieve the common good, to prohibit stealing and killing, and to insure the honoring of one's father and mother. The reason of every man, "of itself," knows these principles to be undeniable because, like *"Every whole is greater than its parts,"* they are definitions of the social life that are essential to the perfection of man's nature.[21] But what actions are required by these principles remain for Aquinas – unlike Cicero – to be decided as a practical question.

Although the prohibition of stealing is a self-evident principle of natural law, even whether private property is desirable has to be established. And the arguments that Aquinas offers for private property are all practical: that each man looks after his own more carefully than after what is common to many or to all; that human affairs are conducted in a more orderly fashion when each man is made responsible for some particular task because confusion arises where anyone may take charge of anything indeterminately; and that peace is better preserved when each man knows what belongs to him, whereas quarrels easily arise among people who share in common without a clear division of goods. None of these arguments is indisputable because they cannot be *deduced* from

[20] Ibid., I–II, 94, 2.   [21] Ibid., I–II, 91, 3; 94, 2.

natural law. The desirability of private property follows from natural law by "determination" because it cannot be demonstrated as a matter of logical implication from first principles. It is a conclusion that is more plausible or persuasive than any proposed alternative.

The content of laws about property is even more disputable than the general conclusion that private property is desirable because the connection between the particular laws governing property and natural law is even more remote. Aquinas makes the same argument as Aristotle: Since law is concerned with matters that are "singular and contingent" and might always be other than they are, there can be no certainty about which laws are most desirable. Speculative reason can reach indisputable conclusions because it deals with unchanging things, but human laws "cannot have that inerrancy that belongs to the demonstrated conclusions of science."[22] While this does not prevent decisions about what laws are desirable from being rational, it does oblige men to make and use law in the manner that is appropriate to practical matters. As the natural law "cannot be applied to all men in the same way on account of the great variety of human affairs,"[23] there is bound to be great diversity in positive laws. In short, far from being a set of commands, natural law in the Thomistic sense leaves the question of the right laws for any time or place necessarily disputable. The few conclusions that can be deduced from natural law, such as the prohibition of unwarranted murder that follows indisputably from the principle that one should do no harm, Aquinas describes as "the law of nations," holding for all men, in contrast to the variety of civil law, which is derived from the law of nature "by way of determination."[24] Natural law is unchanging because it requires that justice should be preserved, which is a "never-failing principle."[25] But just what laws justice requires cannot be known with certainty and is bound to change with time and place.

That Aquinas' natural law has not always been understood in this fashion is partly due to a tendency to assimilate his doctrine to Cicero's very different idea of natural law. But misconceptions are encouraged also by the ambiguity of certain passages. Aquinas speaks of the natural law as a "participation" of human reason in Divine Reason that gives men knowledge of "certain general principles."[26] He also says that for "the volition of what is commanded" to have the nature of law, "it needs to be in accord with some rule of reason" and that if the sovereign's will is not in accord with reason, it "would savour of lawlessness rather than of law."[27]

---

[22] Ibid., I–II, 91, 3.   [23] Ibid., I–II, 95, 2.   [24] Ibid., I–II, 95, 4; 95, 2
[25] Ibid., I–II, 100, 8.   [26] Ibid., I–II, 91, 3.   [27] Ibid., I–II, 90, 1.

In the discussion of Divine Law, he says that laws in conflict with Divine Law "must nowise be observed."[28] But he does not explain how disagreements about whether a law conflicts with Divine Law can be settled or how such disagreements can be avoided. In his discussion of obedience, he says that "Man is bound to obey secular princes in so far as this is required by the order of justice. Wherefore if the prince's authority is not just but usurped, or if he commands what is unjust, his subjects are not bound to obey him, except perhaps accidentally, in order to avoid scandal or some particular danger."[29] If such passages are read without regard to Aquinas' understanding of the relation between man and the cosmic order, between Christian faith and knowledge, and between theoretical and practical reasoning, they might suggest, as many have supposed, that natural law provides a substantive prescription for legislative enactments. That this is not what Aquinas meant is definitely established by what he says about the obligation to obey the law.

It should be noticed, first of all, that although Aquinas describes a law that is not directed to the common interest as "tyrannical" and a "perversion of law" because it is "not being according to reason," and although he even declares it to be "not a law," he insists that it nevertheless has "something in the nature of a law." For even a tyrannical law, merely by virtue of being "an ordinance made by a superior to his subjects, and aims at being obeyed by them," contributes to making those who are subject to it "good." What reconciles Aquinas' apparently contradictory remarks is a distinction between two senses of "good." Although the "proper effect" of law is to "lead its subjects to their proper virtue," it may do so "simply" or only "in some particular respect." If the aim of the lawgiver is the true good, his subjects will be made good "simply." But even if he intends to secure no more than what is pleasurable or useful to himself, even if his laws are "in opposition to Divine justice," still they will make his subjects good relatively with respect to a "particular government," insofar as they unify his subjects into an orderly community.[30]

Aquinas agrees with Augustine that just as it is reasonable to call a man "a good robber, because he works in a way that is adapted to his end," so we must recognize that even a bad law, insofar as it is the duly promulgated command of the ruler to his subjects, has something of the character of a law and therefore contributes to the good of those governed by it. That is why it is entirely consistent for Aquinas to say that "A tyrannical law, through not being according to reason, is not a law, absolutely speaking, but rather a perversion of law; and yet in so far as it is something in the nature of a law, it. . . aims at being obeyed by them,

[28] Ibid., I–II, 96, 4.   [29] Ibid., I–II, 104, 6.   [30] Ibid., I–II, 92, 1.

which is to make them good not simply, but with respect to that particular government."[31] In obeying even an unjust law made by their acknowledged ruler, men are subordinated to a higher order by recognizing themselves as members of their earthly city. The obligation to obey the law, even when it is thought to be undesirable, follows from recognizing that men need to be subject to some law – just as the "irascible and concupiscible faculties" should obey reason, so every subject should obey his ruler. Therefore, even an unjust law, insofar as it "retains some appearance of law, though being framed by one who is in power, is derived from the eternal law; since all power is from the Lord God. . . ."[32] The obligation to obey the law does not rest on its being desirable, but on its having been made by an acknowledged ruler.

Sedition is condemned by Aquinas as "a kind of discord, not between individuals, but between the parts of a multitude." Sedition destroys "the unity of law and common good," and therefore it is a "mortal sin" whose gravity is proportionate to the degree in which "the common good which it assails surpasses the private good which is assailed by strife."[33] Although sedition against a tyrant is not ruled out, this does not contradict what Aquinas says about the obligation to obey a "tyrannical law" because he uses "tyranny" in two senses. One sense describes a ruler who makes laws that are not directed to the common good; in the other sense a tyrant is one who rules without law, by arbitrary orders. Such arbitrary tyrants deliberately try to prevent their subjects from establishing even ties of friendship because they fear that friendship might lead to plots. They try to prevent subjects not only from becoming virtuous lest they grow restive under unjust laws, but also from becoming rich or powerful lest they grow strong enough to oppose the tyrant's will. In other words, such tyrants deliberately try to prevent the orderly communal life that government exists to promote. What justifies sedition against such a tyrant is not that his laws are undesirable, but that he rules without law, according to "unbridled passion" rather than reason, and therefore his rule "in no way differs from a beast." All is uncertain and security is absent, for "no reliance can be placed upon that which depends upon the will, or rather the caprice, of another."[34] Sedition against a tyrant in this sense does not destroy an established order because here the tyrant is incapable of maintaining order. The tyrant himself is "guilty of sedition, since he encourages discord and sedition among his subjects, that he may lord over them more securely."[35] Nevertheless, even in this context

---

[31] Ibid., I–II, 92, 1. [32] Ibid., I–II, 93, 3. [33] Ibid., I–II, 42, 2.
[34] De Regimine 17, 19. [35] Summa Theologiae I–II, 42, 2.

Aquinas introduces a serious qualification on the justification for sedition. He points out that it must be considered whether the disturbance created by sedition might not be still greater than the disorder prevailing under tyranny.

In other words, for Aquinas the maintenance of an orderly communal life always takes precedence over promoting a more desirable order. Order cannot exist where there is no law because order is produced by reason, and law is the rule of reason. There can be no doubt that Aquinas rests the obligation to obey law not on its justice, but on its having been issued by the sovereign to which the individual is subject. He expresses the same view indirectly in his discussion of whether the subjects of one city are bound by the laws of another, where he concludes that "the subjects of one city or kingdom are not bound by the laws of the sovereign of another city or kingdom, since they are not subject to his authority." And similarly, the subjects of a given official such as a proconsul are obliged to obey his commands only in those matters where the subject is ruled by a superior power.[36]

In his most explicit and complete discussion of the proper response to a tyranny, *De Regimine Principum*, Aquinas warns that the attempt to overthrow a tyranny may bring evils far worse than those that it tries to cure: "If the tyranny be not excessive, it is certainly wiser to tolerate it in limited measure, at least for a time, rather than to run the risk of even greater perils by opposing it." For one thing, the attempt may fail and "only succeed in rousing the tyrant to greater savagery." But even if the revolt succeeds, the very fact of revolt "breeds strife and grave discord among the populace, either in the moment of rebellion or after his overthrow when opinion in the community is factiously divided as to the new form of government." Or if the rebels call on another ruler to help them, he may seize power and, because he is afraid of "sharing the fate of his predecessor," he may proceed with "even greater severity against his new subjects." The attempt to overthrow a tyrant may introduce a new tyrant who is worse than the old, who, far from abandoning his predecessor's cruelties, only reenforces them. Aquinas reminds his readers of the old woman in Syracuse who, while all other subjects were praying for the death of the tyrant Dionysius, prayed that he would outlive her; and when asked by the tyrant to explain, she replied that when she was a girl, she lived under a tyrant whose death was desired. He was slain and succeeded by another who was worse; again, his death was welcomed, but he was succeeded by Dionysius, who was still worse. And

---

[36] Ibid., I–II, 96, 5.

she felt certain that if Dionysius were removed, he would be succeeded by an even more terrible tyrant.[37]

An additional reason against the argument that a tyrant may become so intolerable that it would be "an act of virtue for the more powerful citizens" to kill him, even at the risk of dying to liberate their country, is found by Aquinas in Apostolic teaching: "For Peter teaches us to obey not only good and temperate rulers, but also to bear reverence to those who are ill-disposed." Thus, the Christians bore the persecution of many Roman emperors with "courage and resignation." The reason why Aioth (Ehud) was not condemned for his assassination of Eglon was that he did not kill "a legitimate, though tyrannical, ruler of the people," but an enemy. And on the same reasoning, "those who slew Joas, King of Juda, were put to death, even though he was an apostate." Aquinas concludes that "It would indeed be dangerous, both for the community and for its rulers, if individuals were, upon private initiative," to assassinate those who were thought to govern tyrannically. Assassins are more commonly unjust men who slay just rulers; and moreover, they may truthfully claim to have suffered unbearably because "the rule of a just king is no less burdensome to the evil than that of a tyrant." In short, it is an act of "presumption" for individuals to take it into their hands to decide whether their ruler is a tyrant who must be deposed.[38]

The better remedy is for those who have the right to appoint the ruler to remove him: "Where a community has the right to elect a ruler for itself, it would not be contrary to justice for that community to depose the king whom it has elected, nor to curb his power should he abuse it to play the tyrant." And in such a case, the community is not guilty of disloyalty even though they had promised "constant fealty" because the tyrant's failure to discharge his duties absolves his subjects of their oath to him. But if the king was appointed by some superior, then the right to depose him belongs with that superior. And if all else fails, there is always recourse to "God the King of all. . . For it is in His power to turn the cruel heart of a tyrant to gentleness."[39]

There is no suggestion whatsoever in Aquinas' discussion of tyranny that a subject may appeal to the natural law to absolve them of an obligation to obey the law of their sovereign. The emphasis falls rather on the dangers of renouncing an obligation to obey duly promulgated law. While Aquinas suggests that the people who elect a king may have a constitutional right to depose him, he does not deny that a king who fails to perform his duties properly is a "legitimate" ruler. And his remark about how burdensome a just ruler may be to the unjust man carries a

---

[37] *De Regimine* 29, 31.   [38] Ibid., 31.   [39] Ibid., 31, 33.

clear warning that there can be no certainty about whether a ruler is a tyrant. That is a practical question, and about practical questions good men may always disagree. Although Aquinas concedes that there may be some grounds for renouncing political obligation where there is no rule of law, he speaks more about the dangers than the benefits of rebellion. Even where there is doubt about whether the ruler's ordinances are rightfully within his power or apply equally to all, which characteristic true laws must have, still it might be well to observe such enactments "in order to avoid scandal or disturbance."[40] In all these different contexts, Aquinas makes it clear that his doctrine of natural law does not give subjects a right to renounce their obligation to obey whatever enactment they choose to consider "unjust." He never identifies *lex* with *Jus*.

What Aquinas says about the obligation to obey the law postulates a distinction between the authority and the justice of law. But Aquinas makes no such distinction explicitly. Nor does he have a distinct concept of authority as English translations of Aquinas suggest by using the word "authority." Nevertheless, there are intimations of a concept of authority such as Hobbes developed. If a man makes a law that "goes beyond the power committed to him," Aquinas says, that law is an act of violence rather than a law.[41] He describes the sovereign as the ultimate source of law when he says that the sovereign is necessarily exempt from the coercive power of the law since "no man is coerced by himself, and law has no coercive power save from the authority of the sovereign." He points out also that the sovereign must be "above the law" because he decides whether or not to change the law and can "dispense in it according to time and place."[42] In all these ways, Aquinas' sovereign is he who has the last word about the making of law. And the only qualification is that the law must be "promulgated" for the obvious reason that a law can be binding only for those who are aware of it: "in order that a law obtain the binding force which is proper to a law, it must needs be applied to the men who have to be ruled by it. Such application is made by its being notified to them by promulgation, where promulgation is necessary for the law to obtain its force."[43] Nor is the sovereign's "authority" qualified by the requirement that the sovereign ought to oblige himself to observe the law because "*whatever law a man makes for another, he should keep himself.*" For the sovereign must observe the law "of his own free will and not of constraint," because no man is above the sovereign. Only God can judge the sovereign for ignoring the law.[44]

[40] *Summa Theologiae*, I–II, 96, 4.   [41] Ibid., I–II, 96, 4.
[42] Ibid., I–II, 96, 5.   [43] Ibid., I–II, 90, 4.   [44] Ibid., I–II, 96, 5.

It does not follow from Aquinas' insistence on an obligation to obey the law when it is duly promulgated that the distinction between just and unjust laws cannot or should not be made. He even says that whereas just laws "have the power of binding in conscience from the eternal law from which they are derived, according to Prov. viii.15, *By Me kings reign, and lawgivers decree just things,*" an unjust law is not binding in conscience. But the fact that an unjust law is not binding in conscience does not by itself destroy the obligation to obey it. Although Aquinas identifies the rule of law with the rule of reason in the universe, which might imply that there is a rational criterion for positive laws, he carefully rejects the conclusion that in order to qualify as law or oblige obedience, a promulgation must conform to a rational criterion. His doctrine of natural law is designed rather to give an account of the rational character of the purpose served by the law, while affirming the human and contingent character of the law itself and the impossibility of basing obedience to particular laws on an appeal to intuitions of eternal verities.

Aquinas' attention to the character of law as a human artifact led him also to provide the first serious explanation of the relation between law and custom. The simple classical view had been that the legal order replaced the variety of conflicting customs by making some customs rather than others clear and obligatory for all through the deliberate enactment of them in written law. Aquinas' discussion concentrated on another and characteristically medieval relationship between law and custom, the fact that custom is sometimes recognized to have the force of law and even allowed to override promulgated law.

Established custom may be as much a product of reason as law, Aquinas argues, because human reason and will are manifested by deeds as well as by speech. What a man selects as the good is as evident from how he acts as from what he says. When men act in a certain way, they express a rational judgment. When actions are repeated again and again, a custom is established, which means that custom is derived from "a deliberate judgment of reason." And therefore, custom can be as rational as law. Moreover, because custom becomes established only when all the members of the community observe it, custom reflects "the consent of the whole people." Taking account of the established ways of doing things is therefore "one of the conditions of law. For it is not easy to set aside the custom of a whole people."[45] Indeed, since the sovereign, in framing laws, acts as the representative of the people, custom is a more direct way of permitting the whole people to make their own laws. For

[45] Ibid., I–II, 97, 3.

although the people may not have the power to legislate or to abolish a law that has been promulgated, if a custom observed by them is tolerated by those who have the power to make law, then the custom obtains the force of law "by the very fact that they [who have the power to legislate] tolerate it they seem to approve of that which is introduced by custom." Custom may also, according to Aquinas, serve as a test of the usefulness of law. For when some change makes the law defective and it is replaced by custom, that is to say, by many repeated acts that disregard the law, "then custom shows that the law is no longer useful: just as it might be declared by the verbal promulgation of law to the contrary."[46]

The contingent character of human existence is, in other words, such that laws may be made to remedy the defects of custom, and customs may arise to remedy the defects of laws. But on the other hand, custom also re-enforces the law, for "custom avails much for the observance of laws." When a law is changed, a custom is "abolished," and consequently "the binding power of the law is diminished." It is not enough, therefore, to think only of what makes a change in the law desirable: "human law should never be changed, unless, in some way or other, the common weal be compensated according to the extent of the harm done in this respect."[47]

Even while the law remains unchanged, however, it can, in Aquinas' view, be adapted to different circumstances because it consists of rules that have to be interpreted for particular cases. The relationship between any given rules of law and judgments according to those rules is the same as the relationship between the fixed precepts of natural law and the various positive laws, or between the precepts of the Decalogue and their application to cases. The Decalogue forbids murder, theft, and adultery, and this prohibition remains unchanged, but "as to any determination by application to individual actions, – for instance that this or that be murder, theft, or adultery, or not – in this point they admit of change. . . ."[48] This follows from the logical compatibility of a variety of particular conclusions with the same general proposition from which they are derived. Because decisions about cases are "determinations" of rules of law, they may change with the circumstances without affecting the rule.

But law may also be adapted to changing circumstances in another way by what Aquinas calls "dispensation." His view of dispensation rests on his acceptance of Aristotle's understanding of a rule of law as a kind of average: "Now it happens often that the observance of some point of law

---

[46] Ibid., I–II, 97, 3.   [47] Ibid., I–II, 97, 2.   [48] Ibid., I–II, 100, 8.

conduces to the common weal in the majority of instances, and yet, in some cases, is very hurtful. Since then the lawgiver cannot have in view every single case, he shapes the law according to what happens most frequently, by directing his attention to the common good."[49] The more particular the question at issue, the more flexible the interpretation may be, for the more particular is always subordinate to the less particular. A law to the effect that "no man should work for the destruction of the commonwealth, or betray the state to its enemies" must be interpreted strictly. But there may be precepts subordinate to it, which indicate "special modes of procedure" that might, if adhered to on some occasions, achieve the opposite of what the lawmaker obviously intended.[50] Thus, if it were required by law that for each ward some men should keep watch as sentries in case of siege, some person might be released from this duty in order to perform a more important one. Even more general rules of law may sometimes be dispensed from because a general precept is apt to fail in some particular cases, either by preventing some important good or by imposing an evil. And therefore, the nature of law requires that there be a power of dispensation. For it is the "motive of the lawgiver" and not "his very words" that matters. Since every law derives its "force and nature," from its being "directed to the common weal of men," and since no lawgiver can take account of all possible cases, it is conceivable that a case might arise where the observance of the law would destroy the common good.[51]

It should be noticed, however, that the example given by Aquinas is one where there is unlikely to be much disagreement about what is required: If "in a besieged city it be an established law that the gates of the city are to be kept closed, this is good for public welfare as a general rule; but, if it were to happen that the enemy are in pursuit of certain citizens, who are defenders of the city, it would be a great loss to the city, if the gates were not opened to them: and so in that case the gates ought to be opened, contrary to the letter of the law, in order to maintain the common weal, which the lawgiver had in view." But Aquinas goes on to say that such a violation of law is justifiable only where there is a "sudden risk needing instant remedy," that is to say, when observing the law would produce an immediate danger, and the necessity of disregarding the law is so obvious as to be nearly indisputable.[52]

Where there is no such emergency, "it is not competent for everyone to expound what is useful and what is not useful to the state: those

[49] Ibid., I–II, 96, 6. [50] Ibid., I–II, 100, 8.
[51] Ibid., I–II, 96, 6. [52] Ibid., I–II, 96, 6.

alone can do this who are in authority, and who, on account of suchlike cases, have the power to dispense from the laws." The power of dispensation, Aquinas says firmly, belongs only to those who have been given the power to do so. To leave dispensation to the discretion of each individual "would be dangerous." Moreover, there is no justification for an official empowered to dispense from the law to allow a precept not to be observed simply because he regards it as undesirable. If he grants permission to disregard the law "of his mere will, he will be an unfaithful or an imprudent dispenser."[53]

In the course of blending a Greek with a Christian view of law, Aquinas offers a subtle exploration of the relationship between the fixity and the contingency of law. The law, in his view, is to be treated neither simply in Augustinian fashion as the imposed basis of peace in an irrevocably alienated worldly society, nor simply in Ciceronian terms as a deduction from or reflection of eternal verities clearly known to men. Rather, Aquinas argues that man has access, through rational participation in Eternal Reason, to natural law, but that the natural law consists only of very general and abstract precepts that cannot be translated directly into universally applicable law, and which must be applied to particular cases only through interpretation. For the most part, laws are made – for better or worse – by rulers whose aims may not be purely to lead men to God; but these laws, often qualified by (or incorporating) custom are nevertheless, Aquinas holds, to be obeyed because they, along with the customs and interpretations that they incorporate, at least convey a rational order (even if not the highest rational order) to society and human life. Only in extreme circumstances should a ruler therefore dispense from his own law; and only when a ruler fails even to create or impose settled law should the subject contemplate revolt. Law is thus rational at root and rationally obeyed. But law should not be conceived as a direct expression of Eternal Reason and should not be disobeyed simply because subjects believe that it conflicts with whatever they consider to be the dictates of Reason.

The Thomistic account of law is, in short, a powerful and explicit attempt to resolve the Aristotelian tension between law as the cement of society (something to be obeyed because it is law) and law as a moral absolute (something to be obeyed because it is an expression of eternal verities). Certainly it is a more powerful and subtle account than the opposing simplicities of Cicero and Augustine. But at the same time, Aquinas leaves intact the other great Aristotelian tension between justice

[53] Ibid., I–II, 96, 6; 97, 4.

and liberty. If, as Aquinas believes, human reason and the law that human reason fashions are ultimately (even if opaquely at a highly abstract level) a participation in Eternal Reason, how can the law recognize and value the desire and ability of human beings to be independent agents, to enjoy liberty? Is individuality or liberty indeed to be valued? Or is the best law – founded on clear, abstract intuition and followed by inspired and wise practical "determination" and interpretation – one that leads men remorselessly along the path of justice to God? This unresolved question, together with doubts about the limits of obedience, inspired by Augustine, formed the basis of the discussion of the idea of law in the early modern period. After Augustine and Aquinas, the leading questions were: If human law is an expression of justice derived in some way from Eternal Reason, how can liberty be protected? And if human law is purely a man-made artifact, what, if any, are the bases for (or limits to) obedience?

Part III
The modern quest

6   Thomas Hobbes

An escape from the tension between justice and liberty was provided by Thomas Hobbes's radical renunciation of the ancient idea of a cosmos where human reason has access to indisputable knowledge. In his attack on Aristotelianism, Hobbes ruthlessly spelled out the implications of living in a Christian universe. By pursuing St. Augustine's rejection of the pagan universe to its logical conclusion, Hobbes unequivocally replaced the concern with law as a link to divinity and an instrument of education with a picture of law as man's only resource against violence in a world that has no anchor to indisputable truth. By exploring the postulates and implications of this picture of law, Hobbes defined a new set of questions and opened the modern discussion of law.

His account of law rests on a division of the universe into two wholly separate domains: a world of concrete contingent being, which men inhabit, confronting another wholly alien world of infinite being, God the Creator. This picture of the universe – which explains the novelty in Hobbes's conception of law – is a radical departure from the ancient and medieval conception of human beings as products of matter informed by God's reason. Instead, Hobbes's human being is a creature made by God out of nothing, not according to any pattern, but as God in his infinite power willed. As this God is a Creator, and not an intelligible principle, the reason of man cannot in any way penetrate His ideas. Human beings are thus wholly cut off from understanding the eternal reality behind the ever changing world of human experience.

To fit this picture, Hobbes invented a new understanding of rationality that was totally purified of the pagan idea of reason as a quasi-divine power. The pagan legacy was denounced by Hobbes for being the root of social disorder because it sanctioned arbitrary claims to possess final truth and "right Reason": "And when men that think themselves wiser than all others, clamor and demand right Reason for judge; yet seek no more, but that things should be determined, by no other men's reason but their own, it is as intolerable in the society of men, as it is in play after trump is turned, to use for trump on every occasion, that suite whereof they have most in their hand."[1] Hobbes's new definition of rationality proposed to explain the predicament of a creature who could ask questions about the order of the universe and produce a variety of answers, but was irrevocably denied any access to indisputable truth.

In accordance with his repudiation of the pagan cosmology, Hobbes rejected the distinction between spirit and matter on which it rested. He was a "materialist," not in the sense of believing that matter was the ultimate stuff of the universe, but because he refused to divide the universe between matter and spirit or even to speculate on what it was made of. Instead of discussing human beings as souls or rational essences, as his predecessors had, Hobbes preferred to speak of a "*person*" which "signifies an intelligent substance, that acteth any thing in his own or another's name, or by his own or another's authority."[2] This meant that a man should be regarded as an individual substance, and not as a dislocated fragment of divinity. When Hobbes spoke of "nature" he meant the nature of the scientists, not of the ancient or medieval philosophers. For he did not identify nature with the rational order of the universe, but with the phenomena that any man could observe, and he proposed to read men in the same manner as Copernicus had read the stars. The laws of nature in Hobbes's view therefore cannot determine the purpose for which men were created, but rather describe the manner in which God's creatures operate and the conditions of their existence. Such laws are discovered by reflecting on the thoughts and behavior of oneself and other people, not by intuiting God's ideas, reasons, or purposes. Understanding of this sort does not then presume to be god-like, i.e., to escape or belittle sense perception in favor of "higher" intuitions. And it renounces any talk of invisible things such as had led to those "insignificant sounds . . . coyned by Schoole-men and pusled Philosophers." Any talk of entities – apart from the Creator – that do not exist in some time or place and have some determinate magnitude, Hobbes assures us, is nothing but absurd speech "taken upon credit (without any signification at all), from deceived Philosophers, and deceived, or deceiving Schoolemen."[3]

The universe postulated by Hobbes is consequently a welter of particulars. Each man's perception of these particulars depends on the objects that happen to impinge on his senses. As a result every man's head may be full of totally different thoughts. If men are to speak to one another, they

---

[1] Thomas Hobbes, *Hobbes's Leviathan*, ed. Richard Tuck (1651, reprint, Cambridge: Cambridge University Press, 1991), 33.
[2] Thomas Hobbes, *The English Works of Thomas Hobbes*, ed. William Molesworth, vol. IV (London: Bohn, 1966), 310.
[3] *Leviathan*, 30, 24.

can do so only by agreeing to assign certain names to certain particulars, and their agreement can rest on nothing other than their will to make it. For human reason is a power of invention, and as there is no natural, given basis for what is invented, there is no natural foundation for agreement among men.

The human predicament thus takes on a wholly new character. It no longer consists in the difficulty of learning to discover and conform to the first principles of things or the order given by Nature. It arises rather out of recognizing that there is no "utmost ayme" or "greatest Good," such as "is spoken of in the Books of the old Morall philosophers," and that there is no natural limit to a man's desires. Everything attained may suggest another object to be desired. As long as a man lives, desire is endless. Nor is there any natural criterion for what is good and bad; what is good is what a man finds desirable; and every man may find desirable something different. There is no pattern for the good life, given by nature, but only a desire for "felicity" which is "a continuall progresse of the desire, from one object to another; the attaining of the former, being still but the way to the later."[4]

When such endlessly moved and moving creatures live among other such beings, they are bound to discover in one another either impediments or means to their ceaseless search for satisfaction. Even if they do not regard one another as enemies, if they wish only to speak together, there is nothing that can decide for them what signification any sound will have. If they wish to act together, they have no standard by which to choose between a better and worse course of action. They can escape from this predicament only by recognizing someone whom they will obey. But there is no reason in nature why they should follow or listen to one man over another, for no one is so manifestly superior in power, intellect, or any other respect that it would be inconceivable for others to try to supplant him. As long as no human being appears to be as a god among men, no one can by nature be acknowledged to have dominion over the others. And this equality of men is the source of the natural disorder of human life. Because each individual is a unique rational substance shut up within the walls of his own consciousness, if man had nothing but his own reason to guide him, men would be doomed to wander aimlessly in a totally mysterious universe, where each person's thoughts wholly and permanently differed from that of every other; and this independently of the fact that each man may see the next as either a means or a threat to achieving the satisfactions he desires.

[4] Ibid., 70.

Religious faith offers no way out of this predicament because, Hobbes repeatedly reminds us, although God may speak to any man, others cannot know that He has done so. They may choose to believe it, as the Jews did with Moses and the Christians with Jesus, but such acquiescence must rest on a will to believe. The words in Scripture can have an indisputable meaning only when the men using them have agreed upon what meaning they shall have. And there is no given ground for such agreements. Indeed wherever we look, if we can act or think in common with others, it is because we have arrived at an agreement for which there is no foundation in nature: "And therefore, as when there is a controversy in an account, the parties must, by their own accord, set up for right Reason, the Reason of some Arbitrator, or Judge, to whose sentence they will both stand, or their controversie must either come to blowes, or be undecided, for want of a right Reason constituted by Nature; so is it also in all debates of what kind soever."[5]

The moral of Hobbes's novel account of the human predicament is that if men hope to agree on anything, they must come to do so without the help of any natural pattern, standard, criterion, sanction, or model. Therefore, to engage in any discourse or take any common action, men are obliged to obey someone whose will can impose unity on the natural diversity. It is possible to distinguish, however, between decisions made by someone whose right to decide is recognized by those who obey him, and the commands issued by someone who imposes obedience by force. And this distinction is what Hobbes offers as a way out of the human predicament. It explains how men can live together without subjecting themselves to the arbitrary dominion of another because, though their association is necessarily based on a command of will rather than reason, they can choose to oblige themselves to obey and therefore need not be enslaved.

When men choose to recognize another's right to decide for them, they "authorize" him to do so, that is, they give him the right to speak for them. They thereby create a "sovereign" who is absolute in the sense that his decisions – simply because they are his decisions and he has been authorized to make them – are the last resort in our disputes. Having authorized him to decide, they are then obliged by their own action to accept his decision even when they dislike it. Otherwise, they convict themselves of self-contradiction. That does not prevent anyone from finding authorized decisions obnoxious. It merely means that we are obliged to obey what we find distasteful. And this obligation to obey

[5] Ibid., 32–33.

the sovereign, even when his will is distasteful, is the foundation of civil peace.

Although referred to as "he," the sovereign is a concept which may in reality denote one, few, or many, i.e., a king, an elected assembly, or a procedure. What defines the sovereign is possessing the authority to make the final decisions for all. But though in this sense the sovereign is "absolute," he cannot be a tyrant exercising arbitrary power because he could not then secure "peace." For peace, Hobbes emphasizes, is not just the absence of physical combat; it is a condition in which men can have stable expectations, and men subject to the ever changing arbitrary decrees of a tyrant suffer from the same insecurity as men in the "state of nature." The war of each against all is a condition in which a man cannot know from one day to the next what is his own, what will be demanded of him, and who will assert supremacy over him. This insecurity may be created by a government which imposes arbitrary orders no less than by the disorder of anarchy. Tyranny then offers no escape from the war of each against all.

To ensure that men may live without fear, Hobbes stressed that the sovereign's authority has to be exercised by making and maintaining stable rules. Such rules constitute the rule of law. And Hobbes's discussion of law is designed to establish ways of distinguishing rules made, interpreted, and enforced by an authorized officer of the sovereign from rules that are not so authorized and that no one is therefore obliged to obey. Hobbes's distinctive achievement consists in making it plain that if we reject the ancient rationalism, any order in human life must rest on abiding by rules made by an authorized legislator. By emphasizing that the source of law must be an authorized legislator, Hobbes explains how, even though it is wholly a human artifact, law constitutes a protection, indeed the only protection, against arbitrary power.

But at the same time, in defining and emphasizing the concept of authority, Hobbes also shows that there is an ineradicable element of arbitrariness in the rule of law. For the rules which we recognize an obligation to obey can never be ultimately justified by reference to any universal, necessary truth that all rational beings are obliged by reason to accept. Our only alternative to chaos is to will to accept the word of someone. That word may be given in many different fashions; the "someone" may be one person or many, a highly intricate institution or a set of procedures developed long ago over many years. We must, however, if we are to avoid barbarism, agree to accept certain decisions simply because we recognize them to have been authorized. Though we may justify the decisions to which we submit in any number of ways, we cannot find an ultimate sanction for what we accept that no man can rationally dispute.

Therefore, at the base of any system of law, if we push it to its foundations, lies a "decision" that cannot be indisputably justified.

By "law" then Hobbes means "Civil Lawes," which bind the members of a "Common-wealth." A commonwealth is constituted by those who agree to authorize a sovereign, that is, to recognize the right of a sovereign to speak for all of them. For Hobbes, as for all of his Greek and medieval predecessors, law pertains to a community that is created by human artifice. Unlike his predecessors, Hobbes explicitly makes the authorization of a representative of the commonwealth, that is to say, a sovereign, the foundation for this community. Because in authorizing a sovereign, the members of the commonwealth oblige themselves to obey the laws that he makes, law should be understood as a command and not a counsel: "Counsell, is where a man saith, *Doe*, or *Doe not this*, and deduceth his reasons from the benefit that arriveth by it to him to whom he saith it."[6] Since the man to whom the counsel is addressed stands to be benefited by that counsel, he remains free to reject it as, in Hobbes's view, each man is, by nature, the ultimate judge of what will promote his own good. But law is a command rather than a counsel because the reason for obeying a law is nothing other than that it has been issued by someone whose authority to make law is recognized by the person commanded. Law is accordingly defined by Hobbes as follows: "CIVILL LAW, *Is to every Subject, those Rules, which the Common-wealth hath Commanded him, by Word, Writing, or other sufficient Sign of the Will, to make use of, for the Distinction of Right, and Wrong; that is to say, of what is contrary, and what is not contrary to the Rule.*"[7] In order that the members of the commonwealth may be able to discern what constitutes an authentic law, there must be agreed upon signs for identifying a law. And an existing law can be abrogated only by a law forbidding it to be executed, for only the sovereign power can repeal law and make new ones whenever he chooses.

Like his predecessors, Hobbes holds that it is of the essence of law to be written and published, but the reason he emphasizes this requirement is that law must display clear signs of having been derived from the will of the sovereign. For otherwise, any man's private will might claim the force of law. Being written is essential to law in order to indicate that all laws "have their Authority, and force, from the Will of the Common-wealth; that is to say, from the Will of the Representative; which in a Monarchy is the Monarch, and in other Common-wealths the Soveraign Assembly."[8] Hobbes accordingly denies that because a rule appears in "the Books of

---

[6] Ibid., 183, 176.   [7] Ibid., 183.   [8] Ibid., 186.

Lawyers of eminence" or in the opinions of judges, it constitutes law. That is not evidence of its having been willed by the sovereign. To ensure the authenticity of law is the reason for "the publique Registers, publique Counsels, publique Ministers, and publique Seales; by which all Lawes are sufficiently verified."[9] These enable everyone to consult the record of the law to discover whether what he proposes to do is permitted by the law or whether what he takes to be an injury is a violation of the law. Similarly, with officers of the law, their authority has to be verified by a written commission or a public seal.

Hobbes did not therefore accept that the judicial decisions that constitute common law are law, but insisted on the subordination of the common law (and the legal profession) to statute law. He denies what some defenders of common law have argued, that natural reason, art, or divinely informed reason are the sources of common law – they can only be the pronouncements of private individuals. Nor is it "the singularity of Process used in any Court; that can distinguish it so as to make it a different Law from the Law of the whole Nation."[10] Against Sir Edward Coke's identifications of *Lex* with *Jus*, which Coke said constitute the Common Law, Hobbes argues that *Lex* and *Jus* must be distinguished, for only "Law obligeth me to do, or forbear the doing of something; and therefore it lies upon me an Obligation." But justice has to do with rights, and "my Right is a Liberty left me by the Law to do any thing which the Law forbids me not, and to leave undone any thing which the Law commands me not."[11] And in any case, a judge's " long study, observation, and experience" cannot ensure the justice of his decisions: "For it is possible long study may encrease, and confirm erroneous Sentences: and where men build on false grounds, the more they build, the greater is the ruine: and of those that study, and observe with equall time, and diligence, the reasons and resolutions are, and must remain discordant. . ."[12]

Moreover, "before there was a Law, there could be no Injustice, and therefore Laws are in their Nature Antecedent to Justice and Injustice, and you cannot deny but there must be Law-makers, – before there [were] any Laws . . . I speak of Humane Justice . . ."[13] What rendered Edward Coke a judge is not that he "had more, or less use of Reason" but "because the King made him so." The law of which Coke speaks is "not the Reason, Learning, or Wisdom of the Judges" but the king's reason:

[9] Ibid., 189.
[10] Thomas Hobbes, *A Dialogue between a Philosopher and a Student of the Common Laws of England*, ed. Joseph Cropsey (Chicago: University of Chicago Press, 1971), 97.
[11] *Dialogue*, 73.   [12] *Leviathan*, 187.   [13] *Dialogue*, 72–73.

"the Kings Reason, when it is publickly upon Advice and Deliberation declar'd, is that *Anima Legis*, and that *Summa Ratio*, and that Equity which all agree to be the Law of Reason, is all that is, or ever was Law in *England*, since it became Christian, besides the Bible."[14]

The only true common law is the king's prerogative, a doctrine for which Hobbes finds support in Bracton: "No Man may presume to dispute of what he [the sovereign] does, much less to resist him. You see by this, that this Doctrine concerning the Rights of Soveraignty so much Cryed down by the long Parliament, is the Antient Common-law, and that the only Bridle of the Kings of *England*, ought to be the fear of God."[15] The theme is the same throughout, that wherever anyone other than the sovereign is permitted to make law, there is bound to be disagreement, contradiction, and destruction of civil peace, and that law is not a product of wisdom or reason, but of the will of the sovereign.

Hobbes recognizes that some laws are not made by the sovereign but are customs that have acquired the authority of law through long usage. But he maintains that what gives a custom the character of law is not the length of time that it has been in force, but the fact that the silence of the sovereign signifies his consent. However ancient the custom that has been recognized as law, the sovereign remains free to repeal it if he should find the custom unreasonable. And the "Judgement of what is reasonable, and of what is to be abolished, belongeth to him that maketh the Law, which is the Soveraign Assembly, or Monarch."[16] What matters is not who first enunciated the law, "For the Legislator is he, not by whose authority the Lawes were first made, but by whose authority they now continue to be Lawes. And therefore where there be divers Provinces, within the Dominion of a Common-wealth, and in those Provinces diversity of Lawes, which commonly are called the Customes of each severall Province, we are not to understand that such Customes have their force, onely from Length of Time; but that they were antiently Lawes written, or otherwise made known, for the Constitutions, and Statutes of their Soveraigns; and are now Lawes, not by vertue of the PrÆscription of time, but by the Constitutions of their Present Soveraigns."[17]

On the adjudication of laws, Hobbes appears to take two different views. He asserts that all law needs to be interpreted, explaining that if written laws are short, the ambiguity of a word may lead to misinterpretation; if long, the ambiguity may affect many words. Therefore, the only way to understand a law properly is to grasp the final cause for which it was made, and that knowledge lies with the legislator. In saying this, Hobbes,

---

[14] Ibid., 62.   [15] Ibid., 74.   [16] *Leviathan*, 184–85.   [17] Ibid., 185–86.

consistent with his general view, makes the will of the sovereign the ultimate criterion of a correct decision. But Hobbes denies that in interpreting the law, the judge ought to look to "the letter of the Law" because that would allow any and every construction to pass as law. Instead, Hobbes argues that the judge must interpret the words of the law according to "the Intention of the Legislator."[18] The obligation of the judge is to "have regard to the reason, which moved his Sovereign to make such Law" and shape his decision accordingly. For only then will the judge's decision be that of his Sovereign, as it should be, and not his own.[19] Hobbes even suggests that the judge may sometimes without danger "recede" from the letter of the law by consulting the preamble to discover the meaning and sense of the law, the time when it was made, and the "incommodities" for which it was made.[20] The oddity here is that, by allowing judges so much latitude to depart from the letter of the law, and by ignoring the difficulty that had so preoccupied his successors, i.e., of discovering the intentions of the legislator, Hobbes ignored the danger of giving judges, rather than authorized legislators, the power to make law. Nor did Hobbes concern himself with the danger of destroying the stability of law by ignoring precedent. He regarded respect for precedent as a lamentable attribution of infallibility to judges and a readiness to forget that interpreting the law should always consist in divining the will of the sovereign.

Hobbes appears to encourage an even more extreme laxity in adjudication, which allows the judge to cease acting as his sovereign's voice, when he says that in the act of adjudicating, the judge must consider what is "consonant to natural reason, and Equity; and the Sentence he giveth, is therefore the Interpretation of the Law of Nature." Hobbes does add that this interpretation is not the judge's private opinion but given by "Authority of the Soveraign, whereby it becomes the Soveraigns Sentence."[21] And here, too, Hobbes emphasizes that as a judge may err in his judgment of equity, his successors are not bound by his decisions. The general effect, however, is to make the judge's decision rest on his view of equity rather than on interpretation of the written law. There is a suggestion of a reconciliation of the two views when Hobbes says, "For the literall sense is that, which the Legislator intended, should by the letter of the Law be signified. Now the Intention of the Legislator is always supposed to be Equity: For it were a great contumely for a Judge to think otherwise of the Soveraigne." But then Hobbes opens a Pandora's box

---

[18] Ibid., 194, 186–87.   [19] Ibid., 187.
[20] Ibid., 193–95.   [21] Ibid., 191–92.

of judicial arbitrariness – which his successors have duly exploited – by adding that where the "Word of the Law does not fully authorise a reasonable Sentence," the judge may "supply it with the Law of Nature."[22]

In the end, Hobbes remains uncharacteristically indecisive on the subject of adjudication: "the incommodity that follows the bare words of a written Law, may lead him [the judge] to the Intention of the Law, whereby to interpret the same the better; though no Incommodity can warrant a Sentence against the Law. For every Judge of Right, and Wrong, is not Judge of what is Commodious, or Incommodious to the Common-wealth."[23] But the ambiguity in Hobbes's view of adjudication seems less surprising in view of later discussions of law, which devoted themselves with great sophistication to this question first raised by Hobbes, without succeeding in arriving at a coherent answer.

As Hobbes is deliberately rejecting the cosmology of his predecessors, he considers, as they do, the relation of civil to natural law. He calls all unwritten laws "Laws of Nature." For if a law obliges everyone, and is not written or published or proclaimed so that it may be authenticated, it can only be a law of nature. That is the only kind of law that can be recognized by and be agreeable to the reason of every man. But the law of nature, as Hobbes understands it, amounts only to one sentence that is necessarily "approved by all the world:" "*Do not that to another, which thou thinkest unreasonable to be done by another to thy selfe.*"[24] Understood in this fashion, the unwritten law of nature (apart from describing what men are) may fill in what the law leaves unsaid.

Laws of nature are not, however, properly laws. They are rather names for qualities that dispose men to peace. Only when such qualities are defined after a commonwealth is established do "natural laws" become true laws. In authorizing statutes and officers to enforce them, the sovereign decides what constitutes justice and makes rules that the members of the commonwealth are obliged to obey. In this sense, Hobbes grants that the law of nature is part of the civil law. But he also describes the civil law, not so paradoxically as it might seem, as a part of the law of nature because it is a dictate of the law of nature that in order to maintain peace, men have to agree with one another to authorize a sovereign and to obey his laws. Thus, although a judge does not receive written instructions to decide in keeping with the will of the sovereign, he is obliged to do so by the law of nature because otherwise the commonwealth could not survive.

---

[22] Ibid., 194.   [23] Ibid., 194–95.   [24] Ibid., 188.

To other questions, which among his predecessors had received hardly any attention, Hobbes gives more definite answers. These are questions that concern the legislator less than the judge, questions about what may excuse or extenuate crimes and how to assess their seriousness. Hobbes emphasizes first of all that a crime must be a violation of the law which appears in an outward act. There may be violations which are not of this nature, he acknowledges, violations which consist in intentions, but these he identifies as "Sin," or *peccatum*. But this he considers a broad category for different kinds of misbehavior: "All Crimes are indeed Sins, but not all Sins Crimes. A Sin may be in the thought or secret purpose of a Man, of which neither a Judge, nor a Witness, nor any Man take notice; but a Crime is such a Sin as consists in an Action against the Law, of which Action he can be accused, and Tryed by a Judge, and be Convinced, or Cleared by Witnesses." Where the civil law ceases, both sin and crime cease and there is no release from the war of each against all. For where there is no sovereign power, there can be no law to define what constitutes a crime, and each man must protect himself by his own powers. In keeping with his view of civil associations and law as a human artifact, Hobbes points out that what constitutes crime will vary from one community to another: "Many things are made Crimes, and no Crimes, which are not so in their own Nature, but by Diversity of Law, made upon Diversity of Opinion, or of Interest by them which have Authority."[25]

His strictness about equating law with written rules does not prevent Hobbes from exploring possible qualifications on the enforcement of those rules in a discussion of "excuses." He considers ignorance of the law a good excuse if the law has not been made sufficiently public and clear. But ignorance of the sovereign power in a man's native place of residence is no excuse since every person ought to take notice of the power which protects him and enables him to live in peace. Ignorance of the penalty attached to violation of a law is no excuse because when a man voluntarily performs an action, he implicitly accepts responsibility for all its consequences. The only total excuse for a crime is something which removes the obligatoriness of the law. Thus anyone who is incapable of knowing the law, such as children or idiots, cannot be obliged by the law. If a man is imprisoned by an enemy whom he must obey or suffer death, his obligation to obey the law ceases, for everyone has a right, according to the law of nature, to preserve his life as best he can when the sovereign has failed to protect him. A starving man who cannot survive without violating the law is equally excused, for example, if in a famine he steals the food he cannot buy.[26]

[25] *Dialogue*, 78–79.   [26] *Leviathan*, 208.

But another sort of excuse sanctioned by Hobbes is less obvious: He argues that if a man or assembly that holds sovereign power, or someone authorized by the sovereign, commands the doing of something that conflicts with an existing law, the subject is excused from obeying because "when the Soveraign commandeth any thing to be done against his own former Law, the Command, to that particular fact, is an abrogation of the Law."[27] Here, as in his remarks on adjudicating according to the intention of the legislator rather than the letter of the law, Hobbes overlooks the possibility of disagreement about whether the new law conflicts with established law, and the need for an authorized settlement of such disputes. However, in saying that when the sovereign power grants a liberty that is inconsistent with the sovereign's duty to protect the subject, the subject may rightfully object, Hobbes does indirectly take into account the possibility of such disputes. For the reason why the subject has a right to disobey is that the sovereign, by making conflicting laws, is failing to defend him. Besides, the right to disobey is not a right to resist authority but to question, in accordance with established procedures, whether it has been rightly exercised. "But if he not onely disobey, but also resist a publique Minister in the execution of it, then it is a Crime; because he might have been righted, (without any breach of the Peace), upon complaint."[28] The distinction between "a right to disobey" and active resistance to officers of the law provides an important insight into Hobbes's concept of authority.

Finally, Hobbes distinguishes different degrees of crime according to the "malignity of the Source, or Cause," the "contagion of the Example," the "mischiefe of the Effect," and the "concurrence of Times, Places, and Persons."[29] Thus he argues that a crime which has been consistently punished is a greater crime than one that has been committed frequently with impunity, because all such cases offer "hopes of Impunity, given by the Soveraign himselfe."[30] A crime arising from a sudden passion should be treated more leniently than one long premeditated because in the latter the perpetrator had plenty of time to consider the law and the consequences of his action, and "to rectifie the irregularity of his Passions."[31] Nevertheless, the fact that crime arises from a sudden passion cannot excuse it. Crimes against the commonwealth are greater crimes than the same acts done to private men because the damage affects all members of the commonwealth. On crimes against private men, Hobbes would have the seriousness of the crime judged according to the damage caused as estimated by the common opinion of men.[32]

---

[27] Ibid., 109.   [28] Ibid., 109.   [29] Ibid., 109.
[30] Ibid., 210.   [31] Ibid., 210.   [32] Ibid., 212–13.

Just as there is no natural or necessary set of crimes, so there is no "natural rational criterion" for the punishment to fit the crime.[33] Instead Hobbes advocates – and is the first to elaborate – the deterrence theory of punishment. He defines punishment as *"an Evill inflicted by publique Authority, on him that hath done, or omitted that which is Judged by the same Authority to be a Transgression of the Law; to the end that the will of men may thereby the better be disposed to obedience."*[34] For Hobbes, punishment is intrinsic to the rule of law because it is intrinsic to the sovereign's prime duty of maintaining civil peace. For where men enter civil society they do not lose their right to preserve themselves, but hand over that right to the sovereign when they authorize or leave to him (and to the sovereign power only) to act for them in preserving peace, thereby agreeing to refrain from taking such action themselves. That the members of the commonwealth should be subject to pain for violating the law is essential because the passions are ever active, whereas reason to resist them is not. Consequently, if the passions can be gratified with impunity they will be indulged. Thus, "excepting some generous natures," it is fear that induces most men to observe the laws.[35] The only exception is a crime committed in self-defense: "A man is assaulted, fears present death, from which he sees not how to escape, but by wounding him that assaulteth him; If he wound him to death, this is no Crime; because no man is supposed at the making of a Common-wealth, to have abandoned the defence of his life, or limbse, when the law cannot arrive in time to assist him."[36] But one who breaks the law because he fears an attack, for which he has had time to seek protection from the sovereign power, or because he wishes to revenge an insult that the law has not seen fit to define as a crime, commits a crime for which there is no excuse because "the hurt is not Corporeall, but Phantasticall."[37]

Hobbes takes care to distinguish punishment from the mere infliction of evil. He defines punishment strictly as evil imposed by a public authority, which punishment is imposed only after a public hearing that authorizes it for an action defined by law as a crime. Any other evil, whether imposed by a public or a private source, is merely a hostile act inflicted by a usurped power. Nor does any failure to receive some desired public benefit constitute punishment because such a failure merely leaves the person's circumstances unchanged and involves no infringement of law. Moreover, evil inflicted for any purpose other than "disposing the Delinquent, or (by his example) other men, to obey the Lawes, is not

---

[33] *Dialogue*, 39.   [34] *Leviathan*, 214.   [35] Ibid., 206.
[36] Ibid., 206.   [37] Ibid., 206–7.

Punishment; but an act of hostility."[38] In short, punishment must be administered only in order to deter violations of the law, and only according to established legal procedures. Hobbes takes care as well to distinguish punishment from pain that may merely serve as the "Price" of a crime. If the harm inflicted by punishment does not exceed the benefits enjoyed as a result of the crime, Hobbes points out, it necessarily becomes "rather the Price, or Redemption, than the Punishment of a Crime."[39] For evil that does not exceed the good achieved by the criminal action cannot deter anyone from crime. On the contrary, it may encourage many to disobey the law.

That only harm inflicted to *deter* men from violating the law of the commonwealth constitutes punishment follows from Hobbes's insistence throughout that punishment is constituted by evil inflicted in order to preserve obedience to the law and hence the commonwealth. Harm imposed on an innocent man, or on one who is not a subject of the commonwealth, even though it be done for the benefit of the commonwealth, does not constitute punishment. And hostilities against enemies of the commonwealth, who are not members of the commonwealth, constitute war. But Hobbes qualifies the strict logic of his argument when he says that in hostilities by subjects who deny the authority of the sovereign, that is, who commit treason, the rebels may be made to suffer whatever evil the sovereign power chooses to impose on them. This follows from the law of nature by which individuals are obliged to constitute a commonwealth to preserve themselves and which consequently justifies hostility against destroyers of the commonwealth. By denying his subjection to the sovereign, the rebel denies the law and therefore such punishment as the law ordains. Thus, he ceases to be a member of the commonwealth and should be treated as an enemy rather than as a criminal. For punishments set down in the law pertain only to subjects, whereas those who "having been by their own act Subjects, deliberately revolting, deny the Soveraign Power"[40] declare themselves not to be members of the commonwealth. And they thereby put themselves at the mercy of the Sovereign's will unfettered by the laws of the commonwealth.

In his discussion of crime and punishment, Hobbes thus introduced new considerations and a new vocabulary into the discussion of law. The absence in Hobbes's world of a rational cosmos to provide a principle of order made it impossible to define order as the rule of reason over passion; order could be maintained only by human artifice, by social arrangements invented to serve particular purposes. And Hobbes defined

---

[38] Ibid., 215.   [39] Ibid., 215.   [40] Ibid., 216.

order as the absence of impediments to the efforts of individuals to pursue the satisfaction of their wants. In making it clear that law is to be understood wholly as a product of human artifice for which there is no cosmic foundation or test, Hobbes denied that justice could have any meaning other than what Aristotle called legal or conventional justice – the law alone defined justice. Above all, by showing that the obligation to obey the law is ultimately arbitrary, Hobbes made the concept of authority the foundation for the rule of law. His argument consists of three points: that there is nothing on which men can by nature agree, that no one is by nature designated to be a ruler, and that no man can be obligated to do what he has not agreed to do. Only if each agrees with all to authorize a sovereign to make rules for all can everyone oblige himself to obey a common set of rules and live with others in peace.

The effect of Hobbes's revision was to make it unambiguously clear that law constitutes a civil order whose only "ayme" is to enable its members to pursue their self-chosen projects and to enjoy their achievements without fear of being arbitrarily molested. Hobbes encapsulated this understanding of law in a new image that compared law not to a pattern for a good life or to a doctor's prescription, as his predecessors had, but to a hedge: "For the use of lawes, (which are but Rules Authorised) is not to bind the People from all Voluntary actions; but to direct and keep them [the people] in such a motion, as not to hurt themselves by their own impetuous desires, rashnesse, or indiscretion; as Hedges are set, not to stop Travellers, but to keep them in the way."[41] To speak of law as a "hedge" unequivocally identifies it with Augustinian non-instrumental rules, that is to say, rules designed to maintain certain conditions, not to direct enterprises. And the complement of the concept of law as a hedge is Hobbes's concept of authority.

Hobbes's reputation as an "absolutist" is due to a gross confusion of respect for authority with submission to amoral, irrational power. This confusion has distracted readers from noticing that Hobbes's insistence on the obligation to obey authentic law has much in common with Socrates' argument in the *Crito* and with Aquinas' argument that even a bad law, if duly promulgated, retains to some degree the quality of law and therefore carries an obligation to be obeyed. In regarding law, even when defective, as the indispensable condition of a civilized life, Hobbes was wholly in accord with his ancient and medieval predecessors. But pushing beyond the point at which Augustine had left off, he elaborated an understanding of law in which it has no cosmic anchor and is wholly a

---

[41] Ibid., 239–40.

product of human will, and he emphasized that it had an ineradicable element of arbitrariness.

In founding law on authority, Hobbes did not suggest or assume that the sovereign (however constituted) or his laws were beyond criticism. On the contrary, Hobbes acknowledges that rulers can commit iniquities both in making and dispensing their laws. Nor does he forbid subjects to recognize or express their awareness of such iniquities. He only insists that punishing the ruler for his iniquities belongs to God, not to his subjects, and that any attempt by subjects to resist the will of the sovereign, even if founded on a justifiable recognition of his iniquity, constitutes treason and reduces the subject to an enemy to be disposed of by the sovereign as he chooses. It is only when a sovereign fails to perform his task of maintaining civil peace that a subject is absolved from his obligation to obey the law. When a sovereign is displaced by another who has conquered the land, then a subject may, in order to preserve his life – the natural right he never gives up – transfer his allegiance. Here Hobbes's argument is clear enough. But about the more likely circumstances, in which it may be disputable whether a sovereign has ceased to perform his proper role, Hobbes says nothing.

Apart from this oversight, however, Hobbes made the authority of law unambiguously independent of its desirability or justice. But the clarity is gained at the expense of losing all those distinctions that are so important in the Platonic, Aristotelian, and Thomist pictures of law and which provided guidance for judging the moral quality of law. Not only the distinction between natural and conventional justice, but also between theoretical and practical reasoning disappears. Hobbes never addressed himself to defining the moral quality or justice of law in the sense understood by his predecessors – as a pattern for distinguishing desirable from undesirable behavior. He offers no hint of how to answer the question: How can just law (in the sense of a morally desirable standard of conduct) be distinguished from unjust law?

He evaded any such question through his translation of justice in the sense of an order compatible with diversity into the concept of authority. In making this translation, he eradicated the tension that dominated ancient and medieval jurisprudence – between justice in the sense of liberty under law and justice as the set of rules which promote "the good life." Justice in the latter sense became meaningless because man could not discover any indisputable ground for deciding whether the order maintained by law is the right order. Thus justice was transformed by Hobbes from a quality of law to a quality defined by law, and the only meaningful question one could ask about law became whether it had been made by someone authorized to make it. The distinction between power and authority became the essence of the rule of law. Hobbes's successors did not, however, recognize the vital connection between this distinction and his repudiation of the ancient cosmos, upon which they agreed with him. The chief conclusion drawn from Hobbes's account of law was merely that he had divorced law from morality and sanctioned "absolutism." The history of the idea of law in modern times thus became an odyssey of a search for a way to restore a rational moral element to law without returning to the pagan cosmos. But the search meandered through byways where inadvertently the pagan cosmos was rediscovered in new guises that provided a comforting, if inadequate, escape from the bleak clarity offered by Hobbes.

7   John Locke

Hobbes's radical break with the classical idea of law and his development of St. Augustine's doctrine were not taken up by his most immediate successor, John Locke. Indeed, Locke wholly repudiated Hobbes's idea of law to father the modern version of natural law theory, which has far more affinity with Cicero than with Aquinas. Locke's view of law has accordingly been treated as a model of how to escape from ancient and medieval metaphysics without succumbing to Hobbes's "extremism" or "amoralism." However, Locke is more rightly seen as a source of the insidious modern confusion about law, which arises from combining an avowed rejection of ancient and medieval metaphysics with treating law as if there were nevertheless available a given and indisputable foundation, or even blueprint, for it.

Although Locke is taken to be a major figure in the history of the philosophy of law, he nowhere sets out a systematic account of the rule of law. He seems to have agreed with his contemporary who described the "punctilles of the law" as a subject in which "the more a man flutters the more he is entangled."[1] The *Essays on the Law of Nature*, discovered by von Leyden, were not published by Locke himself, and he never explained just how his theory of natural law is connected with the rest of his doctrine. There are many scattered observations on positive or civil law, but nothing like an extended discussion. A systematic philosophy of law can, however, be assembled from Locke's writings on a variety of topics.

In a number of contexts Locke undoubtedly advocates the rule of law in a wholly traditional fashion. He says that those who govern are bound to do so by duly promulgated standing laws, which along with "*known Authoris'd Judges*" he contrasts to "extemporary Arbitrary Decrees." Locke emphasizes also, much as his predecessors had, the importance of having such laws in writing: "For the Law of Nature being unwritten, and

---

[1] John Locke, *Two Tracts on Government*, ed. Philip Abrams (Cambridge: Cambridge University Press, 1967), 87.

so no where to be found but in the minds of Men, they who through Passion or Interest shall mis-cite, or misapply it, cannot so easily be convinced of their mistake where there is no establish'd Judge: And so it serves not, as it ought, to determine the Rights, and fence the Properties of those that live under it."[2] He points out that laws have the virtue of having been made before the event to which they might be relevant; he equates "Absolute Arbitrary Power" with "Governing without. . . *standing laws*" and describes subjection to arbitrary power as a "worse condition than the state of Nature."[3] Everyone should be equally subject to the law: the rules are not "to be varied in particular Cases" and the same rule ought to govern both "Rich and Poor . . . the Favourite at Court, and the Country Man at Plough."[4] In traditional fashion as well, Locke argues that what particular form a government takes is far less important than that "the Ruling Power ought to govern by *declared* and *received Laws*, and not by extemporary Dictates and undetermined Resolutions."[5] And Locke's definition of liberty is familiar and congenial to admirers of the rule of law: "*Freedom of Men under Government*, is, to have a standing Rule to live by, common to every one of that Society, and made by the Legislative Power erected in it; A Liberty to follow my own Will in all things, where the Rule prescribes not; and not to be subject to the inconstant, uncertain, unknown, Arbitrary Will of another Man."[6]

In describing the rule of law as the alternative to arbitrary power, Locke is wholly at one with his predecessors. He departs from them in just that aspect of his doctrine that is supposed to have made him such an effective defender of the rule of law and liberty, his theory of natural law.

In his early *Essays on the Law of Nature*, Locke described the truths of natural law as "so manifest and certain that nothing can be plainer."[7] In the *Second Treatise*, he went further to say that natural law is "as intelligible and plain to a rational Creature, and a Studier of that Law, as the positive Laws of Common-wealths, nay possibly plainer; As much as Reason is easier to be understood, than the Phansies and intricate Contrivances of Men, following contrary and hidden interests put into Words."[8] In the *Essay Concerning Human Understanding*, Locke

[2] John Locke, *Two Treatises of Government*, 2nd ed., ed. Peter Laslett (Cambridge: Cambridge University Press, 1967), 376.
[3] *Two Treatises*, 377.
[4] Ibid., 381.
[5] Ibid., 378.
[6] Ibid., 302.
[7] John Locke, *Essays on the Law of Nature*, ed. W. von Leyden (Oxford: Clarendon, 1954), 201.
[8] *Two Treatises*, 293.

explained more fully the suggestions in the early *Essays* about how the truths of natural law became known to man.

They could not be discovered from the opinions, customs, traditions of human beings, nor any other second-hand knowledge,[9] because everywhere there are men, indeed whole nations, whose thought and behavior flagrantly violate natural law, who consider it "praiseworthy to commit. . . such crimes as are utterly loathsome to those who think rightly and live according to nature."[10] The same evidence establishes that knowledge of natural law is not innate in the human mind, for if it were no one could be ignorant of natural law. In both his earliest reflections on the law of nature and his *Essay Concerning Human Understanding*, Locke insisted that the truth of natural law had to be discovered by the proper exercise of reason on the material provided by the senses, without which reason is as helpless as a laborer "working in darkness behind shuttered windows."[11]

The role of reason is that of a passive "discursive faculty. . . which advances from things known to things unknown and argues from one thing to another in a definite and fixed order of propositions."[12] The senses reveal "the magnificent Harmony" of the "visible structure and arrangement of this world," where everything is regularly and constantly made.[13] From observing that the world has a definite order, reason concludes that "some Deity is the author of all these things"[14] and that men are wholly dependent on Him because His will determines whether they are brought into the world, maintained, or taken away.

Being the product of God's workmanship, man is his property and wholly subject to His will. Since nothing in the world is made without a purpose, God must have designated mankind to fulfill some particular end. And since God orders everything in the world by immutable laws, from the idea of an all-powerful Creator and man's dependence on Him there necessarily follows "the notion of a universal law of nature binding on all men."[15]

What is new in this picture of the relationship between God and man arises from Locke's repudiation of traditional metaphysics. Whereas the highly refined metaphysical categories of medieval natural theology allowed for a distinction between different sorts of ends or purposes – between, for instance, a final, material, efficient, and formal cause – no such distinctions were available to Locke. He accordingly reduced the

[9] *Essays on the Law of Nature*, 133–35.   [10] Ibid., 191.
[11] Ibid., 149.   [12] Ibid., 149.
[13] John Locke, *An Essay Concerning Human Understanding*, ed. Peter H. Nidditch (Oxford: Clarendon Press, 1975), 447; cf. *Essays on the Law of Nature*, 133.
[14] *Essays on the Law of Nature*, 133; see also 109–21, 147–59.
[15] Ibid., 133.

relationship between God and man to that of potter and clay, what has been called the workmanship model, in which man is simply "dependent" on God. The law of nature then becomes a "decree of the divine will"[16] prescribing "definite duties. . . which cannot be other than they are."[17] The instructions of natural law seen in this fashion are manifest and indisputable, making it perfectly clear that God wishes us to "do this but leave off that."[18]

That Locke sees laws as instructions for behavior is suggested as well by his argument that the law of nature does not restrict freedom. Men who fail to observe it are slaves of their passions, unable to consider what action will best promote their happiness. In submitting to the law of nature, they are not being restricted, but are being shown how to achieve what they truly, rather than apparently, desire.

Just how such definite instructions could be reconciled with responsibility for sin is explained in the *Essay Concerning Human Understanding*. There man is described as being born with a drive or instinct to seek pleasure and avoid pain, summed up as seeking happiness. That explanation does not contradict Locke's earlier denial that human beings have innate ideas because pleasure and pain have the character not of ideas, but of sensations that give rise to desire. What immediately "determines the Will. . . to every voluntary Action, is the *uneasiness* of *desire*, fixed on some absent good."[19] The great privilege granted to men by making them "finite intellectual Beings" is that they can suspend action in order to scrutinize their desires and deliberate about whether satisfying a desire would interfere with achieving "true Happiness." This constitutes their liberty, which is "improperly. . . call'd *Free-Will*."[20] Human freedom consists in the ability to stop desires from determining what we do until we have considered the consequences. The capacity for such suspension of desire prevents men from being robots who cannot distinguish between will and desire, and when they exercise that capacity they have done their duty.[21] As God "requires of us no more than we are able to do," he would not chastise anyone who failed to master himself under torture. But in ordinary circumstances, the "right direction of our conduct to true Happiness" depends on restraining our disposition to satisfy a present desire until reason has given its judgment.[22] And God has provided an irresistible inducement for such restraint through "The Rewards and Punishments of another life." Even those who lack faith are bound to be affected by the "bare possibility" of such a future state since there is no absolute

---

[16] Ibid., 111.   [17] Ibid., 199.   [18] Ibid., 151.
[19] *Concerning Human Understanding*, 252.
[20] Ibid., 267–68, 263.   [21] Ibid., 267.   [22] Ibid., 268.

proof of its nonexistence.[23] Whatever will secure eternal bliss is action in conformity with God's will.

Even in the shorter run, God has constructed us in such a fashion that a rational calculation of what will produce more pleasure will direct us properly. The pleasure and pain that men experience are the good and evil that attend our observance or breach of God's law; they are the reward and punishment that He has ordained to enforce the natural law. In this way, the *Essay Concerning Human Understanding* explains Locke's assertion in the *Essays on the Law of Nature* that God not only "demands of us that the conduct of our life should be in accordance with his will," but has made clear what things he wishes that we should do.[24]

Bound up with this view of the nature of reason and the relationship between man and God is an understanding of moral conduct that exalts the idea of law. It appears not only in the early *Essays*, but also in the later *Essay Concerning Human Understanding*, where Locke describes a "*Moral Relation*" as "the Conformity, or Disagreement, Men's voluntary actions have to a Rule, to which they are referred, and by which they are judged."[25] And he defines moral good and evil as "the Conformity or Disagreement of our voluntary Actions to some Law, whereby Good or Evil is drawn on us, from the Will and Power of the Law-maker."[26]

Conformity to law given by a superior will is for Locke the essence of moral conduct because there is nothing in the human will by itself that can demand dutiful action. Nor can human reason by itself distinguish virtue from vice. Left to himself man is incomplete, for he is a dependent being. If he did not subordinate his will to another superior will, satisfaction of his own desires would be the only measure of his actions. He would become a god to himself and a slave to his passions.[27] This picture of moral conduct follows from Locke's denial that human reason has a creative power to invent laws for itself and from his view that reason can do no more than discover the laws made by God. That is why Locke concludes that "the formal cause" of law consists of its being "the decree of a superior will" that informs man about "what is and what is not to be done."[28]

Because a relationship in terms of law is defined by Locke as a relationship between a superior and an inferior will, Locke considers enforcement intrinsic to the idea of law and not merely an addition to it: "For

---

[23] Ibid., 281.   [24] Ibid., 151.
[25] *Concerning Human Understanding*, 350.   [26] Ibid., 351.
[27] James Tully, *A Discourse on Property: John Locke and His Adversaries* (Cambridge: Cambridge University Press, 1980), 36.
[28] Locke, *Essays on the Law of Nature*, 111–13.

since it would be utterly in vain, to suppose a Rule set to the free Actions of Man, without annexing to it some Enforcement of Good and Evil, to determine his Will, we must, where-ever we suppose a Law, suppose also some Reward or Punishment annexed to that Law."[29] Apart from the natural consequence of an action, there must be some independent consequence in the form of reward or punishment if an action is to be affected by a rule. Otherwise, "It would be in vain for one intelligent Being, to set a Rule to the Actions of another, if he had it not in his Power, to reward the compliance with, and punish deviation from his Rule."[30] A rule cannot, then, qualify as a law unless it carries sanctions for disobedience. And conversely, whatever carries a sanction can qualify as law. Thus, Locke distinguishes three kinds of law: the will of God made manifest in natural law and Revelation, which is sanctioned by the pleasure and pain attached to good and evil in this world and the next; civil law, which is enforced by the power of the commonwealth to take away "Life, Liberty, or Goods, from him, who disobeys"; and rules of fashion, which are just as much law as the others, Locke insists, because they are enforced by social disapproval, which no man can endure.[31] By thus connecting law with punishment as well as by identifying law with the command of a superior will, Locke makes the exercise of power (or force) an essential ingredient of law.

All laws rest ultimately on natural law and on God because even though natural law is discovered by reasoning from observations of the natural constitution of things, what is being observed is what God has willed. Because recognizing natural law to be God's command is paramount for Locke, he refused to extend toleration to atheists, who, as they do not acknowledge their dependence on God, cannot recognize any duties. Therefore, "The taking away of God, though but even in thought, dissolves all."[32]

Although Locke's claim that knowledge of what is good and evil is given to man by God and nature appears to be at one with his classical and medieval predecessors, he departs radically from them because (with the exception of Cicero) they endow natural law with a fundamentally different character. Since classical and medieval natural law consists of highly abstract principles, it does not, and cannot, provide precise practical instructions or commands and is thereby compatible with significant diversity at the level of practical action. No such room for uncertainty about practical conclusions is acknowledged by Locke. His reputation for taking a modest view of knowledge rests on his description of himself as

---

[29] *Concerning Human Understanding*, 350.   [30] Ibid., 351–52.   [31] Ibid., 353.
[32] John Locke, *The Works of John Locke*, 12th ed., vol. V (London: Rivington, 1824), 47.

only "*an Under-Labourer. . . clearing Ground a little.*"[33] But within the areas that he chose to clear, Locke had a Ciceronian confidence about what had to be done.

The problem of dealing with conflicting interpretations of Revelation never disturbed Locke. He admitted that philosophers have failed to make out a complete system of morality "from unquestionable principles, by clear deductions." Nevertheless, all the truths that men need about moral conduct are manifest in Revelation, which is "the surest, the safest, and most effectual way of teaching" morality,[34] and no one can "be excused from understanding the words and framing the general notions relating to religion right."[35] In the *Essay* as well, Locke says that faith "leaves no manner of room for Doubt or Hesitation,"[36] just as he writes to the Bishop of Worcester that "the holy scripture is to me, and always will be, the constant guide of my assent; and I shall always hearken to it, as containing infallible truth, relating to things of the highest concernment. . . and I shall presently condemn and quit any opinion of mine, as soon as I am shown that it is contrary to any revelation in the holy scripture."[37] When his friend William Molyneux urged him to complete the work that he had begun in the *Essay Concerning Human Understanding* by demonstrating all the truths of ethics, Locke explained that he need not do so because "the Gospel contains so perfect a body of ethics, that reason may be excused from that inquiry, since she may find man's duty clearer and easier in revelation, than in herself."[38]

Although he sometimes expresses doubts about whether all men can discover moral truth, on the whole he is thoroughly persuaded that the knowledge about moral conduct that human reason can achieve is as certain as the conclusions of mathematical demonstrations. While he denies that the human intellect is "fitted to penetrate into the internal Fabrick and real Essences of Bodies," he insists that "*Morality is the proper Science, and Business of Mankind in general,*"[39] and that the certainty of moral knowledge is indisputable. Whether we take a rule from "the Fashion of the Country, or the Will of a Law-maker," Locke assures us that "the Mind is easily able to observe the Relation any Action hath to it; and to judge, whether the Action agrees, or disagrees with the

---

[33] *Concerning Human Understanding*, 10.
[34] *Works*, vol. VI, 140, 147.
[35] Ibid., vol. V, 41.
[36] *Concerning Human Understanding*, 667.
[37] *Works*, vol. III, 96.
[38] John Locke, "Some Familiar Letters Between Mr. Locke and Several of His Friends," in *The Works of John Locke*, 11th ed., vol. X (London: Davison, 1812), 377.
[39] *Concerning Human Understanding*, 646–47.

Rule." As the rule is "nothing but a Collection of several simple ideas. . .
belonging to it,"[40] the results of comparing an action with a rule are
always certain.

What may seem to be qualifications on this fundamentalist view of
moral truth appear in several different contexts. Locke acknowledges that
though natural law is "perpetual and coeval with the human race," no one
can be bound to perform at all times everything that the law of nature
commands because "he can no more observe several duties at once than
a body can be in several places." And Locke concludes that even though
the binding force of the law never changes, there is often a change in
both the times and the circumstances of actions, whereby our obedience is
defined. He gives examples of cases where the "binding force of nature is
perpetual" but "the requirements of our duty" are not, and it is left to
our "prudence, whether or not we care to undertake some such actions in
which we incur obligation."[41] But far from recognizing that to determine
by "prudence" what a rule means in particular circumstances is a contingent and necessarily disputable decision, Locke asserts that "no one can
stain himself with another man's blood without incurring guilt,"[42] without in any way suggesting that it would be pertinent to determine whether
a particular event in which one man caused the death of another constituted murder, self-defense, accidental homicide, or a duty of war imposed
by law or war.

What seems to be an acknowledgment that the interpretation of principles for practical action might be uncertain appears in the discussion of
the imperfection and abuse of words in the *Essay*.[43] In that context, Locke
speaks very much as Hobbes does about the unlimited variety of interpretations that men invent for the same set of words. But even this does
not lead him to temper his convictions about the certainty of moral truth.
He still maintains that the knowledge of moral truth rests on the agreement or disagreement of "those *Ideas*, which are presented by them," and
if the mind proceeds correctly in deducing from them, the conclusions are
determined. All that is voluntary in knowledge is whether or not men
exercise their faculties, but once they are employed, *"our Will hath no
Power to determine the Knowledge of the Mind* one way or other."[44]

He distinguishes between opinion and knowledge (conclusions of a
deduction), but he denies that because a practical decision has not been

---

[40] Ibid., 358.
[41] *Essays on the Law of Nature*, 193–95.
[42] Ibid., 195.
[43] See Locke, *Concerning Human Understanding*, 490–524.
[44] Ibid., 650–51.

deduced and therefore constitutes opinion rather than knowledge, it is any less certain: "most of the Propositions we think, reason, discourse, nay act upon, are such, as we cannot have undoubted Knowledge of their Truth: yet some of them border so near upon Certainty, that we make no doubt at all about them; but *assent* to them as firmly, and act, according to that Assent, as resolutely, as if they were infallibly demonstrated, and that our knowledge of them was perfect and certain."[45] Indeed, in some cases "the Probability is so clear and strong, that Assent as necessarily follows it, as Knowledge does Demonstration."[46] Just why some propositions that we act upon cannot be demonstrated to be indisputably true, Locke neither explains nor considers. Nor could he have done so because he never acknowledged that the human world's irremediable contingency made it impossible to move from universal principles, or general rules, to indisputable practical conclusions about what should be done here and now. Practical reasoning has no place in Locke's philosophy.

Nor does contingency or the uncertainty of practical reasoning enter into Locke's explanation of the diversity of the human world. Though he recognizes and occasionally even emphasizes the existence of diversity, he attributes it to error. He never withdrew his assertion from the early *Essays on Natural Law* that diversity occurs only because men are led astray by habit into following the herd like brute beasts and giving way to their appetites.

When in the *Essay* Locke translated all satisfactions into pleasure and pains, he was able to explain more precisely how diversity is compatible with the universal validity of the conclusions reached by reason about right and wrong. The diversity acknowledged is not, however, a diversity of intelligent responses, but merely a difference in reactions to stimuli. Nothing more is involved in Locke's censure of ancient philosophers for arguing about whether the *summum bonum* consists in riches or contemplation. That he misrepresents the meaning of *summum bonum* and the ancient dispute is less important than that he attributes the pleasure that men get from things to "their agreeableness to this or that particular palate." He insists on this in order to deny that the differences are due to the things themselves. Whether different moral views might arise from diverse ways of understanding and responding to the sensations aroused is not considered by Locke. He is concerned only with establishing the one true conception of moral good – that of "the greatest Happiness" – which consists in having "those things, which produce the greatest Pleasure; and in the absence of those, which cause any disturbance, any pain." Though

[45] Ibid., 655.   [46] Ibid., 685.

the reactions of men differ, the character of the calculations required to achieve the greatest happiness is absolutely uniform. When they make faulty estimates of the pleasure that different courses of action will bring, men go wrong, but about a pleasure or pain that is immediately present there can be no mistake: "the greater Pleasure, or the greater Pain, is really just as it appears," and the apparent and the real good are, in this case, always the same.[47] Only when it comes to comparing present pains or pleasures with future ones, which is "usually the case in the most important determinations of the will," is it easy to judge wrongly.[48]

In making "the greatest Happiness" the ultimate aim of human activity, Locke emphasizes that he is providing a moral and not a utilitarian standard. While men can arrive at what is right by observing what is convenient, he argues, it is only because God made man in such a fashion that a rational pursuit of happiness under the guidance of reason necessarily constitutes virtue. Nevertheless, nothing is right because it is convenient. The rightness of an action does not depend on its utility, but on its conformity with God's will.[49] And the ultimate end is never in doubt: "The Rewards and Punishments of another Life, which the Almighty has established, as the Enforcements of his Law, are of weight enough to determine the Choice, against whatever Pleasure or Pain this Life can shew, when the eternal State is considered but in its bare possibility, which no Body can make any doubt of."[50]

Even when he acknowledges in the *Essay* that differences of temper, education, fashion, maxims, or interest lead men to different notions of virtue and vice, he concludes that in the main men are inclined to esteem the same sorts of things. If we consider not how men behave, but "their innermost ways of thinking," we find there an "internal" law, or "conscience," which brings even those who "act perversely" to "feel rightly" and to recognize that they behaved wrongly. Serious moral diversity is excluded by Locke's philosophy because it confines reason to discovering universal indisputable truth and deducing therefrom. The differences among human beings are therefore due either to different reactions to sensations, which are not the product of reason, or to a failure to suspend desire in order to consider future pleasures and pains, or to an error in making such judgments. None of these gives rise to a diversity rooted in the privacy of human personality.

Since Locke does not see human beings as intrinsically private personalities, his picture of the human world is far from individualistic. The

---

[47] Ibid., 269, 275.   [48] Ibid., 275.   [49] *Works*, vol. VI, 142.
[50] *Concerning Human Understanding*, 281.

difficulty of finding a common ground among the self-enclosed persons that gives rise to the human predicament in Hobbes's philosophy does not exist for Locke. Neither is there the space for individuality allowed by ancient and medieval philosophies in the movement between abstract universal principles to contingent practical decisions. Instead, moral conduct consists simply in subordination to a superior will and obedience to the clear directions given in the natural law.

In the *Second Treatise*, Locke says that the law of nature "teaches all Mankind. . . that being all equal and independent, no one ought to harm another in his Life, Health, Liberty, or Possessions."[51] Locke's insistence that each man has a right to command himself and the resources that he needs to preserve himself without invasion has every appearance of an individualistic declaration of natural rights. From this premise, however, Locke moves off in quite another direction. Access to the law of nature enables men to live together and be free "to order their Actions, and dispose of their Possessions, and Persons as they think fit . . . without asking leave, or depending upon the Will of any other Man."[52] Moreover, the natural law, being a law, provides for its own enforcement. Every man has a right to punish transgressions of the law of nature not only when they are directed against himself, but wherever they occur. If anyone offends against the law of nature, everyone else has the right to punish the offender for it and exact retribution, not simply for personal damage, but to vindicate the rule of "*reason* and common Equity, which is that measure God has set to the actions of Men, for their mutual security."[53] Certainly murder and possibly even thieving may be punished by death, for punishment has to be severe enough "to make it an ill bargain to the Offender, give him cause to repent, and terrifie others from doing the like."[54]

How far punishment is based on retribution or deterrence is unclear, since Locke speaks of them as one when he says that the power to punish is not an absolute or arbitrary power, "but only to retribute him, so far as calm reason and conscience dictates, what is proportionate to his Transgression, which is so much as may serve for *Reparation* and *Restraint*."[55] Yet he also describes these as the two reasons why one man may harm another. It follows that in principle human beings are capable of existing in "*The State of Nature*," which is a "*State of Liberty*" but "*not a State of Licence*." Locke concludes that the whole of mankind belongs to a "Community of Nature."[56]

---

[51] *Two Treatises*, 289.   [52] Ibid., 287.   [53] Ibid., 290.
[54] Ibid., 293.   [55] Ibid., 290.   [56] Ibid., 288–89.

Because it is a natural community, Locke's state of nature is often supposed to have an affinity with Aristotle's *polis*, which is also "natural." But Aristotle's *polis* is natural because it can satisfy the need given by the nature of human beings for the good life; it is not natural in the sense of being established by a nonhuman agency, and Aristotle emphasizes that human beings do not necessarily come into the world as members of a *polis*, which is a human artifact whose members can choose to join or leave. Moreover, the *polis* can come into existence only when there is an established law distinct from the various tribal customs of the members. This law is not a mere attribute of the *polis*, but the bond that constitutes it because the rule of law makes possible a kind of association that could not otherwise exist. As Locke tells the story, however, men come into a world governed by a law that makes them members of one universal community. Civil society differs from the state of nature only in its power to punish transgressions of the law given by nature more systematically and effectively. For what moves men to quit the state of nature is "the irregular and uncertain exercise of the Power every Man has of punishing the transgressions of others."[57]

This explanation is ambiguous in some respects. For Locke also says that "There wants an establish'd, settled, known Law, received and allowed by common consent to be the Standard of Right and Wrong, and the common measure to decide all Controversies," which suggests that law has to be invented. Yet in the very next sentence, he writes that "the Law of nature [is] plain and intelligible to all rational Creatures." He seems to offer a reconciliation of the two assertions in what he calls his "strange Doctrine" that "*every one has the Executive Power* of the Law of Nature,"[58] because it is the defects of this "strange power" that move us to leave the state of nature. Whether this difficulty arises from a failing intrinsic to all men or found only in some is not clear. Sometimes Locke attributes the inconveniences of the state of nature to "the corruption, and viciousness of degenerate Men,"[59] and sometimes to a widespread propensity in people to be "biassed by their Interest" or ignorant "for want of study" of the law of nature, which, as everyone is both judge and executioner, may produce misjudgments of what punishment is required. This inconvenience in the state of nature leads men to seek "*a known and indifferent Judge*" who will have "Authority to determine all differences according to the established Law" and who will never lack sufficient power to execute the sentence.[60] To establish such a judge, men leave their "great and natural Community" and make "positive agreements" to

---

[57] Ibid., 370.   [58] Ibid., 369, 293.   [59] Ibid., 370.   [60] Ibid., 369.

"combine into smaller and divided associations." Upon entering civil society, they surrender the right each has by nature to punish violations of the law to someone appointed "amongst them" who shall exercise that right "by such Rules as the Community, or those authorised by them to that purpose, shall agree on."[61] In other words, when men enter into civil society, they do not become associated for the first time, but merely agree to break up into smaller associations and to accept a more effective instrument for punishing transgressions against the terms of association that previously existed.

Locke's doctrine of natural law thus radically attenuates the importance of the rule of law. Law ceases to be the bond of civil society as it had been for his predecessors. It ceases to be essential for all men, virtuous as well as wicked. For Locke's law of nature is much more than a postulate of civil law or even a standard or measure for civil justice. The law of nature is the civil law writ large. The civil law, far from being essentially different from natural law, as it was for Locke's predecessors, merely fills in details missing from the natural law, above all by providing just and effective punishment of transgressions. In other words, Locke treats the civil law as a corrective for those who are incapable of exercising their faculties adequately enough to perceive and abide by the law, the natural law, which God has made manifest. It follows that the more nearly men approach perfect rationality, the less need they have for civil law. Civil law serves no purpose distinct from the divinely ordained or natural law; it merely provides aid for obeying God's law with greater security. All this derives from Locke's fundamental doctrine of natural law because it denies the independence of the earthly city from the heavenly city.

Given this view, it is hardly surprising that the predicament which led Locke's predecessors to fear civil unrest above all else disappears in Locke's account of law. While this is generally recognized, its implication for law is usually overlooked. It means first of all that in deciding about civil arrangements, the problem is not how to reconcile different but equally worthy opinions about what is desirable, but how best to achieve objectives that everyone who is adequately rational necessarily seeks. And this predicament introduces a radically revised understanding of the subjects of law. They are not, as they were for Locke's predecessors (with the exception of Cicero), independent agents pursuing different projects, but servants of one and the same project. The objective of civil law is not, then, to make possible an association that embraces many diverse projects, but rather to achieve more effectively the project that everyone

[61] Ibid., 370.

necessarily ought to pursue. In other words, law is an instrument of the enterprise that God has assigned to men.

That explains why the obligation to obey the law depends on its rightness. In order to secure its rightness, it might seem, the binding power of civil law should rest on its conformity to natural law: "the *Municipal Laws* of Countries. . . are only so far right, as they are founded on the Law of Nature, by which they are to be regulated and inter- preted."[62] But at other times Locke attributes the obligation to obey civil law to its being a command of a superior and derives that obligation from natural law. This ambiguity is parallel to another about whether man's obligation to obey the will of God rests on God's power or on the rightness of His commands. Generally Locke says that the bond that obliges us "derives from the lordship and command which any superior has over us and our actions" and that we are bound to obey God "because both our being and our work depend on His will, since we have received these from Him." But he adds quite another reason in his remark that "moreover, it is reasonable that we should do what shall please Him who is omniscient and most wise,"[63] which implies that we should obey God's commands because they are undoubtedly right.

Rightness is made the foundation of the obligation to obey civil law when Locke insists that the law must have the "consent" of its subjects. His emphasis on consent is muddled by his speaking sometimes of au- thority in the manner of Hobbes, as when he says that a man leaves the state of nature when "he authorizes the Society, or. . . the Legislative thereof to make Laws for him," and that civil society sets up "a Judge on Earth, with Authority to determine all the Controversies, and redress the Injuries, that may happen to any Member of the Commonwealth."[64] More often, however, Locke couples authority with consent as if the two were synonymous. The confusion arises from his concept of "depend- ency," introduced to explain the relation between God and man, as well as between lawmaker and subject, a concept which is a curious blend of "consent" and "authority."

Because his emphasis on the rightness of laws and consent to them appears to give individuals a greater say in determining their obligation to obey the law, Locke's philosophy of law is assumed to give priority to human individuality. The opposite is more nearly true. Locke's view of law does not respect individuality because a clear idea of authority plays no part in it. And it could not do so given Locke's understanding of obligation and civil association.

---

[62] Ibid., 293.   [63] *Essays on the Law of Nature*, 183.   [64] *Two Treatises*, 343.

As Hobbes explained, authority can be bestowed only by those subject to it. When I recognize someone's authority, I commit myself to acknowledging that person's right to make certain decisions. Consent enters into authorization only when the terms on which authority is granted are being agreed to. In other words, as a subject of law I consent to the rules designating the procedures for appointing law-making officers and defining their duties. In doing so I confer "authority" on the officers who are appointed, which means that I recognize their right to make certain decisions. But my recognition of their authority does not imply that I consent to the substance of the decision that they take in the course of performing their duties. Nor do I consent to the authority of the lawmakers because I recognize their superiority; on the contrary, it is I who endow them with "superiority," in the sense of a right to decide, which they could not otherwise possess. Having recognized the authority of the lawmakers and of the procedures governing their decisions, I become obliged to conform to decisions that are "authentic," that is to say, conform to the authorized conditions.

Obligation that rests on authority is accordingly a wholly human creation. Locke cannot accept the idea of authority because he denies that obligation can rest on a purely human commitment: "it is not to be expected that a man would abide by a compact because he has promised it, when better terms are offered elsewhere, unless the obligation to keep promises was derived from nature, and not from human will."[65] Because Locke denies that men can give laws to themselves, he insists that if men were not bound by the law of nature, which is imposed by God, they could be bound by nothing. That is why "the laws of the civil magistrate derive their whole force from the constraining power of natural law." The only qualification suggested by Locke is that those who have access to Christian Revelation need not rely on natural law because they have access to another source for God's commands. Even when he emphasizes that the obligation to obey a civil ruler is a matter of conscience rather than fear, that the ruler, unlike a tyrant or robber, does not possess merely superior power, Locke still attributes the obligation to obey civil law to the law of nature, which "decrees that princes and a lawmaker, or a superior by whatever name you call him, should be obeyed."[66] Thus, "all obligation leads back to God"[67] because Locke provided no adequate

---

[65] *Essays on the Law of Nature*, 119.   [66] Ibid., 189.

[67] Ibid., 183. For a very illuminating discussion of Locke's religious views, see Richard Ashcraft, "Faith and Knowledge in Locke's Philosophy," in *John Locke: Problems and Perspectives*, ed. J. W. Yolton (Cambridge: Cambridge University Press, 1969), 194–223. A similar emphasis on Locke's religious faith appears in John Dunn, *The Political Thought of John Locke* (Cambridge: Cambridge University Press, 1969).

account of authorization. Just how any lawmaker acquires his superiority remains a mystery.

Locke rests obligation on what human beings do or think only when he confounds obligation with power. That appears both when he makes the power to enforce its requirements an intrinsic part of law, and when, in the course of arguing that the majority within the community has a "right to act and conclude the rest,"[68] he speaks of the majority's "power." However, he seems to equate power with mechanical force in saying that the power of the community "to Act as one Body" is given only by the will of the majority because the "*Body Politick*" will "move that way whither the greater force carries it, which is the *consent of the majority.*"[69] Since authorization plays no part in Locke's understanding of civil society, it is not procedural correctness that determines whether the governing body can oblige obedience, but rather whether the governing body has discharged its "trust." The immediate test for the validity of law is whether it is made by the legislature because only laws made by the legislative body can have the consent of the people.[70] The power of the legislative body is not limited, however, by law but by "*the publick good* of the Society."[71] Therefore, the legislative body cannot oblige obedience from the people unless its acts are "pursuant to their trust."[72] The legislature is accordingly described as a "Fiduciary power to act for certain ends. . . *all Power given with trust* for the attaining an *end*. . . whenever that *end* is manifestly neglected, or opposed, the *trust* must necessarily be *forfeited*, and the Power devolve into the hands of those that gave it, who may place it anew where they shall think best for their safety and security."[73]

In a relationship of trust as in a relationship of authority, one person acts for others, but the nature of the action to be taken and the assignment of the task are different. In authorization the obligation is to abide by the conditions of the office one holds; one's duties are prescribed by the rules defining the office. In a trust the obligation is to achieve a designated objective. An authorized officer has the "right" to take certain decisions; a trustee has a "duty" to perform a particular task, such as managing an estate for the profit of the beneficiary. Whereas authorization is a substitutional relationship, a trust is an instrumental relationship. The power given with a trust is for the attaining of an end designated by the trustor's instructions. No such requirement defines the powers of an authorized officer. If officers observe the rules defining their office, they cannot be accused of violating their authority even though they may have

[68] Locke,*Two Treatises*, 349.   [69] Ibid., 349–50.   [70] Ibid., 374.
[71] Ibid., 375.   [72] Ibid., 374.   [73] Ibid., 385.

acted unwisely or ineffectively. But if trustees act unwisely or ineffectively, they violate their trust. If parliament is authorized to make or alter the laws of the realm, there are two distinct questions to ask about its activities: Have the appropriate rules and procedures been observed? Are the conclusions reached desirable? The former is a legal question, the latter a political one. In Locke's account the legal question disappears, and there is only one question – whether parliament has acted effectively to achieve the task entrusted to it.

That Locke should regard governing as a trust is in keeping with his theory of natural law. Since the purpose of governing is quite precisely given by the law of nature as Locke understands it, the problem of ruling in civil society is not how to unite a multitude of diverse wills, or how, given the variety of opinion and wants, to determine what the public good requires. It is the much simpler problem of how to achieve what everyone knows ought to be done. The legislature is entrusted with power so that it may pursue a known end.

Although the legal idea of trust is a distinctively English idea that first appeared at the end of the fourteenth century,[74] Locke's description of legislative power as a trust is undoubtedly odd, and he appears to recognize as much when he says that the trust may be "tacit." Whereas a proper legal trust involves three parties, the trustor, the trustee, and the beneficiary, in Locke's account of political trust there are only two parties since the people are both trustor and beneficiary.[75] On the whole most students would agree with Dicey that "Nothing is more certain than that no English judge ever conceded, or, under the present constitution, can concede, that Parliament is in any legal sense a 'trustee' for the electors. Of such a feigned 'trust' the Courts know nothing."[76] But whatever the constitutional authenticity of Locke's notion of trust, there can be no doubt that where the government is understood in this fashion, the laws that it makes have the character of an instrument. Thus, John Austin (cf. chapter 8), who had a similarly instrumental view of law, also took up the idea of trust.[77]

Understanding governing as a trust and law as an instrument for serving that trust excludes any conception of civil society as an association

[74] See F. W. Maitland, *Selected Essays*, ed. H. D. Hazeltine, G. Lapsley, and P. H. Winfield (Cambridge: Cambridge University Press, 1936), 141–222.
[75] Otto Gerke, *Natural Law and the Theory of Society: 1500–1800*, trans. Ernest Barker (Boston: Beacon, 1960), xxvi–xxx, 299–300; J. W. Gough, *John Locke's Political Philosophy* (Oxford: Clarendon, 1956), 143–47.
[76] A. V. Dicey, *Introduction to the Study of the Law of the Constitution*, 8th ed. (London: MacMillan, 1927), 73.
[77] John Austin, *The Province of Jurisprudence Determined*, with an introduction by H. L. A. Hart (New York: Noonday Press, 1954), 231.

of independent agents pursuing diverse ends who wish to retain their autonomy. The rights of individuals are instruments for achieving the public good. Even in his arguments for toleration, it is ultimately the public good that is Locke's criterion for how far the magistrate's power should extend.[78] That explains why Locke never describes civil society as an "association," but rather as "one coherent living Body," or as the *Body Politick.*" And that is in keeping with his description of the law as a provision for preserving "Mankind in general" and transgressions of it as "a trespass against the whole Species."[79] Instead of saying, as did Hobbes, that the will of the sovereign is substituted for the wills of those who have covenanted to enter into civil association, Locke says that civil society has an *"Essence and Union,"* which consists not merely of "mutual Influence, Sympathy and Connexion" among its members, but in their having "one Will," which is in the keeping of the legislative.[80]

That Locke's use of the organic metaphor is not merely ornamental or an insignificant adoption of a medieval image is evident in what he says about the regulation of property. There is nothing unusual in Locke's description of the object of government as "the Regulating and Preserving of Property, and of employing the force of the Community, in the Execution of such Laws, and in the defense of the common-wealth from Foreign Injury, and all this only for the Publick Good."[81] The "Regulating and Preserving of Property" and serving the "Publick Good" are abstract aims, that cannot determine concretely what is to be done until they are interpreted for particular circumstances by political deliberation. That Locke meant something else, however, is suggested not only by his indifference to the problem of deriving practical conclusions from general prescriptions, but also by what he says about the duty to regulate property.

It is an obligation of government because "subduing or cultivating the Earth"[82] is a duty assigned by God, who "gave the World. . . to the use of the Industrious and Rational."[83] Locke tells us also that men are obliged "to promote the great Design of God, *Increase* and *Multiply*,"[84] that "numbers of men are to be prefered to largenesse of dominions," and that "the increase of lands and the right imploying of them is the great art of government."[85] The right of individuals to private possession is not, for Locke, fundamental, but a corollary of the *"fundamental Law of Nature,"* which is *"the preservation of Mankind."*[86] Each man's fear of death does not figure in Locke's concern with civil peace because he takes God not to

---

[78] Locke, *Two Treatises,* 353–54.   [79] Ibid., 425, 349, 290.   [80] Ibid., 425.
[81] Ibid., 286.   [82] Ibid., 310.   [83] Ibid., 309.   [84] Ibid., 188.
[85] Ibid., 315–16.   [86] Ibid., 376.

be commanding the individual to seek self-preservation, as Hobbes does, but to be concerned with the survival of the human species. Thus, private property, even if only in the sense of private use of land, is a natural right because otherwise men would not labor to produce enough to preserve mankind. Because this is the given purpose for the acquisition of property, the law of nature prohibits any man from acquiring more than he can consume, since otherwise the rest would be wasted and denied to those who needed it.

It follows that once men invented money, which made it possible for individuals to accumulate more than they could consume without any danger of its going to waste, the government had a duty to regulate and limit property so as to ensure that all had enough. So in *An Essay Concerning Toleration* of 1667, Locke writes: "The magistrate having a power to appoint ways of transferring proprieties from one man to another, may establish any, so they be universal, equal and without violence and suited to the welfare of that society."[87] In *A Letter Concerning Toleration* of 1689 he says: "It is the duty of the civil magistrate, by the impartial execution of equal laws, to secure unto all the people in general, and to every one of his subjects in particular, the just possession of these things belonging to this life."[88] Von Leyden suggests that in this latter passage Locke sanctioned the redistribution of property by government.[89] Even if that contention is disputed, it must be acknowledged, as Laslett[90] points out, that Locke never withdrew nor contradicted those statements. Whether or not Locke recommended control of credit and prices, or whether measures such as nationalization could be justified on his principles, as has been suggested by Laslett, Kendall, and von Leyden, there is nothing in Locke's understanding of law to prevent the use of legislation to do whatever the majority of the society considers desirable in order to subdue and cultivate the earth as God commands.

Civil society, as Locke understands it, is thus an association with a given purpose, and law is the appropriate instrument for achieving that purpose. Locke never speaks of law as a set of adverbial conditions that ought not to direct anyone's behavior. On the contrary, he claims laws should indicate considerations that must be taken into account when deciding what to do. There is no suggestion in Locke's writing for making the traditional distinction between laws imposing taxation, which

---

[87] Ibid., 366, see footnote for §120.   [88] *Works*, vol. V, 10.
[89] W. von Leyden, *Hobbes and Locke: The Politics of Freedom and Obligation* (London: MacMillan, 1981), 108.
[90] Locke, *Two Treatises*, 104.

command the performance of certain actions, and contract law, which stipulates the conditions for making a contract that can be defended at law, but which does not oblige anyone ever to make a contract. Nor is any of this surprising because an instrumental view of law is inseparable from regarding the power of government as a trust rather than as an authorization. If, as in Locke's view, the government is entrusted with power for the sake of attaining a given end, what matters is whether that trust has been effectively discharged. Whether the rules have been adequately observed is unimportant or significant only insofar as it aids or hinders discharging the trust. That this was Locke's view of law is obvious in what he says about both adjudication and prerogative.

The independence of the judiciary did not concern him. He speaks of legislation and adjudication as one: The duties of the legislature are, he says, a power to "decide the Rights of the Subject *by promulgated standing Laws, and known Authoris'd Judges.*"[91] He describes the legislature also as a "Judge on Earth, with Authority to determine all the Controversies."[92] And he couples legislation with adjudication as if they were aspects of one power: in civil society men have "a common establish'd Law and Judicature to appeal to."[93] At the same time, he attributes a judicial power also to the executive, and besides couples the executive power with the legislative when he derives civil society from the right of every man in the state of nature to judge and punish violations of the law of nature. There is not the slightest suggestion that adjudication has to be kept separate in the statement, "herein we have the original of the *Legislative* and *Executive Power* of Civil Society, which is to judge by standing Laws."[94] Instead of seeing adjudication as a distinct legal procedure, Locke regards it as a "pervasive feature" of civil society.[95]

Locke's indifference to the independence of adjudication is consistent with both his blindness to the character of practical reasoning and his view of government as a trust. If law is understood as the foundation of authority, it is essential to keep the rules fixed, and adjudication is needed to interpret fixed rules for different circumstances. To ensure that the rules are made and changed only by those who are authorized to do so and that the law is not changed for particular cases, adjudication and the enforcement of law have to be kept separate from legislation. In other words, regard for the independence of the judiciary is part of a regard for the formalities of law. But those formalities are unimportant for Locke because he does not regard the rule of law as a set of procedures

---

[91] Ibid., 376. [92] Ibid., 343. [93] Ibid., 342. [94] Ibid., 343.
[95] Von Leyden, *Hobbes and Locke*, 126.

that enables people who do not wish to obliterate their disagreements to settle them amicably. Instead, Locke sees the law as a set of instructions for performing the right actions. What determines their rightness is whether they allow the human species to flourish. Since the law is an instrument for achieving a goal, whose desirability is indisputable because it has been designated for man by a superior will, the only thing that matters is the effectiveness of the law for achieving its object. That is why Locke holds that "Law, in its true Notion, is not so much the Limitation as *the direction of a free and intelligent Agent to his proper Interest.*"[96]

That Locke values the rule of law not for its own sake, but rather as the most effective instrument for achieving desirable consequences, is even clearer in his discussion of prerogative. He defines prerogative as the "Power to act according to discretion, for the publick good, without the prescription of the Law, and sometimes even against it."[97] And he gives the same reason for the right of the people to grant or enlarge the prince's prerogative as for their right to limit it: "whatsoever shall be done manifestly for the good of the People, and the establishing the Government upon its true Foundations, is, and always will be just *Prerogative.*"[98] These are not chance remarks: the same view is repeated in different contexts. Locke explains, for instance, that since "a Rational Creature" would not willingly subject himself to another "for his own harm," when he "finds a good and wise ruler, he may not perhaps think it either necessary, or useful to set precise Bounds to his Power in all things." It is entirely reasonable for the people to permit their rulers to "do several things of their own free choice," not only where the law is silent, but "sometimes too against the direct Letter of the Law."[99]

Of course, all admirers of the rule of law have acknowledged that occasions may arise where the law has no answer or gives an answer so violently unsuitable that it must be ignored. To provide for such occasions, even the strictest of constitutions grants emergency powers in some form or other, for times of peace as well as war. Besides, it is always acknowledged that managing relations with other states requires a large degree of discretion. And if that were all that Locke had in mind when he insisted upon the importance of prerogative, he would be saying nothing remarkable. But in fact he is not merely making the traditional qualifications on the rule of law. He assigns the discretion required for dealing with foreign affairs to the "federative" branch of government; the power that he discusses in connection with prerogative belongs to the

[96] Locke, *Two Treatises*, 323.   [97] Ibid., 393.
[98] Ibid., 391.   [99] Ibid., 395.

executive. Moreover, the necessity for ignoring the law at times is not something that Locke deplores; on the contrary, he assumes that the law is there to be observed only insofar as it serves the public good (understood as a project for ensuring that the species flourishes) and that whenever the public can be served better by other means, the law becomes otiose.

He accordingly explains that there is no reason in the abstract for suspecting prerogative, claiming that the English people have traditionally been tolerant of prerogative because it is a power to do good: They "are very seldom, or never scrupulous, or nice in the point," and questioning of "Prerogative, whilst it is in any tolerable degree imploy'd for the use it was meant; that is, for the good of the People, and not manifestly against it."[100] The people have never "contested" what "was done without law"; on the contrary, they have acquiesced in whatever the prince did, regardless of whether it was done "contrary to the Letter of the Law" or how much it enlarged the prince's prerogative, as long as it served the public good. They would not limit the prerogative of "those Kings or rulers, who themselves transgressed not the Bounds of the publick good. For *Prerogative is nothing but the Power of doing publick good without a Rule.*"[101] Where a dispute arises between the executive power and the people about a claim to prerogative, "the tendency of the exercise of such Prerogative to the good or hurt of the People, will easily decide that Question."[102] When the people are blessed with a good prince who discharges his trust faithfully, he "cannot have too much *Prerogative, that is, Power to do Good.*" And conversely, when the prince turns out to be a poor trustee, the people are justified in limiting his power. Merely changing the extent of the prerogative in either direction is no cause for complaint since "the end of government being the good of the Community, whatsoever alterations are made in it, tending to that end, cannot be an *incroachment* upon any body. . . And those only are *incroachments* which prejudice or hinder the publick good."[103]

Locke's view of prerogative is wholly consistent with his theory of natural law as well as with his view of government as a trust, since on neither ground is the rule of law the constituent of civil society or valued for its own sake. The rule of law is merely an instrument designed to serve a given purpose, and whether or not an instrument should be employed depends entirely on how well it can serve its purpose.

In keeping with this depreciation of law, Locke sanctions a right of resistance to governments that fail to promote the public good. There

---

[100] Ibid., 393.   [101] Ibid., 395–96.
[102] Ibid., 393.   [103] Ibid., 394–95.

would be nothing unusual in his discussion of resistance if Locke had argued merely that there are occasions when men might be justified in refusing to obey the established law. That in some circumstances rebellion might be justified has generally been granted by defenders of the rule of law, even, as we have seen, by St. Thomas Aquinas. The novelty in Locke's argument is that he insists on a "right" to resist unjust law. And that is consistent with what he says about the desirability of prerogative because the object that justifies both is the same, promoting the public good. If the legislature is entrusted with power so that it may pursue a known end, then it follows that when those who have entrusted this power find that the legislature has acted contrary to the trust reposed in it, they are entitled to "place it anew where they shall think best for their safety and security."[104]

Earlier on, in his *Tracts on Government*, Locke did not recognize any right to resistance, arguing that if the magistrate abused his powers, it was for God to punish him. Nor did Locke ever withdraw the arguments that he made in the *Tracts* against claims to a right of disobedience based on conscience. When writing later about toleration, he argues that "a toleration of men in all that which they pretend out of conscience they cannot submit to will wholly take away all the civil laws and all the magistrate's powers, and so there will be no law nor government." In a letter of 1660 he altogether repudiates any sanction for resistance. Having from early childhood found himself "in a storm, which has lasted almost hitherto," he now felt bound "both in duty and gratitude to endeavour the continuance of such a blessing by disposing men's minds to obedience to that government which has brought with it the quiet settlement which even our giddy folly had put beyond the reach not only of our contrivance but hopes."[105] Nevertheless, in the *Second Treatise* Locke argues persistently and firmly for a "Right" to resist "the Exercise of a power without right."[106] Whereas in the *Tracts* he emphasizes the gulf between the ruler and the multitude "whom knowing men have always found and therefore called beasts."[107] In the *Treatise* Locke declares rulers to be just as vulnerable as any of their subjects to using "force the way of Beasts."[108]

In the course of defending the right to resistance, Locke occasionally comes close to speaking as if authorization is the ground of government. He says, for instance, that when "*Oaths of Allegiance* and Fealty" are taken to the supreme executive, "tis not to him as Supream Legislator, but as Supream Executor of the Law. . . *Allegiance* being nothing but an *Obedience according to Law*, which when he violates, he has no right to

---

[104] Ibid., 385.   [105] *Two Tracts*, 102; cf. *Political Philosophy*, 178.
[106] *Two Treatises*, 397.   [107] *Two Tracts*, 158.   [108] *Two Treatises*, 407.

Obedience, nor can claim it otherwise than as the publick Person vested with the Power of the Law, and so is to be consider'd as the Image, Phantom, or Representative of the Commonwealth, acted by the will of the Society, declared in its Laws; and thus he has no Will, no Power, but that of the Law."[109] In the same spirit, a tyrant is defined as one who "makes not the Law, but his Will, the Rule,"[110] who "exceeds the Power given him by the Law, and makes use of the Force he has under his Command, to compass that upon the Subject, which the Law allows not."[111]

But Locke's censure of tyranny is never a clear-cut condemnation of lawlessness as such. Censure of a tyrant's arbitrariness is coupled throughout with condemnation of the consequences of his lawlessness. Indeed, Locke explicitly emphasizes that the consequences are what matter. If the lawlessness, the transgressing of the law, did no harm, it would not be a ground for censure: *"Where-ever Law ends, Tyranny begins, if the law be transgressed to another's harm"*;[112] (emphasis added). This qualification keeps Locke's censure of tyranny consistent with his views on the prerogative, and it makes a judgment of the consequences of lawlessness, rather than an obligation to observe authentic law, the ground for opposing tyranny.

Locke does make some qualifications on the right of resistance. The cause for dissatisfaction must be of "sufficient moment,"[113] and the rebel "must be sure he has Right on his side."[114] Not just any individual, but a substantial part of the community must judge that the government has betrayed its trust. In any case resistance is unlikely under other circumstances since a few private men are so powerless to recover what has been taken from them that even the "Right to do so [to resist the established government], will not easily ingage them in a Contest, wherein they are sure to perish."[115]

Rebellion need not, moreover, affect the prince or king if it is directed at his subordinates who have violated their trust: "the *Sacredness* of the person *exempts him from all Inconveniences.*"[116] But if a king arbitrarily dissolves the legislature, he declares a state of war with his subjects, and then the king becomes a rebel. Apart from these qualifications, Locke argues that a right to rebellion is not likely to be interpreted as an invitation to anarchy because people desire peace and security and are naturally disinclined to overthrow an established government, even when their grievances are substantial. He also suggests that the right of resistance is important chiefly as a threat because rulers are less likely to give

---

[109] Ibid., 386.   [110] Ibid., 417.   [111] Ibid., 418.   [112] Ibid., 418.
[113] Ibid., 397.   [114] Ibid., 404.   [115] Ibid., 422.   [116] Ibid., 420.

cause for rebellion if they believe that their subjects are likely to resist misuse of power.

But otherwise, Locke defends a right of resistance to "the exercise of a Power without right." Indeed, the qualifications he makes elsewhere are forgotten when he says that not only the "Body of the People," but "any single Man" has "a liberty to appeal to Heaven, whenever they judge the Cause of sufficient moment. . . by a Law antecedent and paramount to all positive Laws of men. . . . God and Nature never allowing a Man so to abandon himself, as to neglect his own preservation."[117]

Throughout, Locke's emphasis falls on the self-evident nature of the ground for resistance. If the people *"universally have a perswasion*, grounded upon manifest evidence, that designs are carrying on against their Liberties, and the general course and tendency of things cannot but give them strong suspicions of the evil intention of their Governors," they cannot be blamed for resorting to rebellion.[118] Whenever the people come to believe that the legislators have designs on their property, they are "thereupon absolved from any further Obedience, and are left to the common Refuge, which God hath provided for all Men, against Force and Violence. . . [and] have a Right to resume their original Liberty."[119] To those who protest that if the commands of a prince may be resisted by anyone who feels aggrieved, anarchy and confusion will replace government and order, Locke replies, "That *Force* is to be *opposed* to nothing, but to unjust and unlawful *Force*; whoever makes any opposition in any other Case, draws on himself a just Condemnation both from God and Man; and so no such Danger or Confusion will follow, as is often suggested."[120] Furthermore, to say that men are not to be "absolved from Obedience, when illegal attempts are made upon their Liberties or properties" is like saying "that honest Men may not oppose Robbers or Pirates, because this may occasion disorder or bloodshed." Whatever undesirable consequences may attend such resistance should be charged not "upon him, who defends his own right, but *on him*, that *invades* his Neighbours."[121]

Locke's discussion of the right of resistance makes it clear that he regards law as an instrument for promoting the welfare of a productive enterprise, and that he considers conformity to legal procedures as but one means for ensuring that the ruler remains faithful to his trust. If he can discharge his trust more effectively by violating or ignoring legal procedures, he is obliged to do so. If his subjects can better ensure the

---

[117] Ibid., 397–98.   [118] Ibid., 436.   [119] Ibid., 430.
[120] Ibid., 420.   [121] Ibid., 434–35.

effective discharge of that trust by renouncing their obligation to obey the law, they are similarly entitled, indeed have a duty, to rebel. The formalities of the law are to be respected only insofar as obedience produces the desirable consequence of promoting good policy.

All this rests on Locke's assumption that the truth about what is right in human conduct, public as well as private, is not subject to reasonable disagreement. He is nowhere concerned with the possibility of disputes among good and wise men about whether the law has been violated or adequately observed, whether the public good has been faithfully pursued, or what constitutes the public good. Such questions are meaningless for Locke because he did not recognize that practical reasoning about contingent matters, unlike demonstrative reasoning, arrives at conclusions that are ineradicably disputable, and because he believed that moral truth is as undeniable as mathematical truth.

Locke is indifferent to the possibility of such disputes among good and wise men because he assumes that the truth about what is right is manifest. This belief is rendered plausible by his religious faith combined with his rejection of natural theology. Since he did not accept his predecessors' intricate conception of a rational cosmic order and of the law that ruled that order, he had no regard for what that conception implied about the distinction between theoretical and practical reasoning, self-evident first principles, and contingent conclusions. And he did not understand reason as a creative faculty that can produce infinitely various interpretations of experience and responses to it. His defense of natural rights rests ultimately on a simple, fundamentalist conviction that what men need to know in order to conduct their lives has been made manifest in Revelation and that the meaning of Revelation is too plain to allow serious disagreement among believers. As a result, Locke has left a complicated and dangerous legacy for the philosophy of law.

His doctrine of natural law has been interpreted as a teaching about natural rights, and it has been adopted by people without any religious faith, who, at times perhaps even antagonistic to the Judaeo-Christian tradition, are therefore neither influenced nor restrained by any reading of Christian doctrine or Christian theology. Instead, they take their bearings from an unpredictable variety of conflicting compasses. To such an audience, Locke's doctrine, stripped of its Christian underpinnings, becomes a defense of wholly arbitrary claims to "natural rights" or appeals to "principles of reasonableness," which can be and are used not only to encourage violation of established law, but also to denigrate the conception of law as a set of formally authenticated rules on the ground that it hinders the adoption of desirable social policies. Although such doctrines are considerably cruder than Locke's, their presuppositions about human rationality and individuality and the rule of law are essentially the same because they trace obligation not to rights that are established by human contrivance but to indisputable rights given to human beings. Only the exponents of these latter-day natural law theories do not deign to explain how rights can be "given" without emanating from a Divine Ruler. Yet even if their lack of Locke's religious faith may lead them to somewhat different views about what is desirable, the current advocates of natural rights and natural law conclude, just as Locke did, that the rule of law is an expedient for securing desirable social policy. By describing law as a direction to our greater good, they fail to distinguish between the constraints of procedures, which are defined by rules of law, and the constraints of commands. For such latter-day disciples of Locke, the only alternatives are agreement and obedience or disagreement and rebellion.

Locke not only lost sight of Hobbes's distinction between power and authority, but he also departed radically from the pre-Hobbesian understanding of law. Locke's doctrine of natural law, unlike that of any of his predecessors, identifies law for the first time with an instrument for serving a productive enterprise and achieving a given unitary end. He accordingly abandoned the traditional understanding of law as the bond of an association of independent agents pursuing diverse projects. But the true radicalism of Locke's innovation went unnoticed at the time. Nor did the Lockian theme reappear in the conversation about law until the nineteenth century. And it was fully developed only in the twentieth century, though none of those who did so declared or probably recognized their affinity with Locke.[122]

---

[122] For the leading exposition of recent modern natural law theory, see John Finnis, *Natural Law and Natural Rights* (Oxford: Clarendon, 1980).

8   Immanuel Kant

The new way of thinking about law, introduced by Immanuel Kant, has a surprising affinity with the philosophies of both Aristotle and Hobbes. For Kant derives his view of law from the requirements of moral integrity, but does so without appealing to either revelation or transcendent metaphysics. Kant has accordingly been acclaimed as the founder of the modern philosophy of law. Yet he has also been charged with having no philosophy of law.

Both reputations are plausible because Kant saw human beings as inhabitants of two wholly distinct worlds. On the one hand, their bodily existence makes them components of the natural, empirical world where all objects are moved by causes external to themselves. In this respect, human beings are mechanisms whose operation is determined by sensory stimuli in accordance with the laws that govern the natural world. But on the other hand, human beings are rational persons. They are not only capable of exercising "theoretical reason" to discover, as Newton had, the laws of the natural world, but they are also possessed of "practical reason," which enables them to choose which purposes to pursue by means of utterances and actions without reference to contingent wants or circumstances. Human beings are consequently distinguished by the "freedom" to choose and to act as they "will." Their frequent lack of power to achieve their purposes does not qualify this "freedom." And their conduct cannot be said to be directed to their achievement of a single comprehensive end, such as "happiness."

As "free wills," human beings are also subject to laws, but these are moral laws that prescribe what ought to be done in order for freedom to be fully and equally enjoyed by all human beings. These laws are known *a priori*, by being derived from the "categorical imperative" that a rational person is always to be treated as an end in himself and never merely as a means. Moral laws therefore have no concern with the natural, empirical world, i.e., with what happens, how people behave, or how they can best get what they want or need. In short, moral laws have nothing to do with either convenience or the consequences of actions. As moral laws are made by reason wholly independently of experience, rational persons may be said to be their author and to legislate for themselves. Being bound by nothing outside their rational being in obeying moral laws, human beings can enjoy their freedom.

Moral laws come in two varieties, ethical and juridical. The former designate what ought to be done to maintain one's integrity as a rational person, and the only constraint is the consideration that a failure to comply constitutes a denial of one's rational personality. This consideration is the only appropriate motive for obeying ethical laws. Ethical laws accordingly command not only that the right ends be pursued, but also that it be done for the right reason – for the sake of doing one's duty. To obey the ethical law that tells me not to lie, I must refrain from lying not out of fear of losing my reputation or being punished, but solely because I desire to do what is right.

Juridical laws, however, are indifferent to motives and pertain only to external actions, which are physical events in time and only insofar as they affect others. They are concerned with securing to each individual the freedom to exercise choice insofar as is compatible with the same freedom for all others. Whereas ethical law requires that we repay our debts out of a sense of duty, juridical law requires only that we restore what we owe, and whether we do so out of a fear of punishment, hope of gain, or a sense of duty is irrelevant. Nevertheless, juridical laws are a species of moral law because their aim is to prevent anyone from performing actions that are wrong in themselves, such as compelling others to act as means to one's own ends. In short, juridical laws are concerned with ordering the association of human beings in a manner appropriate for their character as free rational persons.

But if it is clear that juridical law, as such, is a species of moral law, the great puzzle of Kant's philosophy of law is how positive laws (the products of human legislative enactments) can be, and can be recognized as, reflections of juridical law. We are told that his *Rechtslehre* (Science of Right) is designed to provide "philosophical and systematic knowledge of the Principles of Natural Right," which are "a real foundation for actual positive Legislation." Without this foundation, positive law becomes no more than an "empirical system," which, because it is "void of rational principles," is "like the wooden head in the fable of Phaedrus, fine enough in appearance, but unfortunately it wants brain." To ensure that positive law is more than this, the legislator has to consult the immutable rational principles of right, which provide "a universal Criterion by which Right and Wrong in general, and what is just and unjust" may be recognized.[1] But

---

[1] Immanuel Kant, *The Philosophy of Law*, trans. W. Hastie (Clifton, NJ: Augustus M. Kelley, 1974), 43–44.

unlike the classical and medieval writers whom Kant may seem to echo here, he nowhere considers how a legislative procedure can be made to ensure that positive law reflects the principles of natural right. On the contrary, when he says that the laws of a state "are to be regarded as necessary *a priori* – that is, as following of themselves from the conceptions of external Right generally – and not as merely established by Statute," he suggests that positive laws are indistinguishable from the principles of right.[2]

Kant emphasized, moreover, that all rights that do and should appear in positive law necessarily exist in the state of nature. He argues, for instance, that a right to private property must be available without positive law because things that can be possessed and used are to be found in the world. If they could not be acquired, that would be tantamount to denying their existence, or to annihilating them. Nor is it possible that the right to property was originally a communal right because, prior to civil union, communal ownership could only have been established by a contract whereby everyone renounced a right of private possession and transformed the land into a common possession. But as there is no record of any such act, the notion that land was originally a common possession is a fiction.

What can be done in the state of nature is to declare by word or deed that something is mine and that others are obliged to abstain from using it even when I am not in physical possession of it. But according to the laws of right, I may not oblige anyone to do anything that I do not equally recognize as an obligation. I cannot therefore oblige others to refrain from interfering with my possessions unless I accord to every other person whom I may encounter a similar guarantee that I will respect their claims. I can then, in the state of nature, establish possession by making contracts with individuals. Possession on this basis, however, has two shortcomings. First, if a dispute should arise about the terms of the agreement, there is no umpire competent to give an authoritative decision. And second, there exists a "natural Inclination of men to play the master over others, and to disregard the claims of the Right of others, when they feel themselves their superiors by Might or Fraud." Since all can discover such a disposition by merely examining themselves, there is no need to wait for "the melancholy experience of actual hostility" in order to be "entitled to exercise a rightful compulsion towards those who already threaten him by their very nature."[3] If someone obstructs or wrongs me, I have a right to exercise constraint to prevent such a wrong because I would be hindering a hindrance to external freedom. In the state of nature then, a right to property can never be secure and is merely provisional.

<hr />

[2] Ibid., 165.   [3] Ibid., 157–58.

Only when everyone is subject to "universal, external, and public Legislation, conjoined with authority and power," can all possessions be secure. That condition appears only in civil society, where there is a common, collective, authoritative will. It follows from the natural right to defend possession by force that there is a "Right to compel every one with whom we could come into any kind of intercourse" to do whatever is necessary to make possession secure.[4] Since only a civil state can provide a "competent external Power" that can secure to each what shall be recognized as his, the principles of right make it obligatory to leave "the state of Nature in which every one follows his own inclinations, and to form a union of all those who cannot avoid coming into reciprocal communication, and thus subject themselves in common to the external restraint of public compulsory Laws."[5] Although no one can be said to wrong anyone in the natural state, not even if they are engaged in war, because what is available to one is available to all, those who fail to enter into a civil state "must be considered as being in the highest state of Wrong."[6]

The civil condition is not the source of the rights enjoyed by its members. Their rights, being determined by reason, exist prior to and independently of civil law. Our rights are the ground, not the consequence, of civil union. If there were no "Laws regarding the Mine and Thine in the state of Nature" that "contain formally the very same thing as they prescribe in the Civil state, when it is viewed merely according to rational conceptions," there "would be no obligation to pass out of that state into another." The only novelty introduced by the civil condition is a "competent external Power" that provides "public compulsory Laws" to restrain individuals from interfering with the rights of others.[7]

Despite his resemblance to Locke in this respect, Kant, far from stressing a contractual element in civil union, describes the idea of an original contract as symbolic. It is a way of representing the rightful constitution of a civil union, whereby all "give up their external Freedom in order to receive it immediately again as Members of a Commonwealth." But Kant emphasizes that the individual is not left with less freedom; rather, in becoming a member of a commonwealth, a person exchanges the whole of a "wild lawless Freedom" for "his proper Freedom. . . in the form of a regulated order of dependence, that is, in a Civil state regulated by laws of Right."[8]

Kant, accordingly, does not regard the laws governing civil union as an artifact but rather as a discovery, or perhaps as a product of the

---

[4] Ibid., 77–78.   [5] Ibid., 164.   [6] Ibid., 158.
[7] Ibid., 164–65.   [8] Ibid., 169–70.

self-discovery of rational persons. But about the role performed by law, two quite different conclusions may plausibly be drawn from Kant's account of civil union. On the one hand, law is presented as the rules for the association of rational persons who could not otherwise reconcile the freedom of each with the freedom of all. Law thus appears to be a means of reconciling unity with diversity that would be no less necessary if all men were perfectly rational. But on the other hand, as human beings have a natural inclination to invade the rights of others through force and fraud, law has the character of a master powerful enough to restrain the circumstantial irrationality of human beings.

A similar ambivalence about the role of law appears in Kant's discussion of the powers of the sovereign. On the one hand, he is the supreme lawmaker concerned with securing the greatest possible freedom for each compatible with the freedom of all. This conception of the sovereign inspires Kant's distinction between a *"paternal"* government, which is the most despotic of governments because it treats its citizens as "mere children," and a "Patriotic Government," which treats people "as Citizens" according to laws "that recognise their independence, each individual possessing himself and not being dependent on the absolute Will of another beside him or above him." The material well-being and happiness of citizens may perhaps "be more agreeably and more desirably attained in the state of Nature, or even under a despotic government." But the "greatest harmony" between the constitution of the state and the principles of right can be achieved only under a patriotic government.[9]

On the other hand, however, the sovereign is a supreme proprietor as well as the supreme commander of the people. As supreme proprietor, he does not possess anything for his private use, but he *"possesses everything"* because all rights to property are distributed by him, and the sovereign may at any time revoke property rights, provided that he compensates those, living at the time, who are deprived. In part, "Supreme proprietorship" is a necessary juridical conception representing the unity of all private property under a universal public owner. But something more than that seems to be implied when Kant says that subjects who have been deprived of their property have no grounds for complaint because "the foundation of their previous possession lay only in the *Opinion of the People*, and it can be valid only so long as this opinion lasts." When it becomes evident to those who lead and represent public opinion that an institution such as church ownership of land has lost the support of public opinion, that institution should be brought to an end.[10]

---

[9] Ibid., 171–73.   [10] Ibid., 183–85.

As supreme proprietor, the sovereign also has a right to demand service in war and to tax in order to maintain the state. Although, in general, taxation should be imposed by the people themselves through their deputies, the state may also impose a compulsory loan by decree if it finds itself in immediate danger. Its rights as proprietor also entitle the state to administer the economy as well as the army and the police. And it has the right to command the police not only to secure public safety and convenience, but also to protect the public against affronts to the moral sense, such as begging, offensive noises and smells, or prostitution, since a public whose sense of propriety has been blunted by such affronts is more difficult to govern by law.[11]

The powers of the sovereign as supreme commander are also of a mixed character. The power to distribute offices and dignities is entailed in sovereignty. But Kant adds a power to impose taxes for the purpose of securing the material welfare of the people, on the grounds that citizens who lack material satisfactions may refuse to submit to law and that if children perish, the state loses power. The sovereign may therefore compel those with sufficient resources to contribute to the preservation of their fellow citizens.

Although Kant acknowledges that it is difficult to provide such care without offending "against Right or Morality,"[12] he does not in any other way recognize that the character he has assigned to the sovereign as supreme proprietor and supreme commander is in any way incompatible with that of supreme lawmaker. As head of a patriotic state, the sovereign's laws are supposed to secure the freedom of all in accordance with the principles of right, whereas the laws of the supreme commander and proprietor are expected to reflect public opinion, to manage resources efficiently, and to increase the power of the sovereign. In the former role, the sovereign has the character of a ruler; in the latter, he is the manager of an enterprise. Yet all the commands of the sovereign appear to be derived from the principles of right and to qualify as law.

A ground for reconciling the different characters assigned to law appears in Kant's teleological view of history. Here Kant argues that as everything in nature has been assigned a purpose by God, man's possession of reason shows that he was meant to be guided, not by instinct or innate ideas, but by the fullest exercise of his rational powers. Nature's device for securing this fulfillment is the "unsocial social" character of human beings. They want to live in society, but they also want to retain their freedom as individuals to do as each pleases. They come into conflict

[11] Ibid., 185.   [12] Ibid., 188.

because they compete for goods, honor, and power. But that induces them to overcome their natural indolence and to take the first steps from barbarism to culture and finally to civil union. The law acts as a master to break man's will and subdue his self-seeking animal inclinations. In this fashion the inclinations that make it impossible for men to live together in peace become the means to their progress, just as trees in a forest, by trying to get the better of their neighbors as they struggle for air and sunlight, compel each other to grow "beautiful and straight," whereas trees that grow in freedom and isolation where they can put out branches at will become "stunted, bent and twisted."[13]

As individuals and states grow more enlightened about their self-interest, more freedom will result. States will come increasingly to recognize that the way to make industry and commerce flourish and to render the state more powerful is to permit citizens to seek their personal welfare in whatever way they choose that is "consistent with the Freedom of all."[14] And just as civil society grows out of the self-seeking of individuals, so a world-wide civil society will emerge from the conflict among states as it becomes evident that peaceful arrangements are a better way than war to settle their differences. States' recourse to *ad hoc* agreements and increasing links among themselves will bring their relationship ever closer to a world state. And the divine plan will be completed when one law, providing for the freedom of all, governs the whole world.

Kant's teleology thus suggests that, in the lower stages of development, laws serve as rules of management to promote progress to that stage where human beings will no longer need a master to break their wills, at which point law can assume its pure character. Law thus provides a solution to the human predicament that arises from the dual nature of man. Human beings can achieve moral perfection only by becoming wholly masters of themselves, but their animal nature drives them to seek satisfactions in ways that are incompatible with preserving the autonomy of themselves and others. By living under law, human beings are subjected to restraints that curb their animal nature without destroying their autonomy because, as rational persons, they give the law to themselves.

By giving this dual assignment to law, Kant revived the tension in the ancient idea of law in an even more difficult form. For he requires the law to be both non-instrumental and instrumental. It is non-instrumental insofar as conformity to law is desirable in itself and not

---

[13] Immanuel Kant, "Idea for a Universal History with a Cosmopolitan Intent," in *Perpetual Peace and Other Essays on Politics, History, and Morals*, trans. Ted Humphrey (Indianapolis, IN: Hackett, 1983), 33.
[14] *Philosophy of Law*, 48.

for the consequences it brings. But as a master for the animal in man and as an agent for moral improvement, law serves as the instrument of a moral enterprise.

That the two roles assigned to law have been less than perfectly reconciled is evident in Kant's emphasis on the connection between law and coercion and in the implications of that connection for determining the authority of law. Unlike his predecessors, Kant presents the use of coercion to enforce law as a logical consequence of the principles of right: if freedom is put to a use that hinders freedom, any coercion employed against that use is a hindrance to a hindrance of freedom. It follows that right entails the authority to apply coercion against anyone who interferes with freedom. As this is a moral rather than an instrumental argument for the use of coercion, Kant concludes that just as a sense of duty obliges us to obey ethical laws, so the coercion that attends disobedience obliges us to obey civil law. And when he says that "the conception of Right may be viewed as consisting immediately in the possibility of a universal reciprocal Compulsion, in harmony with the Freedom of all," Kant attributes the authority of law to its coercive power.[15]

At the same time, however, Kant suggests that whatever is promulgated by a state is authentic law because "Each of them determines the same thing about all, and All determine the same thing about each." Here promulgated law has authority because the will of the people is "personified" in "a political triad" of the state: the legislative power is personified in the person of the lawgiver, the executive in the ruler who administers the law, and the judiciary in the judge who assigns "every one what is his own, according to the Law." Together the three powers of government represent the "universal united Will of the People."[16] It is not clear whether the whole of one branch of the government is the sovereign, as on occasions Kant speaks both of the legislature and of the executive power as sovereign. But certainly the sovereign does not replace the will of all or act for the people. Instead, the sovereign constitutes the unity of the will of the people.

This identification of the sovereign with the will of all makes it unnecessary for Kant to explain how the law acquires authority or to designate procedures for ascertaining the authenticity of law. Instead, he identifies the authority of law with its justice, which is guaranteed simply by the nature of civil union where "*all* determine and decree what is to be Law to themselves," whereby it becomes impossible to "perpetrate a wrong on that other."[17] But at the same time, Kant rests the authority of law on the right to use coercion to ensure obedience. That is the implication of

[15] Ibid., 47.   [16] Ibid., 165–66.   [17] Ibid., 166.

Kant's definition of Right as "the possibility of a universal Reciprocal compulsion, in harmony with the Freedom of all" according to universal laws. It means, he says, "that Right is not to be regarded as composed of two different elements – Obligation according to a Law, and a Title on the part of one who has bound another by his own free choice, to compel him to perform."[18] In other words, justice, authority, and coercion are to be understood as different aspects of law that are inseparable.

This may explain why, instead of concluding that unjust law does not carry an obligation to be obeyed, Kant says firmly and unambiguously that there is no "Right of Sedition, and still less of Rebellion belonging to the People."[19] Although he presents this denial as a principle "involved *a priori* in the idea of a political Constitution generally as a conception of the Practical Reason,"[20] he gives more than one argument against a right of resistance.

One reason why resistance is always and necessarily wrong is that it destroys an existing legal relationship. Because such a relationship is the only one in which men are necessarily treated as ends, any constitution, however inadequate, is better than none at all, and whatever destroys a legal relationship is immoral. In addition, Kant argues that a right of resistance is a logical absurdity. Whoever would restrain the supreme power must possess sufficient power to do so and also be better able to judge what is right. But that makes him the supreme power, which is a contradiction. That a right of resistance is a self-contradictory idea becomes obvious once we ask: "Who is to be the Judge in a controversy between the People and the Sovereign . . . the question shows that the People would then have to be the Judge in their own cause."[21]

Kant reaches the same conclusion by another route: That a supreme will exists, "holy and irresistible,"[22] he argues, is intrinsic to the idea of a political constitution. In their natural condition the people are a multiplicity of wills. They are united by the institution of a supreme power that establishes public right. If a right of resistance were allowed, the supreme power would no longer have the final word and would cease to be the supreme power, which would dissolve the unity into a multiplicity of wills that can neither make nor enforce law. It follows also that what is called a limited constitution, containing an article that allows one power in the state to resist or restrict the supreme authority when it transgresses constitutional law, is an "unreality." The real object of such arrangements, Kant says, is to disguise the "arbitrary influence" of a "powerful

---

[18] Ibid., 47.   [19] Ibid., 176.   [20] Ibid., 258.
[21] Ibid., 177.   [22] Ibid., 257.

violator of popular Rights" by giving the violator the pretext that he is exercising a right of opposition conceded to the people. In short, Kant maintains unequivocally that the people are bound by duty to "bear any abuse of the Supreme Power," however unbearable it might be.[23]

All questions about the origins of civil government, about whether the power or the law came first, or how the existing ruler attained legitimacy, are either pointless or dangerous to the existing state: "It is a duty to obey the Law of the existing Legislative Power, be its origin what it may."[24] Even when a revolution establishes a new constitution, its unlawful origins do not "release the Subjects from the obligation of adapting themselves, as good Citizens, to the new order of things." They cannot honorably refuse "to obey the authority that has thus attained the power of the State." But neither are they entitled to punish the deposed ruler. If he should withdraw into private life within the same state instead of going into exile, he may not be tried for his past misdeeds. On the contrary, even if he should attempt a counter-revolution, he is still within his rights "because the Rebellion that drove him from his position was inherently unjust."[25]

A formal trial to justify the execution of a monarch is even worse than simply assassinating him because "mere violence is thus elevated with bold brow, and as it were by principle, above the holiest Right." Using the forms of law in this fashion perverts the "Principles that should regulate the relation between a Sovereign and his People," for the people "who owe their constitutional existence" to the laws made by the sovereign are thereby made to rule over the sovereign. The state cannot recognize a right of resistance without in effect committing suicide in the name of a principle that also makes it impossible to restore the state.[26]

Defects in an existing constitution, however, may and should be removed gradually by reform. But all such measures must proceed from the sovereign power and affect only the executive, never the legislative power. Giving the people legal power to resist the executive through their representatives in the legislature is the only way in which a constitution may be genuinely limited without being destroyed. But the executive must not be coerced into doing what the people want because that would constitute a usurpation of the executive's power by the people. At most, the people may put up "a *negative* Resistance" by refusing "to concede all the demands which the Executive may deem it necessary to make [on behalf] of the political Administration."[27]

[23] Ibid., 176–77.   [24] Ibid., 175.   [25] Ibid., 181.
[26] Ibid., 179–80.   [27] Ibid., 181.

Hence, without formulating or indeed recognizing a concept of authority, Kant insists more unreservedly than any of his predecessors, even than Hobbes, on an obligation to obey the established sovereign. But it is not easy to reconcile his views on rebellion with his identification of law with right. The difficulty here is analogous to the disparity between the different roles that Kant assigns to law. It might be argued that the identification of law with right is a postulate of law, and that the prohibition of rebellion is a practical recommendation made at a less abstract level. But Kant provides no ground for distinguishing among his prescriptions in this fashion. He nowhere separates the postulates of law from practical prescriptions for law. He says nothing about the legislator's deliberation or the judge's decision to suggest that it is an activity different from that of the philosopher reflecting on the principles of right.

On the contrary, he describes the relationship between the three powers of government as analogous to that of the three propositions in a syllogism. The major premise is laid down by the legislator, who is apparently supposed to arrive at it by deduction from the science of right, and the conclusion as well as the premise is no less exact or certain than an axiom of mathematics: Just as geometry can unequivocally define a straight line, so the "Science of Right aims at determining what every one shall have as his *own* with mathematical exactness."[28] Kant may seem to make a concession to practical considerations when he says that whether a law is just can easily be discovered by asking: Could every person subject to it have consented to it? But the question does not mean, he warns, that everyone has to agree that the law is acceptable. It requires only that there must be nothing in the law that is unacceptable in principle. And this can be known *a priori*. It need be only possible to consent to such a law; that at any time someone, if asked, might refuse his or her consent to it is irrelevant. Far from supposing that the answer might be disputable, Kant is so certain that the answer is self-evident that he does not hesitate to make quite specific prescriptions for the content of law.

He is sure, for instance, that no one could agree to give others a status superior to his own. Therefore, a hereditary aristocracy could not be established in the state of nature and is intrinsically unjust. Even where an aristocracy is permitted, the head of the state is entitled to abolish its privileges at any time because the rank of nobleman, having no foundation in right, is merely a contingent feature of the constitution. When the sovereign decides to abolish aristocratic privileges, as he should do in order to promote justice, he does not deprive a nobleman of his rights

---

[28] Ibid., 49.

because what the nobleman called his own was dependent only on the contingent will of the sovereign. The same is true of the right of primogeniture. Kant is equally certain that reason requires giving men a right to transmit titles of nobility to their wives but not the converse, as well as requiring that officials should have tenure for life.

About marriage, too, the commands of reason are in Kant's view indisputable. Since marriage is a mutual possession of sexual organs, and since possessing a part of a person necessarily entails possessing the whole, monogamous marriage is the only relationship between those engaged in sexual intercourse that does not dehumanize the partners. In binding both the partners to life-long fidelity, marriage commits both equally, and the right that each acquires in marriage entitles each to compel the other, should one partner stray into the possession of someone else, to return to the former relationship. Kant concludes that "if a man and a woman have the will to enter on reciprocal enjoyment in accordance with their sexual nature, they *must* necessarily marry each other" and that this is "necessary in its nature by the Law of Humanity."[29] A contract of concubinage cannot be right because it is a contract to hire a part of a person for the use of another, which reduces that person to a thing subject to the arbitrary will of someone else.[30] As a contract of marriage confers a right to a whole person, "if one of the married Persons run away or enter into the possession of another, the other is entitled, at any time, and incontestably, to bring such a one back to the former relation, as if that Person were a Thing."[31] If the contract to engage in conjugal cohabitation is not fulfilled because of a secret understanding to that effect, the contract is merely simulated and thereby annulled. But if non-consummation is due to an incapacity that arises after marriage, the contract remains in force because non-consummation arises from "a contingency that cannot be legally blamed."[32] It is not, however, contrary to the natural equality of husband and wife if the law says that the husband shall be master and that the wife shall obey him. This right can be "deduced from the very duty of Unity and Equality in relation to the *End* involved" because the husband's right to command is based upon "the natural superiority of the faculties of the Husband compared with the Wife, in the effectuation of the common interest of the household."[33]

Although some consideration of circumstances is allowed to intrude when Kant turns to the law regulating charitable foundations, even there his argument begins from the principles of right. It would seem to prohibit

---

[29] Ibid., 110–11.   [30] Ibid., 112.   [31] Ibid., 111.
[32] Ibid., 113.   [33] Ibid., 112–13.

abolishing or altering such foundations because that would violate the rights of the heirs appointed in the legacy. But that is only according to the letter of the legacy. If we take into account also the intention of the legacy, as we should, then a change in circumstances might make it advisable to abolish such foundations, or at least to alter their form. For example, the poor and sick might be provided for better by giving them a sum of money instead of maintaining them in institutions that are not only costly, but also restrict personal liberty. Some institutions, such as lunatic asylums, cannot be modified in this fashion because the inmates cannot be said to have a right of their own, and the state has to decide what is good for them.[34] But others, such as educational institutions, "cannot be held as founded for all time, so as to be a burden upon the land." The state must be permitted to reconstitute them "in accordance with the wants of the time." Although the founder who hoped to enjoy the glory of being associated with the charitable foundation that he created may dislike having it altered by others, this cannot deprive the state of a right, indeed a duty, to ensure the institution's "preservation and progress" under changed conditions.[35]

No such considerations, however, enter into Kant's prescriptions for punishment. What constitutes just punishment for each crime is wholly a matter of right. Kant derives his prescriptions about punishment from the principle that all people must be treated as ends in themselves. Whether punishment designed to reform the criminal might be thought compatible with that principle, he does not consider, but instead concentrates on condemning punishment for the sake of deterrence. He acknowledges that there is such a thing as "punitive *Expediency*, the foundation of which is merely pragmatic *(ne peccetur)* as being grounded upon the experience of what operates most effectively to prevent crime."[36] But he nowhere indicates how such considerations could or should be combined with his prescription for just punishment. Instead, he insists that deterrence cannot be the moral ground for punishment: first, because it entails using the criminal as a means to the good of others and, second, because it has to be based on generalizations from experience that ought never to intrude on a moral judgment.[37] Besides, as generalizations from experience are necessarily "wavering and uncertain," they cannot furnish a universally necessary criterion for the justice of punishment. The only moral ground for punishment is that the criminal has committed a crime and must suffer for it: "The Penal Law is a Categorical Imperative; and woe to him who creeps through the serpent-windings of Utilitarianism to

[34] Ibid., 250.   [35] Ibid., 253.   [36] Ibid., 244.   [37] Ibid., 195.

discover some advantage that may discharge him from the Justice of Punishment, or even from the due measure of it."[38] The principle of equality tells us that all who inflict an undeserved evil on another are doing an evil to themselves. It follows that the Right of Retaliation (*jus talionis*), which requires a punishment similar and equal to the injury sustained, is the only principle according to which a court can assign a penalty.

From the principle of retaliation, Kant unhesitatingly derives the punishments due to different crimes. About theft, for instance, he argues that anyone who steals from another steals from himself because by stealing he makes all property insecure and thereby destroys his own property. But having lost everything, since he still retains the will to live, he must be supported by others. The state should not do this for free. Therefore, the criminal must be employed by the state in penal labor and so be reduced, for a time or perhaps for life, to a condition of slavery. Kant is even more positive about the punishment due for murder: "whoever has committed Murder, must *die*. There is, in this case, no juridical substitute or surrogate, that can be given or taken for the satisfaction of Justice. There is no Likeness or proportion between Life, however painful, and Death; and therefore there is no Equality between the crime of Murder and the retaliation of it but what is judicially accomplished by the execution of the Criminal." Kant's only qualification is that the execution "be kept free from all maltreatment that would make the humanity suffering in his Person loathsome or abominable."[39] Even if a civil society should decide to dissolve itself, dissolution has to wait until the last murderer awaiting execution has been put to death. Otherwise, the blood of the murderer's victim would stain the hands of all because, by publicly violating justice through their failure to punish murder, they would have participated in the crime. However many people may have been involved in any way in a murder, they should all be executed, "for so Justice wills it, in accordance with the Idea of the juridical Power as founded on the universal Laws of Reason."[40] Kant's only concession to contingency or expediency is for cases where the numbers are so great that, by executing all, the state would cease to have subjects, and the peoples' feelings would be blunted by the spectacle of mass slaughter. As the only alternative is the dissolution of civil society and a return to the state of nature, which would be even worse, the sovereign ought to treat such a case as an emergency in which he imposes a penalty such as transportation in place of death. But his decision should be recognized to be an act of prerogative rather than a sentence carried out according to law.

[38] Ibid., 195–96.   [39] Ibid., 198.   [40] Ibid., 200.

The argument that capital punishment is immoral because no one could have agreed, when entering civil society, to forfeit his life, is dismissed by Kant as sophistry and a perversion of justice. The fundamental error consists in confounding a judgment of reason – that the criminal must forfeit his life – with the will to take his own life. Punishment follows not from anyone's having willed to be punished, but from his having willed to perform a punishable act: To say, "I *will* to be punished, if I murder any one," can mean nothing more than, "I submit myself along with all the other citizens to the Laws." The person who participates in enacting penal law is not the same as the person who is punished according to law because no one, *qua* criminal, can be supposed to have a voice in legislation, "the Legislator being rationally viewed as just and holy." It is only "the pure juridically law-given Reason" in him that promulgates a penal law against himself and others who act as criminals.[41]

Two kinds of killing are, however, excluded from *jus talionis*. Kant denies that the legislature has authority to impose capital punishment for maternal infanticide and for dueling between subordinate officers because both killings are motivated by honor, which the perpetrators have a duty to uphold. Because it is impossible for legislation to remove the shame of an illegitimate birth or the humiliation of an officer, those shamed in this fashion are in a state of nature, that is to say, compelled to act for themselves. If the birth of a child outside marriage becomes known, the mother cannot escape disgrace; moreover, since such a child enters the commonwealth illegally, like contraband goods, it has no claim on the protection of the law. Therefore, the commonwealth is entitled to ignore both its existence and its destruction. Similarly, if an officer of junior rank is insulted, he is obliged by the opinion of his equals to prove that he has the quality that his profession demands, the courage to face death. If the penal law punished such killings, it would declare honor to be a mere illusion, which would be cruel; if the law refused to impose the death penalty, it would be remiss in punishing unlawful killings. The only solution, Kant argues, is to recognize that the Categorical Imperative of Penal Justice, requiring that unlawful killing be punished by death, remains in force, but that the positive law cannot adequately deal with actions motivated by honor.

Uncertainty about what is right need not afflict adjudication any more than legislation. Adjudication completes the derivation from the principles of right begun by the legislator. Since the decision of a court is the conclusion of the syllogism for which the legislator lays down the

---

[41] Ibid., 201.

major premise, adjudication is the last step in the deduction of an indisputable conclusion.

It follows, Kant argues, that considerations of equity can never enter into a judicial decision. He acknowledges that there may be good ground for complaint in some cases. His example is the grievance of a domestic servant who has been paid his agreed wage but, because the currency in which it is paid has depreciated, gets less in real value than he had expected. Nevertheless, his loss cannot be defended in a court of law, Kant says, because there was nothing bearing on it in the contract of service, and a judge "cannot give a decree on the basis of vague or indefinite conditions." A court of equity is a self-contradiction. Although the Crown may, if it chooses, compensate persons for such a loss, in strict right the claim has to be rejected because the "parties in question undertook the performance of the service occasioning the loss, at their own risk." It may be true, as the dictum of equity says, that "the strictest Right is the greatest Wrong," but that sort of evil can be settled only by a "Court of Conscience." A civil court can decide only questions of right.[42]

Although on the whole Kant moves unhesitatingly from the principles of right to prescriptions for positive law, about which he expresses no uncertainty, he does at times acknowledge a distinction between "pure," practical reason which dictates what is right in itself, and "practical reason," which tells us what the positive law ought to require. In his *Lectures on Physical Geography*, he distinguishes between the first principle of civil society, which is a universal law, and the particular laws of a particular region, which, he says, are relative to the soil and inhabitants of the region. And in the *Philosophy of Right*, he points out that "All this is to be here viewed *a priori*, according to the rational Conditions of Right, without taking into consideration how such a Constitution is to be actually established or organized, for which particular Statutes, and consequently empirical Principles, are requisite." He acknowledges that the question, What is right in itself? has to be supplemented by a judgment about What is right as applied to this case?[43] And he even recognizes that different circumstances may require a legal judgment at variance with the judgment of "mere sound Reason."[44] But he does not suggest that these acknowledgments should qualify what he says about what the law ought to be.

Kant also introduces considerations of contingent circumstances in connection with the right of suffrage. He does not ask whether or how a legislature can in practice truly represent the will of the people, but he does consider the qualifications needed by anyone claiming the rights of

---

[42] Ibid., 51–52.   [43] Ibid., 142.   [44] Ibid., 146.

citizenship. These rights belong, he says, only to those who do not depend on the will of anyone else for their existence and sustenance. Anything less is incompatible with the independence of a citizen. Among those who should be classified as dependent, Kant includes apprentices to merchants or tradesmen, domestic servants, resident tutors, ploughmen, itinerant laborers, women, and minors. All such people are entitled to equality and freedom as "*Men* helping to constitute the people" and may claim that whatever positive laws are enacted should not "be contrary to the natural Laws that demand the Freedom of all the people and the Equality that is conformable thereto." But as they lack independence, they are merely "passive" as opposed to "active" citizens and therefore are not entitled to vote.[45]

Otherwise, Kant makes no concession to contingent circumstances in deriving his prescriptions about the content of law from the principles of right. Nor does he anywhere indicate how conclusions derived from principles of right could be qualified by other considerations. In only one context, in his discussion of perpetual peace, does Kant explicitly sanction practice that does not perfectly accord with what the principles of right require. Although he presents perpetual peace as "the ultimate end of all the Right of Nations," Kant says that it is "an impracticable ideal," because once a union of states extends over a vast territory, the protection of its individual members becomes impossible, and then war returns.[46] Therefore, the establishment of universal and perpetual peace must "always remain but a pious wish." And yet, it remains our duty to work for "what may perhaps not be realized" by establishing whatever Constitution seems "best adapted to bring it about." We cannot deny that it is our duty to do so without reducing the moral law to a deception and thereby degrading ourselves "to the level of the mechanical play of Nature."[47]

Kant's acknowledgment that perpetual peace can never be realized implies that practical action and what is right are measured on the same scale, but that the former might never reach as far along the scale as the latter. What is right is impractical in the sense that it cannot be wholly attained; human actions cannot scale the heights of reason. This view is in keeping with Kant's conception of practical reason as distinguished from theoretical reason only by being directed to action. But it also shows that Kant's "practical reason" is a far cry from practical reasoning in the Aristotelian sense, which is concerned with contingent matters and proceeds by a different logic. Although Kant acknowledged that empirical knowledge is needed for the definition of specific duties and

[45] Ibid., 168–69.   [46] Ibid., 224.   [47] Ibid., 230.

occasionally claimed to have taken such knowledge into account, he gave no indication of how thought moves from *a priori* principles to contingent practical judgments. What concessions he made to contingency only prompts us to ask, How "pure" can practical reason be?, and to notice that Kant is far from consistent in his answer. He seems, as Beck says, "always to have been striving for a degree of purity which could be obtained only in the emptiness of Wolff's 'universal practical philosophy,'" which he rejected.[48] Nor could Kant have made room for practical reasoning without abandoning the understanding of reason and rationality that informs his critical philosophy. For he identifies reason with universal value rules or "laws," rational acts with acts bound by such laws, and moral conduct with rational acts, thus wholly excluding consideration of contingency from rational and moral discourse and conduct. Given his conception of reason and his identification of law with reason, Kant could not relate law to the contingency of the human world. And that is why he has been charged with having no philosophy of law.[49]

In one sense then, Kant is Augustinian and Hobbesian. He takes the view that the proper concern of law is not with leading men to God, or translating substantive natural law into positive law, or with satisfying the desires or achieving the goals of its subjects. Whether a law is "just" is a question solely about whether it regulates the relationships of the members of a civil union appropriately. In another sense, he is Platonic or Aristotelian, since by divorcing the moral realm from the empirical world, Kant unequivocally identified law as a moral regulation. But his singular contention, which separates him as much from classical predecessors as from Hobbes and Augustine, is that uncontentious principles of positive law can be derived directly from the principles of right. As Kant is unable to acknowledge the rationality of deliberation about contingent matters or of answers that are neither universal nor indisputable, he could not account for the rationality and objectivity of contingent, controversial, and changing legislation and adjudication. Instead, Kant assumes that since rational people are bound to agree about what the law ought to command, any decision infected with contingency must be irrational and arbitrary. As a result, Kant suffered an ironic fate. He became the patron saint both of those who divorced law from morality and of those who, deprived of an indisputable basis for positive law, made wholly arbitrary prescriptions for law in the name of morality and reason.

[48] Lewis Beck White, *A Commentary on Kant's Critique of Practical Reason* (Chicago: Chicago University Press, 1960), 53–54.
[49] Cf. Stuart M. Brown, Jr., "Has Kant a Philosophy of Law," *Philosophical Review* 71 (January 1962): 33.

9   Jeremy Bentham

Although Bentham also tied the idea of law to a moral theory that does not rely on either revelation or transcendent metaphysics and had no use for the uncertainties of practical reasoning, his understanding of law could hardly be more unlike Kant's. Whereas Kant sought to preserve the moral character of law by divorcing it from the practical pursuit of satisfactions, Bentham made that pursuit the foundation of law. But neither his concerns nor his methods were simple. What we find in Bentham is a medley of five different and not altogether compatible views of law, which sets the pattern for the theories that became dominant in the twentieth century.

I

In textbooks Bentham is described as the father of the positivist philosophy of law, the view that law consists of rules whose validity can and should be distinguished from their desirability. And he is credited with or accused of believing that adjudication consists of interpreting established rules and that maintaining a fixed set of authenticated rules is the essence of the rule of law. This wholly traditional view of law appears in his criticism of common law.

There Bentham argues that the common law is defective because it does not consist of authentically recorded rules made by known legislators. There is an echo of ancient authors in Bentham's insistence that a rule of law can only be predicated on "some certain assemblage of words. . . It is words only that can be spoken of as binding: because it is words alone that are producible with certainty when occasion comes for any individual to be bound."[1] Therefore, the only real law is statute law because we can see "in every instance who made it: when, where, and how

---

[1] Jeremy Bentham, "A Comment on the Commentaries," in *A Comment on the Commentaries and a Fragment on Government*, ed. J. H. Burns and H. L. A. Hart (London: Athlone, 1977), 259.

they made it: we call for and have produced to us at any time the very thing they made." No such object to which the word "law" could be attached is to be found in common law. It is merely an "assemblage of fictitious regulations feigned after the images of these real ones that compose the Statute Law."[2]

Even when judges pretend to find the common law in written records, those are not the records of authentic law: "there are plenty of books purporting to be books of customary or as it is more frequently called *unwritten law*. . . But what are they? Books written not by the legislator but by private individuals: Books not of authoritative but of unauthoritative jurisprudence. In none of all these books is there so much as a single article which can with propriety receive the appellation of a law. It is owing rather to an imperfection. . . peculiar to the English tongue. . . They contain *jus* indeed, but not *leges*: *le droit* but not *des lois*."[3] Though they pretend to report judicial transactions, these reports are often only "abridgements, extracts, digests" of those transactions, further adulterated, moreover, by the interpretations imposed upon them over many years, for the reporter who begins as a historian invariably ends as a metaphysician "creating rules."[4]

As a result, what we take to be common law is in reality no more than someone's conjecture about law. So various and conflicting are the materials from which the common law is derived that only chance could determine which rules are appealed to by either judge or pleader: "A question arises concerning the title to an article of property. A deed copied from one drawn by a conveyancer of great name and since copied from by a thousand others, but now impeached for the first time; a decision badly reported upon the face of it but taken from a printed book of high authority; a decision well reported upon the face of it but taken from a printed book of low authority; a decision indifferently reported and taken from a book without a name; a corresponding string of unprinted cases; an ancient treatise, and the decisions which it quotes and which when examined make against it; these. . . are all candidates at the same time for the prerogative of legislation:– which of all these outstanding authorities ought to carry it? When the circle has been squared, this problem will be solved."[5]

As anyone may be a legislator if he "happens to bestow his thoughts upon the subject,"[6] and as he can extract whatever law he prefers, there is

---

[2] "Comment on the Commentaries," 120.
[3] Jeremy Bentham, *Of Laws in General*, ed. H. L. A. Hart (London: Athlone, 1970), 153.
[4] "Comment on the Commentaries," 331; cf. *Laws in General*, 184.
[5] *Laws in General*, 191–92.
[6] "Comment on the Commentaries," 331.

no limit to the making of common law. It "can never be finished,"[7] but is constantly altering and increasing without being understood to do so. Instead of marking "the line of the subject's conduct by visible directions," common law turns him "loose into the wilds of perpetual conjecture." It has none of that "grand utility of the law," which is "certainty."[8] And because there is no knowing who made it or when, we are beguiled into believing judges like Blackstone who tell us that the common law is sacred and may not be altered by human hands.

At best, common law consists of rules extracted from particular cases by a process called "extrapolation." In reality, "abstract and contentious" fictions such as "natural law," "equity," "reasonableness," "policy," and "*contra bonos mores*" conceal the fact that the "extrapolated" rules are invented by judges. They are necessarily *ex post facto* and can serve whatever purpose judges prefer. We are told that the special skills and experience, which ordinary men lack, enable lawyers and judges to divine rules from particular cases. But this only means that judges and lawyers share habits of thought alien to the ordinary man and to his conception of justice, and that judges and lawyers are joined in a "partnership" designed to extract "on joint account, and for joint benefit, out of the pockets of the people, in the largest quantity possible, the produce of the industry of the people."[9]

The coherence of the common law is supposed to be protected by the requirement that judges "tread in one another's steps." On this adherence to precedent depends what feeble and vacillating degree of security is provided by the common law. Whereas Blackstone no less than Mansfield assumed that the courts could and should adjust law to new conditions, Bentham insisted on strict adherence to precedent in all common law adjudication: "Should there be a Judge who enlightened by genius, stimulated by honest zeal to the work of reformation, sick of the delays, the caprice, the prejudices. . . of popular assemblies, should seek with his sole hand to expunge the effusions of traditionary imbecility, and write down in their room the dictates of pure and native Justice . . . let him but reflect that . . . amendment from the Judgment Seat is confusion . . . that partial good thus purchased is universal evil."[10] In his first published work, *A Fragment on Government*, Bentham argued in wholly traditional fashion

---

[7] Jeremy Bentham, *The Works of Jeremy Bentham*, ed. John Bowring, 11 vols. (London: Simpkin, Marshall, 1843), III:206, "General View of a Complete Code of Laws" (hereafter *Works*).

[8] "Comment on the Commentaries," 95; *Works*, III:206, "General View of a Complete Code of Laws."

[9] "A Fragment on Government," in Jeremy Bentham, *A Comment on the Commentaries and a Fragment on Government*, ed. Burns and Hart, 509.

[10] *Works*, V:478, "Petition for Justice"; "Comment on the Commentaries," 223–24.

that judicial lawmaking upsets confidence in the "stability of any rules of Law, reasonable or not reasonable: that stability on which every thing that is valuable to a man depends."[11] However great the benefit to the party favored, it is outweighed by the evil to the community at large. Besides, judges cannot see the whole as readily as the legislator, and the judge who legislates in the course of adjudication does not attend to the particular circumstances of the parties to a suit, but uses them as examples of some general condition requiring a new rule.

But at the same time, Bentham argued that the benefit of adhering to precedent was secured at a great cost. Respect for precedent assumes that *"Whatever is, is right"* and encourages an unthinking resistance to changing the law. Judges perpetuate ancient regulations which, though they may have been adequate for their time, are hardly likely to suit the circumstances of a later, less barbarous age. Yet the more ancient the precedent, the more compelling it is.[12] Thus, the common law imposes an impossible task on judges. They are asked to serve two incompatible purposes, to keep the law fixed in order to protect security of expectations and yet to make it flexible enough to do justice in particular cases. As no man can do both, judges are compelled to vacillate between hard-hearted rigidity and capricious arbitrariness.

If they respect precedent, it becomes an "avowed substitute for reason"[13] and mechanical judicature replaces mental judicature. Concerned only to "follow their leader, – as sheep follow sheep, and geese geese," judges grow indolent and self-indulgent.[14] Instead of attending to the particular circumstances of each case, they spin their decisions out of "some vague maxim, conceived in general terms without exceptions, and without any regard to times and circumstances: a maxim conceived. . . by persons who have no such case as the particular one in question present to their view." In any case, qualifications that a legislator would take into account are forbidden to the common law judge. If they want to keep the law steady, judges have to become insensible enough to doing justice to tolerate appalling mischiefs; "Hence the hardness of heart which is a sort of endemical disease of lawyers where that part of the law which is in the customary form is predominant in the system."[15] When the consequences of adhering to precedent become too blatantly absurd to be tolerated, judges become wholly arbitrary. Like conjurers

---

[11] "Comment on the Commentaries," 409, fn. p.
[12] *Works*, IX:322–23, "Constitutional Code."
[13] *Works*, X:511, "Extracts from Bentham's Memorandum Book, 1818–19."
[14] *Works*, V:472, "Petition for Justice," IX:322, "Constitutional Code."
[15] *Laws in General*, 194–95, n. 1.

and, with public approval, the judge "draws from the same fountain bitter waters, or sweet."[16] The judge is left free to "give or to refuse impunity to the murderer," for if the murderer is punished, the Justification is *stare decisis*, and if the murderer is acquitted, the judge is praised for his liberality.[17] And whatever the judge does, the accused is punished without warning and absolved without reason. While the rights discovered are "mere illusions," the punishments are "sad realities."[18]

Both the adherence to precedent and the violations of it reduce the law to a maze of technicalities that no layman dares enter. He is driven to collect as many lawyers and opinions as his fortune permits, yet this "ruinous procedure often serves only to create new doubts."[19] The legal profession cannot be made accountable for the simple reason that no one else has access to the materials of their craft. Judges and lawyers are thus left free to satisfy whatever "sinister interests" they choose to serve, and the people have no way of knowing either their rights or duties: Not even slaves in the American South suffer such tyranny.[20]

II

Although Bentham never wavered in his antagonism to the common law, the identification of law with written rules that is central to his attack on the common law disappears in other contexts. In his account of civil society, he takes up Aristotle's suggestion that law derives the validity that ensures obedience from habit. The unity of civil society is constituted, Bentham says, not by a set of rules that all members are obliged to observe, but by a "*habit* of paying *obedience* to a person, or an assemblage of persons, of a known and certain description." Those who possess such a habit are, together with those whom they obey, in "a state of *political SOCIETY*."[21] The person or persons whom they obey is the sovereign. And the readiness of his subjects to submit to his will is what defines his sovereignty. Whether the habit of obedience in his subjects is the cause or the effect of the sovereign's power is not made clear by Bentham, but he certainly regards the possession of power to enforce obedience as the essence of sovereignty.

[16] *Works*, I:326 "Principles of the Civil Code."
[17] *Works*, V:478 "Petition for Justice."
[18] *Works*, V:546, "Petition for Codification."
[19] *Works*, III:206, "General View of a Complete Code of Laws."
[20] *Works*, IX:7, "Constitutional Code," V:547, "Petition for Codification."
[21] Jeremy Bentham, "Fragment on Government," 428.

"An assemblage of signs" declaring the will of the sovereign is a law. So completely is law identified with the will of the sovereign that "in its primary sense," law is an intellectual object that exists nowhere in a material object that we can buy at the bookseller's. Any command issued by the sovereign, whatever its form, qualifies as law. Far from distinguishing law from orders or decrees, Bentham says that any judicial, military, or executive order, "even the most trivial and momentary order of the domestic kind" or a "temporary order issued by any magistrate" may with "equal propriety" be called a law if it emanates from the sovereign.[22] The only reason for preferring the word "law" rather than "order" or "injunction" is that it carries a clear intimation, as the other words do not, of being willed by the sovereign.

But there is an ambiguity in Bentham's identification of law with a command of the sovereign. For he says also that what gives a "volition" the character of law is the likelihood of suffering in accordance with the will of the sovereign for failing to perform the duties it imposes. Here it seems that what defines law is not merely the fact of being willed by the sovereign, but the consequences of disobeying the sovereign's will. In other words, the idea of punishment is intrinsic to the idea of law. And all laws are necessarily coercive or punitive as well as imperative because they prescribe both specific performances and the punishment for a failure to perform. Although the imperative part is addressed to citizens and the punitive to officials, imperative or civil law cannot be isolated from penal law because unless a failure to obey is subject to punishment, the command is not law. Indeed, the imperative part might more easily be omitted because a penal law necessarily presupposes an imperative law: "To say to the judge, *Cause to be hanged whoever in due form of law is convicted of stealing*, is, though not a direct, yet as intelligible a way of intimating to men in general that they must not steal, as to say to them directly, *Do not steal*: and one sees, how much more likely to be efficacious."[23] Ordinarily, however, "principal laws" are imperative, requiring or prohibiting certain actions, and the "subsidiary" or "punitary" part of the law sets forth the punishment for violations of principal laws. As only performances or prohibitions specified in principal laws can give rise to legal obligations, the pain suffered by violators of the law is clearly distinguished from a merely disagreeable consequence, such as a tax that may attend conduct not required by law.

---

[22] *Laws in General*, 1, 12, 3, 4.
[23] Jeremy Bentham, *An Introduction to the Principles of Morals and Legislation*, ed. J. H. Burns and H. L. A. Hart (London: Athlone, 1970), 303.

Whether a law is formulated as a command or as a prohibition does not affect its imperative character. For every command may be turned into a prohibition and *vice versa*: "The law which prohibits the mother from starving her child commands her to take care that it be fed. . . . A mandate prohibiting drunkenness may without any change in its import be converted into a law commanding sobriety: a mandate commanding chastity into a mandate prohibiting incontinence."[24] Since a command excludes both a prohibition and a non-command, it must include a permission; and conversely, a prohibition "excludes both a command and a permission."[25] Every law is therefore either a command or a "*revocation of one.*"[26]

Bentham recognizes that the word "law" is sometimes used to describe permissive regulations, which revoke, rather than create, legal obligations. But as such regulations are "uncoercive" or "discoercive," that is to say, they do not impose any sanction, they are not truly law. On the other hand, "*praemiary*" or "*invitative*" regulations, which offer rewards instead of imposing punishment, do qualify as laws because they impose sanctions "of the praemiary kind." The offer of a reward, no less than punishment, influences the will by providing a motive for obedience. As the law cannot, however, administer pleasure but can only place pleasure within someone's reach, the business of government must rely mainly on punishment.[27]

Bentham acknowledges that laws are rarely phrased in an imperative tone and more usually in an "assertive" or descriptive tone. But he insists that laws formulated in this fashion, giving no intimation "that the will of the legislator or anybody else, has any concern in what is delivered," merely conceal their true character. Correct analysis can always disclose the hidden imperative. The laws concerned with title to property, for instance, appear to be purely descriptive because they state the conditions that must be observed in order to have a legal claim. But this is an illusion. In fact, all property law rests on a basic prohibition of "meddling" with things or persons. That prohibition is qualified by exceptions for those who have acquired a title to certain things or services. Though apparently descriptive, property law consists of the exceptions to the prohibition of meddling. As the exceptions are exceedingly heterogeneous, numerous, and intricate, it is more convenient to list them separately as if they were independent of the basic command and the sanction attached to it. And this separation creates the illusion that there are laws that are neither

---

[24] *Laws in General*, 96.   [25] Ibid., 97.
[26] *Principles of Morals*, 302.
[27] Bentham, *Principles of Morals*, 95–100, *Laws in General*, 136.

imperative nor penal. Thus, the "cause" of our belief that there are purely descriptive laws "is neither more nor less than. . . the want of coincidence or conformity between the typographical arrangement and the logical: between the order of the ideas about which the several laws in question are conversant, and the order of the signs which are made use of to express them."[28] If all the parts of every law were assembled in one place, it would be obvious that all law is necessarily both imperative and penal.

Since all law is necessarily both imperative and penal, every law has a detrimental effect on someone, either directly, by sanctioning the infliction of pain for disobedience, or indirectly, by prohibiting certain satisfactions or granting someone pleasure that thereby becomes inaccessible to others. No law can be universally beneficial, and every law necessarily inflicts more pain on some than on others. One may and should ask whether the evil caused by a law exceeds the benefits bestowed, but it makes no sense to criticize a law, as Adam Smith did, for being contrary to natural liberty: "To say that a law is contrary to natural liberty, is simply to say that it is a law." For every law is established at the expense of someone's liberty – "the liberty of Peter at the expense of the liberty of Paul."[29] To speak of a law by which nobody is bound or coerced is simply to utter "so many contradictions in terms." All laws necessarily coerce and restrict the liberty of those subject to them.[30]

Bentham makes coercion intrinsic to the idea of law because he has no conception of authority. He dismissed it as a misleading fiction and insisted that civil society rests on a habit of obedience. Hume had taught him that civil association did not arise from a state of nature through a contract between people and sovereign. And Bentham assumed that without such a contract there could be no right to command and hence no authority. That there might be an implicit contract or promise to obey, such as Socrates invokes in the *Crito*, Bentham did not consider. Neither did he attempt to answer the parallel questions about his own conception of sovereignty: How does the sovereign acquire his power to command obedience? And why are the people disposed to obey him? Bentham suggested that a disposition to obey might grow by custom out of obedience to the father in a family, but he regarded that as only one of many possibilities: "sovereignty over any given individual is a matter which is liable to much diversity and continual fluctuation. Subjection depends for its commencement upon birth: but for its continuance it depends upon a

---

[28] *Laws in General*, 105–6, 26, 197.
[29] *Works*, III:185 "General View of a Complete Code of Laws."
[30] *Laws in General*, 54, 248.

thousand accidents."[31] All that matters is whether there is a disposition to obey, for that is the "constituent cause" of the sovereign's power.[32] In the distinction that Bentham makes between passive and active submission, what is being distinguished is not power and authority but power exercised over the physical body ("contrectation") as by the executioner over the condemned, from power exercised over the will of another ("imperation") exhibited in a command by an officer to a soldier. Even the subject who obeys the sovereign willingly is acknowledging not his authority but his power to inflict suffering: "In point of fact a man is subject to any and to every sovereign who can make him suffer: whether it be in person (that is in body or in mind) in reputation, in property, or in condition."[33]

That he has no use for the idea of authority does not, however, prevent Bentham from insisting on an obligation to obey the law. But he describes it as a "fiction" in the "logical sense"[34] because "obligation" does not refer to any material thing, which for Bentham is the only kind of reality. Although all fictions breed confusion, he considers legal terms, such as rights, powers, title, and obligation, useful. To make it possible to use such fictions without inviting confusion, Bentham developed a theory of fictions that prescribes the following procedure for determining the real meaning of a fiction: first, use the word in a sentence; second, translate the sentence into others where the word in question does not appear; and finally, identify the fiction with images that make its meaning explicit. For instance, the appropriate image for "obligation" is that of "a man lying down, with a heavy body pressing upon him."[35] That image explains why we speak of someone being under, bearing, or being relieved of an obligation – we mean that that person is being restrained by an external force – and why "obligation" is a useful "fiction."

In other words, Bentham's conception of obligation is nothing like a moral duty. It is the antipode of Kant's view. Whereas Kant tried to purify the notion of obligation from any concern with consequences, Bentham defined obligation as conduct governed by the expectation of certain consequences. We are obliged when we are "exposed to suffer" as a result of a restriction that is appointed or marked out for failure to perform a prescribed action.[36] An obligation exists whenever pain or loss of pleasure is likely to be experienced as a result of failing to conduct oneself in a certain manner.[37] What distinguishes obligations are the different sources of pain. We are restrained by the religious sanction when

---

[31] Ibid., 20.   [32] Ibid., 139.
[33] Ibid., 30, 139.   [34] Works, VIII:199, 126n, "Ontology."
[35] Works, VIII:247, "Logic."   [36] Laws in General, 56.
[37] Works, VIII:247, "Logic."

we fear punishment by God; we are restrained by the moral sanction when we fear pain caused by the bad opinion of other people; and we are restrained by the legal sanction when we fear the punishment imposed by an officer of the law. Each sanction imposes a duty or obligation. The law obliges its subjects because the fear of punishment "binds" or holds them fast to performing or refraining from certain actions.

Bentham vacillates on whether it is simply the likelihood of suffering pain for a prohibited performance or an awareness of this likelihood that gives rise to obligation. He is accordingly said to have either two different theories of obligation, a "predicative" and an "imperative" theory, or else one "mixed" theory.[38] In any case, being obliged is not for Bentham a recognition that acting in a certain manner is "right," but rather a recognition of the fact that painful consequences will attend a failure to comply. What matters is the relation between what one does and what officers of the law might do, not the reason why one conforms. There is no need to call upon figments of the imagination such as conscience. Nothing is more mysterious than when the likelihood of a succession of certain actions, which anyone can observe, constitutes an obligation. The source of obligation is always power, and authority is nothing but a synonym for power.

What is surprising is that even though Bentham does not distinguish between power and authority, he insists that the validity of law is independent of its desirability. Whether a regulation is a law depends on its pedigree, not on its content or consequences. If it was made by the sovereign, or by someone empowered by him, it is valid law. The formalities that attend legislation – the "ceremonies of authentication" – are the recipes for producing authentic law. They serve as "signs for the purpose of making known to the people that such or such a discourse is expressive of the will of the legislator."[39] The fact that the content of a law falls short of what we would like it to be cannot affect its status as law. Thus, the role of Expositor of law differs from that of a Censor. The former inquires into "*facts*" to show us what "the *Legislator* and his underworkman the *Judge* have done *already*"; the Censor tells us "what he thinks it ought to be," discusses "*reasons*," and suggests "what the *Legislator ought* to do *in future*." Though the Censor speaks as a citizen of the world, the Expositor must speak as the subject of a particular sovereign.[40]

---

[38] Cf. A. W. B. Simpson, ed., *Oxford Essays in Jurisprudence*, 2nd series (Oxford: Clarendon, 1973), 139 ff.; H. L. A. Hart, *Essays on Bentham* (Oxford: Clarendon, 1982), 133 ff.
[39] Bentham, *Laws in General*, 126, n.12.
[40] Bentham, "Fragment on Government," 398.

The oddity in Bentham's insistence that validity depends on pedigree is that the validity of a law does not give it authority. Knowing the pedigree of a law is merely a convenience. Just as the stamp on silver tells me that I am buying the sterling that I mean to buy, so the provenance of a law tells the subject that he is obeying a genuine command of the sovereign. Or perhaps the pedigree of a law serves as a signal that pain will attend a failure to conform. Either way, the obligation to obey a law does not arise from its authority.

But neither is there any right or law anterior to civil law that can serve as a ground for repudiating an obligation to obey it. Nothing that the sovereign commands, whether directly or indirectly, can be unlawful. To say that a law is void because it violates the "law of nature" or any other law or "right" is simply a contradiction. No law can violate "rights" anterior to law because all rights exist "in consequence of civil laws and by them alone." The Romanist notion that there are rights that "have subsisted, or still subsist, independent of the laws" and cannot therefore be altered or violated by civil law is one of the many "false reasonings" based on "the law of nature, or the law of nations, or some such other phrase" which have "no existence at all." Natural law is imaginary law invented out of "ignorance, hardihood, and impudence" by the "legislating. . . Grotti and the Puffendorfs."[41] As it is impossible to know whether a law violates the law of nature, anything like the French Declaration of Rights or the American Declaration of Independence is simply an encouragement to take up arms against any law that one finds displeasing: "you can never make a law against which it may not be averred, that by it you have abrogated the Declaration of Rights; and the averment will be unanswerable."[42] Such talk confounds understanding and inflames passions until all can feel justified in disobeying any law they happen not to like, from which it is but a short step to the conclusion that a bad law is no law and to resist attempts to enforce it is a "right." Rebellion follows and civil peace is at an end.

Nevertheless, a sovereign may grant concessions to his subjects and choose to abide by them. Such concessions may have the character of constitutional limitations on his power. But they are "neither commands nor countermands: in short they are not *laws*." Nor do they have the character of a contract: "They are only promises from the sovereign to the people that he will not issue any law, any mandate, any command or

---

[41] *Works*, III:184–85, "General View of a Complete Code of Laws," 220, "Pannomial Fragments."
[42] *Works*, X:215, Correspondence, 1789 Æt. 41, Brissot-Wilson.

countermand but to such or such an effect, or perhaps with the concurrence of such or such persons." Such promises are like the treaties that a sovereign makes with foreign powers: as there are no legal sanctions for violating a treaty, the people cannot keep the sovereign to his promise. But he might be influenced to keep his promises by sanctions of another kind, by the religious and the moral sanction. Fear of punishment for violating his "treaties with the people" by God in the hereafter, Bentham says, is one of the great uses of the religious sanction. Or the sovereign may be moved by the threat that the people will become less disposed to obey his commands and will withdraw their submission to him. In other words, constitutional limitations might prevail because the sovereign finds it impolitic to violate them, not because they have the force of law.[43]

Here we see that, although Bentham is often coupled with Hobbes as an advocate of the "command theory" of law because he denies that the sovereign can be obliged to observe limitations on his will, Bentham's reasons are different. It is not because the subjects have authorized the sovereign to substitute his will for theirs, but simply because the sovereign has a monopoly of power that makes it impossible for his subjects to enforce their will. Even though religious and moral sanctions may influence the sovereign, they do not affect the nature of his relationship with his subjects. It is a relationship between the possessors of more and less power. Only the presence of a disposition to obey the sovereign distinguishes the civil condition from a state of nature. Law is distinguished from other commands only by the supreme ability of the sovereign to compel obedience; it is inseparable from coercion and is in essence an exercise of power.

III

When, however, Bentham turns to discussing what the law ought to be, the identification of law with power disappears, and law acquires the character of an instrument for reconciling conflicting interests. The discovery of the "principle of utility," Bentham believed, made it possible to escape from the difficulty that his ancient and medieval predecessors considered to be intrinsic to mortal life: the difficulty of reconciling the fixity of law with the contingency of human circumstances. Whereas Aristotle concluded that the law could no more give answers that were equally just in all cases than a rigid ruler could adequately measure an uneven surface, Bentham promised that the principle of utility could

---

[43] *Laws in General*, 16.

make the law perfectly flexible without endangering its stability. That was because the principle of utility offered an indisputable measure for the justice of both general rules and particular commands. Thus, Bentham invented the modern dream of enjoying all the benefits of law without suffering from any of its drawbacks: "Until the grand principle of utility had been exhibited; until. . . by the aid of this principle, the end to be pursued, and the means to be employed, had been recognized; until, so to speak, all the legislative apparatus had been provided, and all the fundamental truths had been arranged, it was impossible to form any precise notion of a perfect system of legislation. But if at length these different objects have been accomplished, the idea of its perfection is no longer a chimera. . . though no one now living may be permitted to enter into this land of promise, yet he who shall contemplate it in its vastness and its beauty may rejoice, as did Moses, when on the verge of the desert, from the mountain top, he saw the length and the breadth of that good land into which he was not permitted to enter and take possession."[44]

The principle of utility, which Bentham later called the greatest happiness principle, approves or disapproves of every action "according to the tendency which it appears to have to augment or diminish the happiness of the party whose interest is in question."[45] Happiness is the sum of pleasures, and the principle of utility is nothing but an injunction to maximize pleasure. By pleasure, Bentham means the satisfaction of whatever desires one might have, and his list of pleasures includes fourteen varieties ranging from pleasures of sense to those of wealth, malevolence, and piety.

The principle of utility tells us that the greatest happiness of the greatest number is the only right end of all human action in both private and public life. It is the only true moral principle because it designates what is good without providing any justification for imposing one man's opinion on the rest. All other moral principles consist "in so many contrivances for avoiding the obligation of appealing to any external standard, and for prevailing upon the reader to accept of the author's sentiment or opinion as a reason. . . for itself."[46] They permit rulers to define the happiness of the governed so as to promote whatever they find most beneficial to themselves and to attribute all objections to ignorance of what is "truly good." But if happiness is identified with whatever is desired by the individuals in question, then they can object clearly and forcibly when their wishes are ignored. No government can excuse discriminating

---

[44] *Works*, I:194, "Influences of Time and Place in Matters of Legislation."
[45] *Principles of Morals*, 12.   [46] Ibid., 25.

against the desires of some in order to promote the satisfactions of others on the ground that the former are excluded by a "true" view of happiness. Where the greatest happiness of the greatest number is the governing moral principle, only policies that satisfy the interests of most of the governed can be justified.

The implication of the greatest happiness of the greatest number is reenforced by the "principle of self-preference" according to which, "In the general tenor of life, in every human breast, self-regarding interest is predominant over all other interests put together."[47] This self-preference principle means, first of all, that all people, whether or not they are selfish, necessarily see one another through alien eyes. People react differently to the same circumstances: "in the same mind such and such causes of pain or pleasure will produce more pain or pleasure than such or such other causes of pain or pleasure: and this proportion will in different minds be different."[48] Therefore, every man's preferences are ultimately private, and it is impossible to understand others sufficiently well to know what their interests are. That is why the philanthropic fanatic, however well-intentioned, regularly produces misery, and why each man is the best judge of what is good for him. The self-preference principle does not imply that human beings are incapable of sympathy or benevolence, but it does suggest that it is safer to expect that people might put their own wants first, if only because they understand them better.

As no legislator can know what another man feels and needs, paternalistic legislation is ruled out. Of course, society must put "bridles into all our mouths" to prevent "our doing mischief to one another," but to direct a man for his own good is another matter: "the tacking of leading-strings upon the backs of grown persons, in order to prevent their doing themselves a mischief, is not necessary either to the being or tranquillity of society, however conducive to its well-being."[49] Moreover, as the law can influence behavior only by punishment, in many attempts to curb undesirable behavior the evil of the punishment exceeds the evil of the offense. It is impossible, besides, to define some offenses precisely enough so as to ensure that the innocent are not caught in attempts to punish the guilty. Laws designed to suppress one vice may instead produce other new and more dangerous vices. And in general, the same mean passions that inspired the founders of religious orders move legislators who attempt to shape the lives of their subjects instead of relying on the principle of utility. For all these reasons, Bentham concludes that "The principal

---

[47] *Works*, IX:5, "Constitutional Code."
[48] *Principles of Morals*, 51.
[49] *Works*, III:5, "Pannomial Fragments."

business of the laws, the only business which is evidently and incontestably necessary, is the preventing of individuals from pursuing their own happiness, by the destruction of a greater portion of the happiness of others. To impose restraints upon the individual for his own welfare, is the business of education; the duty of the old towards the young; of the keeper towards the madman: it is rarely the duty of the legislator towards the people."[50]

The law is not, then, an instrument for shaping a good life or for making men good. Its "principal object" is "the care of security." Under the rule of law, men are accustomed to labor for the future instead of using force to acquire what they want from the labor of others. Security is achieved not by rewarding labor but by ensuring that the fruits of labor can be enjoyed, or in other words, by ensuring "a fixed and durable possession which deserves the name of Property." Indirectly, the law contributes in this way also to human perfection by serving the human capacity for anticipating pleasure and pain. The security of expectations established by the law makes it possible to form "a general plan of conduct and to unite our present and future existence." What is secured is the "persuasion of power to derive certain advantages" from some object or condition, whether it be wealth, reputation, bodily safety, power, rank, or condition in life – that is to say, property in its broadest sense – "It is the law alone which allows me to forget my natural weakness" and to "enclose a field and give myself to its cultivation, in the distant hope of the harvest." And therefore, the security that the law brings is an "inestimable good" and "the distinctive mark of civilization," and law "is the most splendid triumph of humanity over itself."[51]

Even without law, people have a "certain expectation of keeping what each one had acquired" and in this sense, there may exist "a feeble kind of property" without civil society. But despite this echo of Locke, Bentham does not conclude that there are "natural" standards for law. He is arguing rather that in framing law, one has to build on whatever expectations already exist and that no legislator can ignore "a multitude of expectations, founded upon ancient laws or ancient usages." If he wishes to make a law that violates established expectations, he must arrange for it to take effect at a time distant enough to allow people leisure "to prepare for the new order of things."[52] The legislator's duty is to maximize the satisfaction of desire for the community as a whole.

---

[50] *Works*, I:163, "Promulgation of Laws."
[51] *Works*, I:307–9, "Principles of the Civil Code."
[52] Ibid., 323.

This view of legislation endows adjudication with a character very different from its traditional one. The judge's task is not to decide what rules of law mean in the circumstances of particular cases or to determine what rights are protected by law. Instead, the judge's function is to resolve conflicts of interests; judges turn into arbitrators. Consequently, if they can settle disputes by mediation without going to trial, so much the better. It is only when the parties refuse to accept mediation that the judge has to impose a decision, as a settlement reached by negotiation is far more desirable than adjudication. Thus, in the context of Bentham's third theory of law, adjudication ceases to be intrinsic to the idea of law and becomes merely a last resort when the arbitration of disputes fails.

IV

Bentham's fourth theory of law appears when he turns to the reform of law by codification, the key to which he had found in the principle of utility. Law codified in this fashion could make the law so accessible to every citizen that they would have no need of intermediaries to disentangle the obscurities of professional jargon or to find the law that pertains to their circumstances. "Every man has his determinate measure of understanding: the more complex the law, the greater the number of those who cannot understand it." Complexity produces not only widespread ignorance of the law and reluctance to consult it on appropriate occasions, but also "false expectations" and deceptions. What is wanted is "a manual of instruction" simple enough in both style and arrangement to be consulted by any individual without the aid of an interpreter.[53] But in law that grows haphazardly there can be neither clarity nor completeness. To look for "a plan" in heaps of ordinances is as hopeless as "searching for an order of architecture amidst the huts of a village."[54] Only a code constructed on the principle of utility can collect and condense "the vast and hitherto shapeless expanse of jurisprudence" into "a compact sphere which the eye at a moment's warning can traverse in all imaginable directions," with no danger of encountering "*terrae incognitae*" or "blank spaces."[55] Clarity and completeness are achieved by systematic formulation in terms of a single "natural" principle that accords with common sense, that is to say, the principle of utility: "The principle of utility directs all reasons to a single centre: the reasons which apply to the detail of arrangements are only subordinate views of utility."[56] A "natural

[53] Ibid., 324.
[54] *Works*, I:159, "Promulgation of Laws."
[55] *Laws in General*, 246.
[56] *Works*, I:162, "Promulgation of Laws."

arrangement and a familiar nomenclature" permit laws derived from the principle of utility to be as simple in form as in foundation.[57] Because everything is "recorded and displayed to view," every citizen has at hand a repository of "the whole system of the obligations which either he or any one else is subject to," and he need but open the book in order to inform himself "what the aspect borne by the law bears to every imaginable act that can come within the possible sphere of human agency: what acts it is his duty to perform for the sake of himself, his neighbour or the public: what acts he has a right to do, what other acts he has a right to have others perform for his advantage."[58]

Against critics who argue that no code could make the law accessible in this fashion because it is impossible to foresee all the circumstances that require regulation, Bentham replied with a distinction between events "in specie" and events "in general:" "I acknowledge that it is not possible to foresee them [events] individually, but they may be foreseen in their species. . . With a good method, we go before events, instead of following them; we govern them, instead of being their sport. A narrow-minded and timid legislature waits till particular evils have arisen, before it prepares a remedy; an enlightened legislature foresees and prevents them by general precautions."[59] The completeness of a code is guaranteed not by the inclusion of rules for all possible events, but by systematic organization: "as every individual is contained within its species, so is every species within its genus."[60] Once the relations of all the parts are openly dis-played, it is easy to move by obvious steps from any one part of the code to another and from general concepts to specific duties. Everyone could then understand what the law is, and lawyers and officials would lose their monopoly in knowledge of the law.

In Bentham's eulogies of codification and in his conception of a code as a system of rules derived from a single principle, law is identified with fixed rules that can automatically yield the right answer to every legal question. Bentham has, as a result, been described as an advocate of "mechanical jurisprudence." That description is mistaken because it ignores much else that he says. For when he addresses himself to the character of adjudication, he draws a very different picture of law. Al-though here, as in his discussion of common law, Bentham condemns judicial legislation and sometimes speaks of the judge in a wholly trad-itional manner as having to decide, for instance, whether a law regulating

---

[57] *Works*, I:324, "Principles of the Civil Code."
[58] *Laws in General*, 246.
[59] *Works*, III:205, "General View of a Complete Code of Laws."
[60] *Works*, IV:538, "Codification Proposal."

the export of corn is relevant for maize,[61] in his detailed proposals for adjudication under a code Bentham advocates wide powers of discretion for judges.

He rejected the traditional regard for separating adjudication from legislation, which had been formulated as a theory of checks and balances by Montesquieu and had become generally accepted in England by Bentham's time. Against this view, Bentham argued that the separation of powers is irrational because it attempts to prevent officials from abusing their power by removing their power. Moreover, dividing government into separate powers violates the principle of simplicity, complicates the machinery of government, and imposes unnecessary and great costs. Perhaps in a corrupt government the independence of the judiciary might be a useful corrective, but in any other circumstances it is intolerable.

For all these reasons, Bentham regarded the limits on the discretionary power of judges imposed by the separation of powers not as a virtue but as a defect. The fear entertained by advocates of the separation of powers, i.e., that allowing judges to depart from established rules would give them arbitrary power, is groundless, Bentham argued, because there is no evil in arbitrary power as such. Only its consequences are evil when they entail harm or pain to individuals: "In the hands of a judge, power, in whatsoever degree arbitrary, is no otherwise an evil, than in so far as its effect is to produce evil in a tangible shape – to wit, human suffering – in the breasts of individuals."[62] In order to decide whether judicial discretion is desirable, we have to ask whether allowing judges to depart from established rules will produce more or less evil than strict adherence to them.

Although he had earlier criticized the common law for failing to provide clear and fixed rules, Bentham later became persuaded that strict adherence to rules produces greater evil than judicial discretion. As rules are devised by legislators for an indefinite number of unknown cases, they cannot be sensitive to the special features of any particular case. Judges who are obliged to rest their decisions on inflexible rules cannot tailor their decisions to the circumstances and interests of the parties before them; the grounds for their decisions are the wholly different circumstances and interests of previous cases. Therefore, where an inflexible rule governs, "the chances against its not producing evil in excess, are as infinity to one." In order to minimize evil, "the main caution is, in no case, on no occasion, to lay down inflexible rules."[63]

---

[61] *Laws in General*, 158.
[62] *Works*, II:31, "Principles of Judicial Procedure."
[63] *Works*, II:31, "Principles of Judicial Procedure."

The intricate maze of the law of evidence and procedure, which grants exclusions and privileges, allows presumptions, and lays down formulas for weighing evidence, serves only to distort adjudication. Of course, evidence, as "even justice itself, like gold," may be bought too dear and "always is bought too dear, if bought at the expense of a preponderant injustice."[64] But the foundation of justice is truth, and more rather than less evidence makes it easier to get at the truth. Procedural rules rest on the supposition that unjust decisions can be avoided by excluding evidence. In reality, "the effect, or tendency at least, of exclusion put upon evidence, is – to give encouragement and increased probability to criminality, and delinquency, and transgression, and wrong, in every imaginable shape."[65] Where abstract rules made by distant legislators exclude evidence, there is likely to be misdecision for want of evidence. All evidence should be *prima facie* admissible, and what is not admissible in a case should be decided by the judge. No case ought to be dismissed automatically for violating procedural rules, for only judges can determine whether the ability of the court to get at the truth in the case before them has in fact been jeopardized.

Indeed, the ideal procedure for a court is the same as that of a domestic tribunal, the only difference between the two being "the necessary enlargement and diversification, correspondent to the difference in magnitude." The domestic tribunal is for Bentham the model of a "natural" system of justice. There anyone can see that doing justice "is in itself simple" and nothing but what "every intelligent father of a family" does, rather than regarding it as a "matter of an art or science." Because there are no rules in a domestic tribunal, professional intermediaries are not needed, and attention is focused, where it should be, on the dispute between the parties.[66]

As another example of a natural system of justice, Bentham cites the Turkish cadi who sits at his gate and informally hears complaints, and without delay of pleading or the intervention of officials issues his definitive command on the spot. Also, even in England, Bentham discovered a golden age ruled by a "natural system." It flourished before the Normans arrived in the Saxon manorial and its hundreds of courts, a judicature that consisted of numerous small local and informal tribunals. Then it was no more likely that a suitor would be denied the services of a judge than that the children in a private family should be excluded from the

---

[64] *Works*, VII:336, "Rationale of Judicial Evidence."
[65] *Works*, VI:87, "Rationale of Evidence."
[66] *Works*, V:438, "Justice and Codification Petitions."

presence of their father. When the Normans replaced the Saxon tribunals with itinerant officials exercising broad powers, the administration of justice became centralized, complicated, and bedeviled by an unfamiliar, technical language remote from the daily experience of ordinary people. From Norman centralization arose the monopolistic, artificial, and inaccessible structure of the common law.[67]

Bentham's attack on rules of procedure and evidence and his advocacy of a "natural system" were in part directed against the mystifying irrationalities of the English law that he knew. A private family with half a dozen members, Bentham said, could not "subsist a twelvemonth under the governance of such rules."[68] His criticisms and suggestions were so much to the point that they played an important part in the reform of the law of evidence in the course of the nineteenth century. But making English law "simpler, more like common sense, better expressed, better known, and better understood" was not Bentham's only concern.[69] But his eulogies of the "natural system" were derived from a corollary to the principle of utility, the "non-disappointment" or "disappointment minimizing" principle, which Bentham praises for giving the true meaning of justice. It requires that "On every occasion, in so far as benefit in any shape is the subject-matter of dispute, the question being, to which of a number of parties the possession, present or future, in whole or in part, shall be adjudged, – the manner in which for that purpose disposition will be made of it, is that by which, among all the *interessees* taken together, least disappointment will be produced." Whereas the legislator ought to give preference to that interest by "which the happiness of the greatest number will be most augmented," judges should balance the utilities of the two parties before them. In this balancing, the utility of non-disappointment carries the most weight. The only way to give "any determinate import" to the term "*vested rights*" is by employing the non-disappointment principle: "In case of a right being taken away from a man, if the attributive *vested* be attached to it, what is thereby meant to be asserted is – that the pain of disappointment thereby produced in his instance is greater than would be produced by the loss of that same right if the attributive *vested* were not with propriety applicable to it."[70]

The non-disappointment principle makes it clear that the aim of justice is to protect expectations, which is the only thing that "men mean, if they mean anything. . . when they appeal to '*the first principles of justice*'." But

---

[67] *Works*, V:448–49, "Petition for Justice," VII:598–9 "Rationale of Judicial Evidence."
[68] *Works*, VI:205 "Rationale of Judicial Evidence."
[69] Hart, *Essays*, 32.
[70] Bentham, *Works*, III:388, 388 n. 212, "Equity Dispatch Court Bill."

justice may be pursued directly or indirectly. When judges are compelled
to abide by rules, justice is pursued indirectly. The rational way is the
direct way whereby judges clearly and self-consciously apply the non-
disappointment principle to arrive at their decisions: "a much better
chance for prevention of disappointment will be obtained, by aiming at
that object *immediately*, than by aiming at it through so unconducive, and
in every respect unapt a *medium*" as rules.[71] The proper way for judges to
arrive at their decisions is to consider within themselves as if they were
each of the parties in the suit before them and ask themselves: What
would impose the least disappointment on themselves? Whatever benefit
is in question, it should be given to that party which will suffer the greatest
disappointment by losing the suit. If the issue is about the keeping of a
contract, it should be decided by the non-disappointment principle, not
by whether the technical procedures for making a contract have been
observed.

Just how the non-disappointment principle could operate in cases
where murder is at issue, Bentham does not explain. It is difficult as well
to see how a judge could compare expectations in cases where one of
the parties is the civil authority. Bentham ignored such questions because
his attention was fastened on private disputes and on the interests of the
individuals involved. Moreover, he understood the "public interest" as
nothing other than a sum of individual interests.

As early as the *Comment on the Commentaries*, where he insists on
stare decisis, Bentham introduced something like his later non-
disappointment principle. The "business of the Judge," he says there, is
to keep "the distribution of valuables and of rewards and punishments. . .
– conformable to what the expectation of men concerning them is, or if
apprized of the circumstances of each case, as he is, he supposes *would
be*." And he also suggested that judges should put themselves in the place
of the parties to the suit and "to pronounce from such lights, and from
such lights only, as can appear to the judges."[72] In this way, judges can
avoid the danger that the measurement of expectation will be distorted by
the efforts of each party to exaggerate the intensity of his expectation.

What changed in Bentham's later advocacy of adjudication on the
non-disappointment principle was not his aversion to judicial lawmaking,
but his belief in the possibility of combining flexibility with stability.
Bentham became persuaded that he had found a way to preserve both
by allowing judges to depart from the code but forbidding them to alter

---

[71] *Works*, III:312, "Equity Dispatch Court Proposal."
[72] "Comment on the Commentaries," 197.

the rules of the code or to set any precedents for later decisions. No judicial decision was to affect anything other than the case to which it pertained. Every decision was to be based on a calculation of the utilities in each particular case without considering the effects on the community as a whole. The judge could, however, propose changes in the code, which would be considered in an emendation procedure quite distinct from adjudication where the legislator will make the final decision on the changes in the law. Thus, the experience of judges would be harnessed to emendation of the code without derogating from the legislator's exclusive power to make law. And security of expectations was protected both by proscribing judicial legislation and by leaving the judge free to do justice to the distinctive utilities in each case.

Because adjudication based on the non-disappointment principle addressed itself directly to satisfying the known interests of known individuals, it did away with the need for special equity courts. All courts would address themselves to doing justice in each particular case. Instead of being hampered by complicated, incomprehensible, and inflexible rules, judges operating on the non-disappointment principle could, without delay, give decisions precisely directed to the circumstances of each case. Thus, Bentham's non-disappointment principle made law one with equity.

V

As so much is provided for by direct appeal to the principle of utility and its corollaries, why should a code be needed? The answer to this question reveals a fifth theory of law.

Bentham suggests several, not wholly compatible, functions for a code. One is that of a handbook for judges, indicating their powers and objectives, reminding them of the utilities to be calculated and compared, and generally focusing their attention on the relevant considerations. Here the code is not a real legal landscape, but a map that enables both the citizen and the judge to trace the route required by the principle of utility regarding any "imaginable act that can come within the possible sphere of human agency."[73] Far from being "a collection of peremptory ordinances," the code is rather a source from which the judge draws inspiration for his reasoning, where he finds "all the *considerations* capable of affording proper *grounds*" for his decision without being constrained by any.[74]

---

[73] *Laws in General*, 246.
[74] *Works*, IV:479, "Papers on Codification."

But the code acquires another, more decisive, role and becomes a real legal landscape when Bentham says that it lays down rules that serve for most cases, and that judicial decisions merely provide the fine tuning to particular circumstances. Here the judge exercises discretion only when equity requires correction of the code and acts as a "counsel" to the legislator, who retains firm control of the scepter: "the simplicity of the legislative plan would be preserved from violation: the corrective applied would be applied, not in the obscure, voluminous and unsteady form of customary jurisprudence, but in the concise and perspicuous form of statute law."[75]

At other times, however, Bentham writes as if a good utilitarian code would make adjudication altogether redundant. The judge is needed for uncodified law because that is full of "oversights and omissions"[76] and fails to specify completely the actions denoted by words such as "murder," "robbery," "fraud," "words of which no tolerable definition seems ever yet to have been given."[77] If judges did not complete the work of the legislator, such law would remain impotent. But codifiers armed with the principle of utility can fill in all the details precisely. They need only be given information on the present laws of a country, its geography, and the manners and religion of the people in order to provide a truly complete legal system. Of course, they would have to observe certain rules "respecting the method of transplanting laws" and calculate the dissatisfaction that a change in laws might arouse; they should introduce more familiar laws first and remain patient if the people are at first antagonistic. But as the same motives and passions operate in all men, if the laws are rational, the people will be able to see the salutary effects at once. The utilitarian codifier can draw up, for any and every country, codes that provide for every contingency.

When he is writing in this vein, Bentham suggests that a good utilitarian code will automatically yield indisputable decisions. It would require neither schools to explain it nor casuists to unravel its subtleties: "It would speak a language familiar to everybody: each one might consult it at his need. It would be distinguished from all other books by its greater simplicity and clearness. The father of a family without assistance might take it in his hand and teach it to his children, and give to the precepts of private morality the force and dignity of public morals."[78] In this context, law becomes a technical calculation that anyone might and should make.

---

[75] *Laws in General*, 241. [76] Ibid., 239. [77] Ibid., 183.
[78] *Works*, III:209, "General View of a Complete Code of Laws."

This view of law dominates Bentham's discussion of the right to resist observance of the law. Although he dismissed the argument that an authentic legislative enactment is not law when it fails to conform to natural law as pernicious nonsense, he commended resistance to law on utilitarian grounds as rational and even obligatory. He found an obvious example of a law deserving such resistance in a statute passed by the English Parliament under Henry VIII, when it "made over its whole power to the King alone." Were that to happen again, Bentham declares himself ready to "take up arms, that is if I can get what I think enough to join with me: else I will fly the country. I well know I shall be a Traitor and a Rebel: and that as such the Legislature would act consistently and legally in setting a price upon my head." Nevertheless, as such a law would destroy the Constitution, which is "more highly conducive to the happiness of those who live under it than any other yet exemplified," there could be no doubt that the mischiefs produced by obeying the law would exceed the mischiefs produced by rebellion.[79]

For each individual a *"juncture for resistance"* is reached when "according to the best calculation he is able to make, *the probable mischiefs of resistance* (speaking with respect to the community in general) *appear less to him than the probable mischiefs of submission."*[80] The mere fact of dissatisfaction is not enough to justify rebellion. One has to calculate carefully: "Of the two masses of evil, – intensity, duration, certainty, all included – which appears to be the greatest, that to which one believes one's self exposed from continued obedience, or that to which one believes one's self exposed by its discontinuance?" In addition, one has to consider whether there is likely to be enough support for rebellion, since disobedience by just one or a few individuals will merely be punished. One has to ask: "On which side is the greatest probability of success? On the side of the satellites of the tyrant, who will endeavor to punish me in case of disobedience? or on the side of the friend of liberty, who will rally around me to defend me against oppression?" Like all other questions about human conduct, this "is an affair of calculation" that "each one must make for himself according to circumstances," which indeed all do make even if they do not realize that they are using the principle of utility.[81]

But in the *Fragment on Government*, Bentham pointed out that though each man may calculate for himself whether resistance is desirable, there is no *"common* signal alike conspicuous and perceptible to all" that makes it

---

[79] "Comment on the Commentaries," 56–57.
[80] "Fragment on Government," 491.
[81] *Works*, III:219, "Pannomial Fragments."

clear that others have reached the same conclusion. And because there is no such common sign, the sovereign's power must be "allowed to be *indefinite*."[82] This qualification disappears once Bentham turns from arguing against doctrines of natural rights to explaining the principle of utility, where one's duty to obey the law rests on nothing other than the balance of utilities. At no time, however, does Bentham allow an appeal to "rights." Claims based on the principle of utility are not universal "rights," he points out, because they are necessarily personal rather than general, and they are bound to fluctuate over time. And there are no non-legal rights: only the sovereign power can create rights.

His belief in the possibility of reaching rational agreement by adopting the principle of utility as the criterion of correct reasoning led Bentham to propose that instead of binding judges by procedural rules, they should be made accountable by "publicity." Different ways of making judges accountable without binding them by procedural rules were considered by Bentham. He devised an administrative structure for the judiciary in which each judge is made answerable to a superior. In the 1790s and again in the 1820s, he advocated that judges be elected and made subject to recall. But most persistently, he extolled the value of "publicity," that is to say, exposing judicial decisions to public censure as the most effective way of controlling judges. He called this the "principle of dependency": "Publicity is the very soul of justice. It is the keenest spur to exertion and the surest of all guards against improbity. . . It is through publicity alone that justice becomes the mother of security. By publicity, the temple of justice is converted into a school of the first order, where the most important branches of morality are enforced, by the most impressive means. . . Without publicity, all other checks are fruitless: in comparison of publicity, all other checks are of small account."[83] Keeping the judge under the eye of the public has the added advantage that not only is justice more likely to be done, but it will also be seen to be done. The security of the whole will be promoted because the "appearance" of justice helps to persuade the public to approve of judicial decisions.

The public is enabled to scrutinize judicial decisions by the requirement that judges give an account of the reasoning that supports their conclusions in terms of the principle of utility. If he departs from the established rules, his reasons will indicate "the evil which, in the individual case in question, would result from compliance with the rule: and with a proof, that by the aberration, either no evil in any shape has been produced, or

[82] "Fragment on Government," 491–2.
[83] *Works*, IV:316–17, "Judicial Establishment."

none but what has been outweighed by concomitant good."[84] The public can then easily check judicial reasoning, and every trial in a court of law is at the same time a trial of the presiding judge before the court of public opinion.[85]

Bentham's faith in exposing officers of government to public criticism appears even in his very first publication, the *Fragment on Government*. What distinguishes a free constitution from despotism, he argues there, is not adherence to stable rules and procedures, but public discussion and judgment of whether those who govern are producing desirable results. What matters is the subject's right of having the reasons for every act of the government publicly assigned and canvassed and the ease with which everyone, whatever class, may make complaints known to the whole community, concert with others, whether through the press or meetings, to express opposition short of actual revolt. There is no need, then, to worry about the difficulty of interpreting judicial decisions or about disappointing expectations by departures from precedent because everything is to be settled by the principle of utility.

Whereas in his early writings Bentham stressed the conflict of interests between ruler and ruled, later his emphasis fell on the likelihood of reaching rational agreement once the principle of utility governed public discourse. A hint of this line of thought appears in the *Fragment on Government,* where he says that a calculation of utilities provides "a plain and open road, perhaps, to present reconcilement: at the worst to an intelligible and explicit issue, – that is, to such a ground of difference as may, when thoroughly trodden and explored, be found to lead on to reconcilement at the last. Men, let them but once clearly understand one another, will not be long ere they agree." What prevents such agreement is merely the "perplexity of ambiguous and sophistical discourse," which on the one hand, "distracts and eludes the apprehension," and on the other, "stimulates and inflames the passions."[86] Later, Bentham altogether dismissed the peremptory nature of law and replaced the idea of obligation with that of rational assent. Assent is achieved by requiring that every legal rule and decision be supported by a public justification that can persuade those subject to the law of its desirability. Mere obedience to the law is no longer enough; how obedience is secured becomes all-important. Where the law is sustained only by fear of punishment, there is no rational assent; one will is merely imposed upon another. Such a regime fails to

---

[84] *Works*, II:32, "Principles of Judicial Procedure."
[85] *Works*, IV:316–17, "Judicial Establishment."
[86] "Fragment on Government," 492.

respect the rationality of its citizens and cannot be stable: "Power gives existence to a law for the moment, but it is upon reason that it must depend for its stability."[87] In order for law to receive rational assent, every law and legal decision has to be supported by reasons that can justify it. The reasons should be articulated in a way that allows everyone to understand and assess them: "The catechism of reasons is worthless, if it cannot be made the catechism of the people."[88] Talk of "justice" is not merely insufficient, but a threat to rational criticism of the law because it appeals to feelings rather than reason and makes it easy to conceal the defects of the laws with colorful language.

The principle of utility provides a language that renders public accounting accessible to all. Everyone can understand it, and no one can use it to impose prejudice and superstition because the principle of utility "holds up to view, as the only sources and tests of right and wrong, human suffering and enjoyment – pain and pleasure. It is by experience, and by that alone, that the tendency of human conduct, in all its modifications, to give birth to pain and pleasure, is brought to view."[89] The principle of utility thus exposes the law and all decisions to rational criticism. Such criticism, far from encouraging popular discontents, offers the best protection against them. Where discontents can be aired, there is no danger of unpredictable explosions of rebellion. Where citizens can scrutinize the laws and decisions by which they are governed and are persuaded that they are desirable, their obedience is rational and willing. Moreover, in the course of assessing the law rationally, citizens learn to think in terms of the greatest happiness. They come to realize that they can gain support only for measures that are beneficial to a substantial number of other people, since "For the gratification of any sinister (i.e., purely private interest) at the expense of the universal interest," individuals "cannot hope to find co-operation and support from any considerable number of his fellow-citizens."[90] In all these different ways, exposing law to public criticism will ensure that the law is obeyed without imposing any bondage.

Thus, in his enthusiasm for the principle of utility, Bentham replaced not just coercion with persuasion, but the rule of law itself with persuasion. He still held that since not everyone may stop to calculate utilities or calculate correctly or abide by the conclusions, punishment is needed.

---

[87] *Works*, IV:310, "Judicial Establishment."
[88] *Works*, I:163, "Promulgation of Laws."
[89] *Works*, VI:238, "Rationale of Judicial Evidence."
[90] *Works*, IX:100, 63, "Constitutional Code."

Here, however, punishment is no more than the rabbit's foot used by the vestryman to prod dozing parishioners.

VI

Each of Bentham's five different theories of law is inspired by a different project: when arguing against the common law, he identifies law with fixed rules that are not to be changed by judges. In opposition to doctrines of natural law and natural rights, he formulates the "command theory" of law, which identifies law with the sovereign's commands enforced by coercion. When using the principle of utility to reform the law, Bentham converts law into an instrument for satisfying the interests of the members of civil society. In considering the adjudication of a case, he identifies law with equity. And finally, as his enthusiasm for the principle of utility becomes boundless, he suggests that law could be replaced by calculation and persuasion.

What is missing in all five of Bentham's theories of law is the idea of authority. Because Bentham dismissed the idea of authority as a misleading fiction and insisted that civil society rests on a habit of obedience, he could not avoid making a legal command indistinguishable from an exercise of power. The principle of utility enabled Bentham to disengage law from an exercise of power without having to acknowledge the idea of authority, but it was at the cost of repudiating the idea of law. Only his wonderful ingenuity preserved Bentham from doing so explicitly.

Bentham's more immediate disciples, who wrote in the *Westminster Review*, lacked his fertility of mind and succeeded in making plausible Dickens's caricature of Benthamism in his picture of Gradgrind, who answered every human question with heartless calculations and syllogisms. The most influential disciple of Bentham was John Austin, who in 1826 became the first professor of jurisprudence in the University of London. He extracted from Bentham's elaborate reflections on law one strand, which became known as the "command theory of law." From Bentham's insistence that mandates, degrees, orders, edicts, and regulations are all laws because anything commanded by the sovereign is law, Austin arrived at a definition of law as a command that excluded any distinction between a general rule stipulating conditions to be met and an order to perform a particular act. Austin also adopted an instrumental view of law, that is to say, he regarded law as the instrument of a government that also acts as a "trustee" of the people, as suggested by John Locke. In addition, Austin's emphasis on the logical distinction between the law as it "is" and the law as it "ought" to be, without any reference to ideas such as Hobbes's concept of authority, led both disciples and critics of his theory to conclude that to insist on distinguishing between what the law "is" and "ought" to be implies that any consideration of why a legal system or a law is desirable is irrelevant to an adequate understanding of the rule of law. This reaction came to be identified as the "positivist" view of law.

It was by association with Austin that Bentham became known as the father of "positivist" jurisprudence. In truth, however, he had a far more complicated view of law. In the course of his many and varied writings on law, he elaborated one or more of the following five themes in jurisprudence: (1) that a legal decision is necessarily an exercise of power; (2) that a legal decision in a court as well as in a legislature is an arbitration among conflicting interests; (3) that what matters in adjudication is not respecting the established rules but reaching the right decision, in other words, that there is no distinction between law and equity; (4) that any uncertainty in a legal decision destroys its legal character; and (5) that the obligation to obey the law rests on assent to it. Bentham's resourceful journey from an assault on the common law to basing civil peace on rational assent encapsulates the much cruder movement in this century from an unwitting repudiation of the idea of authority to the conclusion that the only way to preserve justice is to dispense with the rule of law.

Part IV

The significance of rules

10 From historical jurisprudence to Realism: Savigny, Jhering, Duguit, Holmes, Gray, Frank

The disciples of Kant and Bentham accepted the traditional view that law consists of stable, non-instrumental rules. But they produced highly simplified versions of their masters' theories and ignored or disparaged the need to consider how such rules can accommodate the contingency of the human world. As a result, their critics found it plausible to conclude that equating law with stable, non-instrumental rules turned it into a non-human mechanism. That conclusion provoked a reaction against what was described as "mechanical jurisprudence," which culminated in an attack on the identification of law with rules, an identification which has since become known as legal formalism.[1] The attack moved on to blur or deny the distinction between legislation and adjudication, and ultimately to a repudiation of the traditional idea of law.

Friedrich Karl von Savigny

At first, however, the reaction against mechanical jurisprudence took the innocuous shape of a new interest in the historical character of legal systems. Friedrich Karl von Savigny, who initiated this development with his studies in Roman law, did not in any way challenge the traditional idea of law. What he opposed was the disposition to liken law to a system of mathematics that can be deduced from axioms, an analogy that appealed to those who saw in codification the universal remedy for all defects in a legal system. Savigny argued that the character of law is rather like that of a language, about which rules can be formulated but whose complexity can never be fully expressed by such rules.

---

[1] Cf. P. S. Atiyah and Robert S. Summers, *Form and Substance in Anglo-American Law* (Oxford: Clarendon, 1987); Robert S. Summers, "The Formal Character of Law," *Cambridge Law Journal* 51 (July 1992): 242–62.

Against the codifiers who believed that there were abstract principles from which law could be deduced, Savigny insisted that law can only be understood as a development over time. This does not mean that Savigny substituted principles drawn from history for principles drawn from reason. Although he advised his contemporaries to acquaint themselves with Roman law, it was not in order to discover the essential principles of law, but to become familiar with the texture of a peculiarly rich and orderly legal system.

Because Savigny rejected the entire notion of law's essence consisting in abstract principles, he understood the development of law differently not only from Kant, but also from Hegel. With Hegel he conducted a vigorous debate on the desirability of codifying German law. Hegel regarded law as the concrete embodiment of reason in history, and he saw progress as the increasing incorporation of reason in concrete human institutions. Hegel therefore contrasted the rationality, objectivity, and permanence of the law to the irrationality, subjectivity, and contingency of individual acts of will.[2] Although he had no use for attempts such as Kant's to deduce law from formal universal principles, he saw in codification an advanced effort to give reason objective embodiment and accordingly condemned Savigny's views as an insult both to the nation and to the legal profession.

But if Savigny did not regard law as an embodiment of reason or a deduction from reason, he neither denied its rationality nor opposed changing law. He even praised some attempts at codification. His arguments were directed against those who would jettison a legal heritage by assuming that its subtlety and variety could be comprehended by any one set of men at any given time and place, or by thinking that, as Thomas Jefferson said, "every law, naturally expires at the end of 19 years."[3] Savigny's thesis was that the law, like all human institutions, had been made by thinkers and statesmen who knew which way to turn their feet without knowing the final destination. The law of the present had been developed over many centuries by men working in a variety of circumstances for a variety of purposes. The unintended consequence of numerous acts with more particular intentions was the blending of rules of law into an organic whole that could not be deduced from any simple set of principles. Therefore, both in its structure and in its mode of change, law is not like mathematics or logic, Savigny argues, but rather like language.

---

[2] Frederick Hegel, *Hegel's Philosophy of Right*, trans. T. M. Knox (Oxford: Clarendon, 1942), 140–41.
[3] Thomas Jefferson, *Thomas Jefferson: Writings*, ed. Merrill D. Peterson (New York: Library of America, 1984), 936.

This analogy to language implied that law is to be understood as an abstraction from a totality of ideas and habits and procedures that constitute the life of the community, which Savigny described as the *Volksgeist*. By using this term he did not mean either that there is a generic difference between the laws of different countries attributable to a national spirit or that justice could be dispensed directly from the *Volksgeist* by a leader, as Carl Schmitt later maintained. Lawmaking rightly understood, according to Savigny, is an act of self-conscious articulation of what had previously been embedded in the custom of the community. It does not follow that the law must remain unchanged, but that it does not change by acts of creation out of nothing. There can be no absolute beginning or end to law; all jurists, insofar as they are conversant with the law, must carry in their modes of thought legal concepts and practices of the past; and if they attempt to change the law by applying the dissecting knife of codification, they run the risk of cutting through sound flesh and producing a monstrosity. Any attempt to reduce to a systematic unity what had developed over centuries would necessarily ignore and destroy the complexity that had made the legal inheritance so rich and valuable.

Savigny maintained that interpreting the law is no more mechanical than legislation. No code and no command can relieve the judge of an obligation to interpret the law. Adjudication was described by Savigny as an act of imagination in which the judge reproduces within himself the activity of the legislator. And he warns that either to tie the judge to a mechanical application of a text, or to give him leave to make the law for every case, would destroy the security of law against the encroachments of caprice and dishonesty.[4]

Savigny's contribution to modern jurisprudence lay in his effort to make plain how contingency is combined with stability in the law. He denied that contingency could be eradicated, but believed that nevertheless stability is possible. The stability of the law, he tried to show, is based on continuity.

But this was not what his admirers and would-be disciples drew from him. His admirers learned from his work that it is a mistake to preserve the ancient distinction between law and custom and to identify law with formally recorded rules. Some of his disciples converted his emphasis on

---

[4] See Frederick von Savigny, *System of the Modern Roman Law*, vol. I, trans. William Holloway (Madras: Higginbotham, 1967), 171, iv–v, 13, 16; Savigny, *Of the Vocation of Our Age for Legislation and Jurisprudence*, trans. Abraham Hayward (London: Littlewood, 1831), esp. 64 ff. 96, 101, 106, 108, 135, 139, 182. For a gross misinterpretation of Savigny's views, see Roscoe Pound, *Interpretations of Legal History* (Gloucester, MA: Smith, 1967).

the historical development of law into a source of immutable historical principles. Others were mainly impressed by his denial that a legal system could be spun out of reason by legislators who have purely abstract knowledge of what is right. His emphasis on the relation between a legal system and its cultural context led still others to conclude that if rules of law are not perfectly self-sufficient and decisive, then they have no meaning at all. In this way, by a twist of intellectual fate, Savigny's effort to illustrate how the law combines continuity with change became the basis for arguing that neither rationality nor stability can be attributed to law.

Rudolf von Jhering

Following Savigny's lead, a group that would become known as the Realist school of jurisprudence borrowed from Savigny's emphasis on law's historical character to transform the traditional equation of law with rules made by legislators given the right to do so. Realism began in Germany during the second half of the nineteenth century with Rudolf von Jhering; it was given a distinctive shape by the American jurist John Chipman Gray; and it reached maturity in the works of the American judge Jerome Frank.

The derivation of legal Realism from the connection that Savigny tried to establish between law and its social context followed a very indirect route. Out of the historical principles of law discovered by Savigny, his disciple, G. F. Puchta, constructed a formal system for which he claimed not merely historical truthfulness, but universal philosophical validity. This way of looking at law struck Puchta's student, Jhering, as "jurisprudence in the air," and he set himself to producing a "jurisprudence of realities." The moral that he drew from Savigny's connection between law and other aspects of social life was that law had been produced by efforts to realize a social purpose. Such a purpose was always practical. Law had then to be understood as a means of realizing an objective that was both social and practical.

What Jhering found wrong with the cult of the abstract advocated by *Begriffsjurisprudenz*, as he called both Austin's analytical and Savigny's historical jurisprudence, was that they considered law as if it were an end in itself to be brought to some static perfection, and they denied that law could be shaped by purpose. According to Jhering, their talk about legal logic and the science of law had no connection with real life, for what matters is not the structure or development of the law, but its adjustment to changing social conditions. Law is not to be understood as the product of reason but of will, and this will is not that of any individual, but of a social whole seeking to perfect itself as a whole. The jurist's task is to consider what the social needs are and how law can best serve them.

Although he emphasized that "the good of the individual is never an end in itself but only a means for accomplishing a social purpose," Jhering nevertheless admired Bentham's attempts to found legislation on social utility and thought of his own system as belonging to the utilitarian tradition. But Jhering disapproved of the individualistic and hedonistic implications of the principle of utility as Bentham had formulated it and rejected its use for calculating the priorities among competing purposes. He condemned any such attempt as an unconscious reversion to a doctrine of natural rights.

Unlike his Realist successors, Jhering was explicit about his presuppositions. He assumed both that there was no problem in discerning the social purpose and that the social purpose always took precedence over any that was merely individual. The differences in how individuals conceived of the social purpose, he said, were insignificant compared with their agreement. In any case, "ideals" could not be hostile to one another; nor could the legislator have any problem in determining what constituted the moral consciousness of the nation. He had only to consider the consequences of any course of action to discover whether it served the social purpose.

Thus, Jhering returned to accepting, in another guise, what he had started by rejecting. He had argued in his first publication, *The Struggle for Law* (1872), against what he took to be the "myth of the folk-spirit" propagated by the historical school, that law was produced by the silent work of a folk-spirit. He maintained instead that law was produced by the struggle of everyone for his rights, and that the "idea of the personality" of the individual depended on retaining the notion of struggle, though he also stipulated that the "rights" claimed should be rights "in principle."

But by 1877, when he wrote *Law as a Means to an End*, the notion of struggle had become unimportant. Indeed, the objective of law had become entirely a social and not at all an individual purpose, and what this consisted of appeared to be self-evident truth in the moral consciousness of the community. The general criterion that should guide the legislator was obvious, Jhering now argued. The practical aim of justice is to establish equality: "When the burdens which society imposes upon its members are distributed unequally, . . . The centre of gravity is displaced, the equilibrium is disturbed, and the natural consequence is a social struggle for the purpose of re-establishing equilibrium . . . always a shock to the existing social order." And he defined the equality desired as a *"relative, geometrical* equality, which measures every share in accordance with each one's contribution. . . ." Only when the members of society were compensated for their devotion could the society flourish. Thus, the principle of equality came to be something dictated by the "practical interest in the continuance and success of society" and not any "*a priori* categorical imperative."[5]

Progress, Jhering predicted, would bring with it a continuous increase in the demands of the state on the individual.[6] In return, the individual would receive not merely sensuous and material goods, but also an improved quality of life. Although private property and the right of inheritance would always remain (socialistic and communistic notions of removing it were "vain folly"[7]), the state would increasingly encroach on private property in order to distribute burdens and privileges equally throughout the social body, so that no one part of it would be unduly weakened or strengthened at the expense of the other parts.

A conflict between social and individual purposes is impossible because society is not, as Kant had said, an association for the purpose of realizing the equal freedom of all, but an association with "a common interest" in which all individuals find their place and themselves by working for the good of the whole. Therefore, setting limits to the activities of the state, or thinking in terms of the disadvantages of state action, as did Mill and Humboldt, was futile. Humboldt and Mill, Jhering said, were still wedded to the law of nature for which the individual "is the cardinal point of the whole law and the State. . . an atom without any other purpose in life than that of maintaining itself alongside of the innumerable other atoms." They had fallen into this error, Jhering explained, because they had accepted the Kantian formula according to which the state and the law have the task of "dividing off of the spheres of freedom" of the individual members "in the manner of cages in a menagerie."[8] Contrary to both Mill and Humboldt, Jhering asserted that the state in the future would not "measure restrictions of personal liberty. . . according to an abstract academic formula, but according to practical need."[9]

In making law subservient to purpose, Jhering did not mean to emphasize the contingent character of law. On the contrary, he emphasized that the historical relation of purposes was a necessary one: "One legal purpose is produced out of the other with the same necessity with which, according to the Darwinian theory, one animal species is developed from the other. And if the world should be created a thousand times as it was once created, – after milliards of years the world of law would still bear

---

[5] Rudolf von Ihering, *Law as a Means to an End*, trans. Isaac Husik, with a preface by Joseph H. Drake (New York: MacMillan, 1924), 276–78.
[6] Ibid., 381.   [7] Ibid., 396.
[8] Ibid., 399, 418.   [9] Ibid., 409.

the same form; for purpose has the same irresistible force for the creations of the will in law as cause has for the formation of matter. . . . Law obeys this compulsion willingly or unwillingly. But the compulsion proceeds step by step." Jhering drew from this necessary progression of purposes the conclusion that therefore "It is not the sense of right that has produced law, but it is law that has produced the sense of right."[10]

Unlike his successors, Jhering saw and admitted the consequences for freedom of the will. The notion that the will "can set itself in motion spontaneously without a compelling reason" is, he said, "the Munchhausen of philosophy," who thinks that he can "pull himself out of a swamp by his own hair."[11] The notion of purpose in relation to the will is parallel to the notion of cause in relation to mechanical events. The stone falls because it is pulled by the earth; the will acts because it is pulled by a purpose. Free choice, then, has nothing to do with law. Whereas Kant had removed contingency from law by making it wholly a product of reason, Jhering achieved the same result by making law wholly a product of will, understood to be totally subservient to a historically given social purpose.

In Jhering's terms, it makes no sense to judge law by ethical standards because for him "ethical" describes social conditions. It is the function of law to define what constitutes such conditions and such an adjustment. In that sense the law determines what is ethical. But in another sense, Jhering preserved a degree of independence for ethics. Moral development consisted for him in the progress of human beings from egoism to a recognition of themselves as part of a social organization. As a legal system could be preserved only by men ready to renounce their private desires, the legal system was dependent on the morality of its subjects. There was, then, a circular relationship between law and ethics – law depended on the social devotion and discipline of individuals, but such qualities could not be developed without the law.

Jhering emphasized that precisely what was required either for the conquest of egoism in the individual or for the achievement of the social purpose was never fixed and could not therefore be known *a priori*. What was required at any given time had to be left for the legislature to decide. Of course, it was morally bound to use its power in the interest of society, but to do so well the legislature had to be left free to change the law when and how it considered fit. There could not, then, be any limit on the right of the legislature to make what laws it considered desirable.

[10] Ibid., lviii–lix.   [11] Ibid., 2.

A cruder version of Jhering's idea of law appeared in France in the work of Duguit, Hauriot, and Gény. The features common to all of them are most clearly stated in Duguit's *Law in the Modern State*, which was translated into English by the British socialist, Harold Laski, in 1919. Duguit argues more directly than Jhering against the traditional idea of law as the bond that unites an association whose purpose consists in enabling the individual members to pursue their diverse activities in peace. That idea, Duguit says bluntly, has become obsolete. Evolution has made it evident that the state exists to provide a variety of public services, and that the law is the means for organizing those services effectively.

Duguit accordingly describes the law unequivocally as an instrument for achieving the purposes of a productive enterprise. Legal rules, then, have the same character as the rules of an army, a hospital, or a factory, all of which are designed to promote certain substantive results. Far from being a set of rules designed to make it possible for people to associate in peace while pursuing a variety of projects, the law becomes the means for directing the members of the society to contribute to the same project. In this picture, a legal order is the contrary not of the reign of arbitrary will, but of a regime that allows multiplicity and diversity; order becomes synonymous with unity of purpose, and law is the means for enrolling every individual in the pursuit of this purpose. Thus, Duguit's idea of law successfully escapes from the abstractness of *Begriffsjurisprudenz* by inventing a radically new purpose and character for law.

The Realists

Another theme in Jhering's work – his denial that fixity and rationality are the essence of law – became the central thesis of the American Realists. Their chief preoccupation was with the inadequacy of what Roscoe Pound described as the "automatic," "slot machine," "formal," "conceptualist" view that the law developed by "rigorous logical deduction from predetermined conceptions in the disregard and often in the teeth of actual fact." To oppose the "automatic," "slot machine" view of law, the Realists adopted Jhering's theory and seasoned it with suggestions made by J. H. von Kirchmann, some years before, in *The Worthlessness of Jurisprudence as a Science* (1848). Kirchmann declared a science of law to be impossible because the law was constantly changing, depended on feeling as well as knowledge and understanding, and rested not on nature but on human will. From emphasizing that the law is constantly changing, the American Realists moved to asserting that in order to destroy any pretense that the law is stable, as well as to ensure that this constant change should be deliberately and rightly forwarded, judges should deliberately promote changes in the law.

The doctrine of the Realists can be traced from the definition of law given by Justice Oliver Wendell Holmes in his lecture on "The Path of the Law": "the prophecies of what the courts will do in fact and nothing more pretentious are what I mean by Law." It has been suggested[12] that Holmes did not intend this to be a comprehensive definition of the law, but merely a mark for distinguishing between law and ethics. Nevertheless, Holmes's definition expresses an attitude to the law that regularly distinguishes all his pronouncements and underlies all Realist jurisprudence. This is an attitude of doubt about the usefulness, meaningfulness, and reality of general rules.

The first systematic exposition of this tendency, though in a moderate form, was given by John Chipman Gray in *The Nature and Sources of the Law* (1909).[13] Although he is one of the few jurists who rightly understood Savigny's emphasis on the historical character of law, Gray's interest lay elsewhere – in how rules of law, and what officers of law do, affect the conduct of ordinary people. What matters to the ordinary man is not, according to Gray, what the legislator has enacted, but what the judge decides; any law that the courts fail to adopt is not law. To claim otherwise confuses an ideal with reality. For law "is not that which is in accordance with religion, or nature, or morality; it is not that which ought to be, but that which is."[14] What the law is cannot be discovered by reading a statute because the same statute can result in two contrary decisions. This indeterminancy or uncertain nature of law means that whether, for instance, a man has a property right at law cannot be known until a court has pronounced.

Gray attributes the futile and mistaken insistence on "discovering" or "finding" the law to an "unwillingness to face the certain fact that courts are constantly making *ex post facto* Law," and thus exercising a highly unpopular power. In reality, "the law, except for a few crude notions of the equity involved in some of its general principles, is all *ex post facto*." People go about their business without the vaguest notion of what the law is, Gray maintains, and "the Law of which a man has no knowledge is the

---

[12] See A. L. Goodhart, "Some American Interpretations of Law," in *Modern Theories of Law* (London: Oxford University Press, 1933, reprint, London: Wildy, 1963), 1–20, esp. 9–10 (page citations are to the reprint edition).

[13] Gray's views became current in Britain through Sir John Salmond. See P. J. Fitzgerald, *Salmond on Jurisprudence*, 12th ed. (London: Sweet & Maxwell, 1966).

[14] John Chipman Gray, *The Nature and Sources of the Law* (New York: Columbia University Press, 1909), 90.

same to him as if it did not exist." And if a case comes up for which there seems to be no law and no precedent, as the judge's business is to "maintain the peace by deciding controversies," he will produce a rule of law for the occasion. "That rule is the Law, and yet the rights and duties of the parties were not known and were not knowable by them. That is the way parties are treated. . . by the courts. . . ."[15] Thus the true lawgiver, Gray concludes, is not he who utters the words of a law, but as Bishop Hoadly said, "Whoever hath an *absolute authority to interpret* any written or spoken laws. . ." (emphasis added). It is futile to look for the "sources, purposes, and relations of the rules themselves, and to call the rules 'The Law.'"[16]

The problem, then, for jurisprudence is to consider how the judge arrives at his rules and what gives his rules authority. In many areas of law, Gray points out, it is the judges themselves who decide whether other judges are acting properly. The state may also indicate that the judges are to obtain their law from certain sources and that acts of legislation shall take precedence over all other sources. In addition, judges may draw their rules from "judicial precedents, opinions of experts, customs, and principles of morality (using morality as including public policy)."[17] Acts of legislation seem to be different from these other sources only because the limits set by a statute are more definite than those set by other sources. Nevertheless, because a statute must be interpreted, though the judge's powers of interpretation are restricted within limits, "these limits are almost as undefined as those which govern them in their dealing with the other sources." A statute, then, guides the conduct of the community not directly, but in the shape of a judicial interpretation. Therefore, Gray says, "The Law of the State or of any organized body of men is composed of the rules which the courts, that is, the judicial organs of that body, lay down for the determination of legal rights and duties."[18]

Radical as it was, Gray's doctrine still had "more than a trace of the old philosophy," complained Jerome Frank in *Law and the Modern Mind* (1935). Frank found no more reality in the judge-made rules than in the legislator's statutes. For after all, he argued, rules are merely words, and "words can get into action only through decisions; it is for the courts in deciding any case to say what the rules mean, whether those rules are embodied in a statute or in the opinion of some other court."[19] Law,

[15] Gray, *Nature and Sources*, 97–98.   [16] Ibid., 100.
[17] Ibid., 118.   [18] Ibid., 119, 82.
[19] Jerome Frank, *Law and the Modern Mind*, with an introduction by Julian W. Mack (New York: Tudor, 1935), 123, 125 (hereafter cited as *Modern Mind*).

according to Frank, consists neither in statutes nor in judicial precedents or rules, but simply in a particular judicial pronouncement, that is to say, the judge's decision for a given case: "For any particular lay person, the law, with respect to any particular set of facts, is a decision of a court with respect to those facts so far as that decision affects that particular person. Until a court has passed on those facts no law on that subject is yet in existence. Prior to such a decision, the only law available is the opinion of lawyers as to the law relating to that person and to those facts. Such opinion is not actually law but only a guess as to what a court will decide."[20] Thus, Frank consigns the judges' rules, along with all other rules, to "some among many of the sources to which judges go in making the law of the cases tried before them."[21] The law is reduced to a set of acts by judges; a legal statement is a prediction of what the judge will *do*.

This is indeed the only notion of law compatible with Frank's understanding of general ideas. For Frank, as for his philosophical ally, John Dewey, an idea represents not an understanding of the world, but an "instrument" for changing it. An idea is not a response to other ideas but to problems, needs, hopes, fears, or aversions, and is designed to reconstruct an unsatisfactory situation. All ideas are like legal fictions.

The connection between the true character of ideas and legal fictions had been suggested to Frank by Hans Vaihinger's *The Philosophy of "As If"* (1924), where fictions are described as "constructions of thought, thought-edifices deviating from and even contradicting reality but invented and interpolated by this very thinking in order to attain its end more expeditiously."[22] Vaihinger had been inspired, as Jhering was, by Kant's view that thought is creative rather than passive, and, like Jhering, Vaihinger was anxious to tie this creativity to an empirical rather than to a rational reality. He found this empirical reality in activity directed to changing the world. The function of ideas was to serve as instruments of change. A clear recognition of how ideas are used for transforming the undesirable present to the desired future, Vaihinger believed, appeared in the legal concept of fiction. Vaihinger accordingly praised lawyers for their acceptance of legal fictions. This concept, broadened to include all general ideas, explained the relation between thought and action.

Frank, however, regarded the notion of legal fictions as an unintended achievement. Lawyers did not recognize their true value, but misused

---

[20] Frank, *Modern Mind,* 46.   [21] Ibid., 127.
[22] Hans Vaihinger, *The Philosophy of "As If"*, trans. C. K. Ogden (London: K. Paul, Trench, Trubner, 1924) (hereafter cited as *Philosophy*), quoted in *Modern Mind*, 318.

them as "semi-myths to conceal the actualities of legal change and adaptation." What is needed, Frank said, is "liberated fictional thinking," which would recognize "the correct use of valid fictions" and acknowledge "that all legal rules are relative and instrumental." Such progress depends on the willingness of lawyers to accept nominalism, the view that general ideas denote nothing real. The readiness to accept nominalism, Frank argues, is "the first step towards knowledge of the provisional or relative character of all concepts."[23] Only by adopting a nominalist view of human understanding could lawyers come to see how naively they have been using general ideas and come to recognize the truth pointed out by Vaihinger: "General judgements, when connected with a general subject, only represent convenient methods of expression. There is no such thing as a general subject in reality. . . ."[24] Jurists such as Bentham who denounced fictions did not distinguish, according to Frank, between "legal lies. . . designated to deceive others" and "legitimate legal fictions," which are undisguised instruments for changing the world.[25] Thus, Frank appeared to align himself with jurists of the natural law school who regard legal fictions as salutary ways of stretching established legal concepts to cover new circumstances. But whereas the latter value fictions for preserving the efficacy and stability of rules of law, Frank values them for destroying the pretense that there are rules of law.

Other Realist jurists moved from the belief that legal rules are irrelevant to the conclusion that what matters is something "more real" that determines the behavior of judges. The Scandinavian Realist, Hessel Yntema, found that the "most salient" thing to say about "the mystery of the judicial process" is "that decision is reached after an emotive experience in which principles and logic play a secondary part. The function of juristic logic and the principles which it employs seems to be like that of language, to describe the event which has already transpired."[26] A truly scientific study of the law, according to another Scandinavian Realist, Herman Oliphant, would completely devote itself to a genuinely scientific subject, "which way they decide cases."[27] Karl Llewellyn, a leading figure among American Realists, pointed out that judges have no monopoly on making law. In the first edition of *The Bramble Bush* (1930), he declared

[23] Frank, *Modern Mind*, 315.
[24] Vaihinger, *Philosophy*, quoted in Frank, *Modern Mind*, 315.
[25] Frank, *Modern Mind*, 320.
[26] Hessel E. Yntema, "The Hornbook Method and the Conflict of Laws," *Yale Law Journal* 37 (February 1928): 480.
[27] Herman Oliphant, "Stare Decisis–Continued," *American Bar Association Journal* 14 (March 1928): 159.

quite simply: "This doing of something about disputes, this doing of it reasonably, is the business of law. And the people who have the doing in charge, whether they be judges or sheriffs or clerks or jailers or lawyers, are officials of the law. *What these officials do about disputes is, to my mind, the law itself.*"[28] In the next edition he described these "unhappy words" as "at best a very partial statement of the whole truth" because they failed to take "proper account" of law as "an instrument of conscious shaping."[29] But how this recantation fits into his general view of the law remained unclear.

All the Realists drew not only on the pragmatism of John Dewey, but also on the logical positivism of Bertrand Russell, Ludwig Wittgenstein, and the Vienna Circle when they were still trying to discover the pure sensory core of knowledge. But the strictest juristic disciples of logical positivism were the Scandinavian Realists, most notably Anders Lundstedt, Karl Olivecrona, and Alf Ross, all of whom were disciples of Axel Hägerström. They addressed themselves to disclosing the meaninglessness of all legal notions, even that of legal validity, along with the logical distinction between "is" and "ought." If a word cannot be shown to refer to some act or sensation, they held, it is metaphysical and meaningless. Legal concepts have no common factual core to them. The concept of marriage, for instance, Olivecrona argued, describes an imaginary condition because the life of every married couple is different. Even the idea of cohabitation signifies nothing because all husbands do not live with their wives. Legal concepts are therefore to be condemned and abjured because they compound superstition, myth, magic, and confusion. Similarly, any talk of the "ends" of law is nonsense because "ends" cannot be known scientifically and are merely irrational declarations of feeling: "We like an end or we don't. We strive for it. We are uninterested. We strive against it. That is all."[30] Therefore, the proper study of law has to do with relations between cause and effect, just as in natural science, for this is the only object of rational discourse. A practical implication of Olivecrona's view was drawn in a book with the ironic title of *On Law and Justice* (1958), by Alf Ross, who advocates that jurists should concern themselves with

---

[28] Karl N. Llewellyn, *The Bramble Bush: Some Lectures on Law and Its Study* (New York: Columbia University School of Law, 1930), 3.
[29] Karl N. Llewellyn, *The Bramble Bush: On Our Law and Its Study*, 2nd ed. (New York: Oceana, 1951), 3.
[30] Paul Sayre, ed., *Interpretations of Modern Legal Philosophies* (New York: Oxford University Press, 1947), 543; quoted in Geoffrey Marshall, "Law in a Cold Climate," *The Juridical Review* (Edinburgh: Green, 1956), 261.

"legal politics," which would study not the ends of law, but how to make law correspond to changing ideological conditions.[31]

Whatever variations they suggested, all Realists were agreed on denying the objectivity of the law. Some spoke of law as mere acts of will, while others went so far as to reduce law to apparent acts of will really determined by chemical or physiological processes. That the Realists drew attention to the constant change in law constituted part of their appeal. Even their insistence that this aspect is the whole of the law gained credence because it seemed to do justice to what some of their predecessors appear to neglect – the element of contingency in the law. This contribution led jurists who were not of the "Realist" persuasion, such as Benjamin Cardozo and Roscoe Pound, to praise Realism for voicing a useful protest against the dogma that the law consists of rules applied with mechanical certainty.

Yet for all their insistence on the value of uncertainty, the Realists smuggled a new kind of monarch onto the throne they affected to despise. In one fashion or another, all Realists advocated that everything done in the name of "law" should be ruled by "real social needs." These needs, they assumed, as Jhering said explicitly, can be known with certainty whether by direct intuition or through scientific expertise. From decisions based on this new myth about "social needs," the Realists, unlike their timid ancient and medieval predecessors, promised consequences whose desirability was certain.

The most curious thing about the Realists is their belief that they were destroying an ancient myth fostered by medieval theologians. As we have seen, the recognition that there is an irreducible uncertainty about how to determine what rules mean in particular circumstances is one of the dominant themes in the ancient and medieval discussion of law. But the ancient and medieval writers did not conclude from this that it is impossible to have fixed rules of law. They distinguished, as the Realists did not, between the different kinds of fixity possible at different levels of abstraction, and between theoretical and practical reasoning. The true object of the Realist attack was a modern myth promoted by Kant, that there is only one kind of rational activity, consisting of demonstrative reasoning from universally valid laws, which yields indisputable conclusions. This claim implies that all reasoning has the character of scientific reasoning, and it permits only two conclusions about the law: that either the law is absolutely certain, or else it is irrational and wholly uncertain. Having

---

[31] Alf Ross, *On Law and Justice* (London: Stevens, 1958), 327; See also H. L. A. Hart, "Scandinavian Realism," *Cambridge Law Journal* (November 1959): 233–40.

discovered, as ancient and medieval philosophers had before them, that rules of law cannot yield absolutely certain decisions, the Realists felt obliged to deny that legal rules determine legal outcomes. They accordingly rejected the traditional idea that the law consists of fixed rules that protect its subjects against arbitrary decisions, and they dismissed the objectivity of legal decisions as an illusion. In effect, the Realists reduced law to a miscellaneous source of materials on which judges draw in no regular fashion. Thus, in the1930s when the Realists' influence was at its height, the nature of adjudication became the central preoccupation of the philosophy of law.

11 The defense of rules: Edward Levi, Hans Kelsen, H. L. A. Hart

Edward H. Levi

Although ancient and medieval theorists of law took it for granted, as we have seen, that human law *cannot* produce certainty, only recently has the relationship between the logic of the law and its capacity to combine stability with change and uncertainty been spelled out. In the classic modern work on the subject, *An Introduction to Legal Reasoning* (1948), Edward Levi says bluntly that the law operates under a pretense: "The pretense is that the law is a system of known rules applied by a judge."[1] He goes on to explain that it is a pretense because no rule of law can absolutely specify a decision. This gap between general rules and particular decisions means that rules of law are always ambiguous. The ambiguity is inescapable because of the logical relationship between any general proposition and a more particular one. Any given particular can be fitted into a variety of general statements, and the particulars that could be implied by a general statement cannot be exhaustively stated. Thus, the character of the logical relationship between a general rule and a particular instance makes it impossible for any general rule, however clear, to yield only one correct decision.

Only with general statements of a perfectly abstract nature, as with figures the sum of whose angles is 180 degrees, can the particulars fitting under it be unambiguously identified. In the law, the rules are general but not abstract. To identify the particular instances that fit under a law, we must always abstract from a cluster of attributes. And while we can and do make rules for a proper manner of abstracting, any attempt to eliminate all uncertainty would lead us into an infinite regress of rules. But this ambiguity in law, Levi points out, also contributes to the stability of the law. Where laws are made by an assembly of men or must be acceptable to more than one person and at more than one instance, a degree of

[1] Edward H. Levi, *An Introduction to Legal Reasoning* (Chicago: University of Chicago Press, 1970), 1.

ambiguity makes agreement and acceptance easier. Differences of view, at least within certain areas, can be reconciled under ambiguous words, and the ambiguity can then be left for the court to resolve as each case arises. Such ambiguity is indispensable for civil peace.

Moreover, the ambiguity in laws makes it possible for the law to remain stable while adapting to changing circumstances. Not only do new situations arise, but peoples' wants also change: "The categories used in the legal process must be left ambiguous in order to permit the infusion of new ideas. And this is true even where legislation or a constitution is involved. The words used by the legislature or the constitutional convention must come to have new meanings. Furthermore, agreement on any other basis would be impossible."[2]

What makes this flexibility possible without destroying the stability of the law is reasoning by example, or analogical reasoning. A legal decision can be formulated in a syllogism, and the syllogism is not a deception, but the premises are never self-evident. The problems in legal reasoning arise out of the difficulty in discovering the premises of the syllogism that are designed to conclude in a decision. The major premise is in question until it is decided what rule of law is relevant. If there is agreement about that, as there may be from the outset in some cases, the court still has to establish whether the action in dispute is of the sort designated by the rule or how this case compares with other cases that have come under the rule.

Even a simple speed law can spawn many awkward questions, and a law forbidding "combinations in restraint of trade" provides an inexhaustible subject for argument. Moreover, once a number of cases have been brought under a statute, the judge is faced with the problem of precedent. He must decide whether the case before him most resembles this or that case in the past if he is to see the law as a consistent whole. In deciding such questions, the judge and the lawyers arguing before him must proceed by analogical reasoning in order to establish the minor premise of the syllogism. The question constantly being answered is: When is it reasonable to treat different cases as though they were the same? This problem is not, as Bentham said, peculiar to the common law. Nor can it be resolved by any definition of precedent. A precedent is binding on a subsequent case because the court finds the cases to be similar. But as no two cases are ever identical, what constitutes a precedent and how a rule applies to this case are not known until the court has pronounced. This is what makes the Realists sound plausible when they say that the judge cannot "find" the law.

[2] Ibid., 4.

According to Levi, however, it does not follow that the judge's decision is arbitrary or to be explained only by some irrational cause, as the Realists suppose. The judge arrives at his decision by reasoning; his decision has reasons, not causes. And the system of law dictates that only certain kinds of reasons are appropriate. The judge ought not to ask himself: "Which of the parties is handsomer, more virtuous, has suffered most, will pay me more?" Or: "What decision will strengthen the government?" Or: "Whom can I make happier?" The questions appropriate for a judge to consider are of the order of: "What rule applies to this case? How does this case compare with other cases like it? Which of the analogies presented before me is more persuasive?" In answering such questions, a judge will be concerned only with applying the law as it exists in statutes and precedents, and he does this by considering whether his decision is consistent with past decisions. His concern with preserving the law will inhibit him from doing justice in this case at the cost of destroying the consistency of the law.

It is therefore just as misleading to think that the judge "makes" the law as that he "finds" it. He does not make the law in the sense of giving effect to his will or to arbitrarily selected requirements. What issues from the court is a decision, not a personal fiat. The judge supports his decision with a legal argument; he may not say, "I think him so because I think him so."

Those who insist that these arguments are spurious and look for some "real" cause for judicial decisions, as Realist jurists do, are exhibiting a fallacy that is endemic today, the fallacy of supposing that there are only three alternatives: certainty, science, and irrationality. Either we must arrive at an indubitable answer of the sort possible within Euclidean geometry, or justify our answer in terms of an established scientific theory, or else we must, in this fallacious view, fall into irrationality. If the reasoning of the judge is neither certainly infallible nor scientifically valid, it must be condemned as illusory.

But rational activity is not confined to deductive reasoning from indubitable premises such as mathematical constructs or from universally acceptable premises such as scientific theories. Analogical reasoning cannot, however, produce certainty or even the degree of consensus generally found among scientists in stable areas of research; it can only persuade a given audience that one conclusion is more "reasonable" than another. What is at issue in any case, even if settled easily, is deciding what constitutes the "facts." An appropriate criticism will offer reasons for considering one set of "facts" more reasonable or relevant than another possible construction. But no construction can be indisputable.

Because analogical reasoning cannot reach a conclusion from which no man could rationally dissent, this uncertainty is often confused with irrationality, thereby giving credence to Realist theories of law. But the uncertainty in analogical reasoning does not render its rationality spurious. A decision is rational because it has reasoned antecedents, not social, psychological, or physiological causes. There is an order appropriate to the reasoning and impersonal criteria for judging it. It is therefore rational though not certainly correct. What emotions the judge may have experienced before or during the trial, or in what order the various ideas in his opinion occurred to him should worry his biographer, not the jurist. What matters for the law is that other reasonable men conversant with the statutes, decisions, and procedures of the law should find his decision and reasoning plausible even if they themselves might have reached different conclusions.

The dependence of law on analogical reasoning also explains, Levi points out, what the Realists assert to be desirable and possible, though they cannot show how it comes about – the relation between the law and the moral convictions of the governed. For when a judge finds some analogies more reasonable than others, however objectively he tries to see analogies, he must see them with his own eyes. And a judge, like all other people, has inherited beliefs, acquired convictions, an outlook on life, in short, a "mental background." His judgment always incorporates assumptions about what constitutes a reasonable interpretation of certain words or what constitutes reasonable conduct in a reasonable man. His decision necessarily incorporates judgments about whether conduct is negligent or responsible, malicious or well-intentioned, reasonable or unreasonable. In other words, the judge decides what accords with the law not in a moral vacuum, but in accordance with his understanding of moral conduct, in terms of which he necessarily interprets the words of the law and understands the arguments presented to him. Though the judge is not meant to be and should not be a one man public opinion poll or a student of public opinion, he is obliged to exercise his discretion in the manner of a reasonable man of his time, and this implies that he reflects unselfconsciously about the morality of his time. But he does so in the course of attempting to apply the law as it is. The notion that the judge "finds" the law, while incorrect as a description of the law, is a useful practical maxim that directs the judge to keep his attention fixed on the appropriate considerations.

Once the character of analogical reasoning is recognized, it becomes obvious, Levi says, that a controversy with the Realists about "whether the law is certain, unchanging, and expressed in rules, or uncertain, changing, and only a technique for deciding specific cases misses the point. It is both. Nor is it helpful to dispose of the process as a wonderful mystery possibly reflecting a higher law, by which the law can remain the same and yet change. The law forum is the most explicit demonstration of the mechanism required for a moving classification system."[3] The Realists denied this because they equated rationality with certainty and demonstrative reasoning and failed to grasp the importance of analogical reasoning for maintaining a legal system.

Hans Kelsen

A different kind of response to the preoccupations of the Realists came from Hans Kelsen and H. L. A. Hart, who are known as "Positivists" and who focused on revising the theories of Kant and Austin. Unlike the Realists, they retained, indeed emphasized, the traditional view of law as a set of stable rules that provide the basis for objective decisions by judges. Kelsen and Hart offered new ways of understanding the character of a legal system, which they believed could explain the uncertainty and change in the law so as to establish that the objectivity of the law is not an illusion.

Kelsen regarded legal Realism as a variety of sociological jurisprudence that denied the fundamental difference between the natural and the human world by being concerned only with facts and causes, rather than with norms and the "meanings of acts of will." Sociological jurists accused his "Pure Theory" of law of being "ideological," Kelsen explains, because it concerns itself with legal norms rather than with legal acts and the causes of legal acts. Those who regard that as "ideological" assume that whatever is not natural reality or a description of it is "ideology." If, however, ideology is used correctly to refer to a "nonobjective presentation of the subject influenced by subjective value judgements" that disfigure "the subject of cognition," then the Pure Theory of law can be acquitted of being ideological, for it is uncontaminated by any illicit considerations of justice. It aims only to discover the essence of law by analyzing its structure: "The Pure Theory desires to present the law as it is, not as it ought to be; it seeks to know the real and possible, not the 'ideal,' the 'right' law. In this sense, the Pure Theory is a radical realistic theory of law, that is, a theory of legal positivism."[4]

Kelsen was no more enamored with traditional jurisprudence than the Realists were, but he criticized traditional jurisprudence for another

---

[3] Ibid., 4.
[4] Hans Kelsen, *Pure Theory of Law*, trans. Max Knight (Berkeley and Los Angeles: University of California Press, 1967), 102–06.

defect, i.e., for unconsciously serving as an ideology to justify or oppose an existing social order. All ideology, he said, is rooted in "Wishing" rather than "Knowing," that is, in "subjective values" and interests other than the pursuit of truth.[5] It is therefore concerned with either preserving or attacking reality, and in order to achieve its end it will either glorify or denigrate reality, but will never present it undistorted. The Pure Theory of law, Kelsen is confident, escapes any such danger by denying all "value" to positive law. He believes it to be a true science of jurisprudence with the same object as the social science of ethics. Both, he explains, are normative sciences, not because they prescribe norms for human behavior and thereby command, authorize, or positively permit a certain kind of conduct, but because they describe certain man-made norms and the relationship between men that is thereby created.[6] By describing norms, Kelsen means analyzing the logical relationship between the rules governing men without any reference to the purposes that they might be designed to serve, other than peace or survival, which are biologically given, not man-made, ends. This exclusion of any relation between law and the purpose that it might be expected to serve removes any possibility that positive law as it appears in Pure Theory can either conform to or violate an ideal law. Therefore, Kelsen argues, neither supporters nor critics of the existing order could find a weapon in Pure Theory.

The objectivity of Pure Theory comes by recognizing, Kelsen says, that justice is merely an irrational ideal. It may be an ideal that men need in order to will and to act, but it is not a subject of "rational cognition." The latter knows only "interests" and "conflicts of interests." These may be satisfied by sacrificing some to others, but that one alternative is "just" cannot be established by rational cognition. If, however, justice is thought of as neutrality, it might be admissible. It would then require only that the government remain indifferent to the various conflicting interests and aim to bring about a compromise between them. Such neutrality, Kelsen argues, has the objective justification that "only a legal order. . . which brings about such a compromise between opposing interests as to minimize the possible frictions has expectation of relatively enduring existence. . . [and can] secure social peace on a relatively permanent basis."[7]

But when justice is used in the ordinary sense, it signifies nothing but a rationalization of personal preferences pretending to a spurious universality, or what Kelsen calls "subjective judgment of value." A norm

---

[5] Ibid., 106.   [6] Ibid., 86.
[7] Hans Kelsen, *General Theory of Law and State*, trans. Anders Wedberg (Cambridge, MA: Harvard University Press, 1945), 13–14, 49.

can be "just" or "unjust" only for those who do or do not desire what the norm prescribes, although whoever pronounces a social institution to be just or unjust may be unaware that he or she is expressing a merely private interest. This is especially obvious in appeals to "natural law," which pretend that the norm of justice is immanent in nature, thus displaying a typical illusion due to an "objectivization of subjective interests."[8] Even the claim that men have a natural right to be free or treated equally is really a self-deception "or – what amounts to much the same thing – an ideology," because it pretends that a subjective judgment of value proceeds from some indubitable source such as "nature."[9]

The only correct sense of justice in Kelsen's terms is "legality." It is therefore "just" for a general rule to be actually applied in all cases where, according to its content, this rule should be applied."[10] Used in this way, justice is related not to the "content of a positive order, but to its application," and it is compatible with any legal order, capitalist or communist, democratic or autocratic. A statement that the behavior of an individual is "just" in the legal sense has the same character logically "as a statement by which we subsume a concrete phenomenon under an abstract concept." It is therefore "an objective judgment of value" to be clearly distinguished from subjective judgments.[11]

Justice in any moral sense does not enter into Kelsen's preference for a *Rechtstaat*. He uses the term to describe a legal order, but for a very different purpose than Kant. Insofar as Kant's *Rechtstaat* is an association defined by nothing but the rules governing it, Kelsen would appear to echo Kant when he says, "If it is asked why an individual together with other individuals does belong to a certain state, no other criterion can be found but that he and the others are subject to a certain, relatively centralized, coercive order. All attempts to find another bond that holds together and unites in one unit individuals differing in language, race, religion, world concept, and separated by conflicts of interests, is doomed to failure."[12] Kelsen is not, however, asserting that the members of a *Rechtsstaat* are autonomous persons, but he is asserting that there is no reality to any notion of national character or spirit, nor to any ideology, metaphysics, or mysticism about the state. He is concerned not with establishing the incompatibility of a "common objective" with "freedom," but with eliminating any ground for passing judgment on the existing

---

[8] Ibid., 14.
[9] Hans Kelsen, "The Pure Theory of Law and Analytical Jurisprudence," *Harvard Law Review* 47 (1941): 55.
[10] Kelsen, *General Theory of Law*, 14.
[11] Ibid., 14.
[12] Kelsen, *Pure Theory of Law*, 287.

legal order. His aim is to identify an object of legal cognition that is untainted by "values" and therefore is a proper subject for scientific investigation. Ultimately, like Kant, he wished to remove any impediment to a world state.

The Pure Theory of law accordingly discovers what the law "is" and not what it "ought" to be. Kelsen regards this distinction as a departure from Austin's command theory; what he and Austin share he confines to a disposition to proceed solely by analysis of positive law. But there can be no doubt that Kelsen significantly differs from Austin when he substitutes the concept of a "norm" for that of a "command" to explain the character of law.[13]

Law cannot be a command, Kelsen argues, because a command is the expression of the will of an individual directed to the conduct of another individual. There is a command only so long as both the will and its expression are present. But legal rules remain valid even if the individuals who made them have ceased to be. In fact, some legal obligations that exist probably do not represent the "real will of anyone." When the members of a legislature die, the statutes enacted by them remain in force, and although a statute is directly contrary to the will of those legislators who voted against it, the statute is regarded as an enactment of the whole legislature. Moreover, a large proportion of the members of a legislature who vote for a bill either do not know its content or know it very superficially.[14]

At most, then, to call a law a command is, Kelsen says, only a figurative expression. It is based on the analogy between enacting or prescribing and commanding. But the former two occur "without any psychic act of will." Therefore, law is better described as a "depsychologized" command; more precisely it is a "norm." Whereas a command prescribes a particular act, a norm prescribes a manner of conducting oneself. To think of laws as commands is to introduce a "superfluous and dangerous fiction of the 'will' of the legislator or the state."[15]

The concept of a norm makes it possible, Kelsen believes, to keep clear the distinction between "is" and "ought," as Austin failed to do. A norm states what "ought" to be done, but to describe the law as a system of norms is to say not what it ought to be, but only what it is. Thanks to the concept of a "norm," it is possible to describe the law without either leaving out its prescriptive character or entering into the realm of "ought." His new concept also enables Kelsen to reject Austin's characterization of a law as "enforceable" without denying that coercion is

---

[13] Kelsen, "Analytical Jurisprudence," 54–55.
[14] Ibid., 55–56.   [15] Ibid., 56–57.

central to the law. A law does not, Kelsen argues, force men to obey its commands. Nor is it at all certain that the lawful behavior of individuals is brought about by fear of the threatened sanction. Rather, a law is a "norm which provides a specific measure of coercion as sanction." This sanction follows upon a "delict," that is, illegal conduct.[16] Or in other words, the law says that certain consequences "ought" to follow upon certain sorts of behavior.

A legal system consists of a hierarchy of norms. The hierarchy has the character of a series of more and more confining frames. Interpretation of legal norms, or movement from a more general to a less general norm, consists in fitting a smaller frame into a larger one. When the judge applies the law to an individual case, he fits the particular case into an appropriate frame.

Kelsen opposes this conception of the law as a frame to what he takes to be the traditional view that law can render certain decisions by an "act of cognition." At the same time, he dismisses analogical reasoning as a worthless description of interpretation because analogies can lead to diverse results, and "no criterion exists to decide when the one and when the other should be applied."[17] As he cannot, therefore, credit analogical reasoning with rationality, Kelsen assumes that the traditional insistence on the rationality of law must mean, as it does for Kant, that there is only one logically correct interpretation of the law. This conclusion, he argues, is a fiction that, though useful for supporting legal security, is not a legitimate part of a scientific description of positive law.

The act of interpretation is not, Kelsen emphasizes, an act of cognition because there is always more than one possible object that will fit into a given frame. The designation of one of several possibilities must then be, according to the Kantian dichotomy between reason and will, an act of will. And it is an act of will that "creates" law. If the interpretation is being done by a "law-applying organ" it is an authentic creation of law.[18] Thus, by a very different route Kelsen unwittingly arrives at the same conclusion as the Realists. By describing every movement to a more particular norm as an act that "creates" law, he denies the traditional distinction between legislation and adjudication.

But this view of law contradicts Kelsen's conception of validity, which he treats as a logical criterion. The validity of a norm is always derived from a higher norm, and in this context Kelsen describes the relation between higher and lower norms as that between a major premise and the conclusion derived from it.[19] This means, Kelsen emphasizes, that the

[16] Ibid., 58.   [17] Kelsen, *Pure Theory of Law*, 352–53.
[18] Ibid., 353–55.   [19] Ibid., 194.

whole legal order can be understood as a logical system. At the same time, however, Kelsen felt obliged to explain, as Kant had not, the uncertainty of the law. To solve this problem he introduced the notion of law as a "frame." The result is a self-contradictory account of a legal system that unwittingly describes it both as a chain of deductive reasoning and as an act of will.

But to the problem of explaining the ultimate justification of the norms that constitute a legal system, Kelsen proposed a more consistent and ingenious solution. A valid law should be obeyed, according to Kelsen, because it has been issued by someone who is authorized by a higher norm to make such a law. As this leads to an infinite regress of norms that could never give validity to the system as a whole, what is needed, Kelsen concluded, is a norm at the base of the legal system that is not enacted. This ultimate norm cannot be "directly evident," in the sense that it emanates from reason, "because the function of reason is knowing and not willing, whereas the creation of norms is an act of will."[20] As the validity of the ultimate norm can neither be derived from a higher norm nor its reason questioned, it must then be a "hypothetical" norm or, in other words, the presupposition of a "law-making authority whose norms are, by and large, observed, so that social life broadly conforms to the legal order based on the hypothetical norm." Kelsen calls this presupposition the "basic norm."[21]

Kelsen's "basic norm" has the same epistemological status as the categories of Kant's transcendental philosophy. Just as the categories are not data of experience but conditions of experience, so the basic norm is a condition of juridical science. The hypothetical basic norm answers the question: "how is positive law possible as an object of cognition, as an object of juridical science; and, consequently, how is a juridical science possible?"[22] A legal system can then be identified as a hierarchy of norms whose validity can be traced to the same basic norm, which hierarchy also constitutes their unity.

But Kelsen is not content with a merely formal solution. He adds an empirical condition for the validity of the legal system as a whole. The norms of a valid system remain valid, Kelsen tells us, "only on the condition that the total order is efficacious; they cease to be valid, not only when they are annulled in a constitutional way, but also when the total order ceases to be efficacious."[23] This condition saves the efficacy of the legal system from being questioned because a particular law or laws have become ineffective.

---

[20] Ibid., 196.   [21] Kelsen, *General Theory of Law*, 437.
[22] Ibid., 437.   [23] Ibid., 119.

But it also introduces a significant uncertainty. Kelsen appears to suppose that whether or not a legal order is "efficacious" is self-evident. Yet the difficulty of deciding after World War II whether the legal order in Nazi Germany could be said to have broken down, or whether it was sufficiently in effect to justify acts accepted as valid by it, suggests that Kelsen's ultimate criterion of "efficacy" may yield judgments not wholly uncontaminated by "subjectivity." Moreover, to say that the validity of a legal system as a whole rests on its "efficacy" equates right with might.

All these difficulties arise out of Kelsen's anxiety to disengage the concept of a norm from any suggestion that it has to do with acts of deliberation or choice. Although he distinguishes the world described by natural science from that described by a science of norms, he refuses to attribute free will to men. Free will, he believes, denies that a man's will is "causally determinable." The law need make no such assumptions. Indeed, it cannot make such assumptions because a "normative, behavior-regulating order" would not be possible if human behavior were not determined by causes. For a norm "commanding a certain behavior" can only signify "the cause of a norm-conforming behavior."[24]

The law needs to assume only that a man may be held responsible for what he does. This means, according to Kelsen, that a man's will may be considered the end point of a relationship of "imputation," which is as central to the normative sciences as causality is to the natural sciences. Thus, a criminal act may be "imputed" to a man when he has violated a norm. A punishment is then imputed to his crime; "by imputation we understand every connection of a human behavior with the condition under which it is commanded or prohibited in a norm."[25] In this fashion, by substituting cause and imputation for choice and deliberation, Kelsen believes himself to have given a pure, scientific account of the law without confusing the science of norms with natural science, or allowing any illegitimate references to human purposes or understanding.

Nevertheless, Kelsen recognizes that he must explain an apparently serious difference between imputation and causation. Whereas in a causal relationship described by a law of nature the effect necessarily follows the cause, in a relationship by imputation the connection may or may not come about because the judge may or may not find the defendant guilty. Kelsen solves this difficulty by saying that when a man lies or speaks the truth, he is causally determined. But he is not determined by a law of nature "according to which one must always speak the truth or always lie." He is determined rather by "another law of nature," for example, by

---

[24] Kelsen, *Pure Theory of Law*, 94.   [25] Ibid., 92.

"one according to which man chooses that behavior from which he expects the greatest advantage."[26] Causality, then, is not incompatible with uncertainty about the relation between two events, and imputation is not essentially different from causation.

The shortcoming in Kelsen's solution is that this second "law of nature" is a rhetorical flourish covering a self-contradiction. For if a man "chooses," he is not determined by a law of nature; he deliberates and decides. If he is "determined" by a law of nature, he is not understanding and considering alternatives, and so he cannot be choosing. Moreover, if every choice is determined by a consideration of what will produce the greatest advantage, there can be no objective judgments and no way of distinguishing legal decisions from the pursuit of self-interest.

Kelsen's Pure Theory of Law restored the equation of law with impersonal rules that the Realists repudiated. But on the other hand, Kelsen reenforced the Realist view of law by excluding from a true understanding of law any moral judgments both about the legal system as a whole and about particular laws. By coupling his definition of law as a set of "norms" with a prohibition of "value" judgments, he suggested that seeing the law as a set of rules requires denying that considerations of justice have any relevance to the law.

H. L. A. Hart

H. L. A. Hart set himself the same task as Kelsen, but phrased it in more matter-of-fact terms: "to give an account of what it is for a legal system to exist."[27] And his style reflects the fact that his affinity is with Bentham rather than Kant.

Although Hart accepts Kelsen's criticism of Austin, he offers different corrections. The command theory of law, he says, affords no way of distinguishing the gunman's order from the policeman's warrant. What matters for Hart is that although the gunman may get his way, his victim feels no obligation to obey him, but only a need to do so in order to avoid being shot. For the same reason Hart rejects the Realists' view that what defines a legal system is that it makes possible predictions of when one is likely to suffer. In the Realist view, he argues, any obligation to obey the law would disappear whenever one could confidently expect to avoid punishment.[28] In Hart's view, the existence of a legal system implies that

---

[26] Ibid., 95.
[27] H. L. A. Hart, *The Concept of Law* (Oxford: Clarendon, 1961), 110.
[28] Ibid., 82.

the citizen has an obligation to obey regardless of whether he will or will not in fact be punished for disobeying. This obligation cannot be explained by what citizens do, but only by how they understand their relation to the laws. A description from an "external point of view" necessarily ignores this "internal aspect" of rules because it can only indicate regularities of conduct. It cannot show why a man who commits a crime may not only predict a "hostile reaction," but may also recognize a *"reason* for hostility."[29]

Hart criticizes both Austin and Kelsen for having too restricted a view of what law does. The former, in his Command Theory of law, reduces law in effect to a policeman halting a motorist at an intersection; Kelsen reduces law to telling officials what to do if somebody commits a crime. Hart regards Kelsen's view as an improvement on Austin's, but holds that Kelsen, too, has fallen far short of an adequate analysis because he fails to recognize two other kinds of laws.

The first kind gives private persons the security of knowing that the contracts, wills, and other private arrangements they make in accordance with the law can be enforced in the courts. Such laws are enabling acts granting new powers to private persons rather than making any behavior criminal or obligatory. They set conditions for engaging in certain activities, but they command nothing. By treating laws of this kind as parts of an order to officials to apply sanctions, Kelsen obscures the fact, so Hart argues, that such rules are "an additional element introduced by the law into social life over and above that of coercive control." They are designed not for the "bad man," but for any "man who wishes to arrange his affairs."[30]

Besides, Hart distinguishes rules of a totally different kind because they are rules for making or recognizing rules. Primitive societies make do with only "primary rules," which govern the activity of the members directly. But a legal system appears only when primary rules are supplemented by "secondary rules," whose function it is to eliminate the uncertainty that arises as soon as primary rules become at all complicated. Hart identifies three kinds of secondary rules. A "rule of recognition" is fundamental because it specifies marks by which rules may conclusively be known to have the force of primary rules. By connecting what would otherwise be discrete unconnected rules into a unified set, the rule of recognition introduces the idea of a system. When the rule of recognition is supplemented by "rules of change," it becomes possible to alter old primary rules or introduce new ones in a deliberate fashion. Lastly, there are "rules

[29] Ibid., 88.   [30] Ibid., 39–40.

of adjudication"[31] that empower certain persons to determine authoritatively whether a primary rule has been adequately observed. They indicate who is to decide such questions and according to what procedures. In other words, they define concepts such as judge, court, jurisdiction, and judgment.

All these distinctions enlarge the notion of law from that of a ground for private litigation or prosecution to a manner of controlling, building, and planning "life out of court."[32] The old notion of law as coercive orders or rules makes it impossible to see this larger function of law. For the coercive aspect of law, in Hart's view, is only incidental to its general task of introducing or modifying "general standards of behavior to be followed by the society generally."[33]

Identifying secondary rules is also vital because they help explain the idea of validity, which is as central to the concept of law for Hart as it is for Kelsen. Whereas Kelsen resorts to a hypothetical "basic norm," which is itself not a legal phenomenon but a "presupposition" of legal phenomena, Hart points to definite rules or procedures on which the validity of laws in a given legal system is based. Moreover, this distinction enables Hart to keep the validity of a legal system independent of its efficacy. For Kelsen, the obligation to observe the laws of a legal system disappears once the legal system ceases to be effective; Hart argues that if laws have been made in accordance with established secondary rules, they remain valid, even when the legal system is no longer efficacious. By emphasizing the internal aspect of law, he is saying that what matters is not only how laws are made, but how laws are understood to be made. This claim suggests that "beliefs" about law are as important as observable phenomena such as orders and acts and carries intimations of a concept of authority.

Hart also departs from Kelsen by admitting considerations of justice to the concept of law and emphasizing the distinction between what the law "is" and what it "ought" to be. The Scandinavian Realists are wrong, according to Hart, when they declare words such as 'just' and 'unjust' to be devoid of meaning. The fact that "concepts like justice" depend on "implicit varying and challengeable criteria," Hart says, "does not render them meaningless when applied to law." They are like other variable standards such as those indicated by "long," "short," "genuine," "false," and "useful."[34] The idea of fairness, that is, of treating like cases alike and different cases differently, Hart considers essential to law.

---

[31] Ibid., 94.   [32] Ibid., 39.
[33] Ibid., 43.
[34] H. L. A. Hart, "Scandinavian Realism," *Cambridge Law Journal* 17 (November 1959): 235.

Besides, Hart holds that something can be salvaged from theories of natural law. But they have to be disentangled from the "teleological point of view," which is "latent in our identification of certain things as human *needs* which it is *good* to satisfy and of certain things done to or suffered *by* human beings as *harm* or *injury*."[35] A minimum natural law can be constructed without resort to metaphysical notions simply by considering "contingent" facts "which could be otherwise" but in general are not.[36] Such a fact is the desire of men to survive. We cannot demonstrate the necessity of this desire but can agree that it persists.

There are a number of such "natural facts" that have a "rational connexion" with certain legal and moral rules. This connection, Hart is careful to point out, is "not mediated by *reasons*; for they do not relate the existence of certain rules to the conscious aims or purpose of those whose rules they are."[37] But as men are vulnerable creatures, they must exercise mutual forbearance and compromise if their lives are not to be nasty, brutish, and short. As their altruism is limited, and the things that they need in order to survive are relatively scarce, it follows that some form of property arrangements must exist. Then, too, the division of labor brings with it a need for dynamic "rules enabling men to transfer, exchange, or sell their products" and recognize promises. And as human understanding and strength of will are limited, there must also be "sanctions" to "*guarantee* that those who would voluntarily obey shall not be sacrificed to those who would not."[38] These conclusions are all untainted by metaphysics or reasons or purpose; they are "simple truisms," Hart maintains, that "disclose the core of good sense in the doctrine of Natural Law." They can be admitted to a positivist theory because they modestly recognize the rational connections of certain facts, contingent though persistent, with certain laws.[39]

Hart will have none of the Realists' skepticism about rules of law. His answer to their charge that rules of law must be meaningless because they do not produce perfectly predictable decisions rests on a distinction between the "core" and "penumbra" of a law. By the "core" Hart means those particulars that are clearly known to belong to the class of acts or things designated by a rule of law – what he calls "the standard case;" in the "penumbra" he includes those particulars that were not in the minds of the legislators but are offered later as new candidates for inclusion. The Realists make the mistake, according to Hart, of neglecting

---

[35] Hart, *Concept of Law*, 186.   [36] Ibid., 188.
[37] Ibid., 189.   [38] Ibid., 192–93.
[39] Ibid., 194.

the "core" in every rule of law and supposing that a rule consists only of the "penumbra," although he agrees that what the Realists say about a law applies to the penumbra.[40]

There is an unintended resemblance between Hart's view on this point and the Realist one he means to refute. For if the core of a law consists of "standard cases," a law appears to have the character of a class of particulars, rather than that of a rule. If a law is no more than a collection of particulars it would seem reasonable to conclude, as the Realists do, that rules of law have no independent claim to attention. Furthermore, in drawing out the implications of the "penumbra," Hart takes over the Realists' reliance on judicial intuition of social needs. When the judge is faced with a case in the penumbra, as he cannot decide in terms of logic, Hart says, he can only consider which decision would produce the most desirable social consequences. In such cases, judges who pretend to be applying the law as it "is" are really enemies of social progress.

Hart consequently interprets the decision of Justice Rufus Peckham in *Lochner* v. *New York* (1905) – that regulating bakers' hours of labor by state legislation was an unprecedented interference with the right of free contract – as an attempt to "give effect to a policy of a conservative type." What is taken to be an excessive use of logic in law, Hart explains, consists in giving "some general term an interpretation which is blind to social values and consequences (or which is in some other way stupid or perhaps merely disliked by critics)."[41] Thus, in cases belonging to the penumbra, justice or morality and law intersect in a way not allowed for by utilitarian theory. The qualifications on utilitarianism that he proposes, Hart believes, can save the reality of rules of law while allowing for the truth that inspires some jurists to disown them.

But in saving the reality of rules of law by distinguishing between a "core" and a "penumbra," Hart has failed to provide a genuine alternative to Realism. He assumes that rules of law can sometimes produce a certainty that they can never produce. Cases that appear to belong to the "core" are not logically different from cases in the "penumbra;" they are merely less likely to be highly disputable. At the same time Hart unwittingly joins the Realists in denying the possibility of separating the powers of judge and legislator when he permits judges to decide cases in the penumbra in terms of what they consider desirable social consequences; then it becomes true, as the Realists argued, that a man cannot know what the law is until his case has been decided.

---

[40] H. L. A. Hart, "Positivism and the Separation of Law and Morals," *Harvard Law Review* 71 (November 1958): 607.
[41] Ibid., 610–11.

Nor is Hart's notion of "validity," for all its superiority to Kelsen's, competent to explain why rules of law are obligatory. Here again Hart is handicapped by his allegiance to a positivist epistemology that has no way of accounting for abstract ideas that cannot be traced to sense perceptions. This allegiance to a positivist epistemology prevents Hart from admitting to his understanding of law the only idea that could solve the problem that concerns him – the concept of authority.

"Indeed, law's validity falls short in making it obligatory for several reasons." Hart argues that if a law is "valid," observing it is obligatory. But to say that a valid law is obligatory does not indicate why it is obligatory. The concept of validity only pushes the question back onto a prior or higher law – this law should be obeyed because it conforms to other laws. That, however, leads to an infinite regress, and the real difficulty persists at every stage of the regress. The real question raised by making "validity" the source of legal obligation is: Why should I obey any law that has consequences that I consider undesirable?

The question can be rendered irrelevant only if we take the view that a law can be shown to be desirable by a demonstration from indubitable premises. Then the desirability of the law becomes a necessarily true conclusion that is irresistible to any rational creature. Indeed, after such a demonstration it would be superfluous to say that a law is obligatory because a man cannot be obliged to accept what he necessarily cannot reject (though perhaps a law might still be "obligatory" for human beings who are not perfectly rational and prevented by their passions from recognizing rational necessity). The Realists replace obligation with social necessity. If men must adjust to or change social reality in order to survive, and if a judicial decision attuned to social needs indicates what is necessary to achieve this result, then men who wish to survive are obliged to obey the orders enabling them to do so. Thus, the Realists make practical rather than rational necessity the ground for accepting the law.

If, furthermore, a political association is not thought of as an association of individual human beings, but as an organism of which the members constitute organs, as many Realists suggest, all questions about the obligation to observe the law become irrelevant. For these questions arise from the supposition that the purpose of a political association is to promote the well-being of its members, individually considered. This is what gives its members the right to ask: Why should I obey a law? But if the end of a political association is independent of the ends of its members, then the latter have no rights; they can but serve and suffer. Then all questions concerning the validity of laws belong to the world of fantasy and need concern no one.

But if laws are intended to regulate the behavior of persons as individuals, and if no law can be shown to be necessarily desirable, then even good and wise men may deny the desirability of any particular legal prescription. Then the question arises: Why should I obey a law that I consider undesirable? Hart answers this question by asserting that a law must be obeyed when it is made in a certain fashion that renders it "valid," regardless of whether it is desirable in content. To say that the concept of validity is central to the law does not, however, explain why a valid law that is not desirable is nevertheless necessarily obligatory.

Where does this necessity come from? It is put there by lawmakers observing the prescribed procedures. But if the lawmakers' acts cannot claim the sanction of a divine or eternal law, what obliges people to recognize this man-made necessity? The only answer is that the lawmakers have been given the authority to make rules obligatory. It is this idea of authority that is missing from Hart's account. Though he speaks of secondary rules giving an "*authority* to legislate,"[42] he does not explain why the authority of law is independent of the justice of its content. This lacuna in the response to the Realist attack was fully exploited by jurists who were bent on repudiating altogether the traditional idea of law.

Yet in his famous debate with Lon L. Fuller[43] about whether a law duly promulgated in Nazi Germany could be considered a valid law, Hart defended something like the Hobbesian concept of authority. Fuller took the modern natural law view – which differs from that of Aquinas – that an unjust law cannot be a valid law. Hart's reply, that the German law at issue was valid even though iniquitous, was taken by some of his critics to signify that he considered any question about the justice of law to be irrelevant for deciding whether to observe it. That was not Hart's view. But Hart could not adequately rebut his critics because he had not addressed the question of why we need or value a legal system. Only by answering this question could Hart have given a satisfactory explanation of why the law as it is should be distinguished from what the law ought to be, and why insisting on this distinction, far from denying that law is a moral institution subject to a variety of moral judgments, is intrinsic to the moral quality of law. In other words, what is missing from Hart's account is an account of why distinguishing law's authority from its justice follows from recognizing why the rule of law is a desirable or just institution.

[42] Hart, *Concept of Law*, 57.
[43] Hart, "Positivism and the Separation of Law," 593–629; Lon L. Fuller, "Positivism and Fidelity to the Law – A Reply to Professor Hart," *Harvard Law Review* 71 (November 1958): 630–72.

Moreover, Hart contributed to the further development of the tendency in Realism that he opposed by his distinction between the law's "core" and "penumbra." This distinction was designed to explain the uncertainty of adjudication. But instead it suggested that if there is any uncertainty about how to interpret a rule, then the rule is an illusion. This suggestion has been implicit in all modern reflections on law, which nowhere differentiate, as Aristotle and Aquinas did, between the logic of theoretical reasoning and the logic of practical reasoning. Only on the basis of this distinction – because it explains how judicial decisions can be rational and yet yield conclusions that may be rationally disputed – can the Realists be adequately answered. But Hart's positivist epistemology can no more than Kelsen's provide any ground for differentiating theoretical from practical reasoning. Instead, Hart's distinction between the "core" and the "penumbra" of law opened the way to an all-out attack on Hart's central contention that "law essentially comprises *rules*."[44] A new defense of this contention, based on a broader understanding of the concept of law, has most recently been undertaken by the advocates of law's "formalism," led by Robert S. Summers.[45] But this defense of law's formalism was provoked by a more direct and destructive attack on the idea of law than that of Realism.

[44] Neil MacCormick, *H. L. A. Hart* (London: Arnold, 1981), 26.
[45] Cf. P. A. Atiyah and R. S. Summers, *Form and Substance in Anglo-American Law* (Oxford: Clarendon, 1987); R. S. Summers, "The Formal Character of Law," *Cambridge Law Journal* 51 (July 1992): 242–62; Joseph Raz, *Practical Reason and Norms* (London: Hutchinson, 1975); Joseph Raz, *The Authority of Law* (Oxford: Clarendon, 1983); Raz, *The Concept of a Legal System* (Oxford: Clarendon, 1970).

Part V

The idea of law repudiated

12 Marxist theories

Although the lengthy history of law's study has produced many different questions and many different answers, until the nineteenth century there was agreement on two points: First, that law is a way of ordering communal relations that must be chosen and can be rejected by those subject to it; and second, that law is superior to other forms of regulation. Both points have been denied by Marxist writers on law.

Just how the Marxist view influenced subsequent developments in the philosophy of law is not immediately obvious. Echoes and intimations of Marxist ideas appear in later writers. But whether they were directly derived from Marx remains to be established. The Realists, who contributed to the repudiation of the idea of law, do not explicitly draw on Marx and were not known to be Marxists. Direct acknowledgments to Marxism in the philosophy of law became noticeable only after mid-twentieth century, in Critical Legalism and Feminist Jurisprudence. But however Marxism affected attitudes towards law, it is an important part of this history because it so clearly highlights the postulates of the idea of law that have been definitely rejected by others subsequently.

The rejection of law rests on the Marxist definition of man as a "species-being." When Marx said that man is a "species-being," he meant that individual human beings are manifestations of the human species in the same way as leaves are manifestations of the life of the tree on which they hang. Or, as Marx put it: "The individual is the social being. . . The individual and the species-life of man are not different, although, necessarily, the mode of existence of individual life is a more particular or a more general mode of species-life or the species-life is a more particular or more general individual life."[1] Just as leaves exist to enable the tree to survive, so men and women exist to perpetuate the human species. Just as leaves on a tree are united by the dependence on the stems and branches

---

[1] Karl Marx, *Economic and Philosophical Manuscripts*, in *Karl Marx: Early Texts*, trans. and ed. D. McClellan (Oxford: Blackwell, 1971), 150–51.

from which they grow, so human beings are held together by *"natural necessity,"*[2] that is to say, by the relations that they develop in the course of their efforts to produce what they need to survive. These relations are not chosen by men but imposed upon them by the conditions of their productive activity: ". . . men create and produce their communal nature by their natural action, they produce their social being which is no abstract, universal power over against single individuals, but the nature of each individual, his own activity, his own life, his own enjoyment, his own wealth. Therefore this true communal nature does not originate in reflection, it takes shape through the need and egoism of individuals, i.e., it is produced directly by the effect of their being. It is not dependent on man whether this communal being exists or not. . ."[3]

In other words, the conception of man as a "species-being" presupposes that what distinguishes human beings from animals is their capacity for "labor" or "production," which is the power to transform nature rather than merely to use what is given as animals do. Although "labor" is the activity of making goods needed for the survival of the species, it also enables human beings to give real expression to their personality because it embodies their activity in concrete objects that are "visible to the senses."[4] Whether productive activity is the essence of humanity is no more disputable than whether human beings are part of the human species. But if men cannot choose whether to engage in productive activity, they can be more or less self-conscious about how their lives are shaped by the productive activities in which they engage. Greater self-consciousness cannot, however, alter these productive activities. For these productive activities have a natural, given pattern of development that unfolds over time and are therefore part of a "process."

The fundamental relationship between human beings which determines all others is that in which they seek the satisfaction of their substantive needs: that is, a relationship of work, or an association in a productive enterprise governed by some particular mode of production. In respect of this relationship human beings are said to compose *bürgerliche Gesellschaften*. These are not necessarily *bourgeois* societies, which classification denotes a particular corrupt "mode of production"; nor are they, properly speaking, *civil* societies, which are associations in terms of non-instrumental legal conditions. They are local associations for the

---

[2] Karl Marx and Frederick Engels, *The Holy Family, or Critique of Critical Criticism,* in *Karl Marx, Frederick Engels: Collected Works,* trans. Jack Cohen et al. (London: Lawrence and Wishart, 1975), IV:120.
[3] Marx, "On James Mill," in *Karl Marx: Early Texts,* 194.
[4] Ibid., 202–03.

satisfaction of common or reciprocal needs. Thus, human beings are not, as they sometimes imagine themselves to be, primarily related in terms of some moral or legal or "*political*" conditions; these, where they exist, are secondary and derivative considerations. It is sheer superstition, Marx writes, to think (as some still do) that productive association must be held together by legal and political conditions ("*the state*"); on the contrary, a "*state,*" when it exists, is held together by the considerations of productive enterprise.[5]

The Marxist view of man accordingly denies that all human beings have an independent destiny that they choose for themselves and seek to achieve. It denies that individuals may choose to associate with one another in different ways: all such differences are illusory. And it denies the possibility of any form of association that is not, or is not determined by, an engagement to satisfy needs. Thus, whereas Aristotle distinguished a *polis* as an association in terms of moral considerations ("the good life") and thought it to be a superior form of association to that of a tribe or a household because it was (not like them) concerned with something higher than the satisfaction of economic needs, for Marx "communist" association was superior to tribal or household association only in respect of its superiority as a productive enterprise. And this superiority derived from its conscious, express, and exclusive recognition of the "species-being" of its members reflected in a "mode of production" appropriate to their alleged characters.

All the distinctions that pervade *bourgeois* society – between the various aspects of production, between production and distribution, between public and private, between one nation and another – are attributed by Marx to what he calls "the division of labor." He charged the division of labor with producing a "fragmentation of productive forces," with giving labor the illusory character of being only one among many possible activities, and with preventing individuals from recognizing their labor as the activity that unites them to other men and enables them to express their humanity. That is why, he explained, the division of labor, and the private property associated with it, gives rise to alienation, which is the illusion in human beings that they have or can have independent, private purposes.[6] For whenever production becomes geared to consumption, to satisfying private desires, it is no longer a "species-activity." The translation of the value of goods into money and the buying and selling in the

[5] Marx and Engels, *Holy Family*, 120–21.
[6] Karl Marx, *The German Ideology*, trans. Jack Cohen et al. (Moscow: Progress, 1976), 94–96.

market directed to satisfying consumption are "alienating" arrangements because they distract man from seeing himself as a producing being, whose nature is fulfilled by laboring for the maintenance of the species and not for the satisfaction of private wants.

One of the worst illusions fostered by alienation is the idea that freedom consists in the unhindered pursuit of private satisfactions. Real freedom, Marx argues, consists in emancipation from all distinctions so that individuals have, and can recognize themselves as having, only one sort of relationship, that of producers who spontaneously work together to satisfy their needs as parts of the human species and are not tempted by the illusion of private claims: "Only when the real, individual man reabsorbs in himself the abstract citizen, and as an individual human being has become a *species-being* in his everyday life, in his particular work, and in his particular situation, only when man has recognised and organised his *forces propres* as *social* forces, and consequently no longer separates social power from himself in the shape of *political* power, only then will human emancipation have been accomplished."[7] The abolition of private property and the division of labor becomes possible once the organization of production develops to such "a degree of universality that private property and division of labor become fetters. . . ."[8] Once "the total productive forces" are appropriated by "the united individuals" and all distinctions are obliterated, the intercourse of individuals will become "the intercourse of individuals as such," and a person's particular way of gaining his livelihood will "become accidental" because it will have no effect on his life.[9] That is why the only society in which the genuine and free development of individuals ceases to be a mere phrase is communist society, where individual development is determined not by the separation but by "the connection of individuals, a connection which consists partly in the economic prerequisites and partly in the necessary solidarity of the free development of all, and, finally, in the universal character of the activity of individuals on the basis of the existing productive forces." This will bring about a complete change in the individuals' consciousness of their mutual relations. Love will become as irrelevant as egoism. All relations will be derived from "the concept of man."[10]

Marx held this view of human progress because he understood the relation of the human world to nature very differently than his predecessors. Whereas they considered the human world to be fundamentally

---

[7] Karl Marx, "On the Jewish Question," in *Karl Marx, Frederick Engels: Collected Works*, III:168.
[8] Marx, *Ideology*, 464.   [9] Ibid., 97.
[10] Ibid., 465, 454–55.

different from the natural world (in the sense of physical and biological nature), Marx taught that what goes on in the human world is merely a reflection of what is given by nature. He thereby made it impossible to think of law as a way of ordering human relations that can be chosen or rejected by human beings because his view of the relation between the human world and nature denies that human beings can make of their experience what they choose. Nevertheless, Marx and Engels and their disciples have acknowledged that there is in European civilization a phenomenon such as law, that is to say, a set of authentically recorded rules, which are made by human beings and subject to being changed by them, for the regulation of communal life. And they have made various attempts to explain this phenomenon in accordance with Marxist doctrine.

Marx and Engels themselves devoted relatively little attention to law as such. Marx concentrated on denouncing the illusion that law is a human invention, or, as he put it, a matter of "mere will." Jurists tell us, he says, that individuals can choose to enter into relations with others through making contracts and that the content of these relations rests "purely on the individual free will of contracting parties." But in fact neither the general nor the private will can determine the existence of property, and legal titles as such are meaningless, for the legal owner who cannot command the capital to cultivate his land really "owns nothing as a landed proprietor."[11] The true nature of law can be grasped only by recognizing its connection with the state.

Because the ruling class asserts itself by setting up the institutions that constitute the state, it is supposed that law rests on will, "indeed on the will divorced from its real basis – on *free* will." But in reality the law, like all political institutions, is an instrument through which the ruling class exercises its power to satisfy its interests. What the *bourgeoisie* describe as the freedom to make legal arrangements is only the reflection of the forms of intercourse in production at any particular time. Nor does the belief that law presupposes equality, a belief fostered by the ruling class, correspond to any reality because law arises from the dominance of one class over others. Although law makes it possible for the "personal rule" of the dominant class to "assume the form of average rule," law is nothing but the expression of the will, that is to say, the common interests of the ruling class.[12] But it is as wrong to blame the *bourgeoisie* for this, Marx warns, as to credit them with the development of law, for that, like everything else

---

[11] Ibid., 100–01.
[12] Ibid., 99, 348.

in the human world, is determined by the conditions of production. The fact that the will of the ruling class is enforced in the form of law, and thereby made "independent of the personal arbitrariness of each individual among them," no more depends on their "idealistic will" or their "arbitrary decision" than does the weight of their bodies.[13] The idea that law is a human invention is just one of the errors propagated by Enlightenment scholars, who had not yet acquired the science that could have enabled them to account for the forms of human relationships. They therefore tried to render the law less mysterious by describing it as an arbitrary dream that appeared out of the blue. In reality, law, like religion, is a category brought into being by historically given conditions.[14]

Law arose together with private property as a result of the disintegration of "the natural community" of the tribe. This development began with the Romans but was accelerated once the "feudal community was disintegrated by industry and trade." When the development of industry and trade made private property more important, Europe took over the "highly developed Roman civil law." But then law expressed only a spurious "nominal" will, not a real "dominant will." The genuine development of law began only in the sixteenth century, and as new forms of intercourse arose, so "the law has always been compelled to admit them among the modes of acquiring property." Until the development of the productive process makes competition superfluous, law cannot be abolished, for whatever men may try to do, competition would reassert itself and, with it, the institutions belonging to that form of production. To suppose that men can impose what they choose "before relations have developed far enough to make the emergence of such a will possible," is "only in the imagination of the ideologist."[15]

What constitutes an obligation to observe the law is nowhere discussed by Marx. Instead, he points out that violations of the law are as much an expression of the underlying productive relations as the making of law. Whether the law is observed has nothing to do with a recognition of authority, but depends entirely on whether the conditions of production promote or impede the domination of the ruling class. Just as the "right" defined by law is not a product of will, so crime does not depend on how individuals regard the law. Although he defines crime as "the struggle of the isolated individual against the predominant relations,"

[13] Marx, "Moralising Criticism and Critical Morality," in *Karl Marx, Frederick Engels: Collected Works*, VI:319; cf. Marx, *Ideology*, 348.

[14] Karl Marx, "Preface to First Edition," in *Capital*, trans. Ben Fowkes (London: Penguin Books, 1976), 89–93.

[15] Marx, *Ideology*, 99–100, 349, 101, 349.

Marx emphasizes that crime is "not the result of pure arbitrariness," but is determined by the same productive conditions that produce the domination of the ruling class: "The same visionaries who see in right and law the domination of some independently existing general will can see in crime the mere violation of right and law."[16]

Engels said even less about the law as such and treated it entirely as a phenomenon of the bourgeois state. But in his account of how the state developed, Engels lays more stress on the conflict among classes. Once the organization of production gave rise to classes with conflicting interests, he explains, it became necessary to have a power that seemed to stand above society in order to restrict the conflict and keep the antagonisms from consuming society in an endless struggle.[17] Elsewhere, Engels describes the veneration for law as "the classical world view of the bourgeoisie," a kind of "secularization of the theological," in which "human justice takes the place of dogma and divine right, and the state takes the place of the church."[18] In *Anti-Dühring* (1885), he explains that once "the struggle for individual existence based on the former anarchy of production, the collisions and excesses arising from these have been abolished, there is nothing more to be repressed which would make a special repressive force, a state, necessary. . . The interference of the State power in social relations becomes superfluous in one sphere after another. . . The government of persons is replaced by the administration of things and the direction of the processes of production. The state is not 'abolished'; it withers away,"[19] and the law disappears with it, since law is merely the machinery by which the ruling class under capitalism coerces the ruled into obeying its commands.

From the contradictions in their remarks about law, it is clear that Marx and Engels found it difficult to account for a phenomenon that they felt obliged to acknowledge but could not fit into their scheme of things. In his *Critique of the Gotha Programme* (1875), Marx condemns the law for being unjust because it treats everyone equally. The right of each worker to equal payment for equal work done, he said, "*is therefore right of inequality in its content, like every right.* Right by its very nature can only consist in the application of an equal standard; but unequal individuals (and they would not be different individuals if they were not unequal) are only measurable by an equal standard in so far as they are brought

---

[16] Ibid., 349.
[17] Cf. Frederick Engels, *The Origin of the Family, Private Property, and the State*, in the light of the researches of Lewis H. Morgan (New York: International Publishers, 1942).
[18] Frederick Engels, "Juristensozialismus," *Der Neuen Zeit*, 2 (1887).
[19] Frederick Engels, *Herr Eugen Duehring's Revolution in Science (Anti-Duehring)*, trans. Emile Burns, ed. C. P. Dutt (New York: International Publishers, 1939), 306–07.

under an equal point of view, are taken from one *definite* side only. . .
everything else being ignored."[20] In the *German Ideology*, however, he
insists that "differences of *brain* and of intellectual ability do not imply
any differences whatsoever in the nature of the *stomach* and of physical
needs," and different forms of activity therefore do not justify any form of
inequality.[21] But Marx never attempted to reconcile his condemnation of
inequality with his condemnation of law for regarding individuals as
equals.

Engels explicitly acknowledged that the existing legal institutions did
not perfectly conform with what Marx's doctrine seemed to require. But
he attributed this discrepancy to the fact that the law could not be a
"blunt, unmitigated, unaltered expression of the domination of a class,"
because this would readily destroy the illusion that the law is a means to
justice. Besides, the law was required to be consistent within itself: "In a
modern state, law must not only correspond to the general economic
position and be its expression. . . which is consistent in itself. . . And in
order to achieve this, the faithful reflection of economic conditions is
more and more infringed upon." The development of law had consequently been complicated by the effort "to do away with the contradictions arising from the direct translation of economic relations into legal
principles, and to establish a harmonious system of law," and by
"repeated breaches made in this system by the influence and pressure of
further economic development, which involves it in further contradictions." All this happens, however, without the awareness of those who
are operating the legal system – "the jurist imagines he is operating with
a priori principles," but they are "really only economic reflexes." Nevertheless, Engels went on to conclude that although law is in reality an
"*ideological conception*," it nevertheless in turn reacts upon its economic
basis and may even, to a limited degree, modify it.[22] But just what that
modification might be Engels never explained.

It took a Soviet Russian jurist to produce a more adequate Marxist
account of law. *In Law and Marxism: A General Theory*, published in
1929, Evgeny Bronislavovich Pashukanis attacked Engels's thesis that the
state and law emerged to prevent the struggle between the classes from
destroying society. He recognizes that the idea of law presupposed an

[20] Karl Marx, *Critique of the Gotha Programme*, ed. C. P. Dutt, trans. Martin Lawrence
(London: Lawrence and Wishart, 1933), 12–13.
[21] Marx, *Ideology*, 566.
[22] Frederick Engels, "Letter to Conrad Schmidt of October 27, 1890," in *Soviet Legal
Theory: Its Social Background and Development*, ed. Rudolf Schlesinger (London: Kegan
Paul, Trench, Trubner, 1945), 21.

understanding of human nature and history that is anathema to the Marxist. In his explanation of why this is so, he revealed more than have many defenders of the traditional idea of law, what view of the human world necessarily makes it impossible even to understand the rule of law. Pashukanis charged Engels's explanation with being self-contradictory. For if it meant that the state "perpetuates the relationship of equilibrium and is therefore a force standing above the classes," it followed that the state is not an instrument of the ruling class as Engels maintained. Or else, it meant that the state emerges as a result of the victory of one class or another, in which case it follows that the state is not needed to prevent the struggle between the classes. In any case, this sort of explanation was unacceptable, Pashukanis maintained, because it evaded the real question: "Why does class rule not remain what it is, the factual subjugation of one section of the population by the other?" Marxists were obliged to explain why class rule should have detached itself from the mere exercise of power and acquired the form of the state and the legal system, which is "an impersonal apparatus of public power, separate from society." Although it was undoubtedly true that the legal apparatus provided the ruling class with an "ideological smokescreen," which enabled it to "conceal its hegemony," that did not explain how such an ideology arose "independently of people's will." A proper Marxist account of the ideology of law had to disclose what connects the existence of law with the distinctive "material relations which it expresses."[23] Those few Marxists who did concern themselves with legal questions regarded the coercion associated with law as its distinctive trait because they supposed that this provided an alternative to the "ideological, purely speculative systems of legal philosophy based on the concept of the subject with its capacity for self-determination."[24] But these Marxists have provided nothing more than a "history of economic systems with a fairly faint juridical tinge, or a history of institutions, but by no means a history of law."[25]

Pashukanis was even more disdainful of "The so-called sociological and psychological theories of law" because, unlike idealistic theories of law, they seemed to promise a genuinely materialistic account of law. But in fact they did not even recognize the problem posed by law because they disregarded the legal form as such or, when they did consider it, simply dismissed juridical definitions as "fictions," "ideological illusions," "projections," and so on.[26]

---

[23] Evgeny B. Pashukanis, *Law and Marxism: A General Theory*, trans. Barbara Einhorn, ed. and intro. Chris Arthur (London: Ink Links, 1978), 139–40.
[24] Ibid., 39.   [25] Ibid., 53.   [26] Ibid., 53.

A satisfactory explanation of law must recognize, Pashukanis insisted, that in formally granting freedom and equality and the autonomy of the personality, law is something more than "an instrument of deceit and a product of the hypocrisy of the bourgeoisie" or distinguished only by the fact that "it is maintained by the organised violence of one class."[27] The establishment of a legal order has real and distinctive effects on human relations and has produced "profound, universal changes of an objective kind." The transformation of human relations into legal relations has liberated the land from "relations of dominance and subservience" and has converted political authority into a separate power.[28] When power is used to guarantee market exchange, it "not only employs the language of law, but becomes one with the abstract objective norm." It becomes a "social and public. . . authority representing the impersonal interest of the system."[29]

Every legal action, Pashukanis insisted, "is an objective fact which has its place outside the consciousness of the parties to it in just the same way as the economic phenomenon which it mediates." And he emphasized that the peculiar impersonality of this form of regulation is what enables the law to accommodate a great variety of relationships and to be indifferent to their character. While from the "historical point of view," every parliamentary resolution is a decision reached by a group with "class-orientated motives," from the legal standpoint, there is only, on the one hand, an impersonal, abstract, legal subject and, on the other hand, "the impersonal abstraction of state power functioning with ideal stability and continuity in time and space." The existence of the state is identical with the "organisation of the bureaucratic machine, the standing army, the treasury, the means of communication. . ."[30] Although the relationship of dependence between retailer and wholesaler, peasant and landowner, debtor and creditor, proletariat and capitalist is the "real basis" of the state, the legal system functions as "an autonomous force, set apart from all other individual and social forces." It "belongs to no one in particular, and stands above *everyone*, and addresses itself to *everyone*."[31]

Throughout, Pashukanis draws attention to the oddity of the legal subject, and he attributes this oddity to the complete divorce of the legal subject from the natural man, from "the organic bond which exists, for example, between the mother animal and its young, or between the clan and each of its members."[32] He also points out that every legal subject is independent of other legal subjects, each of whom has his own, differentiated, private interests. And this, he argues, is what distinguishes

[27] Ibid., 40, 83, n.16.   [28] Ibid., 40.   [29] Ibid., 137.
[30] Ibid., 44, 119.   [31] Ibid., 146–47.   [32] Ibid., 155.

legal regulation from "technical regulation," which presupposes a "unity of purpose."[33]

This distinction is central to Pashukanis's account of law and enables him to explain the fundamental difference between the Marxist and the traditional view of human relationship. Technical regulations are like the "norms" of rail traffic. They are "technical," Pashukanis explains, because they presuppose a common aim, such as maximum efficiency, of the enterprise. But the norms that govern the railways' liability are "legal" because "they are predicated on. . . differentiated interests." In legal regulation, the coercion that enforces it is "no longer considered under the rubric of expediency, but from the point of view of formal, that is of legal, admissibility." The mere form of statutes or decrees, Pashukanis warns, does not signify the existence of law. Train timetables, a plan for mobilization, or a brief for investigating crime are all regulations, but of a kind distinct from legal regulation such as appears in the law concerning the liability of the railways, a law covering universal conscription, or criminal proceedings in a court.[34] Technical regulations are concrete and continually modified in accordance with changing conditions, whereas legal regulations consist of "more or less fixed and unchanging formal limitations on, and regulations for, legal intercourse between autonomous subjects. . . and of organs which help to sort out tangles in such transactions by means of judgments in lawsuits (courts, arbitration committees, and so on)."[35] And because the distinctive character of law consists in its being a regulation governing social relations among people who are self-determining and pursuing their own, different objectives, a sharp distinction between private and public rights is intrinsic to a legal order.

To account for the law, Pashukanis pointed out, one had to explain how the concept of a self-determining subject came into being. Idealist theories of law tried to arrive at the concept by "purely speculative means," but as a Marxist, Pashukanis claimed, he could demonstrate how the legal subject arose historically from the organization of the productive process. And the crucial fact for that demonstration is the exchange of commodities, which is the distinctive feature of capitalism:

In Marx, the analysis of the form of the subject follows directly from the analysis of the commodity form. Capitalism is a society of commodity-owners first and foremost. This means that social relations in the production process assume a reified form in that the products of labor are related to each other as values. The commodity is a thing in which the concrete multiplicity of use-values becomes simply the material shell of the abstract property of value, which manifests

---

[33] Ibid., 79, 81–82.   [34] Ibid., 79–82.   [35] Ibid., 131–32.

itself as the capacity to be exchanged with other commodities in a specific relation. . . . as Marx says: "Commodities cannot themselves go to market and perform exchanges in their own right. We must, therefore, have recourse to their guardians, who are the possessors of commodities.". . . . At the same time, therefore, that the product of labor becomes a commodity and a bearer of value, man acquires the capacity to be a legal subject and a bearer of rights. "The person whose will is declared as decisive is the legal subject."[36]

This transformation of productive relationships into the exchange of commodities is traced by Pashukanis through different aspects of the productive system. When property can be freely disposed of in the market, it becomes the basis of the legal form. That is why, he argues, Marx said in *Capital* that the significance of legal ownership of land and soil is that "the landowner can do with his land what every owner of commodities can do with his commodities."[37] Similarly, when the worker "enters the market as a free vendor of his labor power" and disposes of his labor as a commodity, his relationship with the capitalist becomes the subject of legal contract.[38] Thus, when the development of the productive process reaches the stage of an economy based on commodity and money, human relations are "constructed as relations between subjects," and the conditions are present for a legal form with a "superstructure" of formal statutes, courts, trials, lawyers, and an antithesis between "the subjective and the objective, between the private and the public." Once the conditions are given, a legal order emerges "with absolute inevitability."[39] And the "capacity to be a legal subject is definitively separated from the living concrete personality, ceasing to be a function of its effective conscious will and becoming a purely social function. The capacity to act is itself abstracted from the capacity to possess rights. . . As a result bourgeois-capitalist property ceases to be unstable, precarious, purely factual property which may at any moment be contested and have to be defended, weapon in hand. It is transformed into an absolute, fixed right which follows the object wherever chance may take it, and which. . . has been protected the world over by laws, police and law courts."[40]

The prototype of relationships within bourgeois society is the contract because it is essential to the commercial relations that arise under commodity production. Because a commercial relationship is compatible with

---

[36] Ibid., 110–13; Marx, *Capital*, 178; cf. Bernhard Windscheid, *Lehrbuch des Pandekten-rechts*, 9th ed. (Frankfurt: Rütte & Loening, 1906), vol. I, section 49; quoted in Pashukanis, *Law and Marxism*, 110.

[37] Karl Marx, *Capital*, vol. III, trans. Samuel Moore, Edward Aveling, ed. Frederick Engels (Moscow: Foreign Languages Publishing House, 1961–62), 602; quoted in Pashukanis, *Law and Marxism*, 110.

[38] Pashukanis, *Law and Marxism*, 110.   [39] Ibid., 41–42.   [40] Ibid., 115.

a great variety of diverse relationships of another character, the commercial relationship is impersonal, and that is why the exchange of commodities gives rise to the "legal standpoint."[41] For the exchange of commodities presupposes an atomized economy, where the link between isolated private units is maintained by successfully concluded business deals. As such deals would not be possible without a legal system, "The legal relation between subjects is simply the reverse side of the relation between products of labor which have become commodities."[42] In effect, the legal subject is the abstract owner of commodities "raised to the heavens." The real basis of his legal character is his desire "to alienate through acquisition and to profit through alienating. . . Hence the contract is a concept central to law. . . Historically speaking, and in real terms, the concept of the legal transaction arose. . . from the contract; . . . the legal form, too, in its purest and simplest form, acquires a material basis in the act of exchange."[43] Once this development is identified, it becomes evident that "law as a form, does not exist in the heads and theories of learned jurists," and does not come into existence by "conscious choice," but is produced "by virtue of the same necessity which transforms the product of nature into a commodity. . ."[44] Legal intercourse is merely the reflection of the exchange relation, which "presupposes the existence of more or less fixed general patterns, an elaborate casuistry and, finally, a particular organisation which applies these patterns to individual cases and sees to the compulsory execution of sentences."[45]

Although Pashukanis took great trouble to support his arguments with quotations from Marx, in fact his view of the connection between law and coercion departs radically from Marx's doctrine that the monopoly of coercion by the dominant class is the essence of law. Instead, Pashukanis maintains that the use of coercion merely enables the state to operate legal regulation more effectively, and he explicitly acknowledges that "legal intercourse often manages even without its support, using the law of custom, voluntary arbitration, self-help, and so on."[46]

Pashukanis went so far as to consider a question about law that has generally been dismissed as meaningless by Marxist theoreticians – the obligation to observe the law. It is properly understood, Pashukanis argues, as a "liability" rather than as a "duty" because the legal claim appears in the form of "an external claim emanating from a concrete subject who is also, as a rule, simultaneously the bearer of a corresponding material interest." Bourgeois legal theory, however, has refused to

[41] Ibid., 82.   [42] Ibid., 85.   [43] Ibid., 121.
[44] Ibid., 68.   [45] Ibid., 162.   [46] Ibid., 162.

recognize this and has accordingly become hopelessly entangled in the difficulty of distinguishing between legal and moral obligation. If bourgeois theorists maintain that law is independent of morality, then the coercion associated with law becomes its defining feature, in which case law becomes one with the state and its moral quality disappears. But if law is regarded as distinct from the state, then the significance of law "as a socially necessary minimum is immediately lost,"[47] and law becomes indistinguishable from morality.

As a result, bourgeois legal philosophy has wavered between two contradictory views, between assimilating legal obligation to subjection, to external coercion and assimilating it to "free" moral duty. And this contradiction is not surprising because it reflects the contradiction in the real life of bourgeois society "between the individual and the social, between the private and the universal," which is the basis of a society of commodity producers because it "is embodied in the actual interrelations of people who cannot regard their private endeavours as social aspirations except in the absurd and mystified form of the value of commodities."[48]

Unlike bourgeois theories, Pashukanis explains, Marxism regards both law and morality as reflections of a pathological social order in which individuals are not related by an "organic bond," but are treated as independent subjects. The concepts of law and morality are meaningful only in a "commodity-producing society" because they are designed to provide a relationship between individuals whose natural social ties have been destroyed by a system of production that reduces them to autonomous beings. The phenomenon of moral obligation is peculiar to bourgeois society because it cannot occur where "the limits of the individual self" are blurred by an emotional or productive tie, any more than the legal relation can occur where individuals are not pursuing egoistic interests. Kant recognized this and "gave a logically perfected shape to the form which atomised bourgeois society sought to embody in reality, by liberating the personality from the organic fetters of the patriarchal and feudal epochs. Hence the fundamental concepts of ethics lose their significance if considered in isolation from commodity-producing society, and if one attempts to apply them to any other social structure. The categorical imperative is by no means a social instinct, for its most important determinant is that it is effective where there is no possibility of organic, supra-individual motivation of any kind." In short, morality and law are both "modes of intercourse utilised by commodity-producers," who do not act

---

[47] Ibid., 162–63.   [48] Ibid., 165.

in order to fulfill their "individual historical destiny" or "social function," but to satisfy their private interests.[49]

The meaningfulness of the concept of justice is also acknowledged by Pashukanis, though he says that it "does not contain anything substantively new, apart from the concept of the equal worth of all men" and that it "lends itself admirably to interpreting inequality." Nevertheless, he maintains that justice is connected with the reality of the relations among those exchanging products – "the circulation of commodities, is predicated on the mutual recognition of one another as owners by those engaged in exchange." This acknowledgment may take the shape of an inner conviction, but it is "sufficient for commodity owners to act *as if* they acknowledged one another mutually as proprietors."[50] The real distinction between law and morality is that, for law, only performance matters and motive is irrelevant. And it would seem to follow that justice is to be equated with observing the law.

Despite his acknowledgment of the objectivity of the law and his depreciation of the importance of coercion in connection with law, Pashukanis remained a thorough-going Marxist because he did not take human beings to be self-determining agents capable of accepting or rejecting legal regulation. He insisted that legal relationships are imposed by the productive process, and he did so in the classical Marxist fashion of equating any denial of the Marxist creed, that a legal order is peculiar to capitalism, with a belief that the legal order is a "universal and eternal phenomenon."

Pashukanis granted that there were approaches to law in other societies, but he insisted that they were necessarily rudimentary and partial. In Rome, "the idea that all people are equal, possessing the same 'soul', that they all have the capacity to be legal subjects, and so forth – was forced on the Romans by the practice of trade with foreigners. . ."[51] But there was no true law in Rome because the *jus civile* of ancient Rome was a public law, and the distinction between public and private that is essential to a legal system was absent since the *jus civile* "was founded on, and originated in membership of a gens-organization."[52] In the Middle Ages there was only a rudimentary legal subject, for he was in fact only a bearer of concrete privileges rather than "the universal abstract bearer of every conceivable legal claim."[53] In both these societies power bore the traces of patriarchal or feudal relations, since "Equality between subjects was assumed only for relations which were confined to a particular, narrow

---

[49] Ibid., 154–55.   [50] Ibid., 161–62.   [51] Ibid., 156.
[52] Ibid., 136.   [53] Ibid., 120.

sphere," and social relations generally had a theological rather than a commercial character.[54]

The most remarkable feature of Pashukanis's theory of law is his insistence that what defines a legal regulation is its non-instrumental character. By arguing that legal regulation is indifferent to the purposes and projects of its subjects, and that in a society regulated by a legal system the more powerful are just as subject as the least powerful to legal rules and their sanctions, Pashukanis cast doubt on the fundamental tenet of Marxist doctrine: that every human activity is instrumental, that every institution is an instrument of production, and that in every non-Communist society, political institutions are only instruments for maintaining the power of the ruling class. Pashukanis himself did not doubt any of these propositions. He therefore addressed himself to explaining how a form of regulation which is divorced from the natural character of production, and accordingly non-instrumental, could have arisen necessarily out of the character of production and thus could be shown after all to be instrumental (although in a more indirect and intricate fashion than Marx had supposed). By disclosing "the logical structure of social relations which are concealed behind individuals and which transcend the bounds of individual consciousness," he had established, Pashukanis claimed, that what Marx had said about the economic categories, that they "express the forms of being," was "directly applicable to juridical categories as well."[55] Law understood as the reflection of commodity exchange in no way detracted from the importance of the conflict between classes and the struggle against capitalism. On the contrary, it clarified the nature of that struggle: "the philosophy of law based on the category of the subject with his capacity for self-determination. . . is actually, basically, the philosophy of an economy based on the commodity. . . This view is the basis for the critique by communists of the bourgeois ideology of freedom and equality and of bourgeois formal democracy – that democracy in which the 'republic of the market' masks the 'despotism of the factory.' This view leads us to the conviction that defense of the so-called abstract foundations of the legal system is the most general form of defense of bourgeois class interests, and so forth."[56]

Although Pashukanis did not treat law as an instrument of the power of the ruling class, and so lent considerable credence to the belief that the worker under capitalism can dispose of his labor as he chooses and is therefore in an important sense free and independent, for some years his theory dominated the Soviet juristic establishment. The criticism, when it came and brought Pashukanis's life as well as his career to an end in 1936,

[54] Ibid., 119, 136.   [55] Ibid., 70.   [56] Ibid., 39.

was directed not at his dissociation of law from power, but at the closeness of the links he had established between law and capitalism. Pashukanis had insisted, at least until he came under attack, that there was no place for law under communism because law is associated with the exchange of "commodity values," under the bourgeois organization of society, which is constrained "to retain an equivalent relation between expenditure and compensation of labor."[57] Under communism, there is no exchange; people work spontaneously according to need. Since society is organized as a single enterprise, and all activities are directed to achieving the success of this enterprise, there is no room for a distinction between public and private or for any recognition of individuals as pursuers of independent projects. Without these distinctions, a legal system is impossible. There might still be some sort of regulation, but Pashukanis insisted that it would necessarily have the character of technical regulation since it would be directed at achieving a single purpose, and could not be, as legal regulation is, compatible with a variety of purposes.

That something like "market exchange" persisted within the Soviet economy, Pashukanis acknowledged, but he explained that as "under proletarian dictatorship. . . conflicts of interest are abolished within nationalised industry. . . the legal form as such does not contain within itself those unlimited possibilities which lay before it at the birth of bourgeois capitalist society." Wherever there are isolated social elements, they will resort to law and exchange. Although the enterprises in the Soviet State "actually fulfill a communal task," they still had something like separate interests and were therefore obliged to enter into legal intercourse. But "The ultimate victory of a planned economy will transform their relationship into an exclusively technical expedient, thereby doing away with their 'legal personality'."[58] For then economic life would function as a "natural economy," and the "social link between units of production" would appear not in the artificial commodity form, but in "a rational, undisguised form." Their relations would be directed by "technically-determining prescriptions in the form of programmes, plans for production and distribution, and so forth." Such prescriptions are concrete and are continually being modified in accordance with changing conditions. Consequently, they are totally distinct from legal regulations.[59]

Nor would there be any need for law to deal with crime because crime, in the *bourgeois* sense, would have become meaningless. Undesirable *behavior* would be seen as a medical problem, to be dealt with by the

---

[57] Ibid., 63–64.   [58] Ibid., 132–35.   [59] Ibid., 131.

appropriate technicians and not by jurists "with their 'evidence', their codes, their concepts of 'guilt', and of 'full or diminished responsibility', or their fine distinctions between complicity, aiding and abetting, instigation and so on. . . ."[60] Pashukanis acknowledged that penal codes and criminal law existed in Soviet Russia, but he attributed their existence to the fact that "remnants" of bourgeois society still survived.

Pashukanis's denial that law had any place under communism was in keeping with the canonical texts of Marx and Engels. Marx's *Critique of the Gotha Programme* was directed against the "idealization" of the state. Whatever form the state took, he said, it was an instrument of coercion; communism rejected coercion; and it followed that neither the state nor its law had any place under communism. Engels had said that under communism, the social regulation would differ from law both in form and content and would not ignore, as the law necessarily did, differences in individual abilities and needs. This new kind of regulation would be enforced not by "a special organism separated from society through division of labor" but by public opinion.[61] Nevertheless, the attack on Pashukanis, both within and outside the USSR, took the line that he had maligned communism.

In the West, an attack was formulated at the end of World War II in *Soviet Legal Theory* (1945) by Rudolph Schlesinger, who attributed Pashukanis's deviation to the influence of pre-1917 "legal Marxism": "In a vulgarized economic interpretation of history under the title of 'economic materialism' the Marxian conception of 'relations of *production*' was replaced by the Buecher-Bogdanovian conception of *distribution* of products as being the really fundamental fact of social relations." Schlesinger went on to argue that law was essential to the Soviet State because the unity of purpose that made law unnecessary was absent. Pashukanis's argument that legal regulation would be replaced by technical regulation was essentially the same as Engels's assertion that once classes were abolished, the rule over men would be replaced by the administration of things. But class conflict still had to be fought in the USSR since there could be no "unity of purpose between the Soviet State. . . and the speculator." And Schlesinger boldly supported his assertion by the argument that "the very fact of the existence of a Penal Code proves the existence of conflicting private interests."[62] Schlesinger went so far as to denounce even the expectation that unity of purpose could be established as a utopian vision. In Russia, the railway regulations, which Pashukanis

---

[60] Ibid., 64.
[61] Karl Marx, *Critique of the Gotha Programme* (London: Lawrence & Wishart, 1933), 30.
[62] Rudolph Schlesinger, *Soviet Legal Theory: Its Social Background and Development* (London: Kegan Paul, 1945), 153, 159.

had described as "technical," were legal regulations because, since there
was no unemployment in the USSR, "Non-compliance with technical
rules" was punished by penalties "more serious than those which the
management of the railway could inflict upon its employees" in capitalist
countries. And indeed, in Soviet Russia generally, because there were no
economic sanctions, "the scope accorded to Criminal Law is rather wider
than elsewhere. . ."[63]

Moreover, it was not true that Soviet enterprises were less independent
than capitalist enterprises. Although they had to conform to a plan,
whether "they will make this contract or another" still had to be decided.
The Soviet State had set up industrial enterprises "as separate legal
entities" in order to leave the management free to decide how it would
organize production. The only plausible meaning that one could attach to
Pashukanis's argument that technical regulation would replace legal regulation, Schlesinger concluded, was that under communism there would be
less need for compulsion than under capitalism or the transitional society
because "class-divisions" would have been abolished.[64]

In his eagerness to establish that law would not disappear under communism, Schlesinger denied that law was a phenomenon peculiar to
capitalist society. There was, he affirmed, "a well-elaborated feudal law
in the medieval village, and its study makes a much larger contribution to
the understanding of contemporary Criminal Law than could an analysis
of the growth of commodity exchange in the towns." He denied also that
law was necessarily an instrument of "subordination." Even under "class-
rule," he said, there is "a strong interest on the part of the ruling class in
the regular and predictable working of the judicial and legal machinery,
including its predictable working against individual members of the ruling
class who violate its common interests. In this sense, every legal system is
a system of co-ordination." The role of law in the USSR was essentially
the same as in the US. Anti-trust law in the US played the same role as the
law against speculation in the USSR – in both cases, law provided the
necessary "social machinery."[65]

And so Schlesinger entreated Marxists to acknowledge the value of
maintaining "stable social relations." Such stability could be preserved
only if judges did not legislate, but restricted themselves to establishing
"the recognised content of the legal order. . . for the Judge, *qua* Judge, the
social interest exists in so far as it is embodied in the legal order, and
nowhere else." And unless a state recognized this, it could not "achieve
that normality and smoothness in the social machinery which may
be demanded of any political system, once it has outgrown the initial

---

[63] Ibid., 161–62.   [64] Ibid., 160–61.   [65] Ibid., 157–59.

difficulties of its revolutionary origin."[66] The only possible defense for supposing, as Pashukanis did, that communism could dispense with law is a mistaken identification of law with the apparent revival of capitalism under the NEP programme in the early 1920s. Otherwise, Pashukanis's argument was no more than an apology for either capitalism or lawlessness and an evil encouragement to "anarchy or arbitrary rule."[67]

Schlesinger's doctrine is a more sober and elaborate version of the official denunciation in 1938, by Vyshinsky, who charged Pashukanis with promoting a nihilist attitude to Soviet law. Vyshinsky's insistence on the importance of law under communism was coupled with an argument for the necessity of a strong state. This was the theme of Stalin's report in the following year to the 18th Party Congress, where he declared that the "withering away of our socialist state" was not to be expected in Soviet Russia because it could take place only when socialism had triumphed in all countries. And he repeated with approval Lenin's definition of the dictatorship of the proletariat as "*the legally unlimited dominance of the proletariat over the bourgeoisie, resting on violence, and enjoying the sympathy and support of the toiling and exploited masses.*"[68] Thus, a new task was set for Soviet theorists of law. They had to show that law was intrinsic to "the dictatorship of the proletariat" and compatible with legally unlimited violence.

This feat was managed by S. A. Golunskii and M. S. Strogovich in *The Theory of the State and Law*, which was published in 1940. They defined law as a form of "guidance," which had to be exercised by the Communist Party alone, although it was always actively supported by the proletariat: "In the socialist state, a new law extending the application of state constraint to cases to which it was heretofore inapplicable is enacted only when a majority of the toilers recognizes its propriety." This meant that the dictatorship of the proletariat was "dictatorial after a new fashion."[69] By quoting Lenin to the effect that, "Will, if it is the state's will, must be expressed as *legislation* established by *authority* – otherwise 'will' is an empty concussion of air by an empty sound,"[70] they identified

---

[66] Ibid., 231–33.   [67] Ibid., 164.
[68] Joseph V. Stalin, "Report to the 18th Party Congress, March 10, 1939," in *Soviet Legal Philosophy*, trans. Hugh W. Babb, intro. John N. Hazard (Cambridge, MA: Harvard University Press, 1951), 343; S. A. Golunskii and M. S. Strogovich, "The Theory of Law and State," in *Soviet Legal Philosophy*, trans. Hugh W. Babb, 359; A. Y. Vyshinsky, "The Fundamental Tasks of the Science of Soviet Law," in *Soviet Legal Philosophy*, trans. Hugh W. Babb, 303–04.
[69] Golunskii and Strogovich, "Theory of Law," 361, 363.
[70] V. I. Lenin, "Contradictory Positions," quoted in Golunskii and Strogovich, "Theory of Law," 365.

"dictatorship" with "authority." And that identification was reenforced with a quotation from the *Communist Manifesto*: "Your law is merely the will of your class, erected into legislation – a will whose content is defined by the material conditions of the existence of your class." This proposition, they argued, established that law of any sort is merely "the will of the dominant class elevated into legislation" by being "precisely formulated and given universally binding force, becoming a rule of conduct binding upon all."[71] It was still true that law expressed the will of the dominant class, but in a socialist society it expressed the will of the ruling working class, "and – since exploiter classes have there been destroyed, and the worker class (to which the state guidance of society belongs) expresses the interests and aspirations of all the toiling people – socialist law is the will of the soviet people elevated into legislation. . ." It was a mistake to think that law is distinct from the state or that one preceded the other – law and the state are two sides of the same phenomenon: "class dominance, which is manifested (a) in the fact that the dominant class creates its apparatus of constraint (the state), and (b) in the fact that it expresses its will in the shape of rules of conduct which it formulates (law) and which – with the aid of its state apparatus – it compels people to observe."[72]

The question that had concerned Pashukanis, How could the law be objective?, is never raised by Golunskii and Strogovich. They treat law simply as an instrument of power. Any other view of it was dismissed for reflecting the typical bourgeois error of failing to "start from the foundation of law – which consists of social conditions, production relations, and class conflict," and so failing to "discern in law the will of the dominant class erected into legislation."[73] The canonical Marxist conclusion that followed from this understanding of law, that law like every social arrangement belongs to a particular historical stage of capitalism and to no other (which their book was dedicated to denying), was cavalierly endorsed by describing law as a "historical phenomenon" that, like the state, would disappear at the same time as the "causes which evoked it."[74] Once people had been taught by "the conscious discipline of the communist social order" to observe the "rules of life," "voluntarily and unconstrainedly," then there would be no need for law: "Communist morality and communist customs will stand in the place of law. Governing things

---

[71] Golunskii and Strogovich, "Theory of Law," 365; Karl Marx and Frederick Engels, *Communist Manifesto*, in *Karl Marx and Frederick Engels: Selected Works* (Russian ed., 1933), quoted in Golunskii and Strogovich, "Theory of Law," 365.
[72] Golunskii and Strogovich, "Theory of Law," 366.
[73] Ibid., 401.   [74] Ibid., 366.

and production processes will take the place of governing people." Or, in other words, once the unity of tribal order was restored on a new industrial basis, and human beings learned again to think of themselves as parts of a productive enterprise, there would be no need for law. But this could not happen, they warned, just as Stalin had, until there was no longer any need to "struggle against hostile encroachments on the part of capitalist encirclement."[75] They ignored the distinction that traditional jurists insisted on between rules and orders by speaking of "legal norms," in which they included every sort of regulation. Whether a law took the shape of "a rule, an order, a requirement" was declared irrelevant, and the fact that all Soviet legislation was officially described as a decree went unnoticed. The distinction between instrumental and non-instrumental rules was similarly ignored. Law, Golunskii and Strogovich said, has "a definite goal which the dominant class attains with its aid."[76] That coercion is intrinsic to law followed necessarily from their definition of law as "norms" established by the *"coercive force of the state. . . to the end of safe-guarding, making secure, and developing social relationships and arrangements agreeable and advantageous to the dominant class."*[77]

Law is distinguished from morality by two traits. Moral norms are not enforced by direct constraint on the part of the state, and they lack the unity characteristic of law because law represents the will of the dominant class, whereas moral norms within a single state might differ from class to class. The example given of such differences in moral norms – that strike-breaking was considered moral by capitalists but immoral by the workers – made it clear that Golunskii and Strogovich made no distinction between private and public, such as Pashukanis had considered essential to a legal system. Thus, Golunksii and Strogovich established that "Socialist law is a completely unique type of law," because it is the "first law in the history of human society which is not exploiter law: it banishes exploitation, and gives expression to the interests and will of all the toiling people – of the socialist worker-peasant state." Both in form and substance it differs from any law that has ever existed in any exploiter state because it consists "of norms expressing the will and guaranteeing the interests of a people freed from exploitation. . ." Such a condition can be found only where exploiter classes have been destroyed. Therefore, socialist law is founded upon "public socialist property (the indefeasible basis of the socialist social order) and not upon private property; upon the principles of the proletarian dictatorship which is carrying into effect the state guidance of society."[78]

---

[75] Ibid., 399–400.   [76] Ibid., 368–69.
[77] Ibid., 370.   [78] Ibid., 368, 384–85.

Marx's criticism of law for treating unequal people equally was lightly disposed of as a criticism of the bourgeois law that prevailed in societies where there is private property and consequently no true equality. Moreover, the formal equality of bourgeois law was described as a veil for "the factual inequality created by capitalist exploitation," the fact that the workers could not make use of the rights that they had been granted. Insofar as private property persisted under socialism, inequality persisted and the law accordingly retained elements of "bourgeois law." But socialist law, even though it may temporarily preserve a certain inequality, "is itself a means of mitigating, and gradually eliminating, that inequality."[79] The absence of distinctions considered essential to law in bourgeois societies was recognized but explained away as one of the virtues of socialist law. For these distinctions were inspired by the bourgeois effort to make it impossible for workers to use the law. Since a socialist state wants the law to be known "to the widest possible strata of the toilers," socialist law is "incomparably simpler and more accessible in form – as well as far richer in content," than is bourgeois law.[80]

That the Soviet State sometimes ignored the law was also acknowledged. But such exceptions were shown to be entirely compatible with, indeed intrinsic to, the idea of "socialist law." For the socialist state had "historical tasks" to realize, and the law was only one of the state's instruments for achieving those tasks. It was therefore entirely fitting that the law should be set aside whenever it became an impediment instead of an aid to the state's proper activity: "Accordingly, while socialist legality is constant and stable, it is nevertheless no set form, dissociated from the conditions and tasks of the class struggle and socialist building: it does not, therefore, negative the possibility of applying to class foes extraordinary measures necessarily evoked by the conditions of the class struggle and the resistance of class foes to the measures of soviet authority."[81]

Golunskii and Strogovich end their treatise with a conscientious review of "bourgeois legal theory," which they divide into three kinds: theories that base law on divine authority, theories that base law on race or nationality, and theories that derive law from a higher, independent norm. All of them are found to have failed to recognize the relation of law to real life. As legal norms are "instruments of the class struggle in the hands of the dominant class" and are binding because "behind them stands the exceedingly real authority of the state – with its police, judges, troops, prisons, etc.," only "Trotsky-Bukharin wreckers" would deny that

---

[79] Ibid., 388–89.   [80] Ibid., 391.   [81] Ibid., 393.

Soviet legislation consisted of "legal norms," just as did bourgeois law. But whereas bourgeois theory divides the human world from the physical world and therefore denies that the "law of causation" is just as pertinent to the human as to the physical world, under socialism the true source of law in social relations is revealed because "The worker class, defending the interests of all the toilers, has no need to conceal either the class character of its legal norms, or to conceal whose strength establishes and maintains them and whose interests they defend."[82]

For Golunskii and Strogovich, it is a cardinal sin to suggest, as social democrats did, that the law could be used to reorganize capitalism into socialism without a revolution. And this was long accepted by Western Marxists, who accordingly dismissed the law as an "ideological screen" designed to mask the iniquities of capitalism. Marxists were obliged only to expose the unreality of law. Since the Second World War, however, Western Marxists have changed their attitude toward law. The change was inspired partly by the Althusserian revision of Marxism, which emphasized that "ideology," though produced by economic forces, in turn influenced the organization of society. And it was inspired partly by the recognition, promoted by the teachings of the Realist school of jurisprudence and the disposition generally to interpret law sociologically, that law could be used to destroy the established legal system.

This new attitude to law led Western Marxists to comb Marx and Engels for evidence that they had rejected economic determinism and believed that law could affect the material structure of society.[83] There followed a flood of anthologies and discussions of what Marx and Engels wrote on law. Another curious consequence was the restoration of Pashukanis as the leading Marxist theorist of law on the ground that in order to use the law effectively, it is essential for Marxist revolutionaries to understand the distinctive character of law. There was no serious effort to deal with the conflict between the view of law as an instrument of revolution and the basic tenets of Marxism. Any such question was simply dismissed with the argument that "law is appropriate as an object of

---

[82] Ibid., 423–24.
[83] See Maureen Cain and Alan Hunt, *Marx and Engels on Law* (London: Academic, 1979), xiii. A similar effort to deny Marx's view that law is "merely" ideology appears in C. Sumner, *Reading Ideologies: An Investigation into the Marxist Theory of Ideology and Law* (London: Academic, 1979). The current restoration of Pashukanis to favor is evident in P. Bevine and R. Sharlet, eds., *Pashukanis: Selected Writings on Marxism and Law*, trans. Peter B. Maggs (London: Academic, 1980). There are, besides, a number of anthologies that do not concentrate on Marx, but have select readings that display a conception of law as an "instrument of social control": C. M. Campbell and P. Willes, *Law and Society* (Oxford: M. Robertson, 1979); V. Aubert, *Sociology of Law* (Harmondsworth: Penguin, 1969).

struggle provided that the real material object to be achieved is not lost sight of, that the legal formulae are not fetishized." Law was still described as an instrument of class rule, but this definition was turned on its head to prove that even under capitalism, the working class may as easily make the law serve their purposes as do the capitalists: "Marx argued that the bourgeoisie, having established and fixed a political arena, is constrained by its own rules of legality, its own ideology. Although this constraint is not absolute, but is itself a function of political pressure, it means that there are moments when the workers achieve more by using the law than is possible even for the dominant classes. Means, like law, are created in order to be exploited, used, in political action. The working classes too can play this game, but neither side, least of all the working class whose conceptions and purposes are not embedded in the law, can afford to mistake the means for its real concrete objective."[84]

At the same time, the Marxists who repudiated "economic determinism" and urged that the law be used to destroy capitalism argued that the working class is necessarily engaged in a struggle with the capitalist class and that every human idea must be understood as an instrument of power. But as these convictions rest on a Marxist understanding of human beings, they are incompatible with expecting the law to determine social relations because then the law can only be an instrument of the ruling class. If the Marxist understanding of man as a "species-being" is rejected, the reason for preferring communism to capitalism disappears. In short, the effort to reconcile Marxism with law cannot escape self-contradiction.

There is a fatal self-contradiction even in the highly ingenious efforts of Pashukanis to acknowledge that bourgeois law treats workers and capitalists alike. For if it is possible for capitalism to coexist with a state that is not an instrument of the ruling class, as Pashukanis's account establishes, then the Marxist's conception of human beings and history (which Pashukanis retained) must be false. But the Soviet doctrine that replaced Pashukanis's theory is hardly more consistent in maintaining that the dictatorship of the proletariat is a form of law. That doctrine not only travesties the idea of law both in theory and by the practices that it entails, but also contradicts the Marxist view of history as a process in which each stage necessarily has a different form of political organization.

Indeed, the only view of law that a Marxist can hold at all consistently is that of Marx and Engels, who said very little about law just because they dismissed it as an epiphenomenon, a "superstructure," or "ideology"

---

[84] Cain and Hunt, *Marx and Engels,* 214, 217–18.

that merely disguises the real struggle for power. Of course, they could not explain why "ideology" should have taken such a bizarre form under capitalism. Nor could they acknowledge the existence of law in societies as diverse as ancient Greece and Rome, or medieval and modern Europe. But they did recognize that the individuality of human beings, their character as independent agents who choose what to do and be, is intrinsic to the idea of law because the law imposes a unity that does not destroy the pursuit of independent projects. If, however, "labor" is taken to be the distinctive human activity, and human life is supposed to be governed by "the productive process," and if man is understood as a "species-being," as Marxism teaches, it follows that men are not independent agents. Independence becomes a disease, a pathological "alienation" from the organic unity that is the natural condition of mankind. As the rule of law postulates that such an organic unity is neither natural nor desirable, the only consistent Marxist conclusion is that the rule of law must be repudiated. Although the Marxist conception of man as a "species-being" has never been explicitly adopted by writers who have either deliberately or implicitly rejected the idea of law, the unselfconscious spread of this understanding of human beings made the repudiation of the traditional idea of law comprehensible and plausible. At the very least it accounts for much of the confusion that has bedeviled reflection on the idea of law in the late twentieth century.

13   Political jurisprudence I: From Realism to feminist jurisprudence

The Realist criticism of law which was being nurtured in the 1930s flowered after World War II into what H. L. A. Hart calls "the nightmare theory of law." It dismissed the conventional image of the judge as an objective and experienced declarer of law, who could and should be sharply distinguished from the legislator, as "an illusion" which was bound to disappoint the expectations which it excited.[1] By the 1960s, the attack on the distinction between judges and legislators became dramatically more far-reaching. Instead of being concerned with merely destroying the myth that judges decided cases in terms of fixed rules, jurisprudence became preoccupied with discovering an altogether novel understanding of adjudication. This effort was most marked in the United States, where discussion concentrated on political scientists' studies of the role of the Supreme Court in constitutional review. But the conclusions carried, and were meant to carry, much broader implications for adjudication generally and for the nature of law.

The new school became known as "political jurisprudence." They agreed with the Realists that the law consists in the decisions of judges rather than in the contents of statute books. But political jurisprudence added a new insistence on treating judicial decisions as part of the political process. It emphasized that the courts do not belong to a sheltered legal haven; that they are not a "unique body of impervious legal technicians above and beyond the political struggle," that they are merely one government agency among many, a part of the American political process. Rather, the courts serve as a political battleground, and the judge is a politician acting upon and being acted upon by other political forces. And this is what the courts must and should be in an age of "positive government." It follows that the search for judicial neutrality is a futile quest, and that the concept of a political court has to replace the concept of a

---

[1] H. L. A. Hart, "American Jurisprudence through English Eyes: The Nightmare and the Noble Dream," *Georgia Law Review* 969 (1977): 972.

court of law.[2] Attempts to find impartial legal standards for judicial decisions are dismissed for being inspired by nostalgia, by the childish vision of law with a capital "L" that prevailed in the past. They are condemned for refusing to face the truth that the courts cannot avoid satisfying one interest at the expense of another and that there can be no single, accepted standard for balancing interests. Since the judge is bound to decide according to some preestablished hierarchy of values or social goals, he necessarily decides which social preferences or goals will be given priority.

Against the old-fashioned, "idealized" view – that justice can be blind and provide an even-handed application of known principles to known facts – political jurisprudence summons witnesses from all fields of learning in all ages, each holding widely different opinions: Plato, Karl Manheim, Gunnar Myrdal, Michael Polanyi, Reinhold Neibuhr, Herbert Butterfield, Alfred North Whitehead, and Isaiah Berlin are all called in to testify that neutrality or objectivity is unattainable, both in the social sciences and in the natural sciences, since even facts involve a judgment of value. Because every human activity involves a choice among values, and because such choices are determined by the biography and heredity of the man making them, a wholly disinterested person or activity is impossible. The Supreme Court of the United States has rewritten history just as much as Soviet Communists have; the dissenting opinions of Holmes, Brandeis, and Stone in the late 1930s were no more neutral than the decisions that had earlier developed the substantive due process doctrine from the economic theories of Adam Smith and David Ricardo.[3] Although the advocates of political jurisprudence acknowledge that many cases are decided in accordance with "principles derived from past experience," they point out that the most important decisions are made in those areas of law where judges are divided by conflicting values. In such areas, only those whose battle has already been won plead for judicial self-restraint and insist that the function of the court is to defer to the legislature. They do so because the legislature is promulgating just what they want.

But even if judicial neutrality is impossible, objectivity can still be preserved, political jurisprudence argues, by requiring the judge to set

---

[2] Arthur Miller and Ronald Howell, "The Myth of Neutrality in Constitutional Adjudication," *University of Chicago Law Review* 27 (1960): 689, 659; M. Shapiro, *Law and Politics in the Supreme Court* (London: Macmillan, 1964), 23.

[3] Miller and Howell, "Myth of Neutrality," 665, 682–83, 675. See also: W. Murphy, "Lower Court Checks on Supreme Court Power," *American Political Science Review* 53 (1959): 1017.

out "in explicit form his value preferences as he understands them." If
that were done, the "resulting judgment, were it not for the semantic
problem, might even be termed 'objective'."[4] To explain and promote
this view of the courts, we now need a teleological jurisprudence that is
"purposive in nature" rather than "impersonal" or "neutral." Such a
jurisprudence would reject the old mechanistic view of the social process
and try "to provide purposive direction to the flow of social events."
Teleologic jurisprudence recognizes that the nature of government has
changed and that many of the jobs once done by the three traditional
branches of government are now being done administratively. The legislature merely formulates "broad policy guidelines for the conduct of our
government" and it is the executive and administrative agencies that relate
these guidelines to the complex facts of everyday life. In the same way the
courts have lost power. They now decide only the pathological case that
eludes the other branches of government or involves a "clash of values."
In settling cases of the latter sort, the court acts "as a national conscience
for the American people" and articulates "a broad norm" that transcends
the particular dispute and provides a standard "toward which men and
governments can aspire."[5]

All this happened, we are told, because nowadays "a dwindling minority of Americans espouse views of *laissez-faire*," and the old agreement on
goals, postulated by *laissez-faire*, no longer exists. We have to recognize,
the advocates of political jurisprudence urge, that the "social process" is
not governed by something called reason, as jurists once believed, but "is
a set of interlocking and interacting power relationships." These power
relationships have changed because those who had been suffering have
now become numerous and strong enough to exercise considerable lever-
age. And their political battles have become judicial in nature, which has
turned the courts into a political battleground. In the new picture, reason,
far from being the life of the law, is merely the language of political battle,
and the court is "a power organ which aids the shaping of community
values." The only question is whether it does so avowedly or abashedly.
The court is part of a welfare state, and it cannot avoid being concerned
with welfare. It can choose only whether to do so chaotically or explicitly
and systematically.[6]

A court that clearly recognizes this will see that the most important
question about a judicial decision is what effect it has on the realization
of "societal values." Such a court will see that disputes "should avowedly

---

[4] Miller and Howell, "Myth of Neutrality," 683, 678.
[5] Ibid., 693, 685, 687.   [6] Ibid., 687, 689.

be settled in terms of the external consequences of their application."[7] In decisions on antitrust laws, for instance, the judges would act as "political economists engaged in solving problems of economic organization" and would exercise "a freewheeling economic power."[8] To guide the judiciary in this operation, there are a number of suggestions, including a "law of human dignity"[9] and a "jurisprudence of welfare."[10]

All advocates of political jurisprudence pride themselves on rejecting the old "phonograph theory of justice" and replacing it with an "affirmative jurisprudence."[11] But this does not mean, they insist, that the judge will become arbitrary. It means that the judge will be "engaged in 'operational analysis' – in purposive directional thought – which is both a recognition of the creative nature of his job and a consideration of the forces that limit that creativity." Nor does it mean that the judiciary will become subservient to the state: "The judge may as easily act against the State as in support of it."[12]

The new political jurisprudence goes much further than its Realist predecessors in rejecting the traditional view of law. Even Thurman Arnold, Realist though he was, acknowledged some virtue in what he called Professor Hart's theology: Without "the shining but never completely attainable ideal of the rule of law above men. . . we would not have a civilised government. If that ideal be an illusion, to dispel it would cause men to lose themselves in an even greater illusion, the illusion that personal power can be benevolently exercised."[13] But the advocates of political jurisprudence do not believe that despotism is the only alternative to the rule of law, and they insist that what is expedient for the community provides a "more viable point of departure for a jurisprudence of the age of the positive state."[14]

Outright calls for a political jurisprudence are supplemented by more sophisticated suggestions for concentrating on an analysis of the problem of language and power by using a combination of semiology, phenomenology, and Marxism, by consulting the work of writers such as Levi-Strauss, Habermas, Barthes, and Althusser. Still other suggestions concentrate on explaining that legitimacy is only one "possible kind of effect of casting a political decision in legal form," the virtue of which has

---

[7] Ibid., 691.   [8] Shapiro, *Law and Politics*, 48.
[9] M. S. McDougal, *Perspectives for an International Law of Human Dignity*, American Society of International Law Proceedings, 1959.
[10] A. H. Pekelis, *Law and Social Action* (Ithaca: Cornell University Press, 1950).
[11] Miller and Howell, "Myth of Neutrality," 692.
[12] Ibid., 693.
[13] T. Arnold, "Prof. Hart's Theology," *Harvard Law Review* 73 (1960): 1311.
[14] Miller and Howell, "Myth of Neutrality," 695.

been vastly exaggerated, thus preventing "a more painstaking examination of the real factors which explain conforming behaviour." Or we are told that law should be regarded rather as a factor in the production of collective goods that depend on "mutual coercion."[15] But however much their programs differ, all these suggestions make a point of explicitly denying the distinction between a legal and a political decision that is central to the traditional idea of law.

The reduction of law to politics appears to be strongly opposed by those who have been trying to find new ways of establishing the objectivity of the law. These writers assume that doubts about the objectivity of judicial decisions arise from the lack of adequate statements of the criteria that govern adjudication, and they devote themselves to spelling out such criteria.

One of the more conservative suggestions is that of Professor George F. Christie, who argues that what is wanted are "fixed reference points" for legal reasoning that can be found in *uninterpreted* statutes and cases. He suggests that for the traditional question, Which is the true or correct rule for which a case or group of cases stands? we substitute the question, What factual differences distinguish one group of cases from another? This would reduce disputes about judicial decisions to "disputes about the significant factual differences among cases," which is a question that can be answered much more easily. Rigid adherence to precedent is not desirable, but because the court is required to demonstrate a plausibly significant difference in the facts of two cases that it proposes to decide differently, past cases cannot be lightly overruled.

Despite his concern for objectivity, however, Professor Christie does not exclude altogether the influence on the judge of personal values and goals. Since law is a purposive activity, he says, it must be founded on the human preferences and values often grouped together under the rubric "policy." One can only place limits on the judge's attempts to promote the goals and policies he favors: "In deciding new cases in accordance with the model, courts inevitably must and do legislate, but they can do so only in a restricted and stylised manner."[16] That Professor Christie's conception of law seems to differ from that of political jurisprudence makes it all

---

[15] Cf. Mark Tushnet, "Post Realist Legal Scholarships," *Wisconsin Law Review* (1980): 1383; R. Cover and O. Fiss, *The Structure of Procedure* (1979); Karl Klare, "Law-Making as Praxis," *Telos* 123 (Summer 1979): 40; John Griffiths, "Is Law Important?" *New York Law Review* 54: 339. The plausibility of political jurisprudence is re-enforced by such studies as J. A. G. Griffith's *The Politics of the Judiciary* (London: Fontana, 1977), designed to show the many ways "in which the judges can fulfill their political function and do so in the name of the law," p. 216.

[16] George C. Christie, "Objectivity in the Law," *Yale Law Journal* 78 (1969): 1311.

the more striking that he goes so far toward accepting its view of adjudication.

A more ambitious program for objectivity has been proposed by Professor Richard Wasserstrom. The problem, as he sees it, is to provide "natural" and "individualistic" adjudication that is at the same time objective. That a mechanical application of fixed rules and regard to precedent cannot provide justice has, he argued, always been recognized. Although that sort of decision "procedure" can provide certainty and efficiency, it applies legal rules to cases for no better reason than that they are extant legal rules. If the object is to dispense justice, it is obviously undesirable to apply rules in this manner because "the sterile unfeeling application of extant laws," which ignores the merits of each particular case, cannot secure justice. And that is why it has long been felt that only the procedure of equity, where each case is decided without reference to rigid rules and precedents, produces justice.[17]

But this conviction has not been found generally acceptable, Professor Wasserstrom says, because in the past those who advocated equitable procedures assumed that the only basis for such procedures was intuition. Since intuitions are essentially private affairs, there can be no evidence for the correctness of the conclusion other than that the 'intuitor' believes that he has had the proper intuition. Experience has shown that something more stringent is required to save us from arbitrary rule. Nevertheless, all is not lost. The benefits of an equitable procedure can be had without the drawbacks, Professor Wasserstrom suggests, if we accept a two-level system of justification.

In such a system, the court would be required to justify its decision, just as in the traditional view, by appealing to some legal rule. This insistence on invoking a rule to justify a decision would replace the amorphous intuitions of other proposals for equitable procedures. But appeal to a legal rule would not be mechanical and unfeeling because the rule itself would have to be justified on utilitarian grounds: "Thus, in contrast to the model of precedent, the process of justification does not come to an end once the relevant rule of law has been located and applied. On the contrary, a legal rule is a valid justification for any particular decision if and only if that rule is itself justifiable on utilitarian grounds. And unlike the model of equity, legal rules do play a role in the process of justification. Consideration of justice or utility are relevant, but only to the evaluation of rules of law, not to the decision in a particular case."[18]

---

[17] Christie, "Objectivity in the Law," 1338.
[18] R. Wasserstrom, *The Judicial Decision: Toward a Theory of Legal Justification* (Stanford, CA: Stanford University Press, 1961), 84.

Professor Wasserstrom's suggestion seems to accomplish the miracle that has always eluded legal systems, the marriage of objectivity with doing complete justice to the particularity and contingency of each case: Requiring the courts to justify their decisions by appealing to legal rules secures the litigants against judicial arbitrariness. Allowing judges to disregard precedent and established rules in favor of some other rules, when the principal of utility requires it, eliminates the drawbacks of applying general rules. And in assuring such objectivity, Professor Wasserstrom's proposal seems to be the very antithesis of political jurisprudence.

But the conception of law and adjudication that inspires his proposal makes the contrast somewhat less striking. Professor Wasserstrom's judge is not an officer authorized to decide what established rules mean with regard to particular occurrences. His job is not to decide whether what some person or persons have said or done conforms to the conditions stipulated by law. Professor Wasserstrom's judge is something very different – an arbitrator of conflicting interests who tries to produce "the most equitable" consequences for all parties. Far from supposing that justice has to be blindfolded because it requires deciding only one question – whether obligations laid down by the law have been met – Professor Wasserstrom asks the judge to consider whether the consequences of his decision are "more desirable for the litigants than those of any other possible decision." In other words, the judge is not bound to decide merely whether the accused had exploded a bomb to cause the death of the alleged victim and in so doing has violated the law; he has to decide whether using one rule or another will produce "a minimum of discomfort and a maximum of satisfaction vis-a-vis the two litigants." That the decision has to be filtered through a rule does not affect the central point of Professor Wasserstrom's jurisprudence, that its concern is with satisfying the interests of the litigants: "The consequences to them of deciding the case in one way rather than another are alone relevant to the question of what shall be regarded as justifiable decisions."[19]

The role of a legal rule in such a system is that of a working hypothesis, whose acceptance or rejection depends on whether its consequences are found to be satisfactory. That is why, although Professor Wasserstrom favors using the principle of utility to decide whether rules are desirable, he does not exclude the possibility of "sociological decisions" that would use "the best evidence obtainable from all fields of empirical inquiry."[20]

[19] Ibid., 122.   [20] Ibid., 114, 115, 114.

Nor does the introduction of rules make the judge less of a legislator in Professor Wasserstrom's system than in the other proposals of political jurisprudence. Indeed, he says explicitly that there is no reason why the legislator's question should not also be the judge's question. His system is designed to permit the judge to revise the established rule or practice "whenever it can be demonstrated that the introduction of a new rule or practice is more justifiable on utilitarian grounds." To do otherwise, to refuse to permit rules to be revised by the judge, he points out, "seems little better than an uncritical acceptance of the moral and social *status quo*."[21] Since in his system the courts are not bound to maintain the established rules, they would not be bound by the errors of earlier procedure. This means that they would be unhampered by tradition: "They could meet each case as it came along and feel free to decide it and nothing more."[22]

Professor Wasserstrom has not just refined or supplemented the traditional idea of equity but radically transformed its role in the legal system. Although it is true, as he says, that Aristotle wrote in praise of equity, Aristotle understood equity as an occasional qualification on the usual operation of the law. It is a qualification designed to correct the most flagrant anomalies produced by adjudicating according to fixed rules, which for Aristotle constituted the essence of law. Others, however, have emphasized the dangers of equity. It was denounced by Kant as "a dumb goddess who cannot claim a hearing," and by John Selden as "a roguish thing." And William Blackstone warned against "the liberty of considering all cases in an equitable light. . . lest thereby we destroy all law." But Professor Wasserstrom, for all the complexity of his two-level system, reduces the whole of law to equity. As a result, the judge in Professor Wasserstrom's system understands himself in much the same way as in all political jurisprudence – as a part of the political process. Although he writes his opinions in a different manner and is required to think in terms of the interests of the litigants rather than of the goals of the community or group that he wishes to promote, he is just as remote from the judge who is obliged to do nothing but interpret established law.

Critical Legal Studies (CLS)

At first, political jurisprudence claimed merely to be answering questions overlooked by their predecessors. But in the 1970s a more aggressive

---

[21] Ibid., 174–75. See also: F. V. Harper, "Some Implications of Juristic Pragmatism," *International Journal of Ethics* 39 (1929): 269.
[22] Wasserstrom, *Judicial Decision*, 134, 130.

warrior entered the lists – the Critical Legal Studies Movement (CLS) whose headquarters was at Harvard and disciples everywhere. Led by Roberto Unger and Duncan Kennedy, the CLS movement candidly announced that they were out to prove that the rule of law as we know it is a fiction. They were not all in perfect agreement. Some were avowedly Marxists; others were not. But all the Critical Legalists, like all the other advocates of political jurisprudence, were agreed in opposing what they call "liberal legalism" – the view that law is distinct from politics.

CLS scholars focused their attack not on the idea of rule of law directly, but on the merits of liberal society. They were intent on proving that the assumed connection between liberalism and the rule of law is erroneous, and that in reality liberalism creates hierarchical oppression and gross inequalities. According to Critical Legalists, liberalism places individual liberty as its central value. Consequently, individuals are free in liberal societies to choose for themselves what values they will embrace and how they will live. All values thus become subjective and law functions to protect citizens from illegitimate power as they go about pursuing their own self-interest.[23]

Critical Legal Studies exceeded the efforts of previous critical theories by moving beyond specific criticisms of various aspects of the legal system to an all-out attack on the system itself. In *Knowledge and Politics* (1975), a chief CLS text, Roberto Unger calls for "total criticism," as opposed to the "partial criticisms" of the past.[24] He boldly stated that CLS is devoted to making not merely a legal but also a cultural and political revolution. He envisioned the birth of a new egalitarian society where the law would serve to promote equality rather than domination.

Liberalism and the rule of law are inconsistent because liberal political theory contradicts liberal legal theory. Andrew Altman explains this CLS postulate: "The legal side is committed to the rule of law. The political side is committed to neutrality and to moral, religious, and political pluralism."[25] The pluralism of values extant in liberal states defeats the rule of law by producing widespread contradictions, inconsistencies, ambiguities, and gaps in the law. CLS scholars followed the lead of the Realists by seeking to demonstrate the existence of these difficulties, but transcended their efforts by linking such problems to a denial of the rule of law. According to Unger, liberalism creates the problem of deciding

---

[23] Andrew Altman, *Arguing About Law: An Introduction to Legal Philosophy*, 2nd ed. (Belmont, CA: Wadsworth, 2001), 302.
[24] Roberto Unger, *Knowledge and Politics* (New York: Free Press, 1975), 2.
[25] Andrew Altman, *Critical Legal Studies: A Liberal Critique* (Princeton, NJ: Princeton University Press, 1990), 104.

how the rules that govern society are to be justified. In the midst of competing and even contradictory values, how can lawmakers create laws that citizens will find authoritative and binding? Inevitably, Unger writes, "legislation has to choose among competing individual and subjective values, and to give preference to some over others."[26] The pluralism of values will thus be translated into society's governing rules, creating a system of law built on conflicting principles. So, Unger says, "there can be no coherent, adequate doctrine of legislation. . . on liberal premises."[27] Critical Legalists have produced a substantial body of research that documents the contradictions and inconsistencies prevalent in all areas of law, both public and private. Obviously, this made more sense as a critique of those twentieth-century liberal political theories which found the authority and justification for law in the true moral principles it embodied, rather than in agreement, as emphasized by other liberal theories.

Perhaps a more important, and deeper, source of conflict in the law stems from society's commitment to totally contradictory philosophies. Duncan Kennedy's article, "Form and Substance in Private Law Adjudication," argues that the law is shaped by two mutually exclusive ideologies, individualism and altruism. He describes individualism as the ethic of self-reliance and self-interest, which he opposes to altruism, the ethic of self-sacrifice and sharing.[28]

Kennedy's discussion of individualism and altruism makes an important distinction between rules and standards. Laws written in rule form are advantageous in minimizing judicial lawmaking and in maximizing certainty, but are disadvantageous in that they engender over- and under-inclusiveness. On the other hand, standards are flexible and can be altered to meet specific circumstances, reducing inclusiveness problems; but they are also more likely to produce arbitrary application and uncertainty. The virtues of rules are thus the vices of standards, and vice versa. Kennedy finds a strong association between rules and individualism and standards and altruism.

What Kennedy calls the rule of law "model" consists of the belief that legal rules are deduced from first principles like free will and that rules are mechanically applied to "fact" situations by a strictly neutral judge. The rule of law is necessary in an environment of individualism to preserve personal liberties in the face of extensive disagreement over political and

---

[26] Unger, *Knowledge and Politics*, 85.   [27] Ibid., 83.
[28] Duncan Kennedy, "Form and Substance in Private Law Adjudication," *Harvard Law Review* 89 (1976): 1767.

moral beliefs. Thus, the implied connections that he sees between the rule of law and individualism are many and various, and not at all unusual. Both were associated, he says, with *laissez-faire* and based on the belief that the less the state intervenes, the better the economic results. Both individualism and the rule of law reject "result orientation. . . in favour of an indirect strategy," that is to say they reject the view that legal decisions should be shaped so as to achieve desired results.[29] Both conceive of the legal system as a "limited set of existing restraints imposed on the state of nature" and refuse to "extend those constraints to new situations."[30] Both emphasize self-reliance – thus in contract law, since rules are knowable in advance, anyone who comes out badly from a contract has only himself to blame.[31] In short, the argument for rule enforcement is the twin of the argument that those who fare badly in the economic struggle should not be rescued by the intervention of the state. It is because the individualist wants to restrict sharing and sacrifice that he opposes broadening liability or liberalizing excuses and prefers a strict enforcement of rules. Individualism thus provides good reasons for choosing rules over standards when forming law.

The embrace of liberalism by Western culture has resulted in a legal system dominated by rules. Indeed, Kennedy writes, "The rhetoric of individualism so thoroughly dominates legal discourse at present that it is difficult even to identify a counter-ethic." But Kennedy believes just such an ethic exists in the philosophy of altruism. Altruism "is the belief that one ought not to indulge a sharp preference for one's own interest over those of others. Altruism enjoins us to make sacrifices, to share, and to be merciful. It has roots in culture, in religion, ethics and art, that are as deep as those of individualism." Altruism's focus on self-sacrifice and sharing translates into the redistribution of goods, and its legal equivalent, distributive justice.[32] The altruist, as opposed to the individualist, does not insist on the enforcement of rules, but prefers standards which only direct the judge to seek certain results. That way, the altruist believes, the judge will be encouraged to intervene to secure greater distributive justice and to save the weak from their own folly. The altruist accordingly denies that the legal arguments can be separated from moral, economic, and political considerations. He denies also that the judge can avoid making political judgments. For example, according to the altruist, when the judge refuses to interfere with freedom of contract, he is not enforcing the will of the legislature but giving private parties, and usually the dominant party, what they want.[33] This is a political outcome that the

[29] Ibid., 1741.   [30] Ibid., 1736.   [31] Ibid., 1739.
[32] Ibid., 1717.   [33] Ibid., 1761.

altruist deplores. He believes "that the judge should accept the responsibility of enforcing communitarian, paternalist and regulatory standards wherever possible."[34]

Now that it has become obvious that *laissez-faire* does not secure the splendid economic results that were once expected of it and more and more people have become converted to the altruistic vision, Kennedy informs us, the law has moved steadily toward altruism. Thanks to altruist scholarship, judges appear more competent to make "altruistic" interventions, and "virtually all the rules in our legal system" can be understood in at least one sense to already impose "altruistic duty" and are in effect standards and not rules.[35] Therefore when the altruist urges the abandonment of rules for standards, he is not proposing something new but only recognizing what is already there.

The history of law, according to Kennedy, is a progress to altruism in the course of a continuous struggle against individualism. Like most CLS scholars, Kennedy finds the most telling illustration of this in the development of contract law. It consists, according to Kennedy, of increasingly numerous and successful attempts to compensate for the fact that contracts are not always or even mainly made between perfectly equal partners and that the weaker is made to suffer in the name of the strict enforcement of legal rules. Over the years, judges moved by altruism have actively enlisted state supervision to ensure that each party gets what he *ought* to get, regardless of what was promised or performed. Thus, as moral sensibility has grown, the law has become increasingly cluttered with makeshift expedients introduced to remedy inequality. But these expedients leave the fundamental inequalities untouched and make the law a jumble of contradictions, containing both individualist rules and altruist standards.

This dual commitment to rules and standards, individualism and altruism, undercuts the consistency and clarity of the law. Kennedy concludes, "we are divided, among ourselves and also within ourselves, between irreconcilable visions of humanity and society, and between radically different aspirations for our common future."[36] The plurality of both individual and societal values leads one CLS commentator to describe law as "a patchwork of irreconcilable ideologies," which "faithfully reflects the fragmentation of our political culture."[37]

---

[34] Ibid., 1767.   [35] Ibid., 1721.

[36] Ibid., 1685. Kennedy also sees this conflict between individualism and altruism as shaping the history of law in the modern era; see later discussion.

[37] Andrew Altman, "Legal Realism, Critical Legal Studies, and Dworkin," in *Introduction to the Philosophy of Law*, ed. Jefferson White and Dennis Patterson (New York: Oxford University Press, 1999), 134.

Critical Legalists find important implications for the rule of law in the law's contradictions. They argue that for the rule of law to serve its end of protecting liberty in liberal societies, there must be some method of legal reasoning whereby citizens can come to know the meaning of the nation's authoritative laws and resolve their disagreements. Furthermore, if people are to feel an obligation to obey the law, judges must be able to justify their decisions on legal grounds, wholly independent of moral or political reasons. Unger recognizes that "if the law applier cannot justify his decisions [on purely legal grounds], because they appear to rest on his own personal and subjective values, liberty will suffer. Those to whom the law is applied will have surrendered their freedom to the judge."[38] Unger believes that the plurality of beliefs in liberal societies creates the need for a formalist method of legal reasoning, which he defines as "a commitment to, and therefore also a belief in the possibility of, a method of legal justification that can be clearly contrasted to open-ended disputes about the basic terms of social life."[39] This vision of adjudication infers a high level of legal determinacy, allowing people to accurately predict judicial decisions.

One of the major themes of CLS is that the contradictions within the law produce a high level of indeterminacy. They argue that if the law is mostly indeterminate then legal reasoning is a myth and law is merely politics. Altman explains the CLS argument: "doctrinal rules contain so many gaps, conflicts, and ambiguities that they must be supplemented by an appeal to underlying principles in order to attain a degree of determinacy acceptable to liberalism and consistent with the commitment to the rule of law."[40] Unger thus reasons that "formalism presupposes at least a qualified objectivism" for legal reasoning to be possible given the principles of liberalism.[41] This objectivism clearly does not exist given the conflicting political and ethical principles manifest in the law, leaving judges to choose by some extralegal method which of several competing principles to adopt. As there is no prescribed method for judges to choose between opposing principles, they are left with great freedom to choose according to the values they personally hold. Unger thus believes that "the judge will inescapably impose his own subjective preferences, or someone else's, on the litigants."[42] The contradictions and inconsistencies

---

[38] Unger, *Knowledge and Politics*, 89.
[39] Roberto Unger, "The Critical Legal Studies Movement," *Harvard Law Review* 96 (1983): 564.
[40] Altman, *Critical Legal Studies*, 118.
[41] Unger, "Critical Legal Studies Movement," 565.
[42] Unger, *Knowledge and Politics*, 95.

present in law make it impossible for judges to apply the neutral legal reasoning that is necessary for the rule of law to exist. "An especially important conclusion" for CLS scholars then, "is that no coherent theory of adjudication is possible within liberal thought."[43]

Legal historian Morton Horwitz extends the CLS assault on legal reasoning by dismissing the classical theory of objective causation. He explains that nineteenth-century Tory law was predicated on the notion that it is possible, through the application of the objective laws of natural science, to discover a singular event A that caused event B. This old notion of "objective causation" has been replaced, according to Horwitz, by modern theories which deny the "very possibility of factoring, but one discrete event and seriously viewing it as 'the cause' of another." The truth is that any event is the result of "a multiplicity of contributing causes" and therefore "to impute a determinate causal sequence to any given event is in fact to construct a story that selects its narrative from a literally infinite range of possibilities. There is no particular reason to select one narrative over another." This "acknowledgment of multiple causation" effectively serves to open "the floodgates for judicial discretion," leaving litigants subject to the personal biases of the judiciary.[44] Both Horwitz and Peter Gabel ascribe the old emphasis on objectivity in law to a blindness to human purposes and a misguided attempt to confuse social science with natural science.

In demonstrating the fiction of the rule of law, Critical Legalists also desire to expose the illegitimacy of society's institutions. A recurring theme of CLS literature is that law preserves society's unjust power relationships: "The law's perceived legitimacy confers a broader legitimacy on a social system . . . characterized by power."[45] The CLS attack on law is thus part of a larger attack on an oppressive social order. They believe these illegitimate relationships permeate society, including the "power of capitalist bosses over workers, of judges over litigants, of lawyers over their clients, of teachers over students, of adults over children, of whites over nonwhites, of men over women." All these relationships "are based largely on might rather than right," and "all of them should be dramatically reconstructed so as to create a more egalitarian society in which no one holds illegitimate power over anyone else."[46] Unger sees liberal legalism as the "guard that watches over the

---

[43] Ibid., 98.
[44] Morton Horwitz, "The Doctrine of Objective Causation," in *The Politics of Law*, ed. David Kairys (New York: Pantheon, 1982), 202 (201–13).
[45] David Kairys, ed., *The Politics of Law* (New York: Pantheon Books, 1982), 5–6.
[46] Altman, *Arguing About Law*, 285.

prison-house."[47] By exposing law's role in perpetuating this system, Critical Legalists hope to bring about a cultural or political revolution that will free people from illicit domination.

CLS finds in the current system of law personal alienation and the perpetuation of hierarchical structures. According to Peter Gabel, law is merely a reflection of "the alienation of persons from themselves." It consists, Gabel says, of "moments of interpretive activity arising in concrete social situations as an immediate modeling of social existence. This modeling evokes a structured language that corresponds to exigent relations of material production, yet struggles against this structure towards an understanding that would resolve its contradictions."[48] Diane Polan finds that the hierarchical structure of the law, its "combative adversarial format; and its undeviating bias in favour of rationality over all other values," all indicate that the law is "a fundamentally patriarchal institution" that has no place in progressive society.[49] Any concern to preserve the separation of powers is dismissed by the advocates of critical legalism as "ideology." Thus we are told, as in Shapiro's Law and Politics in the Supreme Court (1964) and Miller and Howell's essay "The Myth of Neutrality in Constitutional Adjudication" (1960), that only a nostalgia for a childish vision of law inspires the attempt to find impartial legal standards.[50] Such attempts simply refuse to face the truth that the courts cannot avoid deciding who should get what advantages; the only choice is whether the judge will do so openly or surreptitiously. What explains the power of the law is that it constitutes and legitimizes dominant power relations without appearing to do so.

In keeping with this basic insight of political jurisprudence, the Critical Legalists have devoted themselves to studying the history of different aspects of the law in order to produce a well-documented, new version of legal history in which the idea of law is replaced by a struggle for power. The law's perpetuation of a hierarchal social order can be tied to liberalism's inability to preserve the rule of law. CLS research, particularly in the area of contract law, is focused on revealing the oppression caused by liberal legalism. Concerning contract law, Karl Klare writes, "The underlying philosophical assumptions of the freedom of contract doctrine parallel those that characterise the classical liberal

---

[47] Unger, Knowledge and Politics, 3.
[48] Peter Gabel, "Intention and Structure, and Contractual Conditions," Minnesota Law Review 61 (1977): 601.
[49] Diane Polan, "Towards a Theory of Law and Patriarchy," in Kairys, ed., The Politics of Law, 301.
[50] Miller and Howell, "The Myth of Neutrality," 689, 659; Shapiro, Law and Politics, 23.

political tradition. . .." that "all values are arbitrary, subjective, and personal," that "society is an artificial aggregation of autonomous individuals who come together solely for the instrumental purpose of maximising personal satisfactions," that "the state should do no more than facilitate the orderly quest for such satisfactions; and that, because values are arbitrary and subjective, only the concurrence, actual or constructive, of individual desires can be standards of ethical obligation."[51]

In his study of the Wagner Act, Karl Klare explains that freedom of contract between workers and employers is a snare and delusion. What he calls "contractualist" jurisprudence either ignores "differences of economic or class power" or regards them as legitimate. The tendency of the freedom of contract doctrine throughout has been to treat as naturally preordained a historically contingent system of class relations. Klare praises the New Deal for producing "new doctrinal formulas" that enabled "progressive courts to brush aside some of the finer concerns and details of traditional private adjudication." In order to make way for the Wagner Act and other New Deal reforms, the distinction between public and private that characterized classical liberal theory had to be removed so as to allow the trade unions, which in the past had been deemed private, to assume the "functions, attributes or powers of quasi-governmental agencies. . ."[52] This hostility to making any distinction between the powers of public and private bodies is a persistent theme in all Critical Legalist writing.

The Wagner Act "became law," according to Klare's history, not when it was promulgated but only when employers were forced to obey its commands by the "imaginative, courageous, and concerted efforts of unheralded workers" who "seized control of their destinies and genuinely altered the course of American history." To the degree that the legal reforms were effective, however, they only helped to reenforce the oppression of the working class, because they reenforced the "institutional bases of that oppression, however much it improved the material circumstances of organised workers."[53] And this was only to be expected from law made by "experts socialised in elite institutions and distant from the lived reality of everyday life in capitalist society." The connection of this form of lawmaking with official violence and coercion, its impersonal, anti-participatory character, its insistence on the presentation of all moral judgments in the form of general supra-historical rules and its exaltation of

---

[51] Karl Klare, "Judicial Deradicalization of the Wagner Act and the Origins of Modern Legal Consciousness," *Minnesota Law Review* 62 (1978): 265.
[52] Ibid., 296.   [53] Ibid., 336.

property over human dignity, all make it inevitable that the result should be "a negation of the human spirit, even when the impulse to do justice and to accommodate to changing social priorities forces its way into the content of legal decisions. . ."[54] And finally Klare tells us that the history of the Wagner Act produced decisions which are "a chaotic amalgam of conceptualism and realism, ruleboundedness and ad hoc balancing, deference to non-judicial sources of law and unhesitating faith in the superiority of the judicial mind, in short a 'hodge-podge' that is characteristic of the self-divided modern legal consciousness."[55] All this is attributed to the "rule of law" ideal which separates law from ethics, and leaves people torn between conflicting aspirations.

While Critical Legal Studies is principally a criticism of liberal legalism rather than a theory of law, a vague constructive vision can be pieced together from its literature. A consistent theme in CLS writings is the need to refocus attention on the importance of group values, such as community and solidarity. This suggestion does not amount to a complete abandonment of liberalism and its focus on individual rights as some have supposed. CLS thinkers insist that they value liberty, but feel strongly that liberalism has gone too far in its emphasis of individualism. Unger thus laments, "the political doctrine of liberalism does not acknowledge communal values."[56] Through a revolution that balances both individual and group values, Critical Legalists hope to establish a new egalitarian society free from domination and oppression. No unified vision or theory for implementing this re-created society exists. Unger advocates a "theory of organic groups," with "the bureaucracies of welfare-corporate and socialist states" assuming increased responsibilities.[57] Others suggest less radical changes, preferring to reform the present legal system. Agreement seems to lie only in an opposition to existing legal practice and the need to reemphasize communal values.

This inability to find a constructive voice, along with other destructive forces, has seriously weakened the significance of Critical Legal Studies in today's legal academy. One major problem has been the movement's inability to accommodate the insights of competing critical theories, such as Critical Race Theory and Feminist Jurisprudence. Consequently, Critical Legalists lost their distinctive voice, and these alternate critical movements have been taken more seriously. Another deflating influence for CLS has been the softened stance several of their leaders have taken of late. Unger and Kennedy in particular have written more acceptingly of

---

[54] Ibid., 337–38.   [55] Ibid., 334–35.
[56] Unger, *Knowledge and Politics*, 76.   [57] Ibid., 23.

liberalism and the possibility of the rule of law.[58] While once offering vigorous criticisms of the rule of law, CLS now seems relegated to watching the Critical Race Theorists and Feminists build on its foundations.

Feminist legal theory

By the 1980s, Critical Legal Studies had helped give rise to a yet more aggressive branch of critical theory, feminist jurisprudence. Adopting the CLS postmodern critique of rationalism, its rejection of the supposed neutrality and objectivity of law, and its pessimism regarding liberal individualism, a burgeoning feminist movement quickly armed itself with the tools needed to undertake a deeper criticism of law and the legal structure.

By the time the CLS movement had reached its peak in the late 1970s and early 1980s feminism had undergone a significant revival. Inspired by the civil rights movement, feminists of the 1960s and 1970s once again asserted the right to equal protection and opportunity under law. Using what has come to be known as the classical liberal argument, feminists scored significant legal victories, from the legalization of abortion to the inclusion of sexual harassment as a form of sexual discrimination prohibited by law, and from the extension of law into the traditionally regarded private family sphere to greater protection against workplace discrimination. Liberal feminists asserted that subordination and inequality are caused by legal and social barriers which preclude women from entering the public sphere. Statutes and norms that discriminate based on stereotypical gender differences are therefore to be rejected based on the liberal assumption that all individuals are born equal and deserve equal treatment under law. The law should be gender blind and the supposed differences between men and women are stereotypical social constructions and should be discarded.

The removal of many of the formal legal barriers, however, exposed more subtle and immanently more pervasive forms of inequality. Feminists turned to arguing that the structure of law itself acted as an informal source of inequality. As a result, many of these early feminists were forced to rethink their previous positions, and, taking a far more critical approach to law and legal theory, they began developing a distinctly feminine legal theory.

---

[58] Altman, *Arguing About Law*, 311 n.12. See Duncan Kennedy, *A Critique of Adjudication* (Cambridge, MA: Harvard University Press, 1997), and Roberto Unger, *What Should Legal Analysis Become?* (London: Verso, 1996).

Feminist legal theorists argue that the traditional dichotomy between rational/irrational, reason/emotion, objective/subjective, principled/ personal, abstract/contextualized, which typifies traditional western thought, is both sexualized and hierarchized.[59] Women have generally been identified as irrational, emotional, subjective, and personal, while men are understood as objective, rational, and principled. Furthermore, the rational, objective side of the dichotomy is granted a dominant position over its irrational, subjective counterpart. Women are therefore subjugated to a subordinate status, a status that consequently renders them unsuited for the practice of law, which is rational, objective, and principled, or in other words, male. Likewise, feminists assert that the hierarchical structure of the legal system, its domination by male practitioners, and its ideologies and methodologies are distinctly male and as such act as informal sources of inequality. The law, they claim, is patriarchal and both intentionally and unintentionally excludes the voice of women. It is, in its present form, a male concoction which systematically oppresses women.[60] Feminist legal theorists thus embarked on a crusade to rid the law of its patriarchal bias, a crusade that would be far more critical of law and the culture it is part of than was the general feminist movement which had preceded it.

Intimations of the new crusade first appeared as early as the late 1960s at a conference on "Women and the Law" in New York. Annual conferences which followed promoted the proliferation of "Women and the Law" courses in law schools and attacks on "gender discrimination." In 1988, the Association of American Law Schools officially recognized Feminist Jurisprudence by devoting to it an entire issue of the *Journal of Legal Education*. For some time now, law journals have banned the pronoun 'he' (writing 'Judge Robert Thomas, she') and regularly carry articles on 'feminist law' by feminist professors.

As they turned to a theoretical and structural critique of law, feminists drew heavily from Critical Legal Studies. Accepting the central assumption of both CLS and its predecessor Legal Realism, feminists assert that law is political; indeed it is political precisely because it is patriarchal. As a result, the belief that the rule of law is designed to provide even-handed application of known rules to the facts of cases at law must therefore be discarded as a deceptive myth. Feminists likewise accept the central tenet

---

[59] See Frances Olsen, "Feminism and Critical Legal Theory: An American Perspective," *International Journal of Sociology of Law* 18 (1990): 199–215.
[60] See Robert Gordon, "New Developments in Legal Theory," in Kairys, *Politics of Law*, 281. John Schlegel, "Notes Toward an Intimate, Opinionated and Affectionate History of the Conference on CLS," *Stanford Law Review* 36 (1981): 391.

of all political jurisprudence, the tenet inherited from Karl Marx, that the human world consists of a struggle for power between weak and strong and that the strong use the legal system as an instrument of domination. To this view of law, feminists add the proposition that sexism is analogous to classism and racism, and that inasmuch as capitalism perpetuates class distinctions, the patriarchal order of society furthers the marginalization and subordination of women.[61]

However, the majority of feminists are quick to move beyond a strictly Marxist/Socialist analysis. They find that the subjection of women cannot be reduced to the principle of class subordination. Gender is more fundamental than class and sexual discrimination will not disappear with the termination of economic inequality.[62] They point to the patriarchal nature of the social structure as a whole rather than the economic structure as a source of female subordination.[63] Likewise, though originally called "Fem-Crits," feminist lawyers soon found the CLS movement wanting as well. At the CLS Conference of 1983, they complained of being "ghettoised,"[64] and argued that CLS had failed to recognize and account for the patriarchal bias of law. Accepting the CLS position that the reformation of law would require a more fundamental restructuring of society, feminists asserted that this restructuring would require the dissolution of patriarchy rather than simply reworking the capitalist socio-economic order.

The revolutionary intentions of feminists are plainly announced. Feminism is "political, methodological, philosophical, and intent upon social transformation," Professor Leslie Bender of Syracuse University declares, though she acknowledges that we cannot know the shape of this brave new world until domination of women is ended in all institutions.[65] Although the fierce denunciations of "patriarchy" and "male domination" and the determination to end the oppression of women both unify as well as distinguish feminist legal theory, the methodological approaches of many feminists, drawing on postmodern and poststructuralist critiques, propose a much more radical objective – an attack on all rational discourse.

---

[61] Catherine MacKinnon, "Feminism, Marxism, and the State: An Agenda for Theory," *Signs: Journal of Women in Culture and Society* 7 (1982): 515.
[62] Carole Pateman, *The Sexual Contract* (Cambridge: Polity, 1988), 134–36.
[63] See Diane Polan, "Toward a Theory of Law and Patriarchy," in *The Politics of Law: A Progressive Critique*, 3rd ed., ed. David Kairys (New York: Basic Books, 1998).
[64] Carrie Menkel-Meadow, "The Fem-Crits Go to Law School," *Journal of Legal Education* 38 (1988): 63.
[65] Leslie Bender, "A Lawyer's Primer on Feminist Theory and Tort," *Journal of Legal Education* 38 (1988): 4.

According to Catherine MacKinnon, the primary project of feminism is to unmask and destroy rationality and objectivity. She asserts that the point of view of male dominance is "the standard for point-of-view-lessness, its particularity the meaning of universality. Its force is exercised as consent, its authority as participation, its supremacy as the paradigm of order, its control as the definition of legitimacy."[66] Because of what MacKinnon describes as the near metaphysical perfection of male dominance, she finds hidden behind the apparent rationality and objectivity of the judicial system a distinctly male superstructure that has marginalized women by placing "maleness" as the "accepted" norm for public discourse. As a result, any attempt to secure sexual equality in the judicial system requires a comprehensive attack on the objectivity, rationality, and process of legal reasoning itself. As Professor Bender asserts, the feminist critique of patriarchy cuts so deep that after extracting the "male biases from our language, methods, and structures, we will have nothing – no words, no concepts, no science, no methods, no law," and there is nothing to regret in this.[67]

The feminist rejection of objectivity, however, is not absolute. Many feminists feel that such a radical attack is unnecessary. Martha Nussbaum, for example, challenges what she calls the "feminist assault on reason," arguing that reason is the weapon of resistance to oppression – not the mode of oppression and that abandoning such a tool will unnecessarily damage the feminist project.[68] Liberal feminists claim that the irrationalities of sexist doctrines can be exposed using the legal system's own norms and procedures. The current legal structure therefore need not be abandoned. However, feminists like Wendy Williams are skeptical about the judiciary's ability to expose inequalities.[69] Finally, others like Katherine Bartlett and Martha Minnow assert that inasmuch as the female voice has been largely excluded from the judicial process, the infusion of a distinctly feminine rationale would significantly improve legal reasoning.[70]

All feminists struggle against the phenomenon of male dominance, but the objective is often nothing so naive as to give women equal rights with

---

[66] Catharine MacKinnon, "Feminism, Marxism, Method, and the State: Toward Feminist Jurisprudence," *Signs: Journal of Women in Culture and Society* 8 (1983): 638–39.
[67] Bender, "Feminist Theory and Tort," 19.
[68] Martha Nussbaum, "Review of Feminist Philosophy," *New York Review of Books* (October 20, 1994): 59, 62.
[69] See Wendy Williams, "The Equality Crisis: Some Reflections of Culture, Courts, and Feminism," *Women's Rights Law Reporter* 7 (1982): 175.
[70] See Katharine Bartlett, "Feminist Legal Methods," *Harvard Law Review* 103 (1990): 829; and Martha Minnow, "Justice Engendered," *Harvard Law Review* 101 (1987): 10.

men. Although they agree that the terms of social discourse have been set by men, there is not so clear a consensus when dealing with the ramifications this has for the concept of equality. Departing from the arguments of liberal feminism, many relational (or cultural) and dominance feminists reject the liberal notion that equality can be gained through equal treatment. Rather, they argue that the concept of equality itself is distinctly male. "Equality" as understood and interpreted by the courts, means "the same as" men, and "different" thus means unequal.[71] Consequently, in order for women to gain equality they must conform to a male standard, which would reduce feminists to the banal level of suffragettes, asking merely to be let in, without correcting the system itself.[72] The ambition of feminist lawyers is, therefore, to purify legal concepts of any male connotations of objectivity and neutrality which, by requiring men and women to be treated equally, in effect subject women to male standards. Concerns with formal legal equality thus horrify feminists because it prevents us from seeing whether actual material conditions have moved closer to "real" or "substantive equality" measured in empirical terms such as income or desegregation in employment, schools, and other institutions.[73]

This feminist attitude toward legal equality is heavily influenced by the research of Professor Carol Gilligan, a Harvard psychologist, who argues that girls tend to score poorly on tests measuring the power of moral reasoning because the tests are based on male norms such as rights and abstract principles of justice.[74] She asserts that the male approach to morality is to abstract the moral problem from the interpersonal level by establishing universal values and principles. The female concept of morality, however, focuses instead on the network of relations wherein the dilemma occurs and then seeks to secure through communication a resolution in the best interest of all. The female ethic is an ethic of care, while the male ethic is an ethic of value or right.[75] The girls, therefore, do badly, according to Professor Gilligan, because their attention is focused on people's dependence on one another. Being child-bearers and having worked as secretaries and cleaning staff, women generally identify with oppressed groups as they know from experience the evils of being an "underclass." But such considerations are necessarily ignored by a system

---

[71] Christine Littleton, "Restructuring Sexual Equality," *California Law Review* 75 (1987): 1282.
[72] Janet Rifkin, "Toward a Theory of Law and Patriarchy," *Harvard Women's Law Journal* 3 (1980): 85.
[73] Bender, "Feminist Theory and Tort," 26f.
[74] Carol Gilligan, *In a Different Voice* (Cambridge, MA: Harvard University Press, 1982).
[75] Gilligan, *In a Different Voice*, 32, 74.

that resolves problems from male vantage points which are distanced, abstract, and acontextual.

Building on Professor Gilligan's insights, relational feminists are prone to divide the world into two kinds of beings: those who "confront problems contextually" with "particularity and sensitivity to feelings and physical needs," and those who think in terms of universals, principles, rules, distinctions, and consistency. Women, they believe, instinctively exhibit the former attitude; the latter is the male view, which has dominated civilization. They adopt the traditional dichotomy between rational/ irrational and its sexualization; however, they reject the hierarchical superiority of rational, objective, and principled, over irrational, subjective, and personal. Equality can therefore only be gained when the legal system is restructured to accept the female side of the dichotomy as equally applicable to legal decision-making.

Whereas both liberal feminists and relational feminists focus on the differences between men and women, thus debating whether women should be treated the same as, or differently from men, dominance theorists, led by Catherine MacKinnon, argue that the affirmation of differences actually guarantees continued inequality. These feminists therefore abhor the traditional distinctions between male and female. Distinctions between what is rational and irrational, objective and prejudiced, principled and arbitrary, as well as private and public, personal and political are not condemned simply for belonging to the cold male outlook, they are rejected primarily because they are the vehicles of male dominance. Catherine MacKinnon explains that the difference approach of liberal and relational feminists fails to recognize that gender itself is socially constructed by men to subjugate women. She explains that the difference between sexes amounts to "the systematic relegation of an entire group of people to a condition of inferiority and attribute[s] it to their nature."[76] Gender is in essence "an inequality first, constructed as a socially relevant differentiation in order to keep that inequality in place," and because of this, "sex inequality questions are questions of systematic dominance, of male supremacy."[77] To formulate the feminist project in terms of equality is therefore a self-defeating approach. Feminists must begin by recognizing that gender, sexuality, and difference are all systematic modes of domination, and to adopt the difference approach and fight for equality without redefining it will continue to reenforce women's inferior position.

[76] Catherine MacKinnon, *Feminism Unmodified* (Cambridge, MA: Harvard University Press, 1987), 41.
[77] Ibid., 42.

Many feminists take an even harder line with what used to be prized as the leading virtue of the law – its formality and abstraction. They deplore the fact that legal rules are made in advance and without knowledge of the particular circumstances in which they will be invoked. They are distressed that judges are obliged to hand down "objective, rule-based decisions supported by notions of individual autonomy, individual rights, the separation of self from others, equality, and fairness." These feminists feel that true justice can be served only when all this is replaced with more "personal" ways of resolving conflicts which would be based on "caring (compassion and need), equity, and responsibility."[78]

But the most comprehensive achievement of feminist legal theory has been its influence on courts and legislators in the specific areas of law such as torts and contracts, its influence on legal education, and its invention of the crime of sexual harassment. Their general convictions are given practical expression in two campaigns: to transform the law schools, and to introduce new legal concepts.

In law schools, feminists seek to replace "authority" in the classroom with "shared leadership," "competition" with "trust" and "cooperation," and exclusive reliance on impersonal knowledge with the acceptance of "personal experience" as a legitimate source of knowledge.[79] Feminists teach that law is above all a support for a hierarchical system, which is reenforced by the submission of students to teachers in classrooms constructed in the shape of an amphitheater. Teachers question unwilling students in a fashion that compels them to recognize the inherently hierarchical logic of the law, by which feminists mean the movement in a legal argument from rules, to the facts of the case, to conclusions about guilt or liability. This kind of reasoning, according to feminists, teaches people to see the real world from above looking down. Law students thus learn to value the theory of law more than the practice of law and to believe that the essence of law is respect for rules rather than concern for real people. Although students enter the law school with an instinctive aversion to the conclusions of the "'reasoned' analysis" that their teachers impose on them, they emerge having learned to think in terms of "rationally derived universal principles" and believing that there are "legally relevant distinctions between acts and omissions."[80]

---

[78] Bender, "Feminist Theory and Tort," 28.
[79] See generally, Nancy Schiedewind, "Feminist Values: Guidelines for Teaching Methodology in Women's Studies," in *Learning our Way: Essays in Feminist Education,* ed. Charlotte Bunch and Sandra Pollock (Trumansburg, NY: Crossing Press, 1983).
[80] Bender, "Feminist Theory and Tort," 33–34.

These distinctions prevent students from recognizing that knowledge and truth are subjective and personal, that human beings are not autonomous, self-interested, and competitive but "interdependent, collective, cooperative, and caring," and that "what were experienced as personal hurts individually suffered" are really "a collective experience of oppression;" in short, that "the personal is political."[81]

Although feminists build on the CLS critique of legal education they also diverge from it. Some feminist legal educators support CLS suggestions for reorganizing law schools so as to destroy the distinction between professor and student, as well as better and worse students, by rotating students and teachers at random among the various law schools.[82] Likewise, they welcome the suggestion that instead of teaching the established doctrine, law schools should concentrate on showing the "indeterminacy and manipulability of rules" so as to "destabilize" or "trash" the study of law and ultimately the whole legal system.[83] However, the majority of feminist scholars replace the CLS desire to teach deconstruction or "trashing" (both techniques of breaking down) with models that depend upon teaching empowerment (building up through collaborative experience sharing), consciousness-raising (seeking new perspectives through similar collaborative experience sharing and personal narratives), and flexible problem-solving strategies.[84] The feminist educational model, explains Carrie Menkel-Meadow, is one in which "building trust, collaboration, engagement, and empowerment would be the pedagogical goals, rather than reinforcing the competition, individual achievement, alienation, passivity, and lack of confidence that now so pervade the classroom."[85]

Overall, the feminist critique of tort law is concerned primarily with its ability to secure justice. Tort law is based largely on a strong conception of individual rights and a notion of how rational individuals would behave and the degree of responsibility they should have for their actions. Feminists contend that these fundamental assumptions and standards are male. Leslie Bender explains that the "reasonable person" standard, like all "universally applicable measures for conduct," is designed to "encourage conformity" with the "dominant ideological stance."[86] The reasonable person, feminists argue, represents men; the "rational man" is male. Professor Bender finds this male bias painfully manifest in the fact

---

[81] Ibid., 9.
[82] Menkel-Meadow, "Fem-Crits Go to Law School," 70.
[83] Mark Kelman, "Trashing," *Stanford Law Review* 36 (1984): 293.
[84] Menkel-Meadow, "Fem-Crits Go to Law School," 81.
[85] Ibid., 81.   [86] Bender, "Feminist Theory and Tort," 20–23.

that the existing law of torts imposes no obligation unless the bystander had a prior duty to the particular person in trouble. It would be less objective, and hence less oppressive, to speak of the care required of a "neighbor" or "social acquaintance." That would acknowledge that we are all interconnected rather than separate, give "safety priority over profit and efficiency" and thus make the law "a positive force in encouraging and improving our social relations."[87] Because of the male focus on "rights, autonomy, and abstraction," tort law now ignores "human needs and hurts."[88] She insists that it should instead give priority for a victim's interest "in having his life saved" over the bystander's interest in minimizing the burden of legally imposed "affirmative duties."[89]

In keeping with such insights, many feminists want to rid the law of its exclusive focus on individual rights and transform it into bundles of group rights. According to Bender, "We need. . . to help change the dominant ideology from individualistic to interconnected. We need to shift from a right-based focus to a focus on both care and rights/justice, from power-over to empowering, from the prioritizing of the market and money to a priority of personal relationships, health, safety, and humanitarian dignity in deciding personal injury disputes."[90] Feminists are anxious to give duties precedence over rights, and would accordingly reform the law of torts so as to impose a duty on *any* bystander to assist *anyone* injured or in danger.

Bender asserts that the reformation of tort law must rest on the proposition that "no one should be hurt," for otherwise people are "decontextualized,"[91] a claim she bases on the formulation of feminine ethics proposed by Gilligan. Other feminists such as L. Finley,[92] Naomi Cahn,[93] and Judith Butler,[94] however, reject Professor Bender's critique. They claim that her effort to formulate a unified feminine approach to tort law falls victim to the same faults she renounces in the male view: oppressing the individuality of experience through the standardization of a uniform experience. The acceptance of a fixed conception of gender identity necessarily creates an exclusionary categorization. MacKinnon

---

[87] Ibid., 30–31.   [88] Ibid., 31.   [89] Ibid., 34–35.

[90] Bender, "Feminist (Re) Torts: Thoughts on the Liability Crisis, Mass Torts, Power and Responsibilities," *Duke Law Journal* (1990): 848.

[91] Bender, "Feminist Theory and Tort," 31, 35.

[92] See Lucinda Finley, "A Break in the Silence: Including Women's Issues in a Torts Course," *Yale Law Journal* 1 (1989): 41.

[93] See Naomi Cahn, "The Looseness of Legal Language: The Reasonable Woman Standard in Theory and Practice," *Cornell Law Review* 77 (1992): 1398.

[94] See Judith Butler, "Gender Trouble, Feminist Theory and Psychoanalytical Discourse," in *Feminism/Post-Modernism*, ed. Linda Nicholson (New York: Routledge, 1990), 325.

goes so far as to reject Gilligan's feminine ethic altogether, arguing that it is essentially the male characterization of femininity.[95] Finally, so dedicated are feminists like Professor Bender to imposing duties that they propose no limit on the kind or intensity of misfortune that strangers to the sufferer should be required to relieve. Nor do they suggest how such a multitude of "affirmative duties" could be effectively enforced by anything other than an awfully efficient police state.

Contract law is another target of the feminist critique, although here they follow a trail well marked by all varieties of political jurisprudence. Like their male counterparts, they regard contracts as at best a nuisance, but more probably sinister. Although, following the CLS model, feminists agree that contract law is largely a means whereby the powerful maintain the status quo, they depart from this critique by shifting the focus of their analysis to gender inequality. They argue that contract law, with its cold, individualistic language and its exclusion from the private sphere of home and family, fails to protect women and thus perpetuates female subordination.[96] As a result, they attach little importance to the niceties of the contract agreed. If a woman sues a moving company for damaging her goods, the fact that she had signed a contract waiving insurance is less important than the fact that she "had not read the contract because the house was really cold and the men were tired and in a hurry to get out." She was "acting like a reasonable woman," explains Professor Mary Joe Frug, because women are "socialised to value other people's feelings highly."[97]

But despite their passionate antipathy to the rule of law as traditionally understood, feminist legal scholars cannot agree on what their new vision of "law" requires. They are divided about whether equal treatment for men and women in education should mean affirmative action favoring women or whether women should attend separate schools because, unless women are treated differently, the results will not be equal. Some feminists demand that "treatment as equals," when applied to pregnant women, should be interpreted as "special treatment" which takes into account biological differences. Against this, other feminists argue that pregnancy should be treated like any other temporary physical disability, because special privileges for pregnant women would prove detrimental to women in the long run, just as protective labor legislation kept women out of higher-paying jobs.

---

[95] MacKinnon, *Feminism Unmodified*, 38–39.
[96] See generally, Nadine Taub and Elizabeth Schneider, "Women's Subordination and the Role of Law," in Kairys, ed., *Politics of Law*.
[97] Tamar Lewin, "Feminist Scholars Spurring a Rethinking of Law," *New York Times*, September 30, 1988.

Even about the treatment of pornography feminists disagree. Catharine MacKinnon advocates allowing injunctions against pornographers who "traffic in materials that can be proven to subordinate women." But she is fiercely opposed by those who regard her suggestions as an invitation to censorship contrary to the spirit of the First Amendment. And black feminists criticize white feminists for ignoring the experiences of non-white women; similarly lesbians criticize heterosexual women, underprivileged women criticize rich women, and Western women are criticized by non-Western women for their ethnocentric approach. Indeed, the disagreements have been multiplying so quickly that feminist jurists now feel compelled to explain that – though their movement at first wanted women to be treated like men – it has progressed to recognizing that women differ not only from men but even from one another. This movement has led to a powerful postmodern, anti-essentialist argument[98] that threatens to fragment feminist legal theory into numerous essentially ineffective individual theories. The ultimate success of feminism as both a legal theory as well as a general social revolution will depend largely on how it meets this challenge.

For the moment, however, there is agreement on the crime invented by Professor Catharine MacKinnon – sexual harassment stemming from a hostile work environment. That invention is only one aspect of her campaign to protect women from unjust subjection. She has toured the United States proclaiming that sexual violence against women often pervades all relationships between men and women, even the voluntary ones. She has campaigned vigorously against allowing courts even to consider in rape cases whether the accused believed that his victim had consented. Professor MacKinnon insists that the victim's (that is, the accuser's) point of view matters most: in harassment cases the intention of the male is less important in determining whether a hostile environment exists.

The latitude now allowed in the USA in cases concerning sexual aggression has exempted women even from the rule that force may be used in self-defense only when there is an imminent threat and only in the degree needed to fend off the attacker. The courts have been persuaded to consider expert testimony on the psychology of battered wives so that a woman who killed her husband in his sleep has been acquitted on grounds of self-defense. That a woman continues to live with her husband no longer counts against her because, it is argued, she does so out of fear

---

[98] See *Feminist Legal Theory: An Anti-Essentialist Reader*, ed. Nancy E. Dowd and Michelle S. Jacobs (New York: New York University Press, 2003).

that he would become more violent if she left. The governors of both Ohio and Maryland have commuted the prison sentences of a number of women convicted of killing or assaulting men on the ground that the women were living "in a constant state of danger of death." In short, the contribution of feminist jurisprudence in this area may be summed up as follows: If a man is alleged to have raped a woman, his belief that she had consented to intercourse may not be considered by the court, however warranted by the apparent facts of the case; if a woman is alleged to have murdered a man, her belief that she was threatened by him will often be accepted by the court, however contrary to the apparent facts of the case. Both are applauded by feminist scholars as the result of casting aside general rules and examining each case on its contextual merits.

Most feminist legal theory makes little pretense of respecting the traditional idea of law. It bluntly repudiates the maintenance of fixed rules and the requirement that judges should decide cases in terms of such rules. Far from seeking to perfect the objectivity of judges or equality before the law, feminist jurisprudence rejects any such concerns as, at best, irrelevant and, more likely, evil. All this follows from regarding the subjects of law not as independent agents pursuing their own projects but as objects of care and compassion, in whatever sense feminists choose to attach to those words.

14   Political jurisprudence II: Ronald Dworkin

Radical as these criticisms are, none constitutes so thorough an attack on the idea of law as the theory of Ronald Dworkin. His attack is all the more effective because, far from identifying himself with political jurisprudence, he claims – at least sometimes – to be defending a strict understanding of the rule of law. His thorough treatment of the systemic restraints surrounding judicial decision-making allows his theory, he says, to solve difficulties that, though recognized, had not been adequately dealt with by his positivist predecessors. Furthermore, by recognizing such restraints, Dworkin addresses the judicial subjectivity thought inimical to the traditional idea of law much more effectively than other political or realist legal theories. By positioning his theory between two leading jurisprudential schools while at the same time presenting it as an exercise in traditional jurisprudence, Dworkin exposes more precisely what is at issue between the new and old attitudes toward law while at the same time successfully disguising the radical nature of his attack.

Dworkin argues that even in hard cases where there are no clear answers, judges are still bound by a web of principles, political theories, and cultural norms. They are not, therefore, free to act as unbound legislatures when existing law dictates no obvious solution. However, in developing his argument Dworkin also asserts that in any judicial action, whether interpreting law and precedent or breaking new legal ground, judges rely on a personal legal theory which combines political, cultural, and legal considerations. In the end, although legal decision-making is restrained by principles, rules, precedent, and the requirements of legal reasoning, a certain judge's political theory often heavily informs if not entirely determines the decision. Thus, according to Dworkin, because legal theory and political theory are inseparably interdependent, legal decision-making, especially in hard cases, is to a very large degree political.

Dworkin's arguments, however, are often intricately complex and seldom easy to understand, a fact that has led numerous scholars to read him on both sides of the issues he deals with. He has been understood by some to be promoting political jurisprudence theories while others see him as a defender of positivism. Natural lawyers accuse him of arguing against any fixed morality in law, while many claim his theories are most properly described as natural law. These conflicting interpretations of theories are often traceable to Dworkin himself as he has been accused of changing positions throughout his writings without admitting it. Regardless however of the complexity, obscurity, or shifting nature of his arguments the relation his theories have to the idea of law is clear. Although Dworkin often appears to be defending the classic formulation of this ideal, or merely to be promoting a restrained political theory of law, when the major body of his work is analyzed and the consequences of the ideas developed therein are identified, it becomes clear that what he is proposing is a radical departure from the traditional idea of law.

Dworkin's theory appeared in three installments, the first two – *Taking Rights Seriously* (1977) and *A Matter of Principle* (1985) – being collections of essays inspired by issues of the day, while the third, *Law's Empire* (1986), is a systematic exposition of law. In each book Dworkin addresses the philosophy of law from a different standpoint and employs a new and distinctive vocabulary. However, the moral of his story has remained the same in all – law and political theory are so inexorably intertwined that law and politics are essentially one.

Dworkin's political digressions from the traditional idea of law are least obvious in *Taking Rights Seriously*, which was regarded by many as a vigorous defense of the independence of law from politics. Indeed, that is what Dworkin himself suggests when he says that the book offers a "liberal" theory of law, designed to correct the failings of the "ruling" theory, " positivism," founded by Jeremy Bentham, and best exemplified nowadays in the work of H. L. A. Hart, Dworkin's predecessor as Professor of Jurisprudence at Oxford.

Dworkin launches his attack on positivism at what is certainly its Achilles heel, i.e., that positivists have not succeeded in explaining what bearing considerations of justice have on our obligation to observe the law, and why the disagreements among lawyers and judges about how cases should be decided do not render all legal decisions questionable. Dworkin blames both these difficulties on the narrow definition of law used by the positivists. Because they hold that there is a clear test for distinguishing legal rules from non-legal standards, he argues, positivists conclude that whenever the judge relies on anything other than legal rules, he must go beyond the law. Consequently, in hard cases where legal rules appear to "run out," the judge is obliged to exercise unconstrained discretion. Moreover, by insisting on a sharp distinction between legal rules and non-legal standards, positivists sever law from morality. If his solution were accepted, Dworkin argues, judges would not be left free to make law as they pleased in "hard cases," and moral considerations would necessarily enter into legal decisions.

Dworkin says that he is defending a strict view of adjudication when he maintains that there is a "right answer" even for hard cases, and that the judge ought never to exercise discretion. This has led Hart to describe Dworkin as an exponent of the "Noble Dream" – "the faith, that, in spite of superficial appearances to the contrary and in spite even of whole periods of judicial aberrations and mistakes," law is never "incomplete, inconsistent, or indeterminate" because "for every conceivable case there is some solution which is already law before he decides the case and which awaits his discovery."[1]

The reason why there is always a right answer, Dworkin explains, is that the law includes not only formal rules and decisions, but also all those principles and standards that are postulated by the formal law. Beyond the statutes, precedents, and the constitutional law of a community, Dworkin argues, there are general principles of fairness and justice that are not explicit, authoritative decisions of any kind, but which can be inferred from the more obvious legal materials. In order to make use of such materials, the judge has to formulate a "political theory" that can coherently accommodate everything that he has found in the law. He can then decide hard cases based on that theory.[2] Each judge is obliged to construct his own theory independently of other judges; what others believe to be the soundest theory should not be taken into account. An additional "theory of mistakes" can enable the judge to discard precedents in a systematic manner, and no questions are excluded from the court's agenda.[3]

At first sight, this may not seem to be a radical view. Ever since law came to be seen as a systematic unity, it has been accepted that any interpretation of a rule of law must somehow take into account its relation to the whole body of law in which it is found. This is what makes it plausible to suppose that Dworkin is not departing from a traditional view of law. That conclusion is supported, moreover, by his emphasis on distinguishing between principles and policies. Principles, he tells us, ascribe benefits to individuals on the ground that they possess a right to them, whereas policies grant benefits on the ground that doing so will promote some collective goal such as national prosperity. Policies are the proper ground for legislative decisions, but not for judicial decisions, which should be based on principles.[4]

---

[1] H. L. A. Hart, *Essays in Jurisprudence and Philosophy* (Oxford: Clarendon, 1983), 132, 138.
[2] Ronald Dworkin, *Taking Rights Seriously* (London: Duckworth, 1977), 81–88.
[3] Ibid., 118–21.   [4] Ibid., 22.

However, inasmuch as Dworkin attempts to use what is undeniably a descriptively successful theory of adjudication as a prescriptive theory of how judges should act or as a jurisprudential theory of what law is, it becomes clear that he is saying something quite different. An illustrative example is his comment on the decisions in the Fugitive Slave cases by Justices Story and Shaw. The Fugitive Slave Acts enacted by Congress made it obligatory to return slaves who had escaped to free states to their masters. And these statutes conformed to Article Four of the Constitution, which provides that the escaped slave "shall not, in consequence of any law or regulation of the latter, be discharged from that service, 'but shall be delivered up on Claim of the Party to whom such service or labour may be due.'" Because the law seemed to them to be perfectly clear, the judges ordered the slaves to be returned to their masters even though they themselves were strongly opposed to slavery.[5]

Dworkin accuses the justices of a "failure in jurisprudence." He argues that if they had acted in terms of his theory, they would have found in the law implicit principles that yielded a clear decision in favor of the slaves. "The general structure of the American Constitution," he says, "presupposed a conception of individual freedom antagonistic to slavery, a conception of procedural justice that condemned the procedures established by the Fugitive Slave Acts, and a conception of federalism inconsistent with the idea that the State of Massachusetts had no power to supervise the capture of men and women within its territory. These principles were not simply the personal morality of a few judges, which they set aside in the interests of objectivity. They were rather, on this theory of what law is, more central to the law than were the particular and transitory policies of the slavery compromise."[6] According to Dworkin, these are the principles that the judges should have enforced in order to discharge their duty to apply the law.

In addition, Dworkin argues that "the law was not already settled against the Slaves, though the judges said it was." Of course, what is "settled" in the law is as disputable as everything else, but it is difficult to imagine how the law could be more clearly settled than it was in these cases. In denying this finality, Dworkin is permitting both himself and the judges a remarkable freedom to decide what is "settled law." He claims a similar freedom in his interpretation of the "principles," which he takes to be the proper ground for the decision in the Fugitive Slave cases since it is by no means clear that his view of the general principles of

---

[5] Ronald Dworkin, "The Law of the Slave-Catchers," review of *Justice Accused*, by Robert M. Cover, *Times Literary Supplement*, 5 December 1975, 1437.
[6] Ibid.

justice and fairness implicit in "the general structure of the American Constitution" is the only possible one.[7] Whereas Dworkin provides no arguments to support his view, simply assuming the modern rejection of intolerance and inequality as self-evident, it would be entirely reasonable, as Hart and others have pointed out, to extract from the same principles quite the opposite conclusion, thereby upholding the decisions against the slaves. Indeed, Dworkin himself admits this possibility, and argues in return that because decisions based on liberal principles will more likely preserve individual liberty, liberals will largely agree with his position.[8]

That such diverse interpretations should be possible is hardly surprising since, as philosophers have pointed out since ancient times, any general proposition may yield a variety of particular conclusions and the more general, the greater the variety. Dworkin's broad and vague "principles" are even more vulnerable than ordinary legal rules to the indeterminacy involved in moving from general to particular propositions. In effect, by allowing, indeed requiring, judges to rest decisions on "principles" and a "political theory" that they have constructed for themselves, Dworkin's theory allows the sort of abuses that Bentham censured when he argued against fictions that permitted the judge to impose his own views under the pretence that he is finding what the law really is. Dworkin himself admits that different judges might construct different theories from the same materials and that it is impossible to demonstrate that any one is indisputably correct. Nevertheless, he insists that truly moral judges will not feel bound by formal rules.[9]

Dworkin's ultimate justification for not relying solely upon formal legal rules is an appeal to individual "rights." Making use of the term "rights" in its strongest sense, he argues that they are indisputable truths by which the law might be judged. He supports his strong understanding of rights by arguing that any government constructed to ensure individual rights must accept rights as not only outside and anterior to the law, but also possibly antagonistic to the law by providing grounds for a claim to new laws or even revolutions. An appeal to "rights" may also justify disobeying the law when it "wrongly invades his rights against the Government." For example, if we recognize the right to free speech, Dworkin says, it follows that a man has "a moral right to break any law that the Government, by virtue of his right, had no right to adopt."[10] He insists that the right to disobey the law is not separate from but intrinsic to all the rights

[7] Ibid.
[8] *Ronald Dworkin and Contemporary Jurisprudence*, ed. Marshall Cohen (Totowa, NJ: Rowman and Allanheld, 1984), 274–75.
[9] Ibid., 112–17.   [10] Ibid., 192.

against the government and cannot be denied in principle without denying those rights. Thus, if a government accepts principles of individual liberty, the denial of any particular fundamental right must come at the great cost of rejecting the very foundation upon which that government is built.

To see how Dworkin arrives at his "rights theory," the first point to notice is how he uses the idea of a "rule." He defines a rule as a proposition, which produces indisputable decisions, as opposed to a "principle," which states moral standards open to a number of different interpretations. This might appear to be, as Dworkin suggests, merely a clarification of accepted ideas about the law because judges and jurists do speak of "principles" and "rules." But they use the two words to distinguish levels of abstraction in the law. Although rules are less abstract than principles, they are propositions of the same logical character, both being indeterminate in relation to any given case. However, stating that "rules are applicable in an all-or-nothing fashion,"[11] Dworkin treats rules as if they were identical with orders, which command a particular performance from a particular person. As a result of this equivocation, he essentially ignores all that his predecessors have had to say about the indeterminacy of rules (as opposed to orders), a notion upon which the traditional understanding of law is based. Furthermore, he writes as if his usage were entirely uncontroversial and bases his entire edifice on this extremely narrow understanding of a rule. Otherwise, he could not attach so much importance to his distinction between "hard" and "easy" cases. For if all rules are necessarily indeterminate (because they are not orders), no cases can be "easy" in Dworkin's sense; "hard" cases are then merely more severely indeterminate than so-called "easy" ones and do not have to be decided in a radically different manner.

Secondly, Dworkin's argument rests on a serious ambiguity about the status of "principles" – he describes them as both within and outside the law. They are within the law when he claims to be defending a strict separation between adjudication and legislation, as in his distinction between policies and principles. But they are outside the law when he argues that in "hard" cases, since the judge cannot rely on the rules and statutes of the law, he must rely on the same moral standards as are used in any political argument. Moreover, by equating "principles" with moral standards, he claims to be restoring the union between law and morality destroyed by positivism. What matters most, however, is that this equation enables him to conclude that it is impossible for legal decisions to be completely distinct from political decisions because the same "moral"

[11] Ibid., 24.

standards, i.e., "principles," have to be invoked in both political and legal decisions. Dworkin thus leaps from an apparently technical discussion of "hard" cases to the conclusion that it is normal and desirable for *legal* decisions to be *political* decisions.

Thirdly, this leap is further obfuscated by Dworkin's discussion of judicial "discretion."[12] He uses the idea of "authorization" as eccentrically as he does that of "rules." For a judge is not acting in an authorized fashion when he selects among the many, and probably conflicting, moral notions prevailing in the community. Such a judge is acting as a *legislator* without having been authorized to do so. Dworkin is right in saying that judges of that sort are making *political*, not legal, judgments. But in approving of such judges Dworkin is endorsing their usurpation of power which they have not been authorized to exercise.

Dworkin presents this view of judicial discretion as essential to the defense of an individual's "right against the State." His assertions to this effect might suggest that he is a defender of liberty. In fact, as Dworkin himself says bluntly, he is out to defend equality, which, he maintains, cannot be reconciled with liberty. "The idea of a right to liberty is a misconceived concept that does dis-service to political thought," Dworkin declares. The "idea of a right to liberty" creates "a false sense of a necessary conflict between liberty and other values when social regulation, like the busing program, is proposed." The law ought to be based, Dworkin says, on the principle of "equal concern and respect,"[13] and he regards the requirements of this principle as so self-evident that he sees no need to defend it. Furthermore, by arguing that "it should be plain how this theory of rights might be used to support the idea . . . that we have distinct rights to certain liberties like the liberty of free expression and of free choice in personal and sexual relations,"[14] he uses this principle as indubitable proof of other much more controversial moral values. Thus, when he advocates reverse discrimination and opposes capital punishment as well as legislation against homosexuality and pornography, he describes his convictions on these issues as necessarily true and indisputable.

Not surprisingly, Dworkin's unabashed bow to postmodernism and political jurisprudence throughout *Taking Rights Seriously* has drawn heavy criticism from traditional conservatives within both the positivist and natural law camps. However, by the end of his account of his new "liberal" theory of law Dworkin also succeeds in alienating many of the postmodernist liberals whose support he had originally gained. He asserts

---

[12] Ibid., 33.   [13] Ibid., 193, 271–73.   [14] Ibid., 277.

that skeptics who say that it is impossible to claim that there is any one right answer in the "hard cases" Dworkin so frequently mentions have yet to put forth an objection that passes the necessary muster. To those who flatly deny the possibility of judicial objectivity, Dworkin replies: "But why not? It may be that the supposition that one side may be right and the other wrong is cemented into our habits or thought at a level so deep that we cannot coherently deny that supposition, no matter how skeptical or hard-headed we wish to be in such matters. . . The 'myth' that there is one right answer in a hard case is both recalcitrant and successful. Its recalcitrance and success count as arguments that it is no myth."[15] With these words, Dworkin ends his account of his new "liberal" theory of law in *Taking Rights Seriously*.

Just how thoroughly Dworkin revises the idea of law becomes more obvious in *A Matter of Principle,* where his central thesis is that it is impossible to distinguish what the law is from what it should be. Whereas in the earlier book, he had emphasized that judges neither should nor need to make law because they can find the "right answer" even for hard cases in existing law, here he argues that whenever judges decide a case, they necessarily make a "political decision" about what the law should be.

This conclusion is supported by Dworkin's contention that all interpretation rests on "normative beliefs." And he explains their significance by an excursion into literary criticism, which starts with the question: Why do critics disagree about what is the best method for discovering the meaning of a literary text? In answer, Dworkin produces his "aesthetic hypothesis," which claims that interpretation consists of reading a text so as to reveal it "as the best work of art." This means that interpretation is determined by a critic's "normative" beliefs. Dworkin then goes on to argue that since normative beliefs shape interpretation, we cannot separate interpreting a work of art from "evaluating" it. We are obliged to recognize that "There is no longer a flat distinction between interpretation, conceived as discovering the real meaning of a work of art, and criticism, conceived as evaluating its success or importance."[16] Therefore, different interpretations of a text, whether literary or legal, are due to different views about what is desirable and not about the meaning of the text.

Dworkin takes trouble to deny that he is putting the objectivity of interpretation in doubt. That interpretation has normative presuppositions, he says, obliges us only to recognize that any dissent from a critic's

[15] Ibid., 290.
[16] Ronald Dworkin, *A Matter of Principle* (Cambridge, MA: Harvard University Press, 1985), 149–53.

explanation of the meaning of a work of art must be due to a different evaluation of its artistic quality. Anyone who pretends to keep his interpretation distinct from evaluation must, according to Dworkin, be equating the meaning of a work of art with the author's intention. And against the possibility of discerning an author's intention, Dworkin draws on arguments that have long been familiar in literary criticism. But he goes further to deny any complete distinction between author and critic: Merely a difference of emphasis separates them because "The artist can create nothing without interpreting as he creates," and the critic "creates as he interprets."[17]

Dworkin insists on this analogy in order to establish that the judge cannot interpret law without making "a political decision" similar to that of a legislator. Adjudication is likened to producing a novel by a chain of authors. Just as each author has to construct a unifying conception of what his predecessors have written, so the judge has to determine what "the point or theme of the practice so far, taken as a whole, really is."[18] Whereas in *Taking Rights Seriously*, Dworkin had argued that judges have to see the law as a whole, here he insists that any interpretation of a legal practice must show "its point or value" in "political terms." A judicial decision must show the value of a legal practice in "political terms" by "demonstrating the best principle or policy it can be taken to serve."[19] And so Dworkin assures us that just as our "commitment" to feminism" or our "dissatisfaction with the rise of the New Right" does and should count "in deciding, among particular interpretations of the works, which is the best interpretation," so must political convictions determine our interpretation of law.[20] Whereas one judge may discover in accident law only "an attempt to reenforce conventional morality of fault and responsibility," a judge who believes that the main goal of law is economic "will see in past accident decisions some strategy for reducing the economic costs of accidents over all." Each chooses the interpretation of accident law which he determines as "a sounder principle of justice." And although "law is not a matter of personal or partisan politics," Dworkin argues that "lawyers cannot avoid politics in the broad sense of political theory."[21] Thus, whatever the judge does, he cannot be neutral; the interpretation of law is, at least in Dworkin's broad sense of the term, "essentially political."[22]

In law as in literature, a judge who attempts to keep his decisions free of his political convictions must be trying to discern the "intentions" of

---

[17] Ibid., 158.   [18] Ibid., 159.   [19] Ibid., 160.
[20] Ibid., 165.   [21] Ibid.   [22] Ibid., 161–62.

lawmakers, that is to say, assuming that the intention of a law is "some complex psychological fact locked in history waiting to be winkled out from old pamphlets and letters and proceedings."[23] In reality, however, the intention of a law is not something "waiting to be discovered, even in principle," but something "waiting to be invented." Those who pretend to be respectful of the text of the Constitution by engaging in "semantic questions" (which is Dworkin's description of arguing from the words of the Constitution) are really displaying their indifference to the text because they are not concerned with the point of having a Constitution or why the Constitution is the fundamental law. They suppose – wrongly – that the Constitution is law because of "a generally accepted theory of the process through which legislation becomes law – in virtue of which the Constitution became law." According to Dworkin, the Constitution is law because the people accept the principles of political morality that it embodies. The judge cannot discover those principles by "finding the law just 'there' in history." He has to construct "a political theory showing why the Constitution should be treated as law."[24] Thus, Dworkin concludes that the judge is obliged to invent an intention for the Constitution.

As an example of the necessity for such invention, Dworkin offers the clause of the Fourteenth Amendment, which guarantees equal treatment without regard to race in matters touching people's fundamental interests. It may give rise, he says, to two opposed interpretations, depending on what the judge takes to be a "matter of fundamental interest." If he regards education as a matter of fundamental interest, he will find racially segregated schools unconstitutional; if not, he will find them to be lawful. He cannot escape choosing between these descriptions by trying to *discover* the "intention" of the clause; and if he tries to rely on the views of earlier judges, he is only treating them as legislators. The judge is therefore obliged to decide "that one rather than the other description is more appropriate in virtue of the best theory of representative democracy or on some other openly political grounds."[25]

That is why all the opinions about the equal protection clause in the Constitution are either "distinctly liberal or radical or conservative." And this proves that "There can be no useful interpretation . . . which is independent of some theory about what political equality is and how far equality is required by justice." Conservative lawyers who pretend to be neutral by using "an author's intentions style of interpreting this clause" are really trying to hide the role played by their own political convictions in their "choice of interpretive style."[26]

---

[23] Ibid., 39.   [24] Ibid., 14, 36–39, 162.
[25] Ibid., 163–64.   [26] Ibid., 164–65.

Since deciding cases is essentially a matter of moral judgment, whatever indeterminacy there appears to be in the law must be due to an "indeterminacy or incommensurability in moral theory." Whether there are "no-right-answer cases" is not then "an ordinary empirical question." Anyone who denies that there is a right answer must be defending "some idea of skepticism, or of indeterminacy in moral theory," a position that Dworkin rejects as unproven.[27]

Whereas the "one right answer thesis" emphasized that judges can *find* a right answer in the law, the new theory of interpretation says explicitly that judges cannot avoid deciding cases in accordance with their idea of what is right. And as Dworkin accordingly insists throughout, this requires that judges must make "political decisions." He supports this conclusion by arguing that interpretation rests on "normative beliefs" and by equating normative beliefs with every sort of presupposition, theoretical and practical, intellectual and moral. However, interpretation is generally distinguished from evaluation by the different kinds of presuppositions that each entails. By equating "normative beliefs" with every sort of presupposition, Dworkin makes it impossible to distinguish interpretation from evaluation and thus converts interpretation into a synonym for evaluation. But this equivocation no more supports Dworkin's conclusion – that what the law is cannot be distinguished from what it ought to be – than the fact that atomic fusion postulates an elaborate scientific theory that makes it impossible to explain what atomic fusion is without advocating that atom bombs be made and dropped. All that the new theory of interpretation really establishes is that Dworkin denies the logical distinction between "is" and "ought."

What Dworkin's denial of the is/ought distinction implies in judicial practice is demonstrated in his discussion of the Weber case. The issue was whether the Civil Rights Act made it unlawful for an employer, the Kaiser Aluminum Co., to use a racial quota system in order to increase the number of black workers in skilled jobs. While the majority of the Supreme Court held that the statute permitted affirmative action plans of this sort, there were dissents from Justices Rehnquist and Burger, which Dworkin criticizes.

He describes Rehnquist's argument – that "the meaning of the words of the act as they stand," clearly excludes the Kaiser plan – as an appeal to "legislative intent" that exploits an ambiguity in that notion. To explain that ambiguity, Dworkin introduces a distinction between "institutionalized intention" and "collective understanding." The former exists where there is a preamble stating the purpose of the act, and though he argues

[27] Ibid., 144–45.

elsewhere that such words are bound to be as ambiguous as any other, here Dworkin says that they could be used to discover the intent of the statute. But as there is no such preamble to the Civil Rights Acts, Rehnquist must mean, Dworkin concludes, "collective understanding." Since there cannot be any "pertinent collective understanding" where there is no "institutionalized intention," there are only two competing justifications for the Act. In basing his dissent on the wording of the statute, Rehnquist made the mistake of assuming that he could choose between competing justifications without making a political judgment.[28]

Justice Burger's argument is dismissed more brusquely because Burger said that, had he been a Congressman, he would have voted to permit plans like Kaiser's. But as in fact Congress had made such affirmative action illegal in the Civil Rights Act, he found that the Kaiser Plan infringed the Civil Rights Act. Dworkin considers Justice Burger's interpretation of the Civil Rights Act wholly irrational because Burger confessed that he himself approved of affirmative action. Here Dworkin repeats his earlier comment on the impropriety of the judges in the Fugitive Slave cases who, though known to oppose slavery, decided contrary to their own moral convictions.

By treating Rehnquist's attention to what the words of the statute meant as an attempt to evade an inescapable political judgment, and by dismissing as irrational Burger's distinction between his own preferences and what the law as it stood actually required, Dworkin disposes without argument of any attempts to justify decisions using rationale based on the intent of the legislature.[29]

Likewise, it is as impossible for the citizen as it is for the judge to distinguish what the law is from what it ought to be. Dworkin restricts civil disobedience only by stipulating that it should be based on principles or rights and not on judgments of policy or collective goals, and he confines his approval to "integrity-based" and " justice-based" civil disobedience. He opposes prosecuting the transgressions that they entail because it is wrong to suppose that "if someone has broken the law, for whatever reason and no matter how honourable his motives, he must always be punished because the law is the law."[30] Whatever the law may require, a person whose motives are superior should not be treated like an ordinary criminal.

Dworkin's chief argument for not punishing civil disobedience is that even though the court has the last word, and we must generally obey its decisions for " practical reasons . . . we reserve the right to argue that the

---

[28] Ibid., 320–30.   [29] Ibid.   [30] Ibid., 114–15.

law is not what they have said it is." The person engaged in civil disobedience is doing the same thing as the Supreme Court does when it strikes down legislation as unconstitutional – preventing the majority from abusing its power at the expense of the minority. The United States Constitution sanctions such behavior, according to Dworkin, because it recognizes "abstract political rights as legal rights." To protect "abstract political rights" is the purpose of efforts to override legislation and, whether done by judges in the Supreme Court or by private citizens engaged in civil disobedience, they are equally legitimate.[31]

Although Dworkin continues to deny that his judges are allowed to make up the law wholesale and insists that they are constrained by the political theory that they are obliged to construct,[32] the nature of that theory remains elusive. Is there only one political theory or many? Is a political theory an interpretation of the law as a whole that seeks to establish the most consistent line or argument in past statutes and decisions, or is it a construction of the law designed to satisfy certain moral requirements, regardless of its fit with the "legal materials?" If there can be more than one political theory, are they all equally objective and desirable? If not, what is the criterion for choosing the best one, and what renders that criterion acceptable? If the theory is designed to satisfy certain moral requirements, how do these become manifest, and what renders them objective or indisputable? Dworkin has endorsed all these conflicting possibilities, sometimes within the same context. In this volume, however, he more consistently emphasizes that what matters is the correctness of the judge's political theory. And he leaves us in no doubt that the correct theory is " liberalism."

Far from attempting to derive liberalism from more fundamental ideas about the capacities or aspirations of human beings, Dworkin points out that it does not rest "on any special theory of personality." Instead, liberalism seems to be an emanation from American public opinion since the 1930s or perhaps from the time of the Constitution. Whatever its derivation, it is the opposite of "conservatism." Not many conservatives would agree, but according to Dworkin conservatives value the ideals of liberty over those of equality, and believe that it is possible to uniformly determine the ideals of a good life and therefore to expect the government to promote them.[33] As liberals claim no such pretensions to the proper mode of life, they recognize the prominence of the moral principle of equality, "that human beings must be treated as equals by their government," over that of liberty. Nevertheless, liberalism is not a form of

---

[31] Ibid., 115–16.   [32] Ibid., 160–62.   [33] Ibid., 189, 199.

skepticism. It insists on the principle of equal concern and respect, "not because there is no right and wrong in political morality, but because that is what is right."[34] The principle of equal concern and respect is what Dworkin calls a moral fact and is no more indeterminate or disputable than the fact that all men are mortal.

From his principle of equal concern and respect, the liberal derives a number of practical and inescapable conclusions. Unlike the conservative, he would qualify the decisions of the market, as well as rights to property and freedom of contract, in order to produce a more equal distribution of wealth. Where people have different talents and handicaps and inherit more or less wealth, "It is obviously obnoxious to the liberal conception" to allow one man to own more because "his father had superior skill or luck."[35] The liberal therefore supports government intervention for the redistribution of goods. And if he finds that an adequate distribution cannot be achieved within a capitalist economy, the liberal would be forced to reluctantly substitute "socialist for market decisions over a large part of the economy."[36]

Dworkin's reformulation of his theory of interpretation and his discussion of liberalism make it clear that what, in his view, ought ultimately to constrain the judge is his allegiance to the principle of equal concern and respect, which enables him to discern certain "rights." These rights are not defined by statutes or past decisions, but they are, Dworkin insists, nonetheless objective and as compelling as the principle of equal concern and respect. It is this relation between rights and the principle of equal concern and respect that leads Dworkin to oppose "principles," which should govern adjudication, to "policies," which are the proper objects of legislation. He proceeds then to use "principles" as a synonym for "rights," and to equate "policies" with "goals."

The opposition between "rights" and "goals" carries an echo of the traditional view that the law ought to set conditions for everyone to observe, rather than to assign satisfactions to anyone, just as the rules of a game do not assign points or decide who should win. However, by describing rules of law as ways of achieving "goals," Dworkin suggests that they assign advantages. Therefore, when he says that "rights" should be "trumps" over "goals," he seems to be saying that the law should not be used to distribute advantages.[37]

But the "rights" ordinarily associated with the rule of law emerge out of established legal rules that define conditions to be observed. A man hurt by careless driving has a right to compensation because everyone is obliged by the established rules to take due care in driving. In Dworkin's

---

[34] Ibid., 203.   [35] Ibid., 195.   [36] Ibid., 196.   [37] Ibid., 66–68.

theory, however, "rights" *are opposed to rules of law* because he identifies the conditions set by rules of law as the "goals" of the majority. When judges decide in terms of "rights" in Dworkin's sense, they are assigning advantages to those denied them by the established rules.

Any doubts about whether Dworkin's emphasis on rights implies that established rules of law may at times be ignored are definitively settled by the leading essay in this volume, originally a lecture to the British Academy, on "Political Judges and the Rule of Law." Here he plainly presents his theory as an alternative to the "rule book conception," which Dworkin describes as the belief that "the power of the state should never be exercised against individual citizens except in accordance with rules explicitly set out in a public rule book available to all. The government as well as ordinary citizens must play by these public rules until they are changed, in accordance with further rules about how they are to be changed, which are also set out in the rule book."[38] Rather than accepting this as the definition of the rule of law, Dworkin argues that it is an understanding of law that should be rejected and replaced with what he describes as the "rights conception" of the rule of law. The rights conception goes beyond the rule book conception by assuming that individuals have "moral rights and duties with respect to one another" as well as "political rights against the state as a whole." It demands that these rights be recognized in positive law to be enforced through the courts at the demand of the citizen.[39] Moreover, Dworkin strengthens his rejection of the rule book conception by stating explicitly: "My point was not that 'the law' contains a fixed number of standards, some of which are rules and others principles. Indeed, I want to oppose the idea that 'the law' is a fixed set of standards of any sort."[40] He then emphasizes that when his theory requires judges to rely on principles not in the rule book, it is requiring judges to do what the rule book ideal prohibits – to legislate and make what he calls "political decisions." And it is precisely these types of political decisions, decisions which may mean requiring interventions by the state to restrict the use of property and freedom of contract and to enforce positive discrimination, that are prohibited by the rule book conception due to their lack of objectivity, fixity, and public acceptance.

The radical nature of Dworkin's revision of the idea of law thus becomes clear. By abandoning the rule book conception and allowing, indeed encouraging,[41] the political decisions required by his rights

---

[38] Ibid., 11.   [39] Ibid., 11.
[40] Dworkin, *Taking Rights Seriously*, 76.
[41] See Dworkin, *Matter of Principle*, 32.

conception, Dworkin plainly rejects the traditional insistence on the separation of powers between judges and legislators. He argues that the judiciary is as justified as the elected legislature to make new law, and given that judges are more likely to protect the rights of the minority, they should do just that.[42] Finally, he does not claim, as he did earlier, to be merely describing the true character of adjudication. He announces that he wishes to promote a radical revision of the idea of law.

However, if Dworkin's rights are not fixed by being recorded in statutes or judicial decisions, how fixed are they? Dworkin does draw a distinction between "legal rights" and "moral rights," and asserts that the boundaries of legal rights are set forth through statute and common law and often reflect moral rights. Moral rights, however, have no such objective definition. In fact, because there is no fixed content for moral rights, they are largely determined by the preferences of the minority, as it is the minority whose moral rights are generally unrepresented in the body of legal rights codified by representatives of the majority. But as there are no God-given majorities or minorities, and today's minority might be tomorrow's majority, the content of rights is bound to shift with every change in public opinion. Dworkin himself points this out when he says that "rights" have to be defined differently in each case depending on the goal to be trumped and that "liberals will disagree about what is needed." And when Dworkin argues that the tyranny of a majority can be prevented by allowing judges to protect the rights of whatever minority is "antecedently likely" to be despised by the majority, he is permitting anyone's guess about the state of public opinion to justify imposing the will of whatever minority he chooses to discover.[43] Rights swinging in the wind of public opinion can provide no secure ground for judicial decisions.

It remains to consider whether the principle of equal concern and respect, from which Dworkin deduces his political theory of liberalism is, as he supposes, indisputable. What distinguishes Dworkin's principle from other egalitarian doctrines is his emphasis on the distinction between "external" and "personal" preferences and the evil of allowing external preferences to determine public decisions.[44] What then makes external preferences so undesirable?

The personal preferences of individuals designate goods or advantages that they would like to have assigned to themselves. Their external preferences designate what they would like to have assigned to others. Wanting a swimming pool because one likes to swim is a personal preference; wanting a swimming pool because one believes it would be good for the community is an external preference. Dworkin argues that people are

---

[42] Ibid., 27.   [43] Ibid., 197–98.   [44] Ibid., 196–97.

not being treated with equal concern and respect as long as public decisions made by a vote of the majority are allowed to rest on external preferences because doing so allows the majority to vote twice – they decide not only what they should get, but also what others should get. Since everything in a democracy is decided by majority votes, the only way to protect minorities against such double counting is to give their preferences (which the majority does not share) precedence over the goals of the majority. These preferences of the minority constitute "rights" and should be immune to modification by decisions of the majority.[45]

However, as Herbert Hart and others have pointed out, external preferences are nothing worse than *disinterested* preferences. When external preferences influence a vote, all that happens is that one person's preferences are being supported by those of another. If, for instance, heterosexuals of a liberal disposition decide the vote in favor of abolishing restrictions on homosexuals, then the vote will have been determined by "external preferences." But no one is being allowed to vote twice. If that were true, denying the vote to heterosexuals would eliminate the double counting. But in fact preventing heterosexuals from voting would be a gross violation of one man, one vote. In short, what Dworkin presents as if it were a purely procedural argument with which no one could disagree – that counting in external preferences is unfair – is no argument at all.

But Dworkin attempts to sustain his condemnation of counting in external preferences with a wholly different argument, i.e., that when people vote on a question and win, they are necessarily saying that the losers are inferior and unworthy of their respect. Unfortunately there is no such necessity. Certainly we can disagree with others for a great variety of reasons; we may even vote against them out of a tender concern for their self-respect. Indeed, democracy as we know it presupposes that we can and should respect those with whom we differ. But if injustice consisted, as Dworkin teaches, in denying satisfaction to the preferences of a minority, then a tyranny that prohibited all publications or all sexual relations would be preferable to a democracy that censored pornography or restricted homosexuals. And as democratic procedures necessarily reject whatever the losing minority prefers, all just persons would have to abandon democracy.

There is much to be said, and much has been said, about the desirability of mitigating the constraints suffered by people who hold unpopular views. Generally, such discussions advocate arrangements that reduce the occasions on which it becomes necessary to make public decisions about which preferences should have precedence. Reducing the area

[45] Dworkin, *Taking Rights Seriously*, 275–77.

controlled by public decisions and securing conditions in which individuals can pursue the projects they prefer without interference is the substance of the traditional concern with preserving "liberty." The echo that it carries of this concern with liberty lends credence to Dworkin's defense of minorities. That his doctrine is designed for a different purpose, however, is evident from his contention that *"liberty" is not a right,* but should always give way to "equality," and that injustice consists wholly in a denial of equality, not liberty.

Whatever its merits, the principle of equal concern and respect cannot bear the burden that Dworkin puts upon it. He admits this unwittingly when he says that it can as easily justify the conservative view that a government should promote the good life as the liberal view that it should be neutral. Herbert Hart's criticism says all that needs to be said: "a notion of equal concern and respect or 'conceptions of the concept' hospitable to such violently opposed interpretations, does not seem to me to be a single concept at all. . . Though the claim that liberal rights are derived from the duty of governments to treat all their citizens with equal concern and respect has the comforting appearance of resting them on something uncontroversial . . . this appearance dissolves when it is revealed that there is an alternative interpretation of this fundamental duty from which most liberal rights could not be derived but negations of many liberal rights could."[46]

That his rights conception cannot serve as an adequate account of the idea of law is also recognized by Dworkin himself in more than one context. He says, for instance, that it is both unnecessary and crude to look to rights for the only defense against stupid or wicked political decisions. More outspoken is his statement that "We need rights, as a distinct element in political theory, only when some decision that injures some people nevertheless finds *prima facie* support in the claim that it will make the community as a whole better off on some plausible account of where the community's general welfare lies."[47] Such passages indicate that the rule book conception of law cannot be replaced by the "rights theory," as elsewhere Dworkin tells us it can, for the simple reason that the rights theory is not designed to provide a jurisprudential philosophy of what law is.

That the rights theory is not designed to provide such a philosophy of law also explains Dworkin's indifference to the fact, which he himself points out, that his doctrine cannot account for criminal law. His

---

[46] Hart, *Essays*, 219, footnote.
[47] Dworkin, *Matter of Principle*, 371.

arguments against restrictions on homosexuals do not exclude, he assures us, all legislation about sexual behavior because "Laws against rape, for example, can be justified by appealing to the ordinary interests of people generally through a theory of justice that does not rely on popular convictions."[48] Decisions about criminal law, made by a majority vote, are permissible because every such decision "is equally in or against the antecedent whole interest of each person, by which I mean the combination of his or her moral and bare interests." People may disagree about how crimes should be defined and what penalties should be imposed, "But since moral harm is an objective matter and not dependent upon particular people's perception of moral harm, no one will think that the majority's decision is unfair in the sense that it is more in the interests of some than others."[49]

This justification for laws against rape and murder fails, however, to explain why they do not deny equal respect to a minority in the same way as do laws restricting pornography. The majority who pass or sustain laws that expose those found guilty of rape or murder to punishment are hardly likely to take a flattering view of the minority of criminals. But that does not seem to worry Dworkin. He does not say that since the minority who are disposed to commit rape or murder are despised by the majority, they are being deprived of equal concern and respect, as he does when arguing against laws banning pornography and homosexuality. Yet he offers no grounds for distinguishing the minority of rapists and murderers from the minority of pornographers or homosexuals. And, conversely, if the "ordinary interests of people generally through a theory of justice" can provide the grounds for laws against rape and murder, why should not the same grounds serve for laws against pornography?

But if *A Matter of Principle* does not offer a more adequate account of the rule of law than *Taking Rights Seriously*, it does reveal why Dworkin opposes the "rule-book conception of the rule of law." According to the "rule-book conception" of law, the obligation to observe a law or to obey a judicial order does not depend on whether it is thought to be desirable, good, or just, but on whether it has been duly promulgated according to the correct procedures. Dworkin, however, has no use for such procedural considerations. He denies that what makes the Constitution of the United States law is that it was accepted by the people in accordance with "the procedures stipulated in the document itself." He takes the only issue about civil disobedience to be whether it is designed to promote a just cause. And he considers the purpose of procedure or "process," as he calls it, to be the distribution of "political power." Procedural rights in

[48] Ibid., 68.   [49] Ibid., 87.

criminal suits, he says, are designed "to compensate in a rough way" for corruption by the interests of the class that administers it. More generally, procedures are chosen for what they contribute to democracy. Although he acknowledges that in the West democracy is identified with procedures "defined independently of any description of the decisions actually reached," he prefers to define democracy in the manner of the "people's democracies," as a system for maintaining equality. But whereas the "people's democracies" aim at an equal distribution of wealth, Dworkin identifies democracy with the equal distribution of political power. And he sees procedure as a means for achieving equality in power.[50]

That is why Dworkin asserts that questions of procedure cannot be decided without regard to "substantive political questions." The Supreme Court, he says, cannot take refuge in procedural arguments based on "the intention of the Framers"; it is bound to make "important political decisions."[51] For as long as judges confine themselves to deciding whether the stipulated procedures have been observed, they will merely be maintaining the existing distribution of power. It has, of course, generally been recognized that the purpose of constitutions is to distribute power by deciding who is qualified to vote and to hold office. But the point of such arrangements is to make it possible to translate all future disputes into issues about procedure, that is to say, into disputes about whether the law has been observed. Dworkin considers this to be impossible. His theory of interpretation assumes that all human utterances are instruments for obtaining satisfactions or power. Accordingly, achieving greater power is the only objective that Dworkin considers in his discussion of procedure, and law is primarily an instrument for redistributing power.

He would have us believe that this theory rests on indisputable moral facts. Unfortunately, his fundamental moral principle is either empty or highly disputable, and he connects law with morality only by rejecting the logical distinction between "is" and "ought". Instead of giving law a moral dimension by repudiating that distinction, the rights theory makes it impossible to tell an authentic legal decision from an arbitrary exercise of power. It allows, indeed obliges, judges to ignore the law in order to satisfy the wants of minorities. And this undoubtedly justifies Dworkin's claim that his theory corrects "the majoritarian bias" of democracy.[52]

But a secret is concealed in what Herbert Hart calls the "Byzantine complexity" of Dworkin's prose – that "the majoritarian bias" is corrected by enabling minorities, who cannot persuade their fellow citizens to agree

---

[50] Ibid., 12, 36, 66, 63, 198, 59.
[51] Ibid., 58, 34, 69.   [52] Ibid., 27–28.

with them, nevertheless to impose their will. In short, if Dworkin's theory were to triumph over "the rule book," minorities who now fail to get their way by constitutional means would be given the power to do as they please by judicial decisions.

Nothing so radical appears in Dworkin's systematic treatise, *Law's Empire*. Indeed, at first sight, he would seem to have renounced his earlier hostility to the traditional idea of law. Whereas earlier he had condemned the judges who decided the Fugitive Slave cases against the slaves and dismissed the statute on which they based their decision as irrelevant, here he adopts as his own the very arguments that were used against him by his critics: "If a judge's own sense of justice condemned that act as deeply immoral . . . he would have to consider whether he should actually enforce it on the demand of a slave owner, or whether he should lie and say that this was not the law after all, or whether he should resign."[53] Dworkin even goes so far as to deny that he has any quarrel with the view "of most laymen," which is also "the anthem of the legal conservative," that "The law is the law" and that "It is not what judges think it is, but what it really is. Their job is to apply it, not to change it to fit their own ethics or politics." This view, "read word by word," Dworkin pronounces as "nothing controversial."[54] And he condemns "activism" in constitutional adjudication on the grounds that justices should "enforce the Constitution through interpretation," not "fiat," and that their decisions "must fit constitutional practice, not ignore it."[55]

As in his earlier books, Dworkin once again introduces a new vocabulary and a new strategy. What had earlier been called "positivism" or the "rule book theory of law" is here described as "conventionalism" (and occasionally also as "matter of plainfact" and "plain-fact" theories, "literalism," "historicism," "passivism," or "semantic theories"). Dworkin's own theory is rechristened as "law as integrity" and presented not as a radical alternative to the "ruling theory," but rather as the moderate middle ground between the two extremes of "conventionalism" and "pragmatism." Pragmatism, which he sometimes also calls "activism," is the view that judges may ignore coherence and "make whatever decisions seem to them best for the community's future." In this moderate mood, Dworkin grants that both extremes possess certain virtues. Conventionalism, by insisting that judges confine themselves to interpreting formal legal rules and observing precedent, provides a sense of security for expectations. Pragmatism, on the other hand, has the flexibility that conventionalism so conspicuously lacks. But against conventionalism,

---

[53] Ronald Dworkin, *Law's Empire* (Cambridge, MA: Belknap, 1986), 219.
[54] Ibid., 114.   [55] Ibid., 378.

he marshals all the earlier criticisms of the "rule book theory." And pragmatism fails, he argues, because it carries flexibility too far by altogether rejecting "the idea of law and legal right."[56]

Nevertheless, although both the introduction of pragmatism as the opposite of conventionalism and the criticism of it are new, for the most part what Dworkin has to say about "law as integrity" is merely a moderated version of the lessons taught in the earlier books, i.e., that law does not consist of explicit formal rules but of the moral principles underlying such rules; that adjudication must be based on a wide-ranging political theory rather than on formal legal rules; and that law is inseparable from politics. The last point receives more emphasis in *Law's Empire* through Dworkin's regular use of "past political decisions" as a synonym for law. But the more important novelty is Dworkin's description of "integrity" as a "political ideal" that should dominate political life.[57] This new theme is important because it holds the clue to the presuppositions of what Dworkin had been teaching all along and of all political jurisprudence.

One of these presuppositions is stated explicitly. Thus, it becomes clear for the first time that Dworkin identifies the essence of law with the coercion sanctioned by it. The central question for any conception of law is, he says, "What can ever give anyone the kind of authorized power over another that politics supposes governors have over the governed?" To answer that question, "A conception of law must explain how what it takes to be law provides a general justification for the exercise of coercive power by the state . . . Each conception's organizing center is the explanation it offers of this justifying force."[58] When law is not simply coupled with the exercise of coercion, it is described as an instrument employed by the "governing power" to "control" the behavior of the governed.

The reason why Dworkin explicitly points out the connection between law and coercion is that the object of his jurisprudence, as he describes it in *Law's Empire*, is to find a conception of law sufficiently "attractive" to persuade people that the coercion sanctioned by the law is "legitimate." And he considers the peculiar virtue of "law as integrity" to be its ability to connect "past political decisions" with "present coercion" by offering a better explanation of how "past political decisions" allow collective force to be trained against individuals. Therefore, "a state that accepts integrity as a political ideal has a better case for legitimacy than one that does not."[59]

---

[56] Ibid., 95; see also 8, 33, 130, 378.   [57] Ibid., 188–91.
[58] Ibid., 190–92, 219.   [59] Ibid., 191–92, 98, 227–28.

The principle of integrity teaches us first of all not to ask whether judges "find" or "invent" the law. Instead, judges are recognized to "do both and neither." For "The adjudicative principle of integrity instructs judges to identify legal rights and duties, so far as possible, on the assumption that they were all created by a single author – the community personified."[60] Although Dworkin has argued throughout for seeing the law as a coherent whole, only in *Law's Empire* does it become clear how his emphasis on coherence differs from the traditional view, which also requires judges to see the law as a coherent whole. In Dworkin's account, the coherence of the law becomes synonymous with "the state speaking with a *single* voice," with seeing the law in terms of a *single* principle, or as the work of a *single* author.[61] Moreover, Dworkin takes great pains to emphasize that "law as integrity" is not to be confused with consistency. On the contrary, adjudication that "accepts that ideal," he points out, "will sometimes, for that reason, depart from a narrow line of past decisions in search of fidelity to principles conceived as more fundamental to the scheme as a whole." The ideal of integrity is far more demanding than consistency. It is "a more dynamic and radical standard" than it seems at first sight because "it encourages a judge to be wide-ranging and imaginative in his search for coherence with fundamental principle." Judges must be ready to see that "an important part of what has been thought to be law is inconsistent with more fundamental principles necessary to justify law as a whole."[62]

The emphasis on equating the coherence of law with a *single* objective, created by a *single* author with a *single* voice, is the most significant novelty in *Law's Empire*. That emphasis springs from the basic presupposition of "law as integrity" and that the "organic" community is the only "true" community. This community is contrasted by Dworkin to the "rule book model" of community where the "concern it displays is too shallow and attenuated to count as pervasive"[63] because unity is achieved "through [such superficial arrangements as] negotiation and compromise,"[64] contractual relationships, the definition of discrete responsibilities, and "Explicit agreements hammered out at arm's length."[65] Dworkin presents the organic community as if it were the only alternative to reducing the idea of a community to a sum of competing interests. He accordingly describes an organic community as "a society of principle" which "takes a more generous and comprehensive view" of a shared understanding. The members "accept that they are governed by common principles, not just by rules hammered out in political compromise." As a

---

[60] Ibid., 225.   [61] Ibid., 217–18, 225.   [62] Ibid., 219–21.
[63] Ibid., 190, 212.   [64] Ibid., 210.   [65] Ibid., 220.

result, politics in an organic community "is a theater of debate about which principles the community should adopt as a system" instead of being an effort by each individual "to plant the flag of his convictions over as large a domain of power or rules as possible,"[66] as in the rule book idea of community.

But what is really at issue here is whether the subjects of law are taken to be independent persons, pursuing projects of their own choosing while observing a common set of rules (as in the traditional view of law), or whether law is to be regarded as the instrument of an enterprise pursuing a single objective. In the latter sort of community, individuals are related like the parts of a machine or the organs of a body, that is to say, their activities are directed to serve a single end, the end of the whole of which they are the parts. It is the latter understanding of a community, it becomes clear in *Law's Empire*, that is postulated by Dworkin's view of law.

If a community is understood in this fashion, it follows, according to Dworkin, that the rights and duties of its members "are not exhausted by the particular decisions their political institutions have reached," but depend more generally on "the scheme of principles which those decisions presuppose and endorse." Why Dworkin has insisted all along that law consists not of formal rules but of moral principles becomes evident when he says that each member of a true community "has duties flowing from that scheme" even though these have never been formally identified or declared. Moreover, Dworkin emphasizes, no member supposes that such rights and duties "are conditional on his whole hearted approval of that scheme."[67] And political obligation is "not just a matter of obeying the discrete political decisions of the community one by one, as political philosophers usually represent it." Instead, political obligation "becomes a more protestant idea: fidelity to a scheme of principle each citizen has a responsibility to identify, ultimately for himself, as his community's scheme."[68] The old concept of political obligation has then to be replaced by a new concept of "associative or communal obligations," which "are complex, and much less studied by philosophers than the kinds of personal obligations we incur through discrete promises and other deliberate acts." "Associative obligations" cannot be defined through explicit rules. They are just part of the community's "scheme." It follows, Dworkin argues, that the emphasis on choice to which we are accustomed is misplaced because the connection between "associative obligation" and choice "is much more complex and more a matter of degree that varies from one form of communal association to another."[69]

---

[66] Ibid., 211.   [67] Ibid.   [68] Ibid., 190.   [69] Ibid., 196.

Dworkin is not advocating the Hobbesian concept of authority, which claims that as long as individuals accept the authority of the reigning legislature, they are obliged to observe the law even when they do not approve of it. Instead, the moral principle that underlies Hobbes's concept of authority – that no man may be obligated save by a choice of his own – is firmly repudiated. In the organic community admired by Dworkin, there is no place for a concept of authority because what individuals approve of is irrelevant. The only thing that matters is maintaining the whole in good working order, or pursuing the objective of the enterprise. That is why Dworkin opposes what he describes as the normal way of arguing about social and political institutions – "by attacking or defending them on grounds of justice or fairness." Integrity, he says, cannot be defended in this normal way because "integrity will sometimes conflict with what fairness and justice recommend." Instead, Dworkin prefers "French revolutionary rhetoric" because it recognized "a political idea we have not yet considered." This new political idea is "fraternity." It is, he tells us, "in the neighbourhood of fraternity or, to use its more fashionable name, community," that we must look for the defense of integrity. Furthermore, a political society "that accepts integrity as a political virtue thereby becomes a special form of community, special in a way that promotes its moral authority to assume and deploy a monopoly of coercive force."[70] This community is an organic whole, not an association of individual persons.

Once we think of a community as an organic whole with a unitary end, it makes sense to say, as Dworkin does, that "Law is not exhausted by any catalogue of rules or principles, each with its own dominion over some discrete theater of behavior. Nor by any roster of officials and their powers each over part of our lives." What defines Dworkin's "empire" of law is "attitude, not territory or power or process . . . It is an interpretive, self-reflective attitude addressed to politics in the broadest sense. It is a protestant attitude that makes each citizen responsible for imagining what his society's public commitments to principle are, and what these commitments require in new circumstances."[71] It is also true that in such a community, "the set of recognized public standards," as Dworkin puts it, "can expand and contract organically . . . without the need for detailed legislation or adjudication on each possible point of conflict." Integrity is accordingly described by Dworkin as "a vehicle for organic change" since judges guided by the principle of integrity cannot be accused of usurping power that does not belong to them when they reject the rules of a statute in favor of promoting more adequately the

[70] Ibid., 188.   [71] Ibid., 413.

underlying "scheme" of the whole. Instead of thinking in terms of "negotiated solutions to discrete problems," citizens governed according to the principle of integrity accept demands on them and make demands on others "that share and extend the moral dimension of any explicit political decisions." Integrity therefore both fuses citizens' "moral and political lives" and "infuses political and private occasions each with the spirit of the other to the benefit of both."[72] All are thus made one; multiplicity ceases to exist.

In short, all the traditional notions about the rule of law, and especially the fundamental belief that there can be no crime without a legal rule defining it, are dismissed. Instead, the citizens of an organic community are governed by a "common . . . scheme of principles." And only a self-interested bigot, or an ignoramus seduced by "conventionalism," would try to pin down a charge brought by officers of the government to a set of words explicitly justifying that charge. Thus, Dworkin rejects what the rule of law has traditionally postulated – that a community governed by law consists of independent subjects pursuing their own projects and associated by their observance of a common set of rules – in favor of "Fraternal association," which is "conceptually egalitarian." And he points out that the "obligations of fraternity need not be fully voluntary," and that the community need not "agree in detail" about what responsibilities each has for one another. The members of a true, organic community accept "associative" obligations; they "share a general and diffuse sense" of "what sort and level of sacrifice" may be expected of them.[73] Moreover, they recognize that "the best defense of political legitimacy . . . is to be found not in the hard terrain of contracts or duties of justice or obligations of fair play that might hold among strangers, where philosophers have hoped to find it, but in the more fertile ground of fraternity, community, and their attendant obligations. . ."[74]

By inventing "law as integrity," Dworkin has attempted to produce what the Russian Marxist jurist, Pashukanis, declared to be impossible – an understanding of the rule of law that would be compatible with a community understood as an enterprise pursuing a single objective. Given this objective, it is hardly surprising that Dworkin's writing is distinguished by a "Byzantine complexity." For he is attempting to produce a square with the formula for a circle. Indeed, Dworkin's project is even more difficult than the one Pashukanis repudiated because Dworkin does not write as a Marxist.

---

[72] Ibid., 188–90.   [73] Ibid., 211, 198–201.   [74] Ibid., 206.

Where there is an enterprise, there must be an objective that the enterprise is seeking to achieve. In other words, an organic community has to have a single objective. There is no such objective for the kind of community postulated by the traditional idea of law because it does not seek to order the activities of its members so as to promote a superior unitary good, but to allow each peacefully to pursue, either alone or in association with others, whatever projects one chooses. As the pursuit of a unitary good is precisely what defines the organic community presupposed by "law as integrity," the government of such a community is dedicated to achieving certain results rather than to maintaining procedures whereby individuals can choose whatever results they regard as desirable.

This poses no problem for advocates of an organic community who are Marxists or socialists like Beatrice and Sidney Webb. They take it for granted that the objective of an organic community is the efficient production of wealth, or what the Webbs described as maintaining "the health of the social organism." The Webbs accordingly emphasized repeatedly that the object of their form of socialism is not equality but ensuring that each individual adequately performs a task required for maintaining the whole. That is also the message of the Marxist slogan: "From each according to his abilities, to each according to his needs," But not even avowed Marxists are willing to commit themselves to an objective of this kind. Nor has any of them adopted the aggrandizement of national power as his aim. As a result, they are left floundering in a swamp of commitments, concerns, ideals, values, obligations, responsibilities, principles, and standards, without being able to grasp any substantial objective for the enterprise that their idea of law is meant to serve. In *Law's Empire* Dworkin addresses this difficulty directly, as he had never done before. And having squared the circle at last, he can speak more moderately about the opponents against whom he had been battling all along, but never so successfully as with his invention of the principle of "integrity," "associative obligations," and an "organic community" in *Law's Empire*.

There it becomes clear why he has so steadily emphasized the concept of "equal concern and respect": It is his solution to the problem of discovering an objective for an organic community that might appear to be compatible with the rule of law. For the concept of equal concern and respect brings to mind the phrase, "equality before the law," and might even be regarded as a synonym for that traditional idea. But in advocating "equal concern and respect" as the single objective of law, Dworkin means something very different from equality before the law. "Integrity" requires, Dworkin tells us, "that government pursue some coherent conception of what treating people as equals means." However, he warns us, "it does not require that particular programs treat every one the same way."[75] In plain words, Dworkin is advocating that the law be used as an instrument for redistributing resources so as to secure equality. To do so the government may be required not to "treat everyone the same way," because securing equal results may require positive discrimination. And he leaves us in no doubt that it is an equal distribution of resources that offers the best explanation of "what it means to treat people as equals." This, Dworkin says, "is the goal of law purified, the community's star in its search for integrity seen from the standpoint of justice alone." Unlike others who have pursued this objective, however, Dworkin proposes to achieve it through handing over power to the "capitals" and "princes" of "law's empire," the courts and the judges.[76] The weapons he proposes to use are as original as the revolution he hopes to make.

Dworkin thus completes an explanation of why law is inseparable from politics. But instead of elucidating the idea of law, in *Law's Empire* the understanding of law that began to take shape in ancient Athens is decisively renounced.

---

[75] Ibid., 223.   [76] Ibid., 407–8.

Part VI

New foundations

15 A skeptical jurisprudence: Michael Oakeshott

One reason why the renunciation of the idea of law has seemed plausible and gained increasing acceptance is the failure of Hobbes's successors to complete his account of law as a purely human artifact. They explored new aspects of the traditional idea by questioning and explicating much that had never before been noticed. But they failed to provide a way of understanding the relation of the rule of law to the civilization that it had shaped. The many refinements on the idea of law offered no adequate anchor for law in a world where human intelligence lacks the power to discover rational certainties such as Plato and Aristotle had relied on. The task of discovering a new kind of anchor for a system of legal rules was completed by Michael Oakeshott in what may be best described as a skeptical jurisprudence.

The originality and significance of Oakeshott's jurisprudence is, however, difficult to grasp. For it rests on the paradoxical character of Oakeshott's skepticism. The pattern for that character was established by David Hume. What makes both Hume and Oakeshott paradoxical is that, although they are skeptics in the sense that they recognize no rational source of indisputable truth, they could hardly be more antagonistic to nihilism. They both insist, without qualification, that men can know truth from falsehood and right from wrong. Nor does their skepticism entail atheism; on the contrary, it is allied to the theology of Augustine and Hobbes, where such skepticism is not merely tolerated but required as the consequence of acknowledging that God is a Creator irrevocably separate from His creatures and utterly unknowable.

Yet it is not surprising that this skepticism has been confounded with nihilism. For it is hardly obvious how, in the skeptic's world of ever shifting sands, we can find a solid rock to stand on. The lack of such a rock has made it plausible to think of legal rules and decisions as products of caprice disguised by elaborate but empty procedures and to repudiate the idea of law. Moreover, Hume invited confusion by emphasizing the destructive part of his project and leaving it unfinished. An understanding of the human condition that could deal with the dilemmas bequeathed by

Hume without renouncing skepticism was provided by Oakeshott. He showed how a skeptic need not, indeed should not, be a nihilist. And in doing so, he solved – or at least showed the way to solving – the skeptic's dilemma by answering the question that has agitated all modern philosophers: How can we reconcile the apparent orderliness of the human world with the conviction that human beings have no access to an infallible source of rational truth?

Other modern philosophers have evaded this question either by returning, more or less surreptitiously, to classical or medieval metaphysics or by trying to relocate the source of infallibility within the human world or else they have thrown up their hands in despair and assured us that it is a delusion to suppose that we can escape from the abyss of nothingness and the dreadful freedom with which it confronts us. The same responses, as we have seen, appear in the history of the philosophy of law. Oakeshott set himself to showing that although the human world has no cosmic anchor, it is nevertheless full of stable and objective standards for thought and conduct.

The pattern of Oakeshott's solution is nowhere clearer than in his account of the rule of law where he provides answers for the most awkward questions that confront the skeptic: If human laws cannot be founded on indisputable truths given to man by a non-human source, how can any law claim to be just or preferable to any other? If the human world is constantly changing, how can fixed rules of law be appropriate? As everything can be other than it is, why are we obliged to obey the established law? How can we distinguish objective legal decisions from expressions of prejudice or arbitrary exercises of will? Defenders of the rule of law have denounced and denied the skepticism that inspires such questions and insisted that the meaningfulness of law can be saved only by recognizing some "absolute standard" such as "natural law" or "natural rights." Their opponents have argued that any claim to objectivity or justice in legal decisions is fraudulent, that we should dispense with rules, and that we cannot be obliged to obey a law of which we disapprove. Oakeshott proposed a wholly new way of thinking about the human condition and hence about law. Understanding it requires learning a new vocabulary and following a fairly taxing maze of distinctions.

The foundation of Oakeshott's solution to the skeptic's dilemma is a radical redefinition of reason. When Hobbes and Hume rejected the old pantheist view of human reason as a participation in the cosmic ordering principle, they reduced reason to a capacity for doing two things: deducing conclusions from premises that could not be questioned, as in geometry, and seeking satisfaction for the desires given by the passions, which Hume summed up in his description of reason as "the slave of the passions." This view of reason intensified the alienation of individuality from rationality, which the ancient pantheist metaphysics made inevitable. In the modern picture, whether derived from Hobbes or from Kant, diversity can arise only from the chaos of irrational desires or from faulty reasoning. But a small step is needed from that conclusion to the nihilist's view that individuality consists in rebelling against reason, rejecting all objective standards and distinctions between truth and falsehood or good and bad, along with all rules of law. Thus skepticism turns into nihilism and makes it impossible to accept the meaningfulness of law.

Oakeshott succeeded in making a complete break with the ancient pantheism by redefining reason as a purely human, but creative power. To avoid any suggestion of a cosmic principle, he speaks of "rationality" or "intelligence" rather than reason. Oakeshott's "rationality" is neither a capacity to discover indisputable truths or universal and eternal patterns, as in the ancient picture, nor is rationality a slave of the passions or a calculating power, as in the modern picture. As understood by Oakeshott, rationality is a faculty for inventing interpretations of and responses to experience. It is a power to choose how and what to see, think, and do. Human beings are not then "rational animals," torn between two warring forces, such as reason and passion, mind and body, or spirit and matter. In Oakeshott's account, human beings are intelligent agents, who are permeated by rationality and are therefore all of one piece. From this standpoint, emotions are no less rational than mathematical calculations because when human beings feel love or fear, they are, as in everything else that they do, making intelligent interpretations of and responses to their experience.

Once human reason is understood in this fashion, the diversity in the human world ceases to be the sinister product of unruly irrational forces or of faulty reasoning. Individuality becomes the inescapable consequence of human rationality. It is a blessing conferred by the fertility of rational activity, and the human world need not be reduced to uniformity in order to make it rational. This understanding of human beings, Oakeshott says, has hovered over European consciousness since ancient times. It is at one with the Christian idea of a person as an immortal soul, which Aquinas understandably found difficult to reconcile with Aristotelian metaphysics. But no one before Oakeshott had explicitly formulated this conception of human rationality.

The second ingredient of Oakeshott's solution to the skeptic's dilemma is the idea of a "practice." Both the diversity and the orderliness of the human world he attributes to a multitude of practices. Tennis, poetry, science, Islam, French cuisine, a market economy, ballet are all "practices." A practice need not be practical; many practices are theoretical. A practice consists of well-defined conditions that shape how people engage in a particular activity. These conditions may be considerations, manners, customs, standards, maxims, principles, or rules. And a practice may arise in any number of different ways. It may be invented *ab initio* or emerge unbidden out of the performances of individuals that, over time, have acquired a definite pattern. Its origins do not affect the nature of a practice.

What makes the idea of a practice so important is that it unifies those engaged in it without dictating what anyone does. This is because the requirements of a practice, being conditions rather than commands or orders, are not obeyed or disobeyed, but subscribed to. When we speak English, we subscribe to a certain grammar, vocabulary, idioms, and usages. But none of these determines what we choose to say. They only enable us to communicate with other speakers of English who may use it to say very different things. As Oakeshott puts it, a practice is not "a fixed stock of possible utterances, but a fund of considerations drawn upon and used in inventing utterances; a fund which may be used only in virtue of having been learned and being understood."[1] And those who are associated in a practice use their rational power in a fashion unlike that which has traditionally been described as reasoning, that is to say, deducing a particular conclusion from a universal premise. We exercise our rationality differently when we subscribe to a practice. Hence the idea of a practice rests on Oakeshott's redefinition of reason.

People who speak the same language may also have purposes or interests in common. But insofar as they are related by their subscription to the practice of English or French or any other, their relationship is *non-instrumental* or adverbial because they are related by a common manner of doing things, not by the pursuit of the same objectives. All speakers of English are united by their reliance on the same grammar and vocabulary, not by saying, doing, or wanting the same things.

This idea of subscription to the non-instrumental conditions of a practice enables Oakeshott to avoid nihilism without renouncing skepticism. For it explains how people can engage in orderly activities, where they recognize and accept common standards, without being reduced to uniformity or having recourse to an infallible or non-human source of truth. The miracle is achieved by separating the conditions or procedures of a practice from the activities in which that practice is expressed. These common conditions or procedures are objectivities given by the practice

---

[1] Michael Oakeshott, *On Human Conduct* (Oxford: Clarendon Press, 1975), 120.

to those who share in it. Although entirely produced by human choices, the conditions of a practice are nevertheless as objective as if they had been derived from a non-human source because they are wholly independent of the immediate purposes or interests of those who draw upon them, and have not been designed to compel anyone to do or say anything in particular. Like all human constructions, the conditions of a practice are constantly changing. But that does not impair their objectivity because, as the changes are non-instrumental and occur bit by bit, the stability of the practice remains unimpaired. Though the English language has been constantly changing, we can still read Shakespeare and, with a little effort, Chaucer.

In the essay on "Rationalism in Politics," Oakeshott attacked the disposition to believe that every practice could and should be formulated as a set of rules, and he also contrasted "rationalism" to respect for tradition. Traditions are practices that have not been explicitly formulated and are maintained by being handed down from one practitioner to another; in other words, traditions are learned by apprenticeship. Oakeshott's concern takes a different turn in his discussion of the rule of law. There he explains a practice that is necessarily formulated in rules. But the rule of law is one variety of the third ingredient of Oakeshott's solution to the skeptic's dilemma – the idea of a moral practice – which need not necessarily be formulated in rules.

For the most part, Oakeshott tells us, human beings become associated voluntarily in order to pursue common ends or interests – to get, make, or do something that they all want. Such associations, designed to achieve an agreed upon objective, Oakeshott calls enterprise associations. Each draws upon one or more practices. In order to run a shoe factory, for instance, we might draw on the practices of English, Italian, engineering, accounting, marketing, and shoe-making. In subscribing to those practices, we are subscribing to non-instrumental conditions. But our subscription to those practices is instrumental because it is a means for achieving a purpose – producing shoes – which is extrinsic to the practices upon which we draw. No such use can be made of the quite different kind of practice, which is called a moral practice. Oakeshott speaks of it also as moral association and as morality. Thus, besides redefining reason and introducing the idea of a practice, Oakeshott has produced a new formulation of the idea of morality.

A moral practice differs from all others because in addition to prescribing standards or criteria for right and wrong in conduct, it imposes obligations. But what is most peculiar about a moral practice is that it involves nothing other than subscription to those obligations. A moral practice has no particular activity, such as speaking English, that belongs to it; neither can it be used as a means to achieving some extrinsic purpose. When we engage in a moral practice, we do nothing other than subscribe to its conditions in whatever activities we undertake. Subscribing to a moral practice means asking ourselves whether this or that constitutes good conduct. This subscription shapes or qualifies whatever other practices we may engage in.

This conception of morality is a far cry from the conception of morality most familiar nowadays, i.e., a list of licences and prohibitions as a ticket to health, prosperity, happiness, or heaven. Nevertheless, Oakeshott's understanding of morality, as of rationality, is not new. He formulated what was long the prevailing conception of morality in England, which was not dominant anywhere else. It explains the peculiarity of that quintessentially English character, the gentleman, who is defined not by the performance of any particular actions or by the observance of a set of rules, but by the considerations and motives that govern his conduct. In other words, it is a view that regards behaving morally as "a kind of literacy." Oakeshott likens it to speaking a language, and like a language, a morality can be subscribed to with more or less delicacy, but cannot tell us what actions to perform: "a morality is not a list of licences and prohibitions but an everyday practice; that is, a vernacular language of intercourse."[2] A morality is changeable in the same way as language is: "Like any other language in its use, it is never fixed and finished. But although it may be criticized and modified in detail it can never be rejected *in toto* and replaced by another." Like any other language, too, a moral language may be used with more or less delicacy, subtlety, refinement – "It may be spoken with various degrees of *sprachgefühl*." But however it is used, a morality "can never tell us what to say or to do, only how we should say or do what we wish to say or do. Thus moral conduct, conduct in respect of its recognition of the considerations of a morality, is a kind of literacy. And just as considerations of literacy do not themselves compose utterances, and just as a practice can never itself be performed, so we may act morally, but no actual performance can be specified in exclusively moral terms."[3] Like all other practices, a morality provides us with objective standards, in particular, with grounds for distinguishing right from wrong conduct (as opposed to expediential or prudential conduct). And all human conduct is qualified by some moral practice, that is to say, by some conception of what is in itself right and wrong. As these standards have been made by human beings, they are never wholly

[2] Michael Oakeshott, "The Rule of Law," in *On History and Other Essays* (Oxford: Basil Blackwell, 1983), 133.
[3] "Rule of Law," 133.

fixed. Nevertheless, they are stable and objective; nihilism is nowhere in sight.

The rule of law is a moral practice. But it is distinguished by the fact that it consists of a set of rules. Oakeshott calls those who subscribe to these rules *cives* or members of a civil association. Unlike other forms of association, civil association consists in nothing other than subscription to the rules of that association. It is analogous to a game, because just as a game is constituted by its rules, so civil association is wholly constituted by the rule of law: "Civil association is a moral condition; it is not concerned with the satisfaction of wants and with substantive outcomes but with the terms upon which the satisfaction of wants may be sought."[4]

Civil association is to be distinguished from a mode of association, which Oakeshott calls "transactional," "in which agents are joined in seeking to procure the satisfaction of a chosen common want or to promote a common interest." Such associates may compose themselves into "a fellowship, a guild, a society, a party, a league, an alliance or a community." They have "a common purpose to the pursuit of which each associate undertakes to devote . . . his time, energy, means, skill and so on. . . The engagement occupies time, it is a call upon resources, it looks to a future, it is inherently terminable and may terminate with the achievement of its purpose or the dissolution of the association. . . The associates are joined in transactions among themselves in which their various skills are directed to the service of the common cause."[5] A state takes the form of this kind of association when its members regard themselves as "joined in the pursuit of a common substantive purpose," such as "the exploitation of the natural resources of its territory (and of resources elsewhere which might be acquired by settlement, force or stealth) for the well-being of the associates"; and when its government is seen "as the 'enlightened' custodian and director of this enterprise; and its 'laws' as the authorization of practices and as instruments for determining priorities and . . . for distributing the product of the enterprise."[6] No such common purpose unites the members of a civil association. They may be "in all other respects total strangers to one another. Or . . . temporarily or durably joined with some others in some other mode of relationship . . . in the exchange of services, in giving and receiving, in sharing and expressing religious beliefs, or in promoting a common *interest*. Indeed, there is no end to the number and variety of the minorities of interest into which they may circumstantially compose themselves or the collocations (sex, family, race, profession, hobby and so on) in terms of which they may from time

---

[4] *Human Conduct*, 174.   [5] "Rule of Law," 122–23.   [6] Ibid., 135–36.

to time recognize themselves."[7] The freedom, like the order and peace enjoyed by the members of a civil association, is not a consequence pursued and achieved. It is inherent in the character of civil association because the freedom of *cives* "is not tied to a choice to be and to remain associated in terms of a common purpose: it is neither more nor less than the absence of such a purpose or choice."[8]

In explicating the "law" to which the members of a civil association subscribe, Oakeshott emphasizes the importance of understanding precisely the nature of the rule of law. He points out that although other kinds of associations have regulations that are called "rules," they are not rules in the same sense because they are concerned with the expediency of conduct: A railroad or a factory is run by rules, but these are designed to make the trains run on time or to produce goods as efficiently as possible. Such rules are designed to achieve certain consequences. Rules of law are not concerned with the consequences or expediency of conduct, but with the *propriety* of conduct. They tell us not what it is useful to do, but what is *right*. And being "right" is an end in itself, not a means to anything else.

Secondly, a rule has to be distinguished from a recommendation or a command, which is an utterance addressed to a particular person, advising that person how to respond to the situation in which he or she finds himself or herself. A recommendation is designed to produce certain results here and now. A rule, however, comes into existence in advance of, and in ignorance of, the circumstances in which it may be invoked or the persons who may be affected by it. Therefore, a rule has to be distinguished both from a managerial decision designed to promote a particular enterprise and from a "policy" such as the Athenian assembly decided in response to Pericles' speech condemning concessions to the Peloponnesians. And whereas a command, decision, or policy is extinguished by being obeyed, a rule is not used up by being observed. Like the conditions of any practice, a rule of law is adverbial and therefore noninstrumental. It tells you not what to do, but what conditions or procedures you must observe if you wish to make a contract that can be defended in a court of law. Or it may tell you that if you engage in the activity of boxing not as a sport, but in order to injure your opponent, you will be doing something that is prohibited. Hence the rule of law "is not concerned either to promote or to obstruct the pursuit of interests." Indeed it is of the essence of law, Oakeshott repeatedly reminds us, not to be "concerned with the merits of different interests, with satisfying substantive wants, with the promotion of prosperity, the elimination of

---

[7] Ibid., 136–37.   [8] *Human Conduct*, 158.

waste, the equal or differential distribution of reputed benefits or opportunities, with arbitrating competing claims to advantages or satisfactions, or with the promotion of a condition of things recognized as the common good." The consideration that we take into account when deliberating about the "propriety" or rightness of law must be "moral, non-instrumental considerations."[9]

The chief impediment to moral association in terms of rules, according to Oakeshott, is the difficulty of determining whether a rule is authentic and distinguishing this from its rightness. It is therefore tempting, Oakeshott warns us, to abandon authenticity in favor of rightness as the ground of moral or legal obligation. This can happen where a rule is regarded as the voluntary utterance of God "whose will was itself also a guarantee of the 'rightness' of whatever is prescribed."[10] Or authenticity can be made to rest on correspondence with natural law or conscience, each of which is also a disguised guarantee of its "rightness." But no such solution is acceptable to a skeptic who denies that what God wills or what the natural law requires here and now can be indisputably known. Even if God were to speak to someone, that person's account of what was communicated to him cannot be indisputably accepted by others. Indeed in a community composed of people with greatly heterogeneous beliefs and projects, there is especially likely to be serious disagreement about the rightness of a rule.

If there is no natural unanimity and no infallible standard for the rightness of rules, and if the rules are obligatory, then the only way to settle conflict is for the will of some to prevail over the will of others. But that violates what Oakeshott describes as the fundamental principle of moral obligation – that no man may become obligated save by a choice of his own. That is not so much a principle as an implication of the understanding of human beings that Oakeshott postulates throughout. For if each person is an independent rational agent, with no access to infallible truth, no one can claim a natural authority to impose obligations on another.

A further reason given by Oakeshott against the contention that a law can be identified by its conformity to justice is that there is no indisputable way of identifying legislators who might be depended on to produce just law. Nor do we have access to indisputable signs by which to recognize the quality of justice when it appears so as "to fend off the threat of anarchy contained in the claim that the voice of 'conscience' is the voice of *jus*."[11] For if the conscience of each individual is separate and

---

[9] "Rule of Law," 154, 141.   [10] Ibid., 135–36.   [11] Ibid., 156.

independent from that of every other individual, there may be as many versions of justice as people. Only if each person's "conscience" were a participation in one, universal and eternal conscience, as pantheists believe, would this problem disappear. These difficulties, Oakeshott says, are recognized by those who try to escape them through declarations of inalienable rights. But no such solution is acceptable to a skeptic. He cannot therefore accept that unjust law is not law.

In the absence of an infallible, uncontentious test for the rightness of a rule, the only alternative is to rest the obligation to observe a rule on its authenticity. That makes the question – how do we establish the authenticity of a rule of law? – central for a skeptical jurisprudence. We cannot consult a rule book as we do in a game, for there is no way of identifying indisputably the relevant rule book. Moreover, in a civil association the rules are far more complicated than in a game. "These difficulties never invade the rules of a game: any question of their authenticity is settled by an accepted rule book, and the arbitrary character of the conditions prescribed by the rules of a game precludes anything but a strictly relativist consideration of their 'rightness,' and there is no temptation to confuse the two."[12] The authenticity of rules of law can be established only by knowing who made them. We can then be certain that only rules which "have been deliberately enacted or appropriated" by those who occupy "an exclusively legislative office" and follow "a recognized procedure" constitute authentic rules of law. Such persons may also deliberately alter or repeal the established rules. The legislature need not be the sole source of law, but a rule, such as a rule of common law, acquires the authority of law by being subject to appropriation, rejection, or emendation in a legislative enactment.[13]

Recognizing the authenticity of law consists in nothing other than acknowledging that it has been enacted by those who have been given the right or authority to do so. The authenticity of a law is thus synonymous with its authority. But acknowledging the authority of law does not entail approval of what it prescribes. For Oakeshott the distinction between acknowledging the authority of a law and approving of it is a logical implication of the fact that the authority of law rests on the authorization of the legislators that necessarily occurs before the law is made. Thus the central question for skeptical jurisprudence is: How do legislators acquire their authority? The authority of legislators cannot be derived from any natural quality such as virtue, prudence, or wisdom because there is no indisputable way of identifying such qualities. The

---

[12] Ibid., 135.   [13] Ibid., 138.

authority of legislators can only be endowed by the office that they occupy: "the authority of legislative enactments lies neither in their terms nor in these having been chosen; it lies in the authority of the procedure in which they were enacted."[14] The authority of an office, that is to say, the right to create obligations, can be conferred only by those obligated. Otherwise, the acquisition of authority would violate the fundamental principle of moral obligation, as the Oakeshottian skeptic understands it, that no person may become obligated save by their own choice.

How the disposition to acknowledge someone's authority arises is irrelevant; it may arise in any number of ways. Hobbes devoted *Leviathan* to showing how the recognition of a sovereign authority might come about in "a state of nature," though he pointed out that it might also be the result of conquest. What matters is not how those subject to the law come to recognize the authority of those who make it, but that those obligated do in fact acknowledge such an authority. In whatever fashion acknowledgment first arises, those who are born into a community and remain to enjoy the protection of its laws are implicitly acknowledging the authority of the legal order. It is the same argument as that of Socrates in the *Crito* when he says that, as he might have left Athens but never chose to do so, he implicitly acknowledged an obligation to obey Athenian law. Today, we implicitly make the same argument when we insist that the freedom to emigrate is a defining mark of a free society. For only then can those who remain be known to have remained willingly and be obliged to observe the laws of that society. And whether we sometimes break the law, Oakeshott emphasizes, has no more bearing on our acknowledgment of its authority than our disapproval of it. The captured burglar, though he struggles to escape, is nevertheless bound to acknowledge the authority of those who restrain him. Acknowledging the authority of law is a conclusion solely about the procedure by which it was made.

The authority of law thus rests on the procedure by which it was enacted, which constitutes an objective standard visible to all that serves as the rock for the law to stand on. Disagreements about whether procedures have been observed can be settled by other procedures that are also defined by authentic rules. The legislature may be constituted in any number of ways, as long as the mode of constituting it and the powers of the office of legislator are specified by law and conform to the procedures laid down by law. In other words, the law is a self-authenticating objectivity consisting in rules for procedures that are visible to and accepted by all those subject to it.

[14] *Human Conduct*, 156.

The principle that no person may be obligated save by choice is protected besides by the fact that obligations are imposed by rules, not by
expressions of "will." That laws are rules and that their injunctions
are not "orders to be obeyed" prevents those obligated to observe them
from being "servile role-performers" because "even the least ambiguous
duty can be fulfilled only by a 'free' agent choosing what he shall do."[15]
The anarchist who feels enslaved by law is really objecting, Oakeshott
says, to managerial rules because they compel him to serve an enterprise
that he would not have joined voluntarily. Thus, the indeterminacy of
rules is regarded by Oakeshott as one of the boons of the rule of law, not
as a defect.

A rule of law, then, does not merely distinguish between right and
wrong in conduct; it is an *authoritative* prescription of conditions to be
subscribed to in acting, and its counterpart is an obligation to subscribe to
these conditions. And the obligation to observe rules of law "is not merely
to feel constrained, nor is it to be confused with having a disposition
usually to comply with what a rule prescribes – what has been called 'a
habit of obedience.' It is neither more nor less than acknowledgment of
the authenticity of the rule. And just as the authenticity or authority of a
rule relates neither to approval of what it prescribes nor to any remunera-
tory or punitive consequences that may be expected to follow compliance
or non-compliance with its prescriptions, so the obligation it entails is
related neither to approval of what it prescribes nor to a hope or a fear in
respect of the consequences of observance or non-observance. And this
obligation is not denied in a failure to comply or even in a refusal to
comply."[16]

Oakeshott accordingly defines an association in terms of the rule of law
as a "relationship in respect of authoritative prescriptions which have a
certain jurisdiction and an ascertainable authenticity." Such an association postulates (what Marxism and Political Jurisprudence obliterate)
"agents engaged in self-chosen actions to promote or procure various
substantive satisfactions." The prescriptions of such an association
impose upon its members obligations "to observe certain adverbial conditions in performing all or any of these actions. These rules are not
designed to promote or to impede the achievement of these satisfactions
and are incapable of doing so, and they are not instrumental to the
achievement of a substantive purpose of their own. And these obligations
may or may not be observed, but they are not denied in a failure to
observe them."[17] Oakeshott concludes that: "The expression 'the rule of

---

[15] Ibid., 157.   [16] "Rule of Law," 130.   [17] Ibid., 131.

law,' taken precisely, stands for a mode of moral association exclusively in terms of the recognition of the authority of known, non-instrumental rules (that is, laws) which impose obligations to subscribe to adverbial conditions in the performance of the self-chosen actions of all who fall within their jurisdiction."[18]

Here then, in the notion of the authority of law, resting wholly on procedural rules, and postulating the idea of a moral practice, are not only the ingredients of a skeptical jurisprudence, but also a model for a solution to the skeptic's dilemma. The idea of a practice explains how individuals may voluntarily cooperate in an orderly fashion without either acknowledging an infallible superior or sacrificing diversity. And the idea of a moral practice enables us to understand how the rule of law can resolve differences of opinion and maintain civil peace without recourse to infallible, non-human truth.

It remains to consider how the desirability or justice of a law can be established. Oakeshott recognizes that insulating authority and obligation from consent or dissent to their demands might seem to render laws "Remote, mysterious, cold . . . clothed in pitiless majesty, they ask neither to be loved nor to be approved," and make it plausible to regard these "stern but unenthusiastic ogres" as "an affront to human dignity." But he dismisses this picture as "the invention of caricature," and he gives three reasons for doing so.[19]

The first is that the idea of law postulates a distinctive morality. We cannot understand the rule of law without recognizing a certain conception of the nature of human beings and of what is due to human dignity. That is one reason why the rule of law is, by definition, not an amoral set of arrangements but a moral practice.

Secondly, the "amorality" of law is qualified by what Lon Fuller has described as "the internal morality of law." This inner morality prescribes "conditions which distinguish a legal order and in default of which whatever purports to be a legal order is not what it purports to be: rules not secret or retrospective, no obligations save those imposed by law, all associates equally and without exception subject to the obligations imposed by law, no outlawry."[20] It is "only in respect of these considerations and their like," Oakeshott grants, that it might perhaps be said that *lex injusta non est lex*.[21] But Oakeshott considers it more precise to think of such requirements as the formal principles or the definition of a legal

---

[18] Ibid., 136.   [19] *Human Conduct*, 157.
[20] Oakeshott, "Rule of Law," 140; Lon L. Fuller, "Positivism and Fidelity to Law – A Reply to Professor Hart," *Harvard Law Review* 71 (February 1958): 645.
[21] Oakeshott, "Rule of Law," 140.

order rather than as criteria of the justice of rules of law. To consider the justice of law, something more is needed.

The third reason why law is not an "unenthusiastic ogre" is that as well as asking whether a law has been properly enacted, we may – and should – ask whether it is right or wrong to have enacted it. In doing so, we evaluate the conditions to be observed quite apart from their authority. Such evaluation is what legislators are deciding when they deliberate about proposals for enactment. Deliberation about legislation is described by Oakeshott as follows: "Nevertheless, rules may also be appreciated in respect of what they prescribe. . . Among makers of rules this may invoke a variety of prudential and consequential considerations (such as the difficulty or probable cost of detecting a delinquency), but for them and for others its central concern is with what may be called, somewhat loosely, the 'evaluation' of these conditions distinguished from the determination of their authenticity. By this I mean not merely the consistency of a rule with the others that compose the set of rules to which it belongs or is designed to belong, but its virtue as a contribution to the shape of this set of rules as the desirable conditions of an invented pattern of non-instrumental human relationships."[22]

By insisting that considering the justice of law is as important as ascertaining its authority, Oakeshott is not, however, opening a Pandora's box of unlimited speculation. He carefully specifies that deliberation about the justice of an enactment is the consideration of certain limited questions. These are "a particular kind of moral consideration: neither an absurd belief in moral absolutes" or "rights," nor "the distinction between the rightness and wrongness of actions in terms of the motives in which they are performed."[23] The justice of a law "is composed of considerations in terms of which a law may be recognized, not merely as properly enacted, but as proper or not improper to be or to have been enacted; beliefs and opinions invoked in considering the propriety of the conditions prescribed in a particular law." Because law is the bond of a civil association and not of an enterprise pursuing a common purpose, the justice of a law cannot be identified with the "merits of different interests, with satisfying substantive wants, with the promotion of prosperity, the elimination of waste, the equal or differential distribution of reputed benefits or opportunities, with arbitrating competing claims to advantages or satisfactions, or with the promotion of a condition of things recognized as the common good."[24] Nor does association under the rule of law require "a set of abstract criteria" for determining the *jus* of a law.

---

[22] Ibid., 130–31.   [23] Ibid., 160.   [24] Ibid., 140–41.

What it does require is "an appropriately argumentative form of discourse in which to deliberate the matter; that is, a form of moral discourse, not concerned generally with right and wrong in human conduct, but focused narrowly upon the kind of conditional obligations a law may impose, undistracted by prudential and consequential considerations, and insulated from the spurious claims of conscientious objection, of minorities for exceptional treatment and, so far as may be, from current moral idiocies."[25]

Oakeshott's concern here is to distinguish the kind of moral judgment involved in evaluating the justice of legislative enactments from other kinds of moral judgments. The proper concern of the legislator, he says, is with "the negative and limited consideration that the prescriptions of the law should not conflict with a prevailing educated moral sensibility." And an educated moral sensibility consists in the capacity to distinguish between "the conditions of 'virtue,' the conditions of moral association ('good conduct'), and those conditions which are of such a kind that they should be imposed by law ('justice')."[26]

Whether a law is "just" is then a judgment made by a particular set of people at a particular time and place and subject to modification. It cannot "specify anything so grand as the conditions of 'human excellence' or of human 'self-realization.'" Yet it would be a mistake to conclude that Oakeshott is recommending what is called "relativism." For he is not equating justice with whatever we happen to like here and now. Deliberation about the justice of law rests on a commitment to a certain conception of law as implicit in a particular understanding of a human condition and the corollaries of that understanding. Moreover, justice is "certainly a moral and not a prudential consideration," as Oakeshott keeps reminding us. And he accordingly excludes from deliberation about justice almost everything that his contemporaries consider to be the heart of the matter.

Deliberating about the justice of legislative proposals, is not, he insists, about an "imagined and wished-for outcome" but about the desirability of "conditions to be subscribed to by all alike in unspecifiable future performances." Neither worldly interests nor unworldly dreams have any place in these deliberations. A well qualified legislator has a "disciplined imagination," the ability to forswear "the large consideration of human happiness and virtue . . . even the consideration of the most profitable or least burdensome manner of satisfying current wants."[27] In short, the proper subject of legislative deliberations is extremely modest – it is some item in the established rules and the comparative merits of

---

[25] Ibid., 143.   [26] Ibid., 160.   [27] *Human Conduct*, 163–64.

alternatives to it. And the arguments for and against it are obliged to ignore any effect on anyone's interests or dreams and to consider only whether it should be included in the *res publica*. Therefore, the model of legislative deliberation for Oakeshott is the debate between Fox and Pitt on the Alien's Bill of 1792 because "Both speakers understood themselves to be deliberating a rule of civil association, not the award of advantage or disadvantage to assignable persons."[28]

Many different considerations have to be taken into account when deliberating about justice. The logic of such arguments is that of practical reasoning in Aristotle's sense: it is an enthymeme in which the major premise is a maxim, a statement about what is generally believed to be desirable, and the conclusion is recognized to be subject to question. Such conclusions cannot, strictly speaking, be refuted, but they can be resisted by arguments of the same sort that the audience may find more or less convincing.

There is no place in any sense, however, for considerations of justice in adjudication. Nevertheless, Oakeshott attaches an unusual importance to adjudication, which arises from his conception of a rule.

According to Oakeshott, it is neither a defect of the law nor unusual circumstances that make us resort to adjudication. It is rather "the unavoidable indeterminacy [of rules]" that "calls for a procedure of casuistry" in which the rules "are related to circumstantial occasions."[29] The "unavoidable indeterminacy" of rules is due to the fact that they "subsist in advance and in necessary ignorance of the future contingent situations to which they may be found to relate." And however free the laws might be from "ambiguity and conflict with one another," their nature as rules makes it impossible for them to "declare their meaning in respect of any circumstantial situation."[30] The casuistry involved in adjudication therefore necessarily enters into all subscription to rules of law. But for the most part, we engage in such casuistry unselfconsciously. Only when a dispute arises and a matter is brought to court does the full analysis have to be spelled out.

As there is bound to be disagreement about the conclusions of the casuistry that relates rules to particular circumstances, adjudication is an essential part of the rule of law. The rule of law must therefore include an office that is endowed with the authority and charged with the duty of determining whether what was said or done on a particular occasion subscribed adequately to the obligation imposed by the law. This office – a court of law – is accordingly concerned with actual performances

---

[28] "Rule of Law," 179, n 1.   [29] Ibid., 135.   [30] Ibid., 144.

"solely in respect of their legality." Its "task is to relate a general statement of conditional obligation to an occurrence in terms of what distinguishes it from other occurrences."[31] It "cannot entertain speculations about the intentions of legislators or conjectures about how they would decide the case" because "to make law and to adjudicate a case are categorically different engagements." Nor may a court decide in terms of what will promote public policy, any particular interests, or even "the public interest" – the rule of law "knows nothing of a 'public interest' save the sum of the obligations imposed by law."[32] Nor is the court "concerned to arbitrate between competing substantive interests" because, since the suitors before the court are to be seen as 'persona' related in terms of the rule of law, these suitors, "like the court itself, have no 'interests.'" Nor may a court decide a case "in terms of so-called substantive 'rights' claimed as a matter of *jus* in some current moral opinion: the right to speak, to be informed, to enjoy an equal opportunity or the advantage of a handicap. The rule of law knows nothing of unconditional 'rights.'"[33] Nor does the opinion of the judge about what is "just" have any place in adjudication. In a court of law, says Oakeshott, justice "must exhibit itself as the conclusion of an argument designed to show as best it may that *this* is the meaning of the law in respect of this occurrence."[34]

On whether judges are obliged to "follow precedent," Oakeshott introduces a new distinction. He grants that the procedural obligations of a court may require it "to take account of decisions in earlier allegedly similar cases." But he denies that such cases are to be recognized by the court as precedents to be followed. Its concern will be rather "with the analogical force of the distinctions they invoked." If, for instance, the issue is to determine whether a trespass had been committed, the judge may be required to consider whether the distinction between a public highway and a private path made in earlier cases is or is not like the distinction made in the case being argued before him. But such analogical reasoning is intrinsic to all legal reasoning. What is always being decided is whether a rule has been adequately subscribed to or violated. Therefore, Oakeshott concludes that, "In respect of the rule of law the expression 'case law' is a solecism."[35]

Neither rigidity, nor an obsessive attachment to the letter of the law, nor indifference to human suffering accounts for Oakeshott's view of adjudication. His view follows necessarily from his understanding of rationality, of moral association, and of rules, and his assumption that

---

[31] Ibid., 144–45.   [32] Ibid., 146.   [33] Ibid.
[34] Ibid.   [35] Ibid., 146–47.

judges do not have access to a source of infallible knowledge about what people ought to do and have – about what is "just." It is because Oakeshott repudiates any claim to indisputable knowledge that he attaches so much importance to procedural rules and to distinguishing legislating from adjudicating.

About punishment, which other theories regard as the essence of law, not much need be said here because Oakeshott regards punishment as an adjunct of law and not as intrinsic to it. Association in terms of the rule of law, he says, "does not presume recalcitrance on the part of its members." But it does provide "for the punishment of those convicted of failure to observe their obligations and perhaps something by way of remedy for the substantive damage attributable to delinquency."[36] The retributive theory of punishment is as alien to Oakeshott as nihilism. To suffer punishment, he says, "is not an acceptable alternative" to fulfilling the obligation to observe the law; "it cannot (and is not designed to) restore the situation to its condition before the delinquency was committed."[37] Fear of punishment may, of course, deter a potential delinquent. And to consider the deterrent effects of the punishment is compatible with the rule of law. But the question being considered is a prudential one and not of the essence of the rule of law.

Oakeshott did not pretend to have invented the idea of the rule of law or the civil association that it constitutes. He was disposed to think that these contrivances had arisen in the manner described in Schopenhauer's story about a colony of porcupines, which he retells as follows:

They were wont to huddle together on a cold winter's day and, thus wrapped in communal warmth, escape being frozen. But plagued with the pricks of each other's quills, they drew apart. And every time the desire for warmth brought them together again, the same calamity overtook them. Thus they remained, distracted between two misfortunes, able neither to tolerate nor to do without one another, until they discovered that when they stood at a certain distance from one another they could both delight in one another's individuality and enjoy one another's company. They did not attribute any metaphysical significance to this distance, nor did they imagine it to be an independent source of happiness, like finding a friend. They recognized it to be a relationship in terms of not substantive enjoyment but of contingent considerabilities that they must determine for themselves. Unknown to themselves, they had invented civil association.[38]

As Oakeshott has emphasized in more than one context, no existing state ever has or could operate purely in terms of the rule of law in the

---

[36] Ibid., 147.   [37] Ibid.

[38] Michael Oakeshott, *Rationalism in Politics and other Essays* (Indianapolis, IN: Liberty, 1962), 460–61.

strict sense. A purely civil association is therefore an abstraction – neither a description of an existing state nor an ideal to be realized. For one thing, the state has to collect taxes to maintain itself, and tax laws are commands, not rules. Nor can the rule of law protect the state against aggression from other states. "One unavoidable contingent circumstance of modern Europe for which the rule of law cannot itself provide" is "the care for the interests of a state in relation to other states, the protection of these interests in defensive war . . . and the pursuit of larger ambitions to extend its jurisdiction. And this is . . . because 'policy' here, as elsewhere, entails a command over the resources of the members of a state categorially different from that required to maintain the apparatus of the rule of law, and may even entail the complete mobilization of all those resources."[39] Unlike Hegel, Oakeshott believed that civil association is severely distorted by war. It is also distorted when the state seeks to provide for those who cannot look after themselves insofar as the government becomes involved in the redistribution of resources and managerial activities. Nevertheless, where the rule of law constitutes the fundamental framework, and where it is not lightly qualified or frivolously abandoned, something approaching a civil association can be and has been maintained. Oakeshott makes no grand claims for the rule of law. Its achievement, as he sees it, is modest but indispensable: "The rule of law bakes no bread, it is unable to distribute loaves or fishes (it has none), and it cannot protect itself against external assault, but it remains the most civilized and least burdensome conception of a state yet to be devised."[40]

Skeptic though he is, Oakeshott has explicated a distinctive understanding of what human beings are and reached the conclusion that association in terms of the rule of law is the "least burdensome of all human relationships" because "it excludes no other and that mitigates conflict without imposing uniformity." It is "particularly appropriate to a state because it is the only morally tolerable form of compulsory association."[41] That is the voice not of a nihilist, but of a philosopher who considers it impossible, and folly to try, to escape from "the unavoidable dissonances of a human condition,"[42] but believed that, without pretending to read the mind of God, or imposing our will on others, or abandoning ourselves to chaos, we have available in the rule of law a mode of association that can enable us both to "delight in one another's individuality and enjoy one another's company."[43]

---

[39] "Rule of Law," 163.   [40] Ibid., 164.   [41] *Rationalism*, 460.
[42] *Human Conduct*, 81.   [43] *Rationalism*, 460.

16   Postscript: Morality, individualism, and law

I

The current repudiation of the idea of law is, as we have seen, at the same time a repudiation of individualism, which is justified as a defense of morality. We are told that if we favor compassion and altruism, rather than the ruthless pursuit of self-interest, we must reject the idea of law as a set of fixed rules designed to make possible an association of people who wish to shape their own lives and pursue their own projects. The traditional idea of law is said to be acceptable only to ruthless individualists who recognize no concern or responsibility for maintaining a decent communal life and securing the well-being of their fellow men.

This way of understanding individualism and the relation between the traditional idea of law and morality arises from a gross confusion. It began with the conclusion that because Hobbes had rejected the ancient and medieval view that linked morality to the governing principle of the cosmos, his idea of law is an amoral concept. The confusion was exacerbated by the message drawn wrongly from Bentham's utilitarianism, that individualism consists in advocating the heartless pursuit of self-interest. In reaction against that message, the opponents of individualism who became influential in the course of the nineteenth century equated morality with altruism or selflessness and contrasted it to individualistic selfishness. Consequently, the moral life came to be understood as a progress of altruism ascending to self-sacrifice. This equation of morality with altruism led to the conclusion that a regard for individuality signifies a disdain for morality. And it was taken to follow that in order to establish justice and peace, everyone must be made to conform to a pattern for moral life that represses the rebellious individuality of human beings. There is disagreement about what form such regulation should take and how far it should go. But the equation of morality with altruism makes it difficult to resist the conclusion that a man's moral quality increases with his readiness to sacrifice his personal wants and aspirations in order to serve some "higher whole," whether this higher whole is identified with the nation, the state, a class, or all of "humanity." In all such versions of the morality of altruism, law has the character of a repressive machine designed to reduce the evil messiness of human life to a "good" orderliness, which citizens who have been properly educated will not resent but submit to gratefully.

Individualists who reject this conclusion are disposed to define human beings as possessors of "rights," which the law should protect. It is the view that we find first in Locke and most recently in Political Jurisprudence. But using "rights" as a standard by which to measure the justice of law merely by postulating that human beings come into the world with a knowledge of what is due to them is usually not recognized as legitimate because universally valid knowledge of "rights" must be naturally available to everyone, and this is not the case. For if there is no non-human source of knowledge about "rights" to which every human being has access, then a "right" can only be a human invention. Rights then become arbitrary claims, and there is no reason why anyone else should be obliged to recognize the rights that I demand because such "rights" cannot be distinguished from "interests," and so cannot serve as a criterion for deciding which interests to satisfy. Nor is there any reason why the various "rights" being claimed by different people should not conflict in the same way as my "interests" may conflict with yours. The only alternative is to have the state or the law define rights. But then "rights" cannot serve as an uncontentious, given test for the justice of law.

There are two ways in which human beings may be supposed to have access to such indisputable, universal truth. Either they may possess a power of perceiving an eternally fixed order outside human life, as Plato, Aristotle, Aquinas, Cicero and Locke believed, though they gave different accounts of the character of this order and of how we come to know it. Or human beings must arrive in the world already programmed by such an order, that is, containing within themselves the imprint of an eternal rational pattern, as Kant assumed. The Marxist theory of history is the most coherent (though not the only) variant of the latter view. But for Marx, the eternal order is imprinted in the organization of the productive activities of human beings. In short, the attempt to find a moral basis for individualism in "rights" must postulate an understanding of human rationality that identifies it with the capacity to discover indisputable and universal truths from which infallible practical guidance can be derived. This postulate makes it possible to explain the great oddity of the human condition, i.e., that though our world is full of confusing variety and irregular change, we can nevertheless rely on some steadiness in it. By discovering something fixed that underlies the variability of our everyday experience, human reason can gain access to truth unaffected by human will and valid for all human beings and can thus enable us to escape from uncertainty about what constitutes justice.

But this understanding of rationality has two irremediable flaws. It is not only incompatible with the modern individualist's rejection of metaphysical truth, such as ancient and medieval philosophers relied on. It also destroys any ground for valuing human individuality. For it obliges us to identify individuality with irrationality: If reason is understood as the power to grasp universal uncontentious truth, the only way of accounting for individuality is to suppose that there is an irrational element in human nature that resists reason and produces a chaos of desires and aversions, operating in no regular fashion. The victory of this irrational element over reason gives rise to the endlessly changing, erratic diversity in human behavior. Human beings must then be regarded as unstable compounds of two warring parts, which have been given different names – reason and passion, spirit and matter, mind and body. But whatever the names and however their relationship is described, man has to be seen as an amalgam of two elements, one being the source of truth, order, and goodness, and the other, of disorder and evil. And to believe that individuals should be free to shape their lives as they choose is tantamount to believing that irrationality should be given free rein. It was this understanding of rationality that led Plato and Aristotle to endorse two conflicting meanings of law, one which identified law with the bond uniting independent agents pursuing heterogeneous projects, and another which identified law with a pattern for the moral perfection of all individuals. In other words, understanding rationality as a capacity for discovering universally valid truth made it impossible to explain why an association of self-moving individuals should be valued and gave rise to the tension between justice and liberty that dominated the ancient discussion of law. Though the tension was eliminated by Hobbes, it has been revived by the efforts of his successors to counteract what they regard as the amorality of his solution.

Individualists are not, however, obliged to renounce either morality or rationality. This is not to deny that there is good reason for the dissatisfaction with Hobbes's manner of escaping from the tension between justice and liberty. For Hobbes retained the picture of man as an amalgam of two warring elements, which picture could account for human individuality only by allying it with the element of irrationality. Nevertheless, there are in Hobbes's philosophy (as in that of Hume) intimations of an alternative understanding of the human condition, and these intimations account for those passages that cannot be reconciled with the view of Hobbes as an amoralist. This alternative has hovered over the

European imagination since the rise of Christianity. But it was not explicitly formulated until very recently.

It was Michael Oakeshott who, for the first time, portrayed a human being as all one, that is, a creature who cannot help being rational. In this picture, if a person's faculties are in good order, he exercises his rationality in whatever he is doing because he is always interpreting his experience and responding in the manner that he selects. This means that whenever a man is aware of anything, he has made something of it. He may see a mountain as a terrifying obstacle, a glimpse of eternity, a challenge to climb, or a store of minerals; he may find joy in weeding his garden or in flying a plane, choose solitude or dote on the noise of a city, work at the craft of his forefathers or wander away to distant lands, feel obliged to endure pain silently or to rail at the heavens, have a genius for laughter or for mathematics. In short, to say that a man is a rational being is to say that he makes of himself what he will and that things appear to him as he chooses to see them. He is not potter's clay being "conditioned," or shaped by a superior or by his circumstances. He does not arrive in the world with a prefabricated destiny; he himself is both potter and clay.

It follows that what a human being does voluntarily is not caused in the way that a trigger sets a bullet in motion, that far from being a mechanical process, human conduct always and necessarily involves choice. A man may have to deal with biological processes within his body and physical processes outside it, and he may be deprived by force of his human faculties. But as long as he retains his reason, he chooses how to understand and to deal with his experience. There is variety in human conduct because a man's interests or wants are what he has learned to think they are, and what has been learned can be learned differently. Human beings are not therefore the passive victims of forces, drives, or needs. They transform their experience into a variety of interpretations, responses, and reflections. Their moral life consists in shaping and maintaining the integrity of their personality and respecting, perhaps assisting, the efforts of others to do the same.

We must then recognize that the morality that can sustain the kind of individualism and the idea of law that Westerners have learned to value rests on the conception of rationality as a creative faculty rather than as a pipeline to certainty. The important novelty in this morality that is crucial for understanding the idea of law is that each man is assumed to possess individuality not in spite of, but because of his rationality. His individuality is not accounted for by a "core" of passions or urges beating against a corset imposed by "reason" or "society." To say that human beings possess individuality means that all are the makers of their own thoughts, that they are capable of shaping a personality, and that they are responsible for what they become. Individuality is not then displayed in egoism, willfulness, selfishness, or rebellion, but in the integrity of a personality. And therefore the individuality of each person need neither threaten nor be threatened by the individuality of others. Men are not obliged either to beat their neighbors or to submit to them; they can as easily laugh with them, ignore, or care for them. The fundamental fact about the human world is not the omnipresence of conflict, but the potentiality for unlimited variety.

With this insight into human nature the human dilemma assumes a totally different form. It has nothing to do with repressing egoism in favor of altruism or asserting the "rights" of individuals against "constraints" imposed by society, morality, or law. Instead, what makes human life difficult is that there are infinite choices, and the problem is how to clear some paths through the jungle of freedom. Individuality is not "given"; men have to learn how to shape themselves, and they may do so more or less elaborately, subtly, or coherently. When they are being educated, they are being initiated into an awareness of the variety of interpretations and responses available to them. What they find in their life in society is a collection of materials on which to draw in order to fashion their lives.

But if understanding rationality in this fashion (as a purely human attribute, instead of as a pipeline to non-human certainties) offers a better explanation of individuality, it also suffers from a great drawback: It allows no escape from the constant flux of human life. And the implications are highly disconcerting. As there is no cosmic necessity for any human contrivance, everything can be questioned. Since rationality allows men to imagine infinitely various alternatives, there are no natural limits to the questions that can be asked. Civilization is therefore vulnerable to being destroyed by the same inventiveness that made it. Of course, anyone who tries to question everything at once will reduce himself to madness or idiocy because a question cannot even be framed without taking some language for granted. But what or how much can be questioned at any time and place without endangering civilized life is far from obvious. In short, human life is surrounded by mystery and is full of fragility, and we can never hope to dispel the mystery or escape from the fragility.

Furthermore, it follows that while there is no ground for depreciating individuality as a vestige of irrationality, neither can our respect for individuality, or even for human life, be indisputably justified. It can only be held as an article of faith. We may give various reasons for respecting human dignity, and we may even find some common ground underlying them. But however long we persist in our questions, we cannot arrive at a reason for which an indisputable justification can be given. However firmly we assert that "every human being is to be treated as an end and never as a means," that understanding must be a commitment because we accept it even though there are alternatives to it that we cannot demonstrate to be necessarily false. We can elaborate and embellish this commitment, but we cannot establish a universal and wholly uncontentious obligation to regard every human being as an end in himself. An affable cannibal may stop to chat before boiling, and the missionary may try to persuade him that men are not for eating. But if he is a sound, stalwart cannibal, and not seduced by soft words or frightened by foreign gods, he will in the end proceed to the pot. And the missionary can save himself only by killing the cannibal. The cannibal's understanding of men does not include the sanctity of human life, and we can offer no rational necessity why it should. That some men think as cannibals do, whether knowingly or not, is an unpleasant but inescapable fact that we are obliged to recognize.

Science is as vulnerable as morality. If we accept a scientific explanation of the precipitation that we call rain, we may confidently say that anyone who expects to produce precipitation by rolling stones is mistaken. Our awareness that we may later change our views on rain need not prevent us from declaring the statement to be true. But we cannot ultimately justify our view to the stone-rolling rainmaker other than by declaring a commitment to a particular manner of explaining such phenomena – the manner which we consider to be "scientific."

In short, once we cease to think of human rationality as a pipeline to eternal verities, we can achieve a coherent understanding of human individuality. But we have to pay the price of admitting that everything we believe is ultimately questionable. And this admission is what makes the rule of law so peculiarly important for those who value the individuality of human beings.

II

If we think of ourselves as possessed of a power to create ideas about ourselves and our world, if we believe that nothing is given to guide us in this creation but what other men have done in the past (or a faith in divine revelation that no individual can oblige another to accept), if we value ourselves for the capacity to be individual personalities, it follows that we want not just to survive, but to make use of resources that are to be found only in a life among other men. We want to be able to profit from the understandings and skills that our ancestors have developed and that our contemporaries are inventing. We want, in short, to learn how to live in a civilized manner, and that is why we value social life. The community we live in is not then merely a protective association, but rather the seed-bed of our individuality. Individualism does not conflict with a regard for communal life and responsibilities. The two are inseparable.

If rationality is understood as a creative power, what makes it difficult for human beings to live together is not so much depravity or aggressiveness as a genius for diversity. Disputes are bound to arise not just because human beings can be wicked, but because they are rational. And even where there are no sharp disputes, there is bound to be confusion arising from the variety of interpretations and responses that human beings can invent. However much people may have in common and however amiable they may be, they will at times arrive at different and perhaps irreconcilable interpretations of the practices they share. Even if everyone were always ready to give way, there would be no way of deciding when the yielding has to stop. The question to be answered is: How can disagreement be settled without reducing men to sheep? And the answer is: By giving some members of the community "authority" to decide some questions for all. The concept of authority was the revolutionary contribution of Thomas Hobbes to the understanding of law as the bond of an association of individuals pursuing heterogeneous projects.

If we recognize that neither nature nor reason can provide indisputable answers to our questions, we are obliged to accept decisions whose authority we acknowledge because otherwise our disagreements must either remain unresolved or be settled by force. The concept of authority offers a way of achieving order without repressing individuality because when we recognize someone's authority, we oblige ourselves only to abide by his decisions, not to agree with them. Order based on respect for authority does not aim to overcome, remove, or dissolve disagreement, but only to provide ways of settling it. It is possible to recognize someone's authority to decide without giving up or denying one's own, different way of thinking. And that is why a community with a respect for authority may include an unlimited variety of opinion and conduct. But it must reconcile itself to an element of arbitrariness in its manner of being governed. For as recognizing authority means giving someone the right to decide a question that has no indisputable answer, such a decision is necessarily in some degree arbitrary because it cannot be shown to be necessarily correct.

The reason for recognizing someone's authority is to secure not just an absence of conflict, but peace in the most profound sense. This sort of peace is a condition in which there can be stable expectations, in which every man can know from one day to the next what is his own, what may be demanded of him, who may assert his will over him, and how he and others can resolve their differences without conflict. The only way of achieving such peace is by living under a system of rules that define who decides what, when, and in what manner. Such a system constitutes the rule of law. In short, if we acknowledge the individuality of men, we can live and work with others in an orderly fashion, i.e., with reasonably stable expectations and ways of reaching agreement, only by acknowledging an obligation to subscribe to laws that are promulgated in an authorized fashion, even when we do not approve of or like the consequences of observing them. The authority of law must therefore be distinguished from its desirability. The point of insisting on certain procedures for passing laws, that is, of defining what constitutes an authoritative ruling, is to enable a multitude to act together, to pursue only one of many possible courses of action, even when they disagree about which is most desirable. If we fail to distinguish the desirability of law from its authority, we destroy the fundamental condition of social peace. Those, like H. L. A. Hart, who insist that the validity of law is independent of its justice are not treating the law as amoral. On the contrary, though they do so unwittingly, they are recognizing that the moral foundation for law lies in a hitherto unacknowledged individualistic morality. By defining the concept of authority so rigorously and boldly, Hobbes provided – what Socrates, in the *Crito*, and Aquinas, in his discussion of the justification for rebellion, were intimating – an explanation of why we are obliged to observe the law even when we find it objectionable. But the moral context of this explanation remained unrecognized until recently.

Hobbes's modern successors, who shared his rejection of the ancient cosmology, either failed to appreciate the moral importance of his invention or found it too difficult to accept its painful implication that, in order to secure social peace, we must reconcile ourselves to accepting an irreducible element of arbitrariness in our social arrangements. Locke reverted to Ciceronian confusion in his attempt to equate law with natural law and confounded acknowledging the authority of law with consenting to it. Kant evaded the problem by replacing the certainties of the ancient cosmology with a foundation for indisputable moral knowledge innate to the structure of human rationality. Bentham invented a variety of technical devices in futile attempts to dissolve any element of arbitrariness in social arrangements and further promoted the confusion of authority with consent. Hart and Kelsen, the former more than the latter, provide intimations of a concept of authority but are too much in thrall to Bentham or Kant to succeed. For Marxists and Political Jurisprudence, the problem – to which the concept of authority offers a solution – does not exist because neither Marxism nor Political Jurisprudence is concerned with securing an association of independent agents, each pursuing individual own projects. Instead they are concerned with promoting one or another enterprise in which the individual members serve as instruments for achieving the aims of the communal project.

III

As authority can only be exercised where there is a system of rules designating who decides what, by what procedures, and under what conditions, the concept of a rule is the necessary complement of the concept of authority in the idea of law. Since ancient times, when so much attention was directed to the equation of law with rules, there has been a great deterioration in the understanding of the nature and place of rules in law. Even the relatively simple but crucial distinction between a rule and an order was obfuscated by Bentham, despite his animadversions against judge-made laws. As Kant's identification of law with eternal verities made him indifferent to the question answered by the concept of authority, the importance of promulgating law as rules was not an issue for him. Marxism and Political Jurisprudence reduce the notion of a rule to a sinister rhetorical device. What distinguishes Positivist Jurisprudence, such as that of Hart and Kelsen, and more recently the Formalism of Summers and Atiyah, as well as the Skeptical Jurisprudence of Oakeshott, is a return to an emphasis on rules as the essence of law.

To appreciate the role of rules in law, we have to bear in mind two important distinctions: between a rule and an order, and between instrumental and non-instrumental rules. The distinction between an order and a rule, which has been largely ignored in modern jurisprudence, was regarded as central to the idea of law in the earliest reflections on law. An order specifies an action to be performed and is designed to produce a predictable change in behavior; the more particular the order, the more unequivocally we can identify whose behavior will be changed and in what fashion. What confuses the distinction between an order and a rule is that an order may be general, that is to say, it may apply to a class of persons. But a command to a class of persons, to do this or that, is still an order and not a rule. Laws drafting every male of eighteen into the army or requiring taxes to be paid are examples of such general "orders."

Whereas Plato and Aristotle emphasize that orders are the instruments of arbitrary masters, or tyrants, Oakeshott emphasizes another aspect of the distinction between orders and rules, namely, that rules are "adverbial." Instead of commanding the subject to perform anything, a rule designates the manner in which certain activities are to be carried out by those who wish to engage in them or a manner of punishing certain actions that are forbidden. A law against murder does not command anyone to refrain from killing, nor does it prohibit all killing. It stipulates that whoever causes the death of another person in a certain manner under certain conditions will be guilty of the crime of murder. It prohibits causing death "murderously." Thus, at the heart of the idea of law is a sharp distinction between an obligation to subscribe to certain conditions in doing what we choose and an obligation to perform this or that action at a given time and place.

Our freedom of choice depends on the extent to which we are governed by regulations that have the character of rules rather than orders. This all-important distinction has been lost in the confusion generated by the talk about open and closed societies, or, more and less, strong and weak government. How free we are to run our own lives depends not so much on the number of "laws" as on whether they are rules rather than orders. Though all "laws," because they apply to classes of people, are couched in terms that give them the appearance of rules, increasingly in recent years many so-called laws are in fact orders.

Nothing like the ancient Greek preoccupation with the distinction between orders and rules appears in modern jurisprudence until H. L. A. Hart. Nevertheless, although Bentham in some contexts dismisses the distinction, it was generally taken for granted. But a deliberate rejection of the need to make any such distinction can be traced from Realist Jurisprudence to its apotheosis in Political Jurisprudence. The concern of advocates of Political Jurisprudence to use the law as an instrument for achieving certain practical results leads them to carry to its logical extreme the Realist tendency to equate law with judicial decisions, which are orders, and to repudiate the importance of legislative rules.

The second distinction between instrumental and non-instrumental rules was first formulated by Michael Oakeshott, though it is implicit in Kant's emphasis on the distinction between moral and utilitarian motives, and in Pashukanis's distinction between technical and legal regulations. But it is implicitly rejected by other Marxist theorists and by all advocates of Political Jurisprudence, as well as by Locke and (on occasion) by Bentham, because they treat law as an instrument for providing certain satisfactions or executing certain projects.

In a community regulated by instrumental rules, the activities of the subjects are directed to serve a substantive purpose, as in a "theocracy" such as Calvin's Geneva, where all regulations are designed to achieve salvation, and no one in the community is allowed to refuse to seek salvation. Today the most familiar example is a country engaged in war, where "laws" may be promulgated in the usual fashion, but all regulations are designed to promote the "war effort." Non-instrumental rules differ from instrumental ones in the same way as the rules of a game differ from the tactics of a team. The tactics are designed to achieve victory; the rules are designed to define the game and enable it to be played. Non-instrumental rules of law define conditions that make it possible for all the members of the community to devise their own projects and to pursue them as they choose without interfering with one another. They accordingly refrain from doing two things: They do not define purposes to be pursued, and they do not hand out advantages. Thus, the laws defining the conditions for making a valid contract do not constrain anyone to enter into any contract; the rules defining property or theft do not distribute property, but they make it possible to know what constitutes property and a secure claim to it. What makes it difficult to understand non-instrumental rules is that the operation of all rules is likely to affect some people adversely and others beneficially. Rules of procedure in a courtroom may be said to work to the disadvantage of would-be perjurers, but the purpose of the rules is to make it possible to distinguish the guilty from the innocent. Though rules defining murder impose disadvantages on certain killers, their purpose is to maintain security of life. Indeed, in connection with every rule of law we may identify people who might find it more or less advantageous, but that is an unavoidable, incidental, unintended consequence, just as in tennis the rule that forbids awarding points to the player whose ball lands outside the court may operate as a handicap on stronger players and as an advantage for weaker players who could not hit the ball so far anyway.

That there can be a purpose for rules other than the distribution of advantages follows from recognizing that human life does not consist solely in the acquisition of wealth or power and that the value of different human lives does not rest solely on the satisfactions acquired. As this is denied by Marxists and the advocates of Political Jurisprudence, they cannot acknowledge the reality of non-instrumental rules. But if power and wealth are not the sole objects of human endeavor, and if human beings can prefer to live their lives in certain conditions because they find such conditions admirable or enjoyable, then there can be rules designed not to distribute advantages, but to maintain a desirable kind of communal life. No doubt there may always be those who think only of what they will gain from this or that arrangement and who will seek to get laws framed accordingly. But the concern in discussions of public affairs with that curious entity that has been variously described as "the common good," "the public interest," "the good of the realm," the "national interest," or "the *res publica*," with which even the most adamant pressure groups try to identify their claims, testifies that we do somehow recognize a distinction between instrumental and non-instrumental rules.

The distinction between instrumental and non-instrumental rules even more than that between rules and orders provides an antidote to the individualist antipathy to connecting law with morality. For it is generally assumed, though rarely acknowledged, that those who insist on a connection between law and morality equate law with a body of instrumental rules designed to achieve a certain pattern of life or goal towards which everyone in the community should be directed. If morality is conceived of in this fashion as a given substantive purpose, then the law must consist of rules instrumental for achieving that purpose. And it would follow that to allow freedom of choice, law must be divorced from morality. But no such consequence follows from a moral preference for non-instrumental rules.

In addition to distinguishing between rules and orders and between instrumental and non-instrumental rules, we have to bear in mind the indeterminacy of rules. This indeterminacy was clearly understood by ancient and medieval writers but has become increasingly obfuscated by modern writers despite their preoccupation with explicating the operation of law. They fail to recognize that, as the law deals with contingent matters, rules of law cannot specify with certainty what is to be done in particular circumstances. There may be such complete agreement on what a rule means in certain circumstances that the indeterminacy goes unnoticed. But the indeterminacy is nevertheless present because of the logical relationship between a general proposition and a more particular one about contingent matters. The particular can be fitted into a variety of general statements, and the particulars that could be implied by a general statement cannot be exhaustively stated. Hence, there can be no certainty about what a rule of law requires.

This uncertainty, vexing though it is, also endows the law with an important intrinsic virtue: The indeterminacy of the law contributes to its stability. It does so in two ways. Where laws are made by an assembly of men, or where laws must be acceptable to a heterogeneous community over a long stretch of time, a degree of indeterminacy makes agreement and acceptance easier. Differences of opinion, at least within certain areas, can be reconciled under general terms, and the exact meaning can then be left for the court to decide as disputes arise. Even more important is the fact that the indeterminacy in laws makes it possible for the law to remain stable while adapting to changing circumstances. Not only do new situations arise, but in addition people's desires change. Law's indeterminacy allows us to take account of what has changed by making a new interpretation of the words. As the words are not repudiated, the rule stands and continuity is preserved even while an innovation is introduced. In short, law can secure stable expectations because, as Levi shows, new and unforeseen circumstances can be recognized as instances of an established rule. Thus, the law can both change and restrict the uncertainty to which members of the community would otherwise be exposed. What has attracted the most attention, however, since the latter part of the nineteenth century, has not been the virtue of the law's indeterminacy, but the difficulties to which it exposes us. These difficulties, while real enough, have nevertheless been grossly exaggerated because certain concepts have been lost sight of. As Realist Jurisprudence became more influential, there was a growing disposition to deny that adjudication should or could be distinguished from legislation. The exploration of law as a constantly altering system of rules led to a greater awareness of how much adjudication changes the law. And it became fashionable to believe that because law is not discovered in Nature, or revealed by God, or imprinted in human reason, as it is not eternally fixed, it cannot be objective. Once law lost its aura of fixity, it seemed to have lost its claim to objectivity.

What was overlooked, however, was that adjudication and legislation change the law in different ways because each is addressed to a different question. The legislator's question is: Can the difficulty before us be resolved by altering the rules? The legislator is authorized deliberately to change the rules. The judge's question is: What meaning does the relevant rule have in the circumstances before us? The judge is authorized to maintain the established rules and not to change the rules. But the accumulation of judicial decisions will unavoidably produce changes in the meaning of the rules. If, however, such changes take place slowly as unintended consequences of interpreting the established law, they need not interrupt continuity or destroy the stability of the law. On the contrary, because the uncertainty of the law allows for such change, the stability of law is the complement of its uncertainty.

The Realists' rediscovery that the law is not deduced from universal and indisputable truths, such as Kant envisages, led them also to emphasize the arbitrariness of judicial decisions. It is, of course, true that the judge's decision is arbitrary in the sense that it cannot be deduced from a rule of law in the way that a conclusion is deduced in a geometrical demonstration. It cannot therefore be demonstrated to be the only and necessarily correct decision. Nevertheless, a judicial decision need be neither irrational nor subjective because it can be supported by reasons, and the system of law dictates what kinds of reasons are appropriate. It is therefore possible for others who are conversant with the statutes, decisions, and procedures of the land to recognize that a decision is reasonable even when they themselves might have chosen another. Whether a decision is a reasonable legal decision depends not on whether we like its consequences, but on whether it can be justified by appropriate legal reasoning. If we preserve a clear distinction between the ways in which judges and legislators change the law, we can preserve stability while adapting the law to a variety of circumstances. But the distinction between judging and legislating can only be preserved if both judges and the public respect the difference between interpreting established rules and deliberately making new law.

IV

It has, however, become fashionable to follow the lead of Political Jurisprudence in denying not only that adjudication can be distinguished from legislation, but even that the law consists of rules that have to be interpreted by courts and should be changed only by authentic legislators. This fashion has flourished because we have lost sight of two further concepts intrinsic to the idea of law, that of a "historical objectivity" and of "practical reasoning." Before the idea of law came under attack, these concepts unselfconsciously formed part of the mental baggage of those who served our legal system and were subject to it. They have by now all but disappeared even from academic reflection on the law.

A historical objectivity, or what Oakeshott calls a "practice," consists of contingent connections between contingent ideas made by human beings. There is no necessity for any of these connections, and they might have been made differently or not at all. But having been made, they constitute an objective order. The character of this order is most obvious in a language, in the narrow sense of French or English. Every language has changed and continues to change, with new words or constructions being introduced and old ones being dismissed as archaic. Nevertheless, those who speak a language can understand past examples of the language and do not doubt that their utterances are meaningful and can be understood by any other speaker of the same language. For they regard their language as an independent, coherent, impersonal public identity that they have found, not made. This view constitutes the objectivity of a language, even though it has been made by many different people over time and has continuously changed. It is a historical objectivity.

A historical objectivity is not something created here and now, but the unforeseen consequence of performances by persons who were thinking of other things. What matters is that a historical objectivity is not created by the agreement of those who submit to it; for them it is just as given as if it were part of the cosmic order. They take it to be given because it has a continuous identity that has been recognized over many generations. Thus, a historical objectivity acquires the character of a "natural" object.

The explicit formulation of an understanding of law as a historical objectivity is the contribution of Savigny, who emphasized the intricacy of the historically achieved coherence of the law and the danger of destroying that coherence by wielding the radical surgery of codification. That his disciples emphasized instead the changeability of law is not surprising because a historical objectivity such as law (or language) lacks a permanent substratum or a given objective or end for the changes within it. But if that prevents it from being fixed, it need not destroy its stability. That was not, however, what Savigny concerned himself with explaining. He did not point out, as Levi did later, how stability could persist amidst change, how – as the new is bound up with what remains of the old – the new acquires the maturity of an established form.

Understanding the nature of law as a historical objectivity has become especially difficult in recent years because that understanding rests on the concepts of authority and practical reasoning, both of which have been neglected by most modern writers. By identifying law as the product of decisions made by those who have been given a right to decide by the subjects of law, the concept of authority explains how law's content can be objectively determined and ceases to be anything like a "subjective opinion." The concept of practical reasoning explains how the judge's interpretation of the law can be objective and reasoned, as well as amenable to objective and reasoned criticism, even though judicial decisions cannot be shown to be indisputably correct and may be overturned by superior courts. How practical reasoning makes it possible to reach objective legal decisions was, as we have seen, first explained by Aristotle, elaborated in modern times by Edward Levi, and later, with a somewhat different emphasis, in Michael Oakeshott's discussion of a "moral practice" and analogical reasoning.

The neglect of practical reasoning and its crucial importance for the law springs from a disposition, encouraged by the influence of Kant, which has dominated modern thought and reflection on the law. This is the disposition to think in terms of a dichotomy between indisputable, universal truth and incoherence. According to this way of thinking, if we cannot know the former, there can be no truth at all, or only the instant certainties of "apocalyptic utterances."[1] Confined, as some have believed, to these alternatives, modern men have clutched at doctrines like Marxism or structuralism, which allow for no contingency, or else have wallowed self-righteously in chaos and cultivated an appreciation of nothingness. Weird combinations of both tendencies are displayed in the doctrines of Political Jurisprudence. But once the law is seen as a

---

[1] Cf. Judith N. Shklar, "Hegel's Phenomenology," *Political Theory* 1 (August 1973): 266–7.

historical objectivity, and we recognize and understand the place of authority and practical reasoning in the operation of the law, the maintenance of stability alongside uncertainty and change, which the rule of law achieves, ceases to be a mystery.

Understanding the concepts of authority, of historical objectivity, and practical reasoning also makes it easier to distinguish the validity of law from its desirability, and to see why the obligation to observe the law rests on the conformity of its promulgation with established legal procedures and not on its "justice" or "morality." But that does not mean that the rule of law requires all subjects and officers of the law to approve of all valid laws. It does not even exclude the refusal to execute or observe a valid law. What the rule of law does exclude is a claim to a "right" to do so.

Citizens who find a law too iniquitous to observe may refuse to comply with it without denying respect for the rule of law if they acknowledge that they are violating the law and accept the consequences stipulated by the law. Similarly, a judge who finds a law too iniquitous to enforce may resign from the bench or register his disapproval in his decision while strictly interpreting the relevant law. But he may not use his power to rectify the law. In all such circumstances, two judgments have to be made: Is this law not merely undesirable but iniquitous? Is the legal system of which this law is part so iniquitous that destroying it is preferable to enduring its injustice? In other words, the refusal to enforce or comply with a valid law must be recognized to be a revolutionary act, justified by a profound moral conviction and not merely by a difference of opinion about the desirability of a particular regulation. Of course, a deliberate violation of the established law, if done openly, may also be an act of protest that will not threaten the system as a whole but may encourage some modification of it. But more serious refusals to observe the law, whether by officers or citizens, must be recognized, as Socrates argued, to threaten the prevailing legal system. In short, acknowledging an obligation to observe or enforce the law does not exclude decisions to refuse compliance, but it does require making a sharp distinction between mere dissent from a valid law and the judgment that it or the system as a whole is iniquitous.

V

The individualist morality identified here enters more directly into the deliberations of the legislator. If we do nothing more than prefer to be ruled by a system of law – as opposed to decrees or tribal customs – we are making a moral choice. If this preference is not merely a momentary whim like preferring chocolate ice cream, it implies a certain understanding of oneself and is a moral preference. Even though the preference for living under the rule of law may not have been chosen self-consciously the understanding postulated by it may not be self-consciously recognized; as is usually the case, a willingness to acknowledge the authority of a system of law expresses a moral preference. Furthermore, because a system of law may take different forms, the moral preference expressed by recognizing the authority of a legal system may be further specified. It is obvious enough that a moral preference is involved when law is seen as an instrument for bringing into existence a certain pattern of life or achieving a certain objective. That a system of law embodies a morality just as much if it consists of non-instrumental rules has yet to be recognized. To prefer to be ruled by a non-instrumental system of law means that one wishes to be associated with others in one fashion and not in another. It means that one does not want to be part of an enterprise for producing wealth or health or happiness, but that one wants to be part of an association that leaves its members free to choose their projects for themselves. Such an association is what Michael Oakeshott calls a civil association and which he distinguishes from an enterprise in which all the members are enrolled in a single project. When, therefore, we say that we wish to live under a non-instrumental system of law, we endow it with a definite moral character.

What distinguishes the government of a civil association is not that it does more or less, but that it conceives of its purpose as doing a certain kind of thing. It is not an organization for either repressing or satisfying self-interest, nor is it an arbitrator of conflicting claims or a dispenser of benefits. A government of a civil association is a council of the whole community, which has been given the authority to make and enforce rules to which everyone is obliged to subscribe. The purpose of these rules is to enable the members of the community to live and work together peacefully, while leaving each free to choose and pursue their own projects. Just as it would be unthinkable for the umpire at a football match to join in the playing, so it is out of character for this sort of government to take control of enterprises, whether industrial or educational. Such a government exercises control over private activities, but only in the manner of making and enforcing the rules of the game.

As Oakeshott points out, no state is or can be a perfect civil association. The law in all Western countries has been a mixture of instrumental and non-instrumental rules. But that does not make it either unintelligible or irrelevant to keep the distinction clear and to recognize the different moral characters of different sorts of rules. Just how instrumental and non-instrumental rules can be combined or how desirable different mixtures may be are practical questions that cannot be answered in the abstract. It can only be said that if people are eager to preserve the character of a civil association, they will observe certain conditions when deliberating about whether to change their laws.

If legislators wish to preserve the character of a civil association, they will start with a strong presumption in favor of achieving any given purpose by means of private efforts. They will recognize that it is essential to do so in order to avoid the danger of converting the government into a manager and thereby introducing two evils in one – installing a manager who is dangerously powerful as well as difficult to make either responsible or efficient, and diminishing the effectiveness of the government as a ruler. If, nevertheless, it is decided that the government should intervene in a managerial fashion, i.e., if it is decided to adopt instrumental rules, a civil association will take care to keep the managerial undertakings sharply distinguished from the activities proper to the government as a ruler.

But there is still another moral dimension to the rule of law that creates considerable confusion about the relation between morality, individualism, and law. A civil association presupposes that the activities of the state do not exhaust communal life, that the members of a civil association associate in a multitude of other ways, and that if they have lived together for a long time they will have in common a "civility." It is here that the differences commonly ascribed to national character, to temperament, climate, or race, become relevant. Civil associations may be noisy or quiet, chaotic or orderly, businesslike or easy-going, excitable or stolid. What is considered a minimum of cleanliness in one place may feel like a hospital regime to another. A civil association may take great pains to cultivate public gardens or hate the sight of them. It may relish large, fast motorcars or ban them altogether. Its members may consider it indecent to walk about the roads without a hat or decent to do so in a bikini.

Whether conduct is regarded as indecent or decent does not make it a proper subject for legal regulation – that is a separate question involving considerations of another kind. What needs to be noticed here is that any community of people who live together in harmony have come to agree on what is decent and indecent, reasonable and unreasonable, offensive and inoffensive, negligent and careful. And this agreement will be reflected in all the laws, whether about abortion or compensation for injury or parking fines. Standards of civility are involved in questions as apparently technical as the location of an airport – no amount of cost-benefit analysis can annihilate the fact that different communities will assess costs and benefits differently. Nor will talk of efficiency avoid the difficulty. What is considered to be an "efficient" location for an airport will depend on whether "rural beauty" or "silence" is given precedence over speedy travel, whether people are more concerned with getting to the remotest corners of the world faster than anyone else or with being able to stay at home in peace. When the members of a civil association come to deliberate about their laws they cannot avoid considering standards of civility. They may not do so explicitly; nevertheless, some standard of civility will shape the way in which they make their laws. In this sense, too, law cannot be divorced from morality.

The great difficulty in a civil association is to distinguish regulations made to preserve standards of civility from the regulations appropriate to an enterprise association like a theocracy. Much of the effort to dissociate law from morality arises from the misconception that any consideration of civility is the same as a theocratic regulation and hence inappropriate to an association of people who do not wish to be managed into heaven. To see how considerations of civility need not turn a civil association into a theocracy, it might help to consider the relation between the rules of grammar and the canons recognized by critics and writers for what constitutes good usage in a language. Neither the rules of grammar nor the canons of good usage dictate what is to be said or in which style. But whereas the rules of grammar describe the structure of the language within which variations are possible, the standards laid down by critics give a general idea of how to use the language with elegance, humor, irony, or clarity. Or to put it another way, men speaking the same language have in common not only a grammar, but also certain notions of what constitutes good and bad usage. In the same way, a commitment to the freedom of each individual "to live his own life in his own way," which characterizes a civil association, carries with it a view of what constitutes a civilized life and what conditions have to be enforced generally to preserve it. To try to enforce such conditions is as compatible with the variety intrinsic to a free society as insisting on clarity in writing is with a variety of form and content in what is written. A civil association allows for a great variety of pursuits and enterprises and modes of conduct, but the variety cannot be infinite. A community worthy of its name is bound to set certain limits to the variety. It cannot avoid doing so without renouncing civilization and becoming a bedlam. What matters is whether in setting these limits the desire to preserve a civil association remains dominant.

How differently moral considerations may enter into deliberations on law may be illustrated by considering possible responses to a question about marriage laws. It may be thought necessary to make or amend such laws because the cohabitation of a man and a woman is believed to have a sacrosanct character and should neither take place nor be dissolved without due recognition of this character. This way of understanding marriage is very likely to be present in a theocracy. But it might also be part of the civility of a civil association. This is not, however, the only conception of marriage compatible with a civil association. Marriage might be understood in many other ways. It might be considered a contract, much like any other contract, which the government will protect if certain conditions are observed, or allow to be broken if certain conditions are not met. Or the cohabitation of a man and a woman might be thought of as an act of friendship that is of no concern to anyone other than the two persons involved. If that were the prevailing view, there might come to be great confusion about who is responsible for looking after children, and to remedy that difficulty it might be suggested that it would be desirable to set up public orphanages or other public institutions for bringing up children.

But if that suggestion were accepted, the civil association would be in danger of adulterating its character by turning itself into a nursemaid as well as a rule-maker. And in order to avoid doing so, it might be decided to regulate the conditions of cohabitation by some sort of marriage laws, so as to make parents responsible for their children. In such a case, laws regulating the conditions of cohabitation, laws that might resemble those in a theocracy, will have been inspired by a concern for personal freedom and not by a desire to impose any particular pattern of conduct. Moreover, even if it were decided that no such law should be adopted, it would not follow that morality had been excluded from the domain of law. That decision, too, would be a moral decision. Considerations other than moral, such as considerations about the cost of enforcement, may have entered into the deliberation. But insofar as the deliberation was set in motion and concluded by moral ideas – ideas about the kind of association wanted and about the civility that distinguished that association – it is a deliberation shaped by moral considerations. Indeed, apart from rules like those designating which side of the road should be used by motorists, it is difficult to think of any subject entirely free of moral considerations.

Unless we recognize that morality is intrinsic to law, we will be unable to defend the rule of law and hence our liberty against its most deadly enemy, confusion about what matters most to us. The threat of such confusion is peculiarly great now because contemporary civilization is founded on a highly complicated and subtle agreement. That is the only kind of agreement likely to be found among people of highly developed individuality who recognize no indisputable criteria for human activities and who are well aware of the variety possible in the human world. To act on such an agreement is an exceedingly difficult task. On the one hand, there is a danger of adopting measures suitable for a theocracy, a tribe, or an enterprise, rather than for a civil association. On the other hand, there is a danger of trying to avoid such measures by denying that law has any connection with morality. But to do so makes nonsense of law because the concept of law is a moral concept.

If we wish to defend freedom for individuality, we must recognize clearly that what is always at issue, in any discussion about law, is communal morality. And this has two distinct aspects. One refers to preserving the character of a civil association, which means preserving the non-instrumental character of law. The other refers to preserving standards of civility when determining the substance of law.

In order to protect the freedom of individuals to live their own lives, we must prevent a civil association from being turned into an enterprise. The pertinent question for that purpose is: How compatible is this measure with maintaining a civil association? The answer will be no more and no less certain or objective than the answer to any other human question. But as arguments and reasons can be advanced and rebutted, lucidly, plausibly and coherently, disagreements can be discussed objectively, though never settled to everyone's satisfaction. But any attempt to escape from such imperfection by decontaminating the law from morality or uncertainty will certainly destroy the law.

What the conversation about law, which began in ancient Greece, reveals above all is that the idea of law offers no simple or easy solutions to our dilemmas. Now that the desirability and even possibility of maintaining the rule of law has been openly denied, that challenge can be met only by promoting a widespread and self-conscious understanding of the morality of individualism, of the concepts of non-instrumental rules, of authority, of historical objectivity, and of practical reasoning, concepts whose relevance for the idea of law has been fitfully recognized in the past but only recently explicitly identified and explained. Such an understanding is needed in order to appreciate fully and rightly the shortcomings of law. For the rule of law cannot remove all arbitrariness and uncertainty. It cannot dispel the mystery surrounding human life. It is itself highly fragile. Indeed, the rule of law can survive only in a community resigned to enduring many evils that human beings understandably yearn to avoid. Nevertheless, the ancient Greeks' veneration of the rule of law was wholly justified. They were acutely aware of what we are in danger of forgetting, that the rule of law is our sole protection against tyranny. But in addition, our long and rich experience of the rule of law has enabled us to see more clearly blessings brought by the rule of law which were barely visible to our predecessors. For we have learned how to escape the tension between justice and liberty, which Plato and Aristotle struggled unsuccessfully to resolve. We have discovered how the rule of law can allow us to shape a civilization where order is preserved while diversity flourishes.

Index

adjudication 35, 43, 98, 99, 100, 102, 127,
149, 150, 152, 153, 155, 156, 168, 169,
170, 171, 172, 173, 174, 175, 180, 181,
185, 187, 199, 208, 213, 218, 247, 248,
251, 252, 253, 254, 256, 260, 262, 264,
278, 279, 281, 284, 289, 291, 296, 297,
298, 300, 322, 323, 324, 338, 339
Aeschines 3
Aliens bill of 1792, debate on 322
Altman, Andrew 255, 258, 259, 260, 264
anagrapheis 1
anarchy 3, 63, 95, 131, 132, 227, 240,
315, 318
ancient Greeks (*see also* Aristotle, Plato) 2,
5, 41, 346
Aquinas, Thomas 1, 41, 48, 68, 69, 105, 106,
108, 217, 218, 309, 327, 333
aristocracy 21, 145
Aristotle 1, 21, 26, 42, 43, 44, 45, 46, 47, 48,
49, 50, 51, 52, 54, 55, 65, 69, 70, 71, 72,
73, 75, 77, 84, 86, 91, 105, 106, 119,
135, 151, 152, 157, 164, 218, 223, 254,
307, 309, 322, 327, 328, 334, 340, 346
Arnold, Thurman 250
Augustine 1, 59, 69, 70, 71, 72, 73, 75, 78,
86, 87, 91, 105, 108, 152, 307
City of God, 60
Societas, 62
Universitas, 62
Austin, John 124, 180, 181, 188, 204, 207,
211, 212

Bartlett, Katherine 267
Bender, Leslie 266, 267, 271, 272, 273
Bentham, Jeremy 1, 153, 185, 189, 196, 201,
211, 277, 280, 326, 333, 334, 335
Berlin, Isaiah 248
Blackstone, William 155, 254
Brandeis, Louis Dembitz 248
Burger, Warren E. 286, 287
Butler, Judith 272
Butterfield, Herbert 248

Cahn, Naomi 272
Calvin, John 335
Cardozo, Benjamin 198
Christie, George F. 251
Cicero 1, 42, 59, 67, 68, 73, 74, 76, 77, 86,
108, 113, 114, 120, 327, 333
Civil Rights Acts 286, 287
civil society 67, 103, 119, 120, 121, 123, 124,
125, 126, 127, 129, 138, 141, 148, 149,
150, 157, 160, 167, 180
Coke, Sir Edward 97
commonwealth 44, 50, 53, 67, 96, 100, 102,
103, 104, 113, 121, 131, 138, 149
Conservatism 288
constitution (general) 1, 9, 16, 17, 18, 22, 25,
30, 31, 32, 33, 39, 53, 81, 98, 113, 124,
128, 138, 139, 143, 144, 145, 150, 151,
163, 164, 176, 178, 201, 209, 278,
295, 296
Constitution of the United States of
America 261, 279, 280, 285, 288,
294, 296
contract 11, 14, 22, 127, 137, 138, 146, 150,
160, 173, 212, 215, 225, 232, 233, 239,
257, 258, 261, 262, 270, 273, 289, 290,
298, 300, 301, 314, 336, 345
Critical Legal Studies (CLS) 1, 221, 254
Critical Race Theory 263
Feminism 1, 221, 263, 264, 284

Decalogue 84
democracy 21, 25, 31, 33, 49, 236, 285,
292, 295
Demosthenes 3, 4, 15
Dewey, John 195, 197
Draco's code 1
Duguit 185, 192
duty 35, 46, 49, 66, 68, 85, 102, 103, 111,
114, 115, 123, 125, 126, 130, 133, 136,
142, 144, 146, 147, 149, 151, 161, 162,
167, 169, 177, 234, 258, 272, 279, 293,
318, 322

347

CPSIA information can be obtained at www.ICGtesting.com
Printed in the USA
LVOW131939180613

339069LV00001B/3/P